June 7. 1951
Mrs. Larry Sorteavair,
From J. Sidonio Nye.

Intravaia
413½ Clark Street
Morgantown, West Va

BOOKS IN THIS SERIES

THE VICTOR BOOK OF

Ballets
and Ballet Music

BY ROBERT LAWRENCE

SIMON AND SCHUSTER · NEW YORK
1950

Radio Corporation of America has given us permission to use "Victor" in the title of this book, "Victor" being exclusive trade-mark owned by that company.

Musical Quotations from:

Facsimile, copyright 1950 by Harms, Inc. Reprinted by special permission.

Fall River Legend, copyright by G. & C. Music Corporation, New York, N. Y. Used by permission.

Fancy Free, copyright 1950 by Harms, Inc. Reprinted by special permission.

Interplay (originally published as *American Concertette*), copyright 1944 by Mills Music, Inc. Used by permission.

On Stage, copyright 1945 by G. Schirmer, Inc. Printed by permission.

DEDICATION

For My Parents,

in their evenings at the ballet

ACKNOWLEDGMENTS

THE author's appreciation is due those who have helped in many ways to bring this work to completion: Miss Gladys Chamberlain, chief librarian of the Fifty-Eighth Street Music Library, New York, and her assistants, Mary Lee Daniels and Lilly Goldberg, for their kindness in making available many books and ballet scores ordinarily difficult of access; Martin and Sally Kamin, who graciously permitted the writer to consult the 1842 (original) piano reduction of *Giselle* and other rare material in their dance bookshop; Anatole Chujoy and the staff of *Dance News*, for patient answers to miscellaneous queries; the staff of the Museum of Modern Art's Dance Archives, for the same courtesy; George Balanchine, for his generosity in giving over several days during a busy season to a discussion of his ballets in abstract style; Doris Humphrey, Ruthanna Boris, Antony Tudor, Michael Kidd and Todd Bolender, for valued counsel on their choreography; Muriel Bentley, Hugh Laing, Paul Godkin and Herbert Bliss for documentation of certain works in which they have danced; Leonard Bernstein, Norman Dello Joio and Morton Gould, for making their full scores available to the author and in some cases, when this was not possible, sending thematic quotations in their own hand, a favor thankfully remembered; Ivan Boutnikoff, for information regarding the Fokine orchestral version of Schumann's *Carnaval*; Max Goberman, for technical pointers on Tudor's use of music by Prokofieff and Delius; Arthur V. Berger, for guidance on American folk elements in the works of Aaron Copland; John Onysko and Walter Alford of Ballet Theatre, Sergei Denham and Doris Luhrs of the Ballet Russe de Monte Carlo, Betty Cage of Ballet Society, Barry Hyams and Martin Feinstein of S. Hurok, Inc., and Isadora Bennett, for their co-operation in the assembling of photographic and other vital materials; Fred Fehl, for permission to examine at length his archives of dance snapshots; Bernard Braddon of the Liberty Music Shops, for enabling the writer to check on many ballet recordings; Marian di Lorenzo Hampden, for faithful assistance in preparation of the manuscript; to all these are acknowledgments gratefully given.

ROBERT LAWRENCE
Phoenix, Arizona

Contents

Contents

Contents

Contents

Contents

Contents

Contents

Contents

xvii

THE VICTOR BOOK OF
Ballets
AND BALLET MUSIC

AN EARLY NINETEENTH CENTURY COMIC BALLET. THE DANCER KISSING THE BALLERINA'S HAND IS FILIPPO TAGLIONI, ONE OF THE OUTSTANDING CHOREOGRAPHERS OF HIS DAY AND FATHER OF MARIE TAGLIONI.

BALLET PERSPECTIVE

IN THE BEGINNING

Ballet, as we know it today, is one of the most recent of theatrical arts. This combination of choreography, music, and décor may be said to have begun professionally in 1661, when King Louis XIV of France granted leave to a learned circle of instructors to form a Dancing Academy and gave them a room in the Louvre for their meetings. Eight years later the monarch granted permission to a pair of now obscure intellectuals, Abbé Perin, poet, and Robert Cambert, court organist, to found a national opera: L'Académie Royale de la Musique et de la Danse. This institution was to include professional ballet as well. After a single season, the two partners were forced to surrender their patent because of grave financial losses and intrigue against them at court. The grant soon passed to the chief intriguer—Jean Baptiste Lully, under whom the Academy was to flourish—and with this transference of authority begins the history of modern theatrical dance.

The art did not, of course, spring into being spontaneously. Roots of ballet had been nurtured in Italy, first as a part of religious spectacles of the late Middle Ages (in which the dance occupied a place generally subservient to poetry and music) and then as an attraction of the Renaissance carnivals. When Catherine de' Medici left her native city of Florence in 1533, married the son of a French king,* and settled in Paris, seeds of ballet from Italy were to find good soil for their growth.

Court splendor first brought them into bloom. When ambassadors from Poland arrived in 1573 to offer the crown of their country to Catherine's son, the Duc d'Anjou, the Queen entertained them with a mighty evening of music and dance. Eight years later she reached the climax of her activities as impresario, dictated more often by political than by artistic considerations, when the spectacular *Ballet Comique de la Reine*, often called the first complete dance-drama, was given before an audience of ten thousand guests to celebrate the betrothal of a princess of the blood, Marguerite de Lorraine, to the Duc de Joyeuse. Several officials of the royal household, supervised by an artistic director, Balthasar de Beaujoyeulx, pooled their talents in a version of the Circe legend, achieving a blend of poetry, music, décor, and dance which—though the tremendous cost of its performance was to cripple the French court financially for some time to come—had a healthy effect on the future of ballet. The lordly masque, which flourished soon after in the England of Ben Jonson and Inigo Jones, was an offshoot of this type of pageantry, but more literary than dynamic in its action.

EARLY DEVELOPMENTS

Once it had established a foothold in the court of France, the new art grew rapidly. Seven years after the production of the *Ballet Comique de la Reine*, a historic treatise was published with rules not only for learning the proper steps in courtly dances, but also for noting them on paper. The author, a canon of the Church named Jéhan Tabouret—who wrote under the pseudonym of Thoinot Arbeau—held forth on dancing and its practice in a series of imaginary dialogues between himself and a young pupil called Capriol, using by way of illustration music for favorite dances of the period.† His work, *Orchesography* ("The Writing Down of Dance"), has survived as a monument of its

* The Duc d'Orléans, later Henry II.
† The British composer Peter Warlock has arranged six of these old tunes in a modern orchestral work, the *Capriol Suite*.

kind, one of the first attempts to codify organized movement, a problem still not solved satisfactorily today.

Arbeau's book and the entertainments of Marie de' Medici, to which it was bound in style and period, were among the early sproutings of ballet. The art as we are familiar with it today began to take shape nearly a hundred years later, during the reign of Louis XIV, who himself appeared in court performances as a young man. The conniving but artistically able Lully (1633–1687), Florentine by birth, composer, dancer, and violinist, led the King's orchestra, moved beside him in the royal ballets, wrote music for the danced interludes (then called *entrées*) which formed an important part of the plays of Molière, and finally—when he got hold of the patent to L'Académie Royale de la Musique et de la Danse—created operas in which ballet played an important role. It was in his era that musical entertainments were finally removed from the floors of royal ballrooms and put upon the stage. The technique of theatrical dance was beginning to function effectively.

THE ENTRANCE OF VIRTUOSITY

With Lully's Academy in working order, the professional quality of ballet was assured and has come down to us in a direct line from this ambitious Florentine; but the style of dance which he favored was soon changed. His successor, the composer Jean Philippe Rameau (1683–1764), and a whole new generation that clustered about the throne of Louis XV preferred another type of movement, the *danse haute*—elevated dance, with leaps and figurations in air—as opposed to the older *danse basse*, which stayed on the ground.

A good technical performance of the *danse haute* called for two evolutionary changes: an abbreviated costume, to relieve the dancers of the cumbersome court dress used at the time of Lully, and a new virtuosity of motion. Both of these factors were not long in coming. Marie Anne de Cupis de Camargo (1710–1770) shortened her ballet skirt, made startling progress in the art of elevation, and, together with her teacher, Françoise Prévost, began the dynasty of noted ballerinas who, through the centuries, have contributed their special gifts of style, imagination, and skill to the development of the art.

TOWARD AN EXPRESSIVE MEDIUM

Just as the history of opera is made up of an eternal conflict between the brilliant and the purely lyrical, so has the story of ballet, ever since the time of Camargo, been given over to pendulum swings between the virtuosic and the expressive. The first to react against Camargo's emphasis on mechanics of the dance was Marie Sallé (1707–1756), not only a performer of distinction but also a choreographer of talent, whose ballet *Pygmalion* (1734) won successful productions in England, France, and Germany. For Sallé, the soul of the art lay in the communication of inner feelings rather than of formal effect. Though always based on a strong technical foundation, her gifts veered in the direction of mime.

The most articulate champion of the expressive in dance, however, as against the predominantly technical, was to be a choreographer of later date than the creator of *Pygmalion*: Jean Georges Noverre (1727–1809), born near Paris but fated for a large part of his life, through intrigues at the French court and general opposition to his theories of dance-drama, to work abroad. On a brief visit to England, from which he was forced to return owing to the outbreak of the Seven Years' War, Noverre was acclaimed by David Garrick as "the Shakespeare of the Dance." Summoned to Stuttgart in 1760 by the Duke of Württemberg, who gave him full scope as choreographer, he created a first-class company. Its fame traveled to France, where the doors of the Opéra were still barred to him, creating a stir in the Parisian theatrical world. Soon the great performer Gaetano Vestris (who, with his son, Auguste, set a historic standard for grace, expressiveness, and virility in male dance) visited Noverre in Stuttgart, absorbed many ideas in the elimination of old-fashioned stage convention, and brought back with him to Paris the master's ballet *Jason et Medée* (1770). It was in this work, with which he scored a full success, that Vestris is said to have been the first dancer in the French theatre to remove his mask and employ the full range of facial expression.*

THE REFORMS OF NOVERRE

At length Noverre did succeed in returning to the French capital as choreographer (1776). His career there proved less brilliant than might have been expected, partly because he had a powerful enemy in the ballerina Madeleine Guimard (1743–1786), who, strongly protected in court circles and popular with every social class for the charm of her dancing, was opposed to him on personal grounds. With the advent of the French Revolution, Noverre's creative period came to an end.

He had, nevertheless, aside from generating new ideas in the sphere

* Some historians claim that the noted dancer Maximilien Gardel (1741–1787) was the first to appear without a mask in 1772 when, dancing at the last moment in place of Vestris, he removed it in order to let the audience know his identity.

of theatrical dance, accomplished one outstanding piece of stagecraft in Paris. Two years after his return, he was to become the collaborator of Christoph Wilibald von Gluck (1714–1787)—his outstanding contemporary in the field of lyric drama, who like himself insisted on the noble and heartfelt as opposed to the brittle and brilliant—in mounting the dances for the great composer's *Iphigénie en Tauride* (1778). All of the surviving operas of Gluck—*Orfeo ed Euridice, Alceste,* the two *Iphigenias,* and *Armide*—demand even today in performance the vision of a contemporary Noverre, so completely are they a fusion of song, dance, and mime.

Still, the full impact of Noverre's *ballet d'action*—a form in which movement and drama were designed to coincide at every point—was to be realized less in his practical works than in the famous series of theoretical *Lettres sur la Danse et sur les Ballets,* addressed to his patron, the Duke of Württemberg, and published in 1760. In this sheaf of articles, Noverre wrote that "ballet must speak through the eyes, as it were, to the very soul of the spectator." For him the technique of the dance, though a required foundation, was secondary to its goal: expressive power. These writings were to give strong direction to the work of future choreographers, among them Salvatore Viganò and Michel Fokine.

Noverre also had pupils to carry on his principles at first hand, notably Jean Dauberval (1742–1806), whose comedy-ballet, *La Fille Mal Gardée,* first produced at Bordeaux in 1786, is the oldest member of today's standard repertory (in a revised, nineteenth-century version). The period of Noverre and Dauberval, though full of disappointments for talented artists—because of the traditionalism entrenched at French theatres—did offer them certain basic opportunities. Dance was still considered an indispensable part of the lyric stage, not only in the majestic operas of a Gluck but in the lighter and perhaps more representative stage pieces of an André Grétry (1741–1813). The production of independent ballets went on as before. Most of the dancing, however, was complacent in quality; and the ideals of Noverre, ultimately to prevail, were lost to Paris for the time in a welter of conventionalism that, despite the beheading of the Bourbons, stayed enthroned on the Parisian stage.

MASTERS OF ITALIAN DANCE

With the turn of the nineteenth century, supremacy in theatrical dance passed briefly from France to Italy. One of the greatest names in the history of the art, Salvatore Viganò (1769–1821), a pupil of Dauberval, presided at Milan's famous opera house, La Scala, as ballet master, producing works in which for the first time members of the *corps de ballet* were made to move as individual artists instead of as a collective mass.

Before his intendancy at La Scala, which began in 1812, Viganò had danced and choreographed in Spain (where he met Dauberval), England, Germany, and Austria. It was in Austria that he collaborated with Ludwig van Beethoven on the ballet *The Creatures of Prometheus* (1801).* An excellent musician himself, he sometimes composed music for the works he produced in the Italian theatre. The French novelist Stendhal, in his travel diary *Rome, Naples, Florence, 1817,* has left striking evidence of how strongly this generation esteemed Viganò, with his massive Milanese dramas that often bordered more on pantomime than dance. The range of subjects was monumental: *Otello, Prometheus* (not to be confused with the earlier *Creatures of Prometheus), La Vestale, The Titans,* all of them set heroically on the immense Scala stage. Not one of them has come down to us. We know these works only through contemporary accounts of them and through reproductions of their wonderful scenic designs by the artist Sanquirico. Beyond a doubt, whatever the disparity between motion and mime, they must have had magnificently stirring moments.

The other leading Italian force in nineteenth-century dance, Carlo Blasis (1797–1878), a cultured man with such varied interests in science and the arts as to suggest a minor da Vinci, was more concerned with the codification of ballet technique than with the extension of its aesthetic range. The principles of systematic practice, exercises, and basic training formulated by Blasis in his famous *Treatise on the Dance* (published in 1820) and *The Code of Terpsichore* (1830) have lasted into the present time as the fundamentals of the *danse d'école*—the formal school on which the mechanics of ballet rest and around which they can be broadened as the expressive need arises. Blasis was appointed director of the Imperial Academy of Dancing and Pantomime at Milan in 1837. His teachings were to be carried by gifted pupils to every corner of Europe; but Italian creative choreography, with the passing of Viganò, was never to recover its short-lived supremacy.

THE ROMANTIC BALLET

Soon again Paris became the center of theatrical dance. The romantic ballet, child of the French literary mind, had brought it back. This type of work—called romantic because of its fantastic, other-worldly

* See page 136.

background but actually, in point of technique, of classic texture—
burst upon the Parisian public in 1831 with the sensational third act
of Meyerbeer's opera *Robert the Devil,* in which Marie Taglioni scored
the first of her many triumphs as leader of a band of ghostly bacchantes. With Taglioni, representing in her soaring movements the
release of the spirit from earthly limitations, all of the ballerinas of the
romantic age were soon to rise on their toes (*sur les pointes*) and stay
there. Her floating powers were exhibited even more impressively a
year after *Robert* in the ballet *La Sylphide* and later in *La Fille du
Danube.* Then, in the same ethereal vein, but with greater dramatic
contrasts within the plot, came the epoch-making *Giselle* (1841). Carlotta Grisi, another adept in the art of elevation, was to dance the title
role.

Not only has this ballet remained important, ever since opening
night, for its uncanny combination of progressive action with formalized dance; it is noteworthy as well for the score by Adolphe Adam
which, whatever its ultimate artistic merits, may well be labeled the
first modern ballet music. Gluck's wonderful score for the danced *Don
Juan,* on which he collaborated with the choreographer Angiolini in
1761, is still a model of dramatic power; yet it is conceived in separate
sections which, though they follow one another in order, are different
entities. The same may be said of Mozart's charming but theatrically
less worthy ballet *Les Petits Riens,* and of Beethoven's impressive *The
Creatures of Prometheus.* With the score of *Giselle,* a symphonic flow
is established in which individual numbers are so masterfully blended
with the course of the choreography as to provide a continuous expressive framework. It is but one step from here to the musical architecture of today's ballets, with their long-lined spans.

CHANGING VALUES

In the France of the 1830's, theatrical dance was a woman's world.
Taglioni and Grisi precipitated the era of romantic ballerinas. Lucile
Grahn, Fanny Cerito, and Fanny Elssler, the last of whom also excelled in character dancing, carried it on. The male dancer in this
period was little more than a cavalier, supporting the ballerina in the
adagios and carrying out the necessities of the plot. Not until the advent, in the next century, of Vaslav Nijinsky and Adolph Bolm were
the traditions of the house of Vestris, with their emphasis on strong,
expressive male dance, to be restored.

With the Opéra itself declining, irrevocably this time, into a place of
business rather than of art, there was little scope in Paris for choreog-

raphers of imagination, once the first glories of the romantic ballet had been diffused. Jules Perrot (1810–1892), husband of Grisi and part-designer of *Giselle*, spent much of his time at the new fountainhead of theatrical dance, the Imperial Theatre of St. Petersburg. In Paris, there remained Lucien Petipa (1815–1900), Arthur Saint-Léon (although he, too, had his Russian interludes), and Louis Mérante (1828–1887). Saint-Léon, most imaginative of the three, brought forth the only ballet masterpiece to be created in Paris between the fading of the romantic movement and the end of the century: *Coppélia*. He enjoyed in this work the musical collaboration of Léo Delibes (1836–1891), whose scores for the dance have taken their place beside those of Tchaikovsky and Stravinsky (in addition to having influenced the latter two formatively) as among the most colorful and idiomatic in ballet literature. Unfortunately, the choreographic worth of the other ballets for which Delibes provided his excellent music came nowhere near that of *Coppélia*.

BALLET IN OPERA

During this same period of the middle and late nineteenth century which saw the decline of ballet in Western Europe, the large-scale "grand" opera came fully into its own . . . and the hub of operatic activity was Paris. Italy, of course, had its great composers of lyric drama, but they came to France for the final accolade. Gaetano Rossini created his *William Tell* expressly for the Paris Opéra; Giuseppe Verdi wrote *Don Carlos* for the same theatre and revised many of his other works for production in Paris. The word "revised" has a special significance here, for the trappings of ballet—if no longer its creative possibilities—lingered in operatic traditions of the French capital and were required as part of the over-all decoration. Foreign works, up for Paris production, which contained no grand ballet with which to dazzle the audience at the height of the evening, must be changed until the desired effect came off. It was on this stone that Richard Wagner stumbled with his Paris version of *Tannhäuser* (1861), refusing to interpolate a ballet in the middle of his second act—the fashionable nook for dance—but placing it, instead, at the very beginning of the opera, in the Venusberg scene. This did not suit Parisian taste of the era and, together with a brace of more personal reasons, caused the work to be hissed.

The requirement of grand ballets for grand operas persisted. When Charles Gounod, who had written *Faust* to be performed at a smaller Paris house, the Théâtre Lyrique (1859), wanted to bring his work into the repertory of the Opéra ten years later, a full-scale dance epi-

LUCIEN PETIPA AND MARIE TAGLIONI

sode had to be added. This tradition of ballet in opera as a kind of sauce over the vocal meat was injected into the Italian theatre through such spectacular works, modeled along Parisian lines, as Verdi's *Aïda* (1871) and Ponchielli's *La Gioconda* (1876), in which brilliant music was combined with a fair amount of academic dance. Gone was the fusion between song, sound, and movement that had marked the operas of Gluck. These new ballet interludes were dragged in by the hair or the heels in a triumphal procession or ballroom scene and, via the still-born quality of their dramatic mood, have contributed largely to the inertia which hangs today over the dance departments of most opera houses.

TOWARD A FREER OPERATIC DANCE

Characters in the classical operas and ballets of the eighteenth century were invariably gods or heroic mortals; those of the nineteenth, either fantastic members of the spirit world or earthy members of a peasant community. The "folk" feeling invaded opera by way of Karl Maria von Weber's *Der Freischütz* (1821), with its fascinating blend of the popular and the supernatural, and ballet through the admirably conceived scenes of peasant life in *Giselle*. By the time of *Coppélia* (1870), it had become the vogue to introduce various national dances into the action of grand ballets as *divertissements* incidental to the plot. When these were carried over into opera, as in Smetana's *The Bartered Bride* (1866), Borodin's *Prince Igor* * (1889), and, in our own century, Jaromir Weinberger's *Schwanda the Bagpipe-Player* (1927), all works of Slavic background, the lyric dramas to which they were added gained, rather than lost, in color and impact.

Aside from these folk moments, the grand ballet—in diluted, unimaginative form—was to remain supreme, a deadening weight to nineteenth-century opera (except where the sheer genius of a Verdi forced it to a triumphant conclusion). Not until the works of Richard Strauss did a new direction reveal itself. In the very period when Michel Fokine, as a young man in Russia, was starting his earliest ballet reforms, the Bavarian composer was at work on an opera, *Salome* (1905), which called for a freely designed dance of the utmost expressivity as its climax. In 1909, Strauss was to repeat this same formula with *Elektra*, in which the singing voice also yielded, at the point of highest emotional intensity, to the flash of a moving body. It seems almost predestined that these two masters, Fokine and Strauss, should finally have collaborated (even when somewhat past their respective primes) on a full-scale ballet, *The Legend of Joseph* (1914), in which a third great creative force, Léonide Massine, then a youth of twenty, made his debut in the title role . . . all under the auspices of the most potent force seen by ballet in this century—Sergei Diaghilev.

THE BIRTH OF RUSSIAN BALLET

Diaghilev (1872–1929) was the first to acquaint Western Europe and America with the full spendor of Russian ballet, when he assembled a company of artists from the Imperial Theatres and presented them in Paris at the Châtelet in May, 1909. To many in the audience, this seemed like an art sprung into birth full-grown; but it had been in the process of evolution since the early 1700's, when the French ballet master Lande was imported by the Empress Anne to give instruction at the newly formed Dancing Academy in St. Petersburg. Later in the same century, Gaspare Angiolini—the choreographer for Gluck's *Don Juan* (Vienna, 1764)—and the great French dancer Charles Le Picq went to Russia at the invitation of Catherine the Great. These foreign

* Completed after Borodin's death by Rimsky-Korsakov and Glazunov.

masters left their mark on the development of native dancers who were eager to progress and seemed to have untold powers of application. The arrival of the famous dancer and choreographer Charles Didelot (1768–1837) during the reign of the Emperor Paul cemented this special quality of technical solidity which has been associated with Russian ballet ever since.

While the vitality of theatrical dance was declining in the West, after the last flowering of romantic ballet, it remained on the ascendant in St. Petersburg. Outstanding dancers, including Marie Taglioni, went to perform as guests, revealing a new poetry and virtuosity to Slavic audiences; eminent choreographers, who had been trained in the best traditions, helped establish a repertory and standards of performance superior to those of any other European capital; and generous grants from the Imperial treasury maintained ballet as an integral part of the Russian scene. Under the leadership of the French-born choreographer Marius Petipa (1822–1910) and his assistant, Lev Ivanov (1834–1901), the Mariinsky Theatre * of the Russian capital became the home of lavishly presented, technically superior dance.

THE REIGN OF PETIPA

Many of the newer ballets at the Mariinsky, under the long intendancy of Petipa (he was connected with the Imperial Theatres from 1847 to 1903), were repetitions of formulas long overworked. Their scenic backgrounds, expensive rather than suggestive, made scarcely more than a passing nod to historical accuracy; their choreographic plan was often a stereotype of what had served successfully on several previous occasions. Yet Petipa, principally of value in his concept of smoothly run performance, of well-knit administrative order, could— when working with a first-class collaborator like Tchaikovsky—turn out a choreographic masterpiece. *The Sleeping Beauty* remains a case in point. Essentially a conservative, Petipa was not actively opposed to change; but at times he did endorse it only under pressure. Such was the case of the visiting Italian dancers.

One St. Petersburg summer after the Mariinsky had closed for the season, Virginia Zucchi (1874–1930), the ballerina of a small Mediterranean troupe appearing at a secondary theatre in town, so electrified her audiences with the brilliance and strength of her technique that Petipa received a court order to engage her at once for his company.

* The Mariinsky Theatre, subsidized by the Czar, was opened as an opera house in October, 1860. Twenty years later, ballet—in addition to the operatic schedule— was transferred there from the Bolshoi Theatre of St. Petersburg, which had served as its home since 1783.

He acceded; and the utter precision of Zucchi's dancing (she had been a pupil of Blasis) greatly influenced the performing standards at the Mariinsky. Other eminent Italian ballerinas followed—Pierina Legnani and Carlotta Brianza; and, in 1887, the noted male dancer, Enrico Cecchetti (1850–1928), joined the company, not only to appear as soloist but later to teach for many years at the Imperial School. Thus Russian ballet, as we know it today, combines elements of French origin, Slavic organic growth, and Italian technical finish.

At the beginning of the twentieth century St. Petersburg saw spectacular productions, impeccable technique. As yet there were no great native male dancers; but under the influence of the Imperial Academy, there had grown up a new generation of Russian ballerinas which included the notable Mathilde Kchessinska, Olga Preobrajenska, Vera Trefilova, and one of the greatest performers of the age, Anna Pavlova (1881–1931). Every stimulus to artistic perfection was present except a sense of expressive power in the choreography for the newer works. Stagnation had set in.

FOKINE AND THE DIAGHILEV ERA

The cycle of conflict between the lyrical and technical elements in ballet had swung round again; and this time, in place of Noverre and Viganò arose Michel Fokine (1880–1942) to demand that music, painting, and dance be fused into one powerful entity. At first, as a teacher in the Imperial School, he met with the expected opposition to ideas contrary to those in practice. In time, he prevailed; and the story of his greater works, nearly all of them produced for the first time outside of Russia during the seasons of ballet begun by Sergei Diaghilev at the Paris Châtelet in 1909, occupies a considerable portion of this book.

Certainly it was Diaghilev who brought out the best in Fokine—*Les Sylphides*, *Petrouchka*, the original opera-ballet version of *Le Coq d'Or* (1914)—just as he succeeded in drawing out the genius of all the great artists with whom he came in touch. First interested in the promotion of modern tendencies within the Russian art world, then in the diffusion of those currents abroad, he was attracted successively to painting, opera, and ballet; and it was in this order that he arranged the demonstrations of Russian art in Paris which were to launch his career as a Western impresario.

In the end, after forming a permanent company of his own and severing official connections with the Russian Imperial Theatres, Diaghilev was to pull up national roots and center his interests on the Côte d'Azur. His range of ballet subjects passed from their initially Slavic phase through Gallic satire to Marxian commentary. In playing the eclectic, courting the purely novel, he was to forfeit, before his death, the artistic vitality of his career in its prime; but any criticisms of sterile pathways followed by the later Diaghilev are as nothing beside his stupendous gifts to contemporary art.

It was he who launched the greatest living composer, Igor Stravinsky, on his creative way, commissioning successively *L'Oiseau de Feu*, *Petrouchka*, and *Le Sacre du Printemps*; who restored the prestige of the male dancer with that most fabulous of performers, Vaslav Nijinski; who encouraged, in this same artist, choreographic powers which, though of more inherent promise than realization, indicated new expressive directions; who discovered and trained Léonide Massine, one of the foremost living choreographers and dancers; who gave scope to the development of another gifted choreographer, Bronislava Nijinska, sister of Vaslav; who presented the finest creative and dancing talents available, from Fokine, Thamar Karsavina, and Adolph Bolm of his earliest years to George Balanchine, Alexandra Danilova, and Anton Dolin of the last period; who took first-class ballet on tour to communities which had never experienced it before; and, finally, who—in engaging the outstanding painters, writers, choreographers, and composers of their times to work side by side, under a centrally guiding hand, on the creation of new ballets—must have fulfilled, on many occasions, the old dreams and yearnings of Noverre. This was a man with incalculable influence on every phase of theatrical dance in our time.

With his death in 1929, his dancers were scattered, some of them coming to America, many of them going to England, and a few remaining in France. Serge Lifar, one of his last disciples, became premier danseur at the Paris Opéra; Anton Dolin was to help establish, with another former Diaghilev dancer and distinguished choreographer in her own right, Ninette de Valois, the Camargo Society in London. Miss de Valois later founded the Sadler's Wells Ballet company, which has since achieved international prominence; Mr. Dolin formed his own troupe with Alicia Markova, eventually coming to America to join Ballet Theatre.

EARLY THEATRICAL DANCE IN AMERICA

The United States enjoyed performances of ballet as far back as 1791. These first manifestations were not of the highest order; but in the course of the 1830's such artists as Paul Taglioni (brother of Marie) and his wife Amélie were to reach New York on tour; and in the years

1840–42 the renowned Fanny Elssler, idol of Paris, Vienna, and London, barnstormed the country with sensational success.

It is a tragic fact that the history of ballet in America during the entire nineteenth century and much of the twentieth has been a succession of illustrious European names appearing as guests rather than the formation of any first-class native company. The early 1900's saw Adeline Genée, Anna Pavlova, and Mikhail Mordkin performing as guests at the Metropolitan Opera House; but that theatre had no *corps* of ultimate distinction with which to surround them. Mme Pavlova's many journeys across the country helped, through the ballerina's exquisite art, to bring the average man closer to theatrical dance; yet her troupe was poor in music and décor. It was not until the Diaghilev synthesis of these arts arrived on tour in 1916 that the United States was exposed to the full range of ballet, its rich potentialities in combining movement, painting, and sound. The impressions created were to take root and remain.

BALLET REVIVAL

Between 1916, the year of the Diaghilev visit, and 1933, when Sol Hurok, indefatigable American manager, brought the René Blum and Colonel de Basil Ballets Russes de Monte Carlo into the St. James Theatre, New York, there was a drought of theatrical dance in this country. In its place had come beginnings of an exceptionally fertile development in concert dance; but this movement, except as it has directly affected the evolution of ballet, is outside the scope of the present accounting. The arrival of the troupe owned jointly by the director of the Monte Carlo Opera Ballet and a former Russian army officer renewed the main line of danced theatre in this country, and audiences were quick to accept it.

Internal warfare in artistic and business direction was before long to split the company into conflicting organizations, all with confusingly similar names and all competing fiercely for the services of available artists and choreographers. But in the first days of the ballet renaissance in America, an interesting repertory was presented, including some of the old Fokine works and new ones by George Balanchine (who had been with the troupe for one season in Europe, from its formation at Monte Carlo in 1932 until 1933); pre-eminent ballerinas were introduced to this country: Alexandra Danilova, Tamara Toumanova, Irina Baronova, Tatiana Riabouchinska (the last three, children of Russian *émigré* families, discovered by Balanchine in Parisian dancing studios, still in their early 'teens at the time of their debuts); and, lastly, the season was brightened by the presence both as dancer and as choreographer of Léonide Massine, who, after an earlier tour here with the Diaghilev company and a subsequent creative prime abroad, had languished in New York for three years (1928–31) as ballet master at the Roxy Theatre.

LÉONIDE MASSINE

Massine's works had their expressive and coloristic origins in the reforms of Michel Fokine, but went on—in certain of his best compositions—to a new plastic resourcefulness and fullness of design. In his famous "symphonic ballets," the first of which—*Les Présages,* to the music of Tchaikovsky's Fifth Symphony—was produced in 1933, the choreographer was to communicate through dance the architectural and emotional quality of an orchestral score as he heard it. Some of the results were striking; others fell short.

This medium of symphonic ballet contains its debatable aesthetic points, and has sometimes led Massine to impose a pretentious literary idea on a purely musical design; but it has also spurred him into producing some notable works. Most successful among them remains the Berlioz *Symphonie Fantastique,* a *ballet d'action* with scenario based on program notes by the composer, realizing to a remarkable extent the dramatic intentions of the mind that molded the music. His more stylized but almost equally commanding treatment of the Shostakovich First Symphony in *Rouge et Noir* also ranks among his finer achievements.

Symphonic ballets aside, perhaps no other choreographer of modern times has varied so radically in the general quality of his output, from the sublimity of a *St. Francis* and dash of a *Three-Cornered Hat* to the futility of an *1814.* Massine has been censured severely on the basis of his shortcomings, while his very real attainments—his wealth of theatrical imagination and unique grasp of the high-dramatic element in ballet—have too often been passed over. He has been critically accepted, rather, for his supremacy as a performing artist, the most commanding stage personality of his time.

GEORGE BALANCHINE

The advent of Balanchine had a profound effect on theatrical and pedagogic dance in the United States. Not only a first-rank choreographer, but a pianist and conductor of ability, he brought to his teaching and to his creative works a crispness of phrasing, musicality of movement, and feeling for absolute design—heritages of the Russian Imperial School, in which he was trained as a boy—that were to grow constantly, during his stay here, in communicative strength from the experimental days of the American Ballet (started by Lincoln Kirstein in 1934) through the more mature and distinguished period of Ballet Society (founded in 1946, with Mr. Kirstein again as moving force), to the culmination of the latter group as the New York City Ballet (1948).

Balanchine's choreographic and musical powers, as represented in his latest output, seem inexhaustible. His is a cool, bright flame as compared to the dark fires of Massine, but steadier. Alone among dance creators of the present day, he has inspired a band of disciples, young choreographers including William Dollar, Todd Bolender, and John Taras, many of whose works were first performed publicly by Ballet Caravan (1936–41) and the American Concert Ballet (1943). Both of these troupes came into being through the efforts of Mr. Kirstein, who, in every field of theatrical dance, scholarly as well as executive, has made important contributions to the progress of the art in this country.

From 1944 to 1946, Mr. Balanchine was also actively associated with one of the later incarnations of the original Blum–de Basil troupe, the Ballet Russe de Monte Carlo, under the direction of Sergei Denham. He raised the performing standards of the company, developed the talents of several notable young dancers, including Maria Tallchief—now his wife—Ruthanna Boris (also a talented choreographer), and Leon Danielian, staging several of his own ballets as part of the repertory. During the season of 1947–48 he was to bring one of his finest works, *Theme and Variations*, to the stage for still another major group: Ballet Theatre.

THE WORK OF BALLET THEATRE

This company, which, perhaps more than any other, has occupied a leading place on the American scene, was formed in 1939 by Lucia Chase and Richard Pleasants—outgrowth of a previous group founded by the late Mikhail Mordkin in conjunction with his ballet school.

The aims of Ballet Theatre's inaugural season were strikingly creative: Antony Tudor, promising British choreographer, was to be in charge of the company's English wing; Eugene Loring, already noted for *Billy the Kid* (Ballet Caravan, 1938), of the American division; and Anton Dolin, director of the classical department. Although many changes in policy and administrative personnel were to take place in

MARIE TAGLIONI AND STULLMÜLLER IN ZEMIRE ET AZOR, AN 1825 BALLET WITH
CHOREOGRAPHY BY PAUL TAGLIONI, BROTHER OF MARIE

the group's early years, with the departure of Loring and the arrival of
a Russian wing, Ballet Theatre has adhered almost constantly throughout a stormy existence to interesting programs and high standards of
performance. Its only grave mishap occurred in 1946, when the management parted company with Mr. Dolin. The classical repertory de-
clined, the rounded grace of Dolin's staging yielding to a hardness of
line appropriate to contemporary themes but out of place in *Swan Lake*.

Ballet Theatre's positive achievements have been many. In the last
years of his life, Michel Fokine provided the organization with a revival of his *Sylphides* and a fresh success in *Bluebeard*; Massine contributed his debatable but effective *Aleko*, later appearing as guest in
several performances of this and other ballets; the young dancers Nora
Kaye, Rosella Hightower, Alicia Alonso, and John Kriza rose from the
ranks to stardom; performances of grandeur were contributed by
Alicia Markova, of earthy appeal by Irina Baronova; and significant
new works were designed by Antony Tudor and Jerome Robbins.

ANTONY TUDOR

Mr. Tudor's fame had preceded him from England and was the basis of his joining the company. His choreography, though based on the classical *danse d'école,* shows the same indebtedness to modern (concert) dance that marks certain of the works of Massine, notably *Rouge et Noir* and *St. Francis*; but Tudor's use of these elements is more consistent. The center of gravity in his ballets lies in the psychological heart of the plot, in the conflict of the subconscious emotions that dominate his characters. When these are turned outward, the result can be repellent but is always dramatically rewarding.

The Tudor ballets, adult experiences, need performers trained in a special idiom of intricate movement and timing. They have been fortunate in the presence of Hugh Laing, who has danced every one of them with authority, and of Nora Kaye, who won her first triumph with *Pillar of Fire.*

JEROME ROBBINS

The other choreographic mainstay of Ballet Theatre, native-born Jerome Robbins, started with the company in 1940 as a member of the *corps,* first came to public attention the following year through a bit part in Agnes de Mille's *Three Virgins and a Devil,* and was soon dancing leading roles, notably in *Petrouchka* and as alternate for Mr. Laing in *Pillar of Fire.* He developed into a stimulating soloist; but his real importance to theatrical dance began with the première of his own *Fancy Free* in 1944. Here was the perfect American comedy-ballet—with overtones of sturdy warmth—masterful in its formal structure, unself-conscious in its use of a native theme. Mr. Robbins later carried over these same gifts for humor to the abstract *Interplay,* for characterization to his brooding *Facsimile,* but was less successful in a subsequent ballet of social significance, *The Guests,* where the etched clarity of design that, along with fundamental rhythmic animation, is the hallmark of his best work, was clouded by political confusion. Unlike Mr. Tudor, who, with the exception of *Undertow,* has always used standard symphonic scores for his ballets, Robbins works directly with contemporary composers from the outset. He has been blessed in his collaboration with Leonard Bernstein, one of the most vital figures in American music, who first made a spectacular debut in the world of ballet by both composing and brilliantly conducting the score of *Fancy Free.*

LORING AND DE MILLE

Further American choreographers of standing, associated during part of their careers with Lucia Chase's troupe, are Eugene Loring and Agnes de Mille. With *Billy the Kid*, his first important composition, Mr. Loring gave promise of becoming a dominant force in dance. This is still the most compelling tragic ballet on a large scale to have come from American roots; Loring's movement patterns, Kirstein's scenario, and Aaron Copland's score were fused into a work of absolute power; but Mr. Loring, in his subsequent productions for Ballet Theatre (1939–40) and Dance Players (1941–42), of which he became artistic director, did not quite recapture the ecstasy of *Billy*. Dance Players, however, did serve a valuable purpose in training promising young dancers, some of whom—among them Michael Kidd and Janet Reed—developed into notable performers. It also enabled Lew Christensen, whose *Filling Station* had been mounted by Ballet Caravan in 1938, to stage another meritorious work, *Jinx*.

Mr. Loring's *Billy*, epic of the Southwest, was to enjoy in time a pendant: Agnes de Mille's diverting little work about the same region, *Rodeo*, produced by the Ballet Russe de Monte Carlo in 1944. Miss de Mille, at her best in themes that command an expressive rather than a formal medium, has brought a wealth of mime to the American dance theatre. Her ability to strike and sustain a dramatic mood—joyous and deeply human, as in *Rodeo*, or macabre, as in *Fall River Legend* (Ballet Theatre, 1948)—compensates for occasional limitations in over-all design.

BALLET IN MUSICAL COMEDY

Much of Miss de Mille's most valuable work has been done in the field of musical comedy. After an initial venture in this medium by Michel Fokine, whose dances for productions by the late Florenz Ziegfeld and other revue magnates during the 1920's represented more of a commercial by-product than a practicing art form, real impetus for the integration of ballet into the popular theatre was launched by George Balanchine with his ingenious *Slaughter on Tenth Avenue*, danced by Ray Bolger in the musical *On Your Toes* (1936). The *Slaughter* episode, a satirical piece dealing with the lives and loves of gangsters, came as the dramatic climax of the evening and proved that, in the hands of an expert choreographer, ballet could offer a fascinating adjunct to Broadway. Mr. Balanchine has since devised the dances for many other successful musical comedies, including *I Married an Angel, The Boys from Syracuse, Cabin in the Sky,* and *Where's Charley?*

Agnes de Mille's contribution to this entertainment medium has been even more solidly organic. Where Mr. Balanchine was content to build his numbers around the story, Miss de Mille's dancers in *Oklahoma, Carousel, Allegro,* and *Brigadoon were* the story. The talented Michael Kidd, with one work, *On Stage,* to his credit in Ballet Theatre's repertory, won distinction in musical comedy through his brilliant dances for *Finian's Rainbow,* inseparable from the molding of the plot. Jerome Robbins, too, has worked productively in the field with *On the Town* (an evolution of his *Fancy Free*), *Billion Dollar Baby, High Button Shoes,* and *Miss Liberty.* Most of the patterns for these Broadway ballets have stemmed not from the *danse d'école,* retained merely as a basis for footwork and "lifts," but from the enormous range of bodily expressiveness which is the contribution of modern dance.

In their enthusiasm for the wedding of ballet and Broadway, some of these choreographers have loaded the scales at the expense of those other component elements of musical comedy, song and dialogue, prompting a hostile critical reaction. Only Helen Tamiris, whose designs for *Annie Get Your Gun* and *Inside U.S.A.* remain a model of their kind—deft, imaginative, mercurial, but never obtrusive—and Mr. Balanchine seem to have respected fully the conventions of this form.

A highly interesting attempt to fuse dance and theatre idioms into an interdependent whole by creating a new medium for them was made in 1948 by the show called *Ballet Ballads.* This group of short plays, danced and sung, with words by John La Touche and music by Jerome Moross, called three different choreographers into service: Katherine Litz for the first of the plays, *Susanna and the Elders;* Paul Godkin for the second, *Willy the Weeper;* and Hanya Holm for the finale, *Davy Crockett. Willy the Weeper,* an inventive work in itself, profited by the appearance of its choreographer in the title role, for Mr. Godkin—more recently soloist with Ballet Theatre—is one of the most prodigiously gifted dancers of the day. *Davy Crockett,* set with humor and imagination by Miss Holm, offered an agreeable experience in theatre dance-song. *Susanna and the Elders,* which had more of whimsy than design, fared least well of the three.

Another field, vast in its opportunities for development, has recently been opened to choreographers: television. Among the leading figures who have already created in this medium are Balanchine, Bolender, and Godkin. No definitive trends have yet emerged; but it is safe to predict that the technical demands of the television camera may soon change the course of ballet more radically than any other single factor in its history until now.

OUTSIDE THE DANSE D'ÉCOLE

A major enigma in theatrical dance lies in the career of Doris Humphrey, who, unequaled among native-born choreographers for her mastery of invention and expressiveness of design, has not yet produced a work at the bidding of any large-scale company. In magnitude of conception, Miss Humphrey's own stage productions—given in small New York theatres or at Bennington College, Vermont—surpass a majority of the more ambitiously mounted ballets which have come our way. This is an inner magnitude, for Miss Humphrey's loftiness of theme and treatment, as in the great trilogy *New Dance, Theater Piece*, and *With My Red Fires* (1935–36), or *Inquest* (1944), are not calculated in terms of massed effect but rather of communicating the dynamic and emotional heart of the dance in a form that is clear, noble, and moving. The choreographer seems neither to accept nor to reject the technique of the *danse d'école*. In her vocabulary, based on the pull of gravity between balance and unbalance, all is admitted which can be integrated legitimately into the art work at hand.

Claude Debussy once wrote, in a penetrating essay which flays the cult of separatism in the arts, that "there is only a single music, be it the symphony or the waltz." His statement may be extended to the unity of theatrical dance, be it the formal ballet or the widely removed aesthetic of Martha Graham. It is not the place of this perspective to inquire into the technical and philosophical bases of Miss Graham's school. These have had their origins outside the traditional medium which, with its lines of development, is the province of this book. Yet ballet is a sphere not unknown to Miss Graham and, on one occasion, was conquered by her triumphantly when, in 1929, she danced the leading role in Massine's version of *Le Sacre du Printemps* at the Metropolitan Opera House. It is simply that her creative interests lie, in general, far from the *danse d'école* or its recent evolutions. Such a divergence is less drastic than it sounds. When Miss Graham, a choreographer and performing artist of consequence, produces convincing theatre pieces and, in the course of their preparation, causes new musical scores by Aaron Copland (*Appalachian Spring*), Paul Hindemith (*Herodiade*), Darius Milhaud (*Imagined Wing*), Carlos Chávez (*Dark Meadow*), William Schuman (*Night Journey*), Samuel Barber (*Cave of the Heart*), Gian-Carlo Menotti (*Errand into the Maze*), Norman

21

Dello Joio (*Diversion of Angels*), and Vincent Persichetti (*Lear*) to be written for her, she emerges not only as a salient figure in the general field of dance but also as a tremendous influence on the musical future of ballet. Outstanding symphonic composers, once they are enticed from the concert platform into the orchestra pit, are likely to remain there for further collaboration.

After nearly three hundred years, ballet (as part of a larger dance theatre) has only begun to try its choreographic wings. Great periods of performing technique lie behind us; but new creative eras, involving a fusion of all the arts, are clearly ahead.

Courtesy Dance News

MARIE TAGLIONI WITH HER BROTHER PAUL IN A BALLET ENTITLED
THE EVENING OF A RAJAH

THE STORIES
OF THE BALLETS

Adélaïde, ou la Langage des Fleurs

THIS ONE-ACT BALLET ("Adélaïde, or the Language of the Flowers"),
with choreography by Natashe Trouhanova, contains both book and
music by Maurice Ravel. After having scored his "Valses Nobles et Sentimentales"—written originally as a group of piano pieces (1911)—for
symphony orchestra, Ravel was asked by Mlle Trouhanova if she might
use the new version as basis for a stage work. The composer not only
agreed but, since he was especially interested in ballet at this time, having recently completed the score of *Daphnis et Chloé*, developed a
dramatic outline for his music. The score was first produced in ballet
form at the Théâtre du Châtelet, Paris, April, 1912, with Ravel conducting. A second edition, with choreography by Serge Lifar and décor by
Maurice Brianchon, was given at the Paris Opéra in February, 1938.
This same music served as background for William Dollar's *Promenade*,
first produced by Ballet Caravan at Bennington, Vermont, in 1936.

The action takes place about 1820, in the salon of a courtesan who expresses her moods through the medium of flowers. As the curtain rises, a
number of her guests are dancing.

Adélaïde, the hostess, pauses before a vase of tuberoses, which for her
signify voluptuousness. The language of the flowers grows even more
specific as Lorédan, a handsome young man, enters and offers Adélaïde
a hawthorn blossom indicating hope.

Unmoved, the hostess produces a white syringa, token of sisterly affection, and hands it to Lorédan; but the young man is not to be discouraged. After a heated interchange, Adélaïde gives him a black iris, which is a confession of deep love.

Adélaïde, however, changes mood. Her interest soon passes from Lorédan to a new admirer, the Duke, who arrives with a bouquet of sunflowers—the promise of riches. As she dances with the noble, Lorédan withdraws into an alcove and looks on jealously.

At last the guests retire. The Duke stays on, hoping for complete success; but, when the capricious courtesan presents him with a branch of acacia—sign of platonic love—he gives up and leaves.

Once more Lorédan advances, only to be thrust aside by Adélaïde with a new floral barrier: a poppy, symbol of forgetfulness. The youth stalks from the room, soon to reappear on a neighboring balcony, a funereal twig of cypress in hand, contemplating suicide. Only then does Adélaïde repent and throw Lorédan a red rose. He dashes from his balcony to her ballroom and she falls into his arms.

HUGH LAING AS ALEKO

Aleko

THIS BALLET in four scenes, with choreography by Léonide Massine, scenario by Mr. Massine and Marc Chagall, artistic collaboration by Henry Clifford, is based on the poem *Gypsies*, by Alexander Pushkin (from which the opera *Aleko*, by Sergei Rachmaninoff, was also derived). Produced at the Palacio de Bellas Artes, Mexico City, by Ballet Theatre, September 8, 1942, it had its first North American performance at the Metropolitan Opera House, October 6, 1942, with Alicia Markova and Hugh Laing as the gypsies, and George Skibine in the title role. Mr. Massine, Anton Dolin, André Eglevsky, and Igor Youskevitch have subsequently appeared in the name part.

Critical reception of *Aleko* at its première was mixed, with the preponderance of opinion verging on the unfavorable. For some groups, however—admittedly in the minority—this ballet remains a colorful addition to the repertoire, a piece with its dancing roots in the romantic past but its theatrical aesthetic in the present, a work in which Massine has achieved as perhaps rarely before—save in *St. Francis*—a singular directness of narrative style, obscured on first sight only by the complexity of the surrounding group dances.

The décor and costumes by Marc Chagall are a major part of the appeal of *Aleko*. Four splendid backdrops, with the sumptuousness of independent canvases but related indispensably to the dramatic action, give final point to Massine's choreography. They are among the most striking in all ballet. The music is that of Tchaikovsky's A minor Trio for Pianoforte, Violin, and Cello, in an arrangement for symphony orchestra by the late Erno Rapee.

SCENES ONE AND TWO

(Set to the first movement of the trio)

Night has fallen across a vast Russian wasteland. A campfire glows dimly in the gloom. At its side crouches an old gypsy woman, at once hag and visionary, her eyes fixed on a point of sky that had been the horizon at dusk. A malignant bird, its feathers still brilliant in the failing light, hovers about the scene. Across from the gypsy woman stands an old man of the tribe, the leader of this wandering band. He too is staring ahead, his face overcast. Grouped about these figures are the motionless gypsies.

Tchaikovsky, in the opening movement of the Piano Trio, plunges without introduction into his first theme, and Massine, in his treatment of the music, enters directly into the dramatic action. The curtain rises in silence. At once, into the midst of the gypsies comes a stranger—the city youth, Aleko. Self-exiled from his community, he is wandering along the plain, looking among the nomads for those human sympathies denied him at home.

The youth seems to find what he is seeking in Zemphira, a gypsy girl, daughter of the chieftain. She is young, swarthy, a Carmen of the steppes. At the bidding of her father, the young men of the tribe rouse themselves and make Aleko welcome.

This is the flood-tide of his love for Zemphira. As the young gypsies frolic at their games and whirl across the background, the pair dance a passionate *pas de deux.*

But a new, languorous melody is introduced in the orchestra, and a rival suddenly appears on stage: a dark-skinned youth of the tribe. He

attracts Zemphira, who turns to him and ignores her lover. All this time, the old woman is staring at the invisible point on the horizon.

The opening motive of the trio returns and, to its sorrowful melody, Zemphira's father tries to console the forsaken Aleko. So do the younger nomads. They jump onto the back of a prancing horse and drag the stranger off to share their wandering life. The scene changes; the gypsies have become part of a traveling circus. Gaiety prevails in the midst of the striped booths. Even Zemphira's father, who presides over the fair, seems to have lost his forbidding appearance.

Aleko works with the gypsy boys, helping unroll the carpets for the performers, watching the antics of the trained bear. But the sight of Zemphira on the fringe of the circus grounds with her new lover distracts him. The spectators dissolve, dusk comes on, and—to the closing bars of this movement, with their brooding augmentation of the opening theme (No. 1)—the dreary atmosphere of the wasteland returns.

SCENE THREE

(Second movement of the trio: Theme and Variations)

Beneath a surrealist sun and sky, three maidens are bathing in a brook. Their privacy is broken by youths who have come to work in the fields near by. As the peasant women, intent on the harvest, also enter to a

Andante con moto

plodding rhythm, the bathers disappear. In early performances of *Aleko* an elaborate ensemble for two soloists and the *corps de ballet* followed at this place—"Butterfly and Pan," conventional in character and only loosely related to the plot. This whole episode has since been eliminated. As now presented, the scene moves from the entrance of the women with their scythes to a vigorous group number for the men.

The beauty of the late summer day proves too much for the workers. Forgetting the harvest, men and women dance joyously together, then rush off; and the brookside is deserted. As the golden light that beats upon the scene changes to a dull red, Zemphira enters with her gypsy lover. They come along the bank with slow, sensuous steps and are seen by Aleko, who—for the first time—threatens them.

They defy him; and Massine has cast this defiance in the form of a bold mazurka. As the dance subsides, Zemphira goes off through the reeds bordering the stream. Her lover looks after her, then disappears. Only Aleko remains, with the figures of the harvesters gliding past him on their way back to the village. The theme of the bathers returns in almost its original form, as if now—within this scene, from opening to closing—the wheels of Fate had run round.

SCENE FOUR

(Third movement of the trio)

Aleko lies in a tortured sleep. All about him are the phantoms of his past in the imperial city of St. Petersburg. A gigantic, rearing white horse and magnificent candelabra dominate the scene—tokens of Czarist splendor. The opening of this finale is still another variation—grandiose and powerful—on the melody of the second movement.

Allegro risoluto e con fuoco

ALICIA MARKOVA AND GEORGE SKIBINE

Confused images dominate Aleko's dream. The staring gypsy hag of the wastelands has been turned into a great lady of the city, mounting the social ladder of the court. Fantastic figures of nobles, flunkies, and monsters, of brutal police lashing at commoners with their knouts, crowd his brain. In his vision, he sees a poet in love with a girl of the town. A youthful Duke approaches, flatters the girl, wins her favor. Irresistibly, Aleko identifies himself with the poet, who challenges the Duke to a duel. The poet is slain but lives on through the immortality of his verse. (It is said that, in the composition of this scene, Massine had in mind, as the original of the poet, the figure of Pushkin himself, who died in a duel at the hands of his wife's brother-in-law, Baron d'Anthès.)

The imperial frolic goes on. Just as the crashing first subject of the finale is restated by the orchestra, the gypsies rush in and join the orgy. Zemphira and her lover appear among the revelers, raised on high by the crowd. The dream figures freeze in the brain of Aleko. He awakens, rises from the ground, and before him—as in the vision—stands the gypsy pair.

The motto theme of the opening movement (No. 1) returns with tenfold intensity. Raising his knife, the youth plunges it first into the body of his rival, who spins to his death, and then into the heart of Zemphira. As Aleko stays motionless beside the girl's corpse, her father—the gypsy chieftain—confronts him. In payment for his crime, the youth is sentenced not to death but to banishment.

Funereal rhythms arise in the music. Tchaikovsky composed this trio as an elegy in memory of his teacher and benefactor, Nicholas Rubinstein; and the yearning theme with which it starts is transformed, at the end, to music of the grave.

Unwanted by his friends of the city, disowned by the nomads, Aleko must live as an outcast. While the gypsies mourn and Zemphira's body is borne away, he returns to his wanderings.

Photo: Wurts Brothers

SCENE TWO FROM THE 1935 RADIO CITY MUSIC HALL PRODUCTION
OF LEONIDOFF'S EL AMOR BRUJO

El Amor Brujo

THIS BALLET ("Love, the Sorcerer"), calling for contralto soloist with orchestra, is based on an Andalusian gypsy tale. The libretto was written by Gregorio Martínez Sierra, and the score by Manuel de Falla. The ballet was first presented at the Teatro de Lara, Madrid, in April, 1915, with Pastora Imperio as featured dancer. There is no available record of the choreographer on this occasion. Probably the work was staged by Imperio herself, as its story—an old folk tale—came to Martínez, the librettist, from Imperio's mother. *El Amor Brujo* was given a concert performance in the same city during the following season under the direction of Enrique Arbos. It reached the United States in symphonic form (1928) under the direction of Arturo Toscanini.

The scenario, folklike in character and flexible in its handling of a dramatic situation, has appealed to more than one choreographer. Argentina danced the work, in her own production, at the Paris Opéra Comique in the 1920's. The late Argentinita restaged it for the Madrid Ballet in 1932; and other versions have been produced in America by such diverse personalities as Adolph Bolm (Chicago Allied Arts), La Méri (Ethnologic Dance Centre, New York), and Gluck Sandor (Dance Centre, New York).

A passionate motto theme, which runs through the ballet, sounds at once in the introduction. Soon the curtain rises on the single Andalusian

scene that is the background of the drama. To the accompaniment of nostalgic contralto singing, Candelas—heroine of the tale—appears. She has been in love with a dashing gypsy, recently dead, who lives in her memory and keeps coming back to haunt her. Always Candelas remains under the influence of this specter. . . . A live and handsome villager,

Photo: Wurts Brothers

VINCENTE ESCUDERO AND CARMITA IN THE 1935 RADIO CITY MUSIC HALL PRODUCTION

Mosso marcato

Carmelo, wants to wed her but the ghost intervenes. Because of his sorcery, she cannot grant Carmelo the kiss of perfect love.

Desperately, Candelas tries to drive off the specter through a ritual fire dance. She fails. Now the adroit Carmelo takes the reins in hand. He will himself trick the ghost, whose habits were known to him in life.

Allegro ma non troppo

Since the deceased always had a strong taste for attractive women, Carmelo decides to use Lucia, a companion of Candelas, as decoy. It is she who will break the spell and deflate the specter for all time. The plan is set in motion. Carmelo comes to woo Candelas, as the orchestra plays one of de Falla's most beautiful melodies. Jealously, the specter

Andantino tranquillo

appears, but when his eye is caught by the pretty Lucia, he ignores Candelas and follows her friend.

Carmelo is now able to convince the girl that his own devotion for her is greater than that of the specter. As morning dawns and the bells of the village sound their chimes, the pair at last exchange the perfect kiss and exorcise the ghost forever.

IGOR YOUSKEVITCH AS APOLLO

Apollon Musagète

THIS NEOCLASSICAL ballet in two scenes was commissioned by the Elizabeth Sprague Coolidge Foundation for a festival of chamber music held in the auditorium of the Library of Congress, Washington, D. C., in April, 1928. Igor Stravinsky, who composed the score, was also allowed a choice of dramatic theme. His aesthetic approach to *Apollon Musagète*, in terms of music and dance, may best be understood from certain passages in his autobiography that express his views on Tchaikovsky's *Sleeping Beauty*: * "It was a real joy to me to take part in this creation not only for love of Tchaikovsky but also because of my profound admiration for classical ballet, which, in its very essence, by the beauty of its ordonnance and the aristocratic austerity of its form, so closely corresponds with my conception of art. For here, in classical dancing, I see the triumph of studied conception over vagueness, of the rule over the arbitrary, of order over the haphazard." This kind of work, in the eyes of Stravinsky, was the perfect expression of the Apollonian principle, which demands full creative consciousness of the artist. Therefore, he determined to write a ballet, a statement of faith, "founded on moments or episodes in Greek mythology plastically interpreted by dancing of the so-called classical school."

Desiring to emphasize melodic structure above all else in his new work, Stravinsky composed the music for strings alone. The sonorities

* As revived in London by the Diaghilev company during the season of 1921. Stravinsky had done a certain amount of respectful editing of Tchaikovsky's music in connection with these performances.

he obtained, largely through the use of added cello parts, are note-worthy and never fail to heighten the effect of the ballet through their resonance. In preparing his dramatic scheme, Stravinsky retold the legend of Apollo's investing the Muses with their various arts. Here, the nine nymphs are reduced to three Calliope (poetry), Polyhymnia (mime), and Terpsichore (dance).

The choreography for the American première of *Apollon Musagète* was arranged by Adolph Bolm, who also danced the title role. Two months later, a Paris performance was given at the Théâtre Sarah Bern-hardt, with the composer conducting. Serge Lifar was the Apollo; Alex-andra Danilova and Alice Nikitina alternated as Terpsichore. André Bauchant contributed the décor, which does not appear to have pleased Stravinsky entirely.

In Paris, the work was staged by George Balanchine, whose authorita-tive version was later seen for the first time in the United States at a performance by the American Ballet at the Metropolitan Opera House in April, 1937, with Lew Christensen as Apollo. On that historic eve-ning—which also included the first American performance of *Le Baiser de la Fée* and the world première of *Card Party*—the orchestra was con-ducted by Stravinsky. With its name shortened to *Apollo,* the Balanchine version was revived by Ballet Theatre at the Metropolitan Opera House in April, 1943, with a brilliant cast consisting of André Eglevsky as Apollo and Vera Zorina, Nora Kaye, and Rosella Hightower as the three Muses. Stravinsky himself conducted. Repeated several times that season, the ballet was acclaimed for the formal beauty of its outline, the inventiveness and masterly design of its choreography, the nobility of its music.

SCENE ONE (Prologue)

The Birth of Apollo

Fragments of the great central melody of the ballet, representing the god himself, are heard in the opening bars of the introduction and then the theme itself emerges. The curtain rises and the nymph Leto is seen

giving birth to Apollo. According to the legend, "Leto was with child, and, feeling the moment of birth at hand, threw her arms about a palm tree and knelt on the tender green turf, and the earth smiled beneath her; and the child sprang forth to the light . . . goddesses watched, giving him for swaddling clothes a white veil of fine tissue, and bound it with a golden girdle." This picture, the only narrative portion of the ballet, is ingeniously carried out in the choreography of Balanchine. The child-god snaps the umbilical cord with a sharp pirouette, and two goddesses lead him to Olympus.

The scene changes, and Apollo, now the full-grown divinity, remains alone.

SCENE TWO

Soon the three Muses appear, each one with her special variation, classical in feeling. Calliope, who receives the stylus and tablets from

Apollo, personifies poetry and rhythmic grace. Polyhymnia, finger on

lips, represents mime. Terpsichore, combining in dance the rhythm of poetry and eloquence of gesture, takes the place of honor among the Muses.

Following these variations comes a magnificent solo for Apollo, in which the god combines his endowments of strength and beauty with that special attribute as inspirer of the Muses from which the ballet takes

its name. He embraces the three divinities lovingly; they intertwine with him and each other in a glowing marriage of the arts. Finally, as the great central theme sounds again in the orchestra and his chariot descends from the sky, Apollo leads the Muses to Parnassus.

Photo: Studio Lipnitzki   SERGE LIFAR AS APOLLO

Appalachian Spring

THIS BALLET with choreography by Martha Graham was first performed by Miss Graham and her company at the Coolidge Festival in the Library of Congress, Washington, D. C., October, 1944. Leading roles were danced by the choreographer, Erick Hawkins, Merce Cunningham, and May O'Donnell. Isamu Noguchi designed the settings, and Edith Guilfond the costumes. Mrs. Elizabeth Sprague Coolidge, moving spirit of the Festival, also commissioned two other Graham ballets on the same program to the music of Paul Hindemith and Darius Milhaud.

The score for *Appalachian Spring* was composed by Aaron Copland, who used, as subtitle to the work, *Ballet for Martha*. The instrumentation called for a chamber ensemble of thirteen. It was expanded to symphonic size, with some of the original music slightly condensed, in 1945, when a concert suite was made by the composer. In May of that year *Appalachian Spring* received both the Pulitzer Prize for Music and the Award of the Music Critics Circle of New York for the outstanding theatrical composition of the season. The symphonic suite was given its première the following October by the New York Philharmonic-Symphony Orchestra, under the direction of Artur Rodzinski.

Appalachian Spring marked a milestone in Martha Graham's career as creative artist. One of the great figures in modern American concert dance, she had been turning gradually to the proscenium as frame and to orchestral tone as support for her projection of deep-seated states of feeling until, in this choreographic landscape—which combined her expressive powers with a score of full musical validity—she produced one of her finest works.

The title, *Appalachian Spring,* was chosen by Miss Graham from the heading of one of Hart Crane's poems, although the ballet is not related to the text itself. This is a story, or rather an evocation, of simple American people, of pioneers in the last century who extended the frontiers of the land through the solidity of their thoughts and deeds rather than through action.

A new farmhouse has been built in the Pennsylvania hills, and the neighbors are on hand to congratulate the young farmer and his bride.

Photo: *Cris Alexander*   MARTHA GRAHAM AND MAY O'DONNELL

After a slow introduction suggesting the mystical nature of the earth that sustains these folk, a joyous procession enters.

Several types from early American communities are presented: the husband and his bride; an old pioneering woman, hale and outgoing; a Revivalist, who stamps on sin, assisted in his extravagant gestures by four young followers. The farmer himself is strong and filled with a sense of pride in the land. His bride can think only of the child to come. In a tender duo they plan for the future.

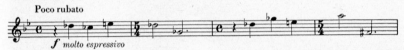

There follow moments of jubilance, with the dancing of the Revivalist and his flock, and of exaltation when the bride thinks of her approaching motherhood. As a great calm comes over the music, an old Shaker melody called "The Gift to Be Simple" is heard.

Soon the neighbors depart, leaving the couple to themselves. The woman sits in a rocking chair on the porch of the new house, whose framework is barely indicated; her husband stands protectingly behind her; and this danced picture, reflecting the doubts, hopes, and achievements of American communal life in the early nineteenth century, comes to an end on a note of strength and fertility.

Photo: Arnold Eagle   MARTHA GRAHAM AND ERICK HAWKINS

Courtesy Museum of Modern Art

L'Après-Midi d'un Faune

THIS "choreographic tableau" in one act, with scenario by Vaslav Nijinsky, was first produced during the Diaghilev season at the Théâtre du Châtelet, Paris, in May, 1912. The scenery and costumes were by Léon Bakst. As musical accompaniment, Nijinsky used the famous orchestral work of the same name by Claude Debussy *—which, in turn, had been inspired by the poem of the French impressionist, Stéphane Mallarmé.

Like so many of the ballets associated more with Nijinsky's prowess as a dancer than with any lasting qualities of their own, *L'Après-Midi d'un Faune* has lost much of its interest for a younger generation. Divorced from the personal performance of its choreographer, it now seems a charming but gratuitous attempt to graft on to the music of Debussy an atmosphere which any sensitive listener might have found there for himself.

In this work, which was Nijinsky's first essay at choreography, the

* Its full symphonic title is *Prélude à l'Après-Midi d'un Faune.*

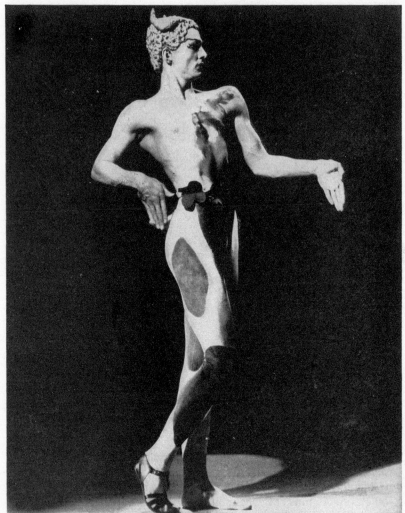

GEORGE ZORITCH

great dancer based his approach on the general mood of Mallarmé's poem. Instead, however, of conforming to the sinuous curves of Debussy's melodic scheme and the rich variety of his harmonic language, Nijinsky introduced sparse, angular movements in profile to evoke the idea of figures crossing the surface of a Greek vase. This attempt at a dimensional sense of antiquity has succeeded on stage, but it does not always coincide with the free, rhapsodic flow of Debussy's music.

Whatever the ultimate merits of this tableau, its chief character has become one of the advertising staples of Russian ballet, inspiring many

grotto in Germany to which the goddess Venus had been banished by Christian theology during the Middle Ages and where she held court attended by a number of renegade knights, among them Tannhäuser. But the original bacchanale of fauns, satyrs, and Graces, and the episode of Leda and the Swan (seen by Tannhäuser in an erotic vision as he lies in the arms of Venus) were infinitely enlarged to suit Parisian taste.* Musically, this orgy in the cave of Venus became one of Wagner's greatest pages.

In the Dali-Massine ballet, the collaborators have used the Venusberg only as a point of departure. The central character in the work is Ludwig II, mad King of Bavaria and Wagner's arch patron. The vagaries of the scene are viewed through his fevered brain, which acts as a center of gravity for whatever action exists.

Emphasis is laid on the distorted and grotesque. Venus is seen on her traditional couch, but hardly as Wagner would have imagined her. Instead of flowing robes, she wears a union suit. Characters out of psychological casebooks wander across the scene. There are Sacher-Masoch and his wife, in an intimate display of incompatability; a satyr,

---

* Certain elements of the Paris public of 1861 were displeased, however, because this important ballet came at the start of the performance instead of in the second act. They were not used to arriving at the opera house so early.

Photo: Maurice Seymour   THREE FIGURES FROM BACCHANALE   *Courtesy Dance News*

with a smaller satyr attached to his leg, knitting industriously; several nymphs in psychopathic dress. In the midst of this confusion wanders Ludwig—seeking some kind of relief from his own harrowing problems.*

Stray allusions to the original Venusberg appear at various points in the action. Leda and the Swan (in this case, a gigantic stationary bird which forms part of the stage setting) perform a *"pas de deux"*; Graces and fauns appear intermittently in extravagant dress and posture; Ludwig plunges blindly through this mass of Wagneriana and falls to his death in the center of the stage. As he does so, four umbrellas open in solemn formation about him.†

This, then, was *Bacchanale.* As a parody on Wagner's mammoth theatrical ideas, it was perhaps welcome; but its effete extravagances, its pulpy pornography, were symptomatic of an era's decay.

* The King was to find no relief in real life. He committed suicide in the Starnberger See, June 13, 1886.

† Here, the Pilgrim's Chorus from *Tannhäuser,* played brassily as a close for the Dali-Massine ballet, was tacked on to Wagner's own poetic ending of the Bacchanale.

VILLAGE FESTIVAL SCENE

Le Baiser de la Fée

THIS BALLET-ALLEGORY ("The Fairy's Kiss") in four scenes, by Igor
Stravinsky, was first presented at the Paris Opéra in November, 1928,
by the company of Ida Rubinstein, for whom it was composed, with
Stravinsky conducting. Bronislava Nijinska arranged the choreography
and Mme Rubinstein appeared in the title role. A later version, imagi-
natively set by George Balanchine, was first given by the American
Ballet at the Metropolitan Opera House in 1937. It is this edition—revived for the Ballet Russe de Monte Carlo at the Metropolitan in April,
1940, with Mia Slavenska in the name part, Alexandra Danilova as the
Bride, and André Eglevsky as the Bridegroom—which has become the
definitive *Baiser de la Fée.** The Balanchine choreographer was introduced to Paris Opéra audiences in the summer of 1948.

In inviting Stravinsky to create the music for this ballet, Mme Rubinstein had suggested that the score contain certain reminiscences of
Tchaikovsky. The première was timed for November, 1928, to com-
memorate the thirty-fifth anniversary of the composer's death. Stravinsky welcomed the opportunity of paying homage to an artist he admired.

* Still another setting, by Frederick Ashton, was produced in London by the
Sadler's Wells Ballet in November, 1935.

He selected a tale by Hans Christian Andersen, "The Ice Maiden," as basis for the libretto—since, in his mind, the Dane's poetic approach resembled that of Tchaikovsky in its sensitivity.

The score of *Le Baiser* evoked not only Tchaikovsky's spirit: it also included several quotations from his music. On the title page, Stravinsky has written the following words: "I dedicate this ballet to the memory of Peter Tchaikovsky.... It was his Muse (like our Fairy heroine) whose fatal kiss, imprinted at birth, made itself felt in all the work of that great artist, and eventually led him to immortality. Thereby does our ballet (with a similar tale) become an allegory."

SCENE ONE (Prologue)

Cradle Song of the Tempest

A lullaby is heard in the orchestra, long-breathed and nostalgic. Then the curtain rises, disclosing the opening scene.

A solitary woman, fondling her infant, is caught in the midst of a storm. Tall, winged creatures appear—mysterious companion spirits of the Fairy. They pursue the woman, separate her from the child, and carry it off.

Now the Fairy herself—dark and beautiful—is seen approaching the child. She kisses it tenderly, then disappears. Peasants pass, find the infant, look vainly for its mother, and, filled with compassion, adopt the child as their own.

SCENE TWO

A Holiday in the Village

In the midst of a typically Swiss landscape, peasants are dancing in Alpine costume. Their village band plays a tune derived from the Tchaikovsky "Humoresque."

Photo: Alfredo Valente   *Courtesy Museum of Modern Art*

DANILOVA, SLAVENSKA, AND EGLEVSKY

The child has grown to manhood and is dancing among the peasants with his girl. Soon the musicians, villagers, and fiancée go off. As if magnetized, the Young Man remains. It is then that the Fairy appears, dressed as a gypsy. She approaches the youth, reads his palm, and foretells great happiness. When the Young Man, struck with her strange powers, asks her to lead him to his fiancée, she consents.

SCENE THREE

At the Mill

Guided by the Spirit, the Young Man finds his girl at a neighboring mill, surrounded by her companions in the midst of games and dances.

The Fairy disappears almost at once. Then comes a joyous *pas de deux* for the young couple, in the mood of their approaching wedding.

As the girl withdraws to try on her bridal costume, the Young Man is left alone. Once more the Fairy appears, this time covered by a long wedding veil. . . . The orchestra plays the melody of Tchaikovsky's "None But the Lonely Heart."

Mistaking the Fairy for his fiancée, the Young Man makes love to her. When she removes her veil, he is confused and tries to escape; but, dominated by her spell, he is carried off at this moment of his greatest earthly happiness to eternity.

SCENE FOUR (Epilogue)

Cradle Song of the Eternal Dwelling Places

The Fairy's companion sprites range themselves * slowly in groups before a décor representing the immensity of celestial spaces. Far above the scene, the Young Man and his Spirit are joined in the embrace of immortality.

* According to the libretto. In Balanchine's version they do not appear at this point, yielding the stage to the two principals.

GROUP FROM BALLET IMPERIAL

Ballet Imperial

THIS ESSAY in classical style, with choreography by George Balanchine, was introduced by the American Ballet on its South American tour in 1941, with Marie-Jeanne in the leading female role. The New Opera Company offered it next at the Broadway Theatre, New York, in November, 1942, with Mary Ellen Moylan, William Dollar, Gisella Caccialanza, and Todd Bolender as featured dancers. Later absorbed into the repertory of the Ballet Russe de Monte Carlo, the work was first given by that troupe at the New York City Center in February, 1945, with Miss Moylan, Maria Tallchief, Nicolas Magallanes, and Herbert Bliss in the leading parts. Scenery and costumes were created by Mstislav Doboujinsky.

Ballet Imperial is performed to the music of Tchaikovsky's G major Piano Concerto, No. 2. It has no plot but is a choreographic impression of the concerto's architectural plan, and—like the score from which it springs—is divided into three separate movements.

In creating this ballet, Balanchine wished to pay homage to the theatre of his boyhood—the great Mariinsky * of St. Petersburg, with its royal-blue décor and crystal chandeliers. This was the home of clas-

* Now the Kirov State Academic Theatre of Opera and Ballet, Leningrad.

sical dance, the workshop of the choreographer Petipa, the proving ground of Tchaikovsky. It was here that the Czar and his court applauded their favorite ballerinas; and in *Ballet Imperial,* Balanchine has re-created a whole era of vanished elegance through spacious choreography and a handsome sense of style.

FIRST MOVEMENT

Allegro Brillante

The concerto has no formal introduction. Its fiery first theme emerges

at once in the opening pages. An elaborate symphonic passage follows, played with lowered curtain, until—on the appearance of the second theme—the action begins.

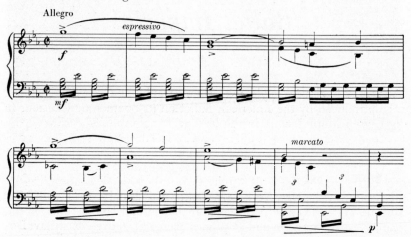

Eight men and eight girls are on stage, framed by the imperial splendor of the Mariinsky. Eight more girls enter, followed by a soloist who, in a short interlude, gives the impression of a noble lady-in-waiting. Finally, the ballerina herself appears briefly, to a cadenza played by the pianist. She seems more than a dancer, communicating, in fact, the idea of a young empress.

As the ballerina leaves the stage, the ensemble continues to dance. . . . She returns almost at once with a male partner who assists her in a

PAULINE GODDARD, MARIA TALLCHIEF, AND YVONNE CHOUTEAU

pas de deux, while the *corps* bows low in reverence. Then both principals disappear, making way for a *pas de trois* by two men and the lady-in-waiting. At the stately close of the movement, the entire corps—which has gone off during the *pas de trois*—comes back for the final measures, with the ballerina in the ascendant.

SECOND MOVEMENT

Andante non troppo

Here, to the phrases of the Andante, a mixed quartet of soloists, assisted by eight girls from the *corps de ballet,* take part in a rendering through spatial design of the music's form and poetry.

THIRD MOVEMENT

Allegro con fuoco

In contrast to the romantic mood of the preceding music, orchestra and piano soloist introduce a vivacious melody.

The ballerina enters on the shoulders of her partner, descends to the stage, and dances. Then she vanishes, to reappear twice more in the midst of the *corps*, the last time followed by a solo by her partner.

Now the lady-in-waiting and the entire ensemble enter. Dominated by the ballerina, they perform a glittering finale.

GROUP FROM LE BEAU DANUBE

Le Beau Danube

THIS WORK was first constructed in two acts for Count Étienne de Beaumont's Paris ballet season of 1924. Nine years later, Léonide Massine redesigned *Le Beau Danube* in its current one-act form for the Ballet Russe de Monte Carlo, with a première at Monte Carlo in April, 1933. The first New York performance took place in December of the same year at the St. James Theatre.

This is an ideal closing ballet. Massine's choreography—which constitutes a Viennese pendant to his later and more popular *Gaité Parisienne*—is sparkling. The arrangement and orchestration by Roger Desormière of Johann Strauss's music, the scenery by Vladimir Polunin, and the costumes by de Beaumont are the perfect complement to this choreographic idyl of Vienna in the 1860's.

The work has lost some of its sheen in recent performances. Scenery and costumes, as first designed, can no longer be used because of legal complications. Mr. Massine's part of the Hussar—in which he was inimitable—has been taken over with less successful results by Igor Youskevitch and Frederic Franklin. Only Alexandra Danilova, of the original cast, still appears regularly and with her accustomed glory, as the Street Dancer. Most of the other roles, designed by Massine for gifted young members of the Ballet Russe de Monte Carlo who rose later to stardom, are now assumed by minor dancers whose futures do not seem so bright. The whole ballet might shine again if entrusted to a group of consistently first-class artists.

Just as the spirit of Vienna dominates this idyl of a Sunday afternoon in the Prater, so does the music of Johann Strauss permeate its every mood and gesture. At the rise of the curtain a typical group of holiday-makers is seen in Vienna's public park, all in costumes of a bygone century. Among them are a gardener tidying up the grounds, an artist, a winsome young girl to whom he is attracted. Their pleasant, trifling by-play is underlined in the strains of a Strauss waltz. This placid mood

is broken off, however, by the arrival of the dashing King of the Dandies, who wins the girl away from the artist. Then other Sunday strollers

come upon the scene, among them a handsome Hussar. With him is a simple Viennese girl—his fiancée—and her family. They mingle with the crowd and, for the moment, are lost to sight.

Now it is the turbulently brilliant Street Dancer who appears. She is escorted by her manager and by an athlete with bulging muscles, who forms part of her act. First the Dancer performs alone for the crowd. Then she is joined by her two comrades in a hilarious ensemble, archetype of all old music-hall turns, grotesque in effect and skillful in construction.

Suddenly the Dancer sees the Hussar . . . an old love of hers. With fine contempt for middle-class propriety, she decides to win him back on the spot. That this involves an onslaught against the Hussar's fiancée does not deter the Dancer. She insults the girl, who retreats at once with her family.

The crowd disperses; the Hussar and his former love are alone. At this moment, the spectator who missed Léonide Massine in the role can

ANGEL ELETA, MARIAN LADRE, AND OLGA MOROSOVA

have no adequate idea of the ballet's electrical quality. One felt in his performance, as the first strains of the "Blue Danube" sounded in the

orchestra, the workings of a basic inner rhythm that was longing for release, for outward expression. When that release came, it bore an exhilarating sense of climax.

As the music mounts, the Street Dancer looks at her former lover and starts toward him. He stands motionless, building a superb crescendo of body tension. Finally, with a gesture of abandon, the Hussar breaks into the waltz, joining the Dancer in a glowing *pas de deux*.

At the height of the reconciliation between Hussar and Dancer, the young fiancée returns by herself. She has slipped away from her family and come to defy her rival in a contest of wills. Not too strangely, she wins—for the old flame rekindled by the strains of the "Blue Danube" has already faded in the Hussar with the end of the waltz. Acknowledging defeat, the Dancer yields her ground. The fiancée's agitated family enters in search of her and, after a few difficult moments—which are smoothed over by the intervention of the girl's charming younger sister —all is set to rights.

A great celebration follows, at which the entire crowd of Prater habitués—in serpentine formation—dance gaily in honor of the Hussar and his future bride. Even the Dancer and her muscular companion join in this final toast to young love, and the curtain falls on an irresistible tide of youth, joy, and animation.

Photo: Maurice Seymour   ZORINA   *Courtesy Museum of Modern Art*

EUGENE LORING AS BILLY THE KID

Billy the Kid

THIS BALLET by Eugene Loring, with libretto by Lincoln Kirstein, is one of the glories of American theatrical dance. Produced by the American Ballet Caravan under the direction of Lincoln Kirstein, it was first performed at Chicago in October, 1938. The following year this work was given in New York by the same enterprising group. Since 1941 *Billy* has been presented intermittently by Ballet Theatre. Its most recent revival, in a restudy by Loring, took place at the Metropolitan Opera House in April, 1948, almost ten years after its première. On this occasion—according to unanimous critical opinion—the ballet seems to have shown new depths and dimensions. Its movement patterns are as elemental as the West from which they spring, its story of the relation of a transgressor to society as fundamental as a Biblical tale.

The basic validity of *Billy the Kid*, the feeling it gives of having been around for years as part of our national dance, has worked in one way to Loring's disadvantage. Most of his creative ideas have quickly become standard vocabulary, liberally used in the works of others. By accepting these ideas as public domain, we are apt to lose sight of their startling inventiveness, the dramatic imagination that brought them into being.

There is a single setting for *Billy*—functional and handsome—by Jared French, which conveys, with its borders of distant cacti, the wide-open quality of the West. Much of the work's ultimate impact comes from the superb score of Aaron Copland. This music matches the choreography in sturdiness and humanity, and is based, in part, on old American tunes. A concert suite, arranged by the composer, has been drawn from the following sections of the ballet: (1) opening (rolling back of the frontiers); (2) street scene and rodeo; (3) card game by the campfire; (4) Billy's capture and general dance; (5) lament on the death of Billy, and finale.

Mr. Loring created the title role in this work and has generally been considered the most convincing of its interpreters. There have been

DANCE-HALL GIRLS FROM THE BALLET THEATRE PRODUCTION

other fine performers in the part—Charles Dickson, Ian Gibson, Michael Kidd, John Kriza—but although all excelled in the later, more agitated sections of the drama, none succeeded in capturing the mood of the twelve-year-old child at the beginning of the story quite so ably as Loring. Marie-Jeanne created the part of the Mexican sweetheart, but more recently Alicia Alonso has made the role her own, dancing it beautifully and investing it with complete understanding. The important part of Pat Garrett has been well taken by Lew Christensen, by Richard Reed, and, with especially notable results, by Peter Gladke.

Billy the Kid is the tale of William Bonney, born in Brooklyn at the close of the Civil War and removed as a child to the Southwest, where his brief career as a killer struck terror to the region. The ballet offers the saga of Billy as a rhapsody on the westward expansion of this country toward new frontiers.

The curtain rises almost immediately after the first bars of music, revealing an empty, shadowy stage. From the orchestra emerges the central theme of the work, a motive sounding like a call and later suggesting—in full orchestration—the steady, migrating stream of courageous men and women.

Pat Garrett, symbol of constructive force, is the first to appear on stage. He is leading a procession of pioneers, who push forward through the shadows, bathed in an occasional flash of light. This mass movement is the Prologue.

Suddenly the scene clears and we see the street of a bustling frontier town. The human types one would associate with such a locale pass in review: vigorous horsemen hurrying by (self-propelled, in Loring's ingenious choreography); a somber cowboy in red; a Mexican on the prowl; three buxom dance-hall girls. The music for this episode is based on a version of the popular tune, "Old Granddad," first given out by piccolo and clarinet.

Soon the full orchestra is heard. Pat Garrett enters, breaking in a bronco. The townspeople cheer him, he rides off, and the prowling

Mexican dances with some dark-skinned girls. Into this highly charged group come the twelve-year-old Billy and his mother. The mother is veiled (significantly, as we shall see later), and Billy—dressed in overalls and wearing a large straw hat—tugs along innocently at her side. There is an extended musical climax at this point, starting softly and building up irresistibly to match the drawn-out crescendo of action on stage. Its theme is the classic melody "Good-by, Old Paint."

Moderato

A fight develops between two of the hangers-on in the crowd. At first the conflict starts in slow motion, hypnotizing the townspeople. Billy's mother draws closer to watch; and then a wild shot fired by Alias, one of the fighters, finds its way to her heart. Billy, in a fury, rushes toward Alias (who is to appear throughout the ballet as a Nemesis in various forms) and stabs him in the back. The slain hoodlum is carried off by the cowboy in red; Pat Garrett tries to console Billy and warn him against his murderous instincts, but the boy slinks away.

It is here that Loring has accomplished a most inventive shift in time and action. The two bodies have been removed; Billy and Pat have gone their separate ways; and yet the crowd stays on, moving in circles, or rather in grooves. As they plod their way up and down the single street of the town, the years seem to pass. Soon Billy appears among these same people as the gunman he was destined to become. Outwardly he is courteous: when the youth makes his entrance, he salutes a frontierswoman. Soon, however, he is alone, and his antisocial nature comes to the surface in a danced soliloquy.

Solitary horsemen cross the scene, which is now the desert. The symbolical Alias—Billy's incentive to murder—turns up as a land agent and plays cards with Billy. He discovers that the youth is cheating, challenges him, and is shot. Billy kicks the body contemptuously and laughs.

Now the young outlaw is seen in still another game of cards (one scene flows into the other uninterruptedly), this time with Pat Garrett, who has become sheriff of the region. The cowboy in red is with them, beside a campfire, and two girls from Billy's gang. A quarrel breaks out between Pat and Billy—again over the matter of cheating. Pat rides off angrily in the darkness.

Suddenly, in the orchestra, the simulated sound of shooting is heard. (This is effected by so-called "rim shots" on the snare drum—hitting the metal rim of the instrument with both drumsticks—and the rapid rat-tat-tat of trumpets.) Billy and his gang withdraw in alarm: Pat Garrett and his posse are on their trail. A desperate fight follows in which Billy's

Photo: Alfredo Valente   *Courtesy Ballet Theatre*
JOHN KRIZA AND PAUL GODKIN

three confederates are killed. The desperado himself is taken captive
by Pat, who rides him off to jail. There follows a dance by the whole
community, exultant at the end of Billy's criminal career. The music is
gawky, raucous, jubilant, as one would expect of such a moment in
pioneer history; and Loring's choreography does not fail it.

If the final scene of *Petrouchka,* with the falling snow, pounding bass drum, and stamping coachmen, may be called the most exciting in ballet, a certain moment in this general dance from *Billy* runs it a very close second. In the midst of the rejoicing, Billy's Mexican sweetheart— a mysterious figure in mauve *tutu*—crosses the stage for the first time (she is not actually to appear in the plot until two episodes later). She moves *sur les pointes*—strikingly alone among the plodding revelers— and is evidently seeking Billy. A few seconds after her electrifying entrance, she disappears like a wraith and the dance goes on—only to yield, as the last celebrant vanishes, to the apparition of Billy and his jailer seen in half-light at the rear of the stage.

Billy's jailer is the resurrected Alias, again primed to be slain. The murder is easily done and the young outlaw escapes, making for the desert. Ironically, it is Alias—now materialized as an Indian guide—who leads him to the refuge of his Mexican sweetheart, where ultimately he is to be trapped.

It is night. Billy lies down in the brush and takes off his boots. A posse, headed by Pat Garrett and the Indian guide, rides by in pursuit but does not see him. As he begins to dream, in the remote stillness of the scene, the sweetheart appears.

She advances toward Billy. He sees her and rises slowly. Then begins a provocative duo in which Billy and the girl dance together but never seem to fuse. Their union is ephemeral, bloodless. It is noteworthy that the role of the Mexican sweetheart is taken by the same dancer who, earlier in the ballet, has played the part of Billy's veiled mother. Shall we say that Billy confuses this living girl's affection with the memory of his dead parent? Or that the sweetheart does not even exist but is a mere variation, in Billy's fantasy, of the mother? These are Freudian implications of the *pas de deux* to which only Loring can know the answer. His choreography for the sweetheart is of a classical purity— even chastity—strikingly at variance with the bold lines of the rest of the ballet.

At length the girl disappears as mysteriously as she has entered. Billy stretches out to rest. Garrett and the Indian guide are lurking near by. Hearing a sound in the darkness, the youth knows he is being stalked. The music in the orchestra stops. A heavy silence hangs on the stage—and Billy speaks. "*Quién es?*" he calls ("Who is it?"). There is no answer. Billy laughs, shrugs his shoulders, and lights a cigarette. At once he is a target for Pat Garrett, who shoots the outlaw dead. The scene fades.

At this point there occurs what, in the opinion of the writer, is the only false note in the ballet. The music softens; a group of mourning women appears, lamenting the passing of Billy, whose youthful charm (in his nonmurderous moments) has become a legend of the Southwest. The labored group-posturing on stage, the contrived sentiment in the orchestra, make for an episode which might well be removed from an otherwise perfect work of art.

When the last of the women has passed, shadows fall and the atmosphere reverts to the epic mood of the opening. This is the Epilogue. The pioneer theme (No. 1) returns in the orchestra. Pat Garrett again leads the settlers on their westward march. But this time, while the persistent measures of the motive are sounded in the pit, the pioneers face to the west, then to the east, constantly shifting in a kind of unresolved, universal march as the curtain falls.

Photo: Alfredo Valente   *Courtesy Ballet Theatre*

NORMA VANCE AND JOHN KRIZA

Photo: Maurice Seymour   Courtesy Dance News
POPOLONI, BLUEBEARD, AND HIS WIVES IN ACT III

Bluebeard

THIS COMEDY ballet in two prologues, four acts, and three interludes—all played without pause—with book and choreography by Michel Fokine, was first presented by Ballet Theatre at the Palacio de Bellas Artes, Mexico City, in October, 1941. One month later, the United States première took place at the Forty-fourth Street Theatre, New York.

The plot of this work is based principally on the nineteenth-century operetta *Barbe-Bleue*, with libretto by Ludovic Halévy and Henri Meilhac and music by Jacques Offenbach. Its orchestral background, skillfully arranged by Antal Dorati, draws upon several theatrical scores by Offenbach for source material. Like Léonide Massine's *Gaité Parisienne* preceding it and Fokine's own unfinished *Helen of Troy* which followed, *Bluebeard* was part of a prolific Offenbach revival movement in America which reached its heights before this country's entrance into war and trailed off with the early moments of combat. *Bluebeard*, however, has remained as a notable comic experience. Its scenery and costumes were designed by Marcel Vertès.

From the point of view of choreographic ingenuity, this ballet may be ranked among Fokine's most successful. The cast is enormous, the action perhaps overlong, but every role has been contrived with fine clarity and resourcefulness, while the group compositions are a study in mobile wit. Its plot, not to be taken too seriously, is an excuse for amusing situations and cleverly devised solo and group dances.

The first performances of *Bluebeard* brought Anton Dolin in his celebrated playing of the title role; Antony Tudor and Lucia Chase as the King and Queen; Alicia Markova as Princess Hermilia; Ian Gibson as Prince Sapphire (a part later taken with distinction by George Skibine); Irina Baronova as Boulotte; Annabelle Lyon as Angelo, the page; Hugh Laing and Jerome Robbins as the Queen's Spanish lovers; and Simon Semenoff, expert mime, in the part of the alchemist, Popoloni.

THE PROLOGUES

I

The weary King Bobiche, assisted by his divertingly collapsible chancellor, Count Oscar, is seen on the banks of a river, carrying a little child, Hermilia, the King's unwanted daughter. Both men move with stealth as they plot to dispose of the infant. After placing a pendant about the baby's neck to identify her at some future time if the need should arise, the King helps Oscar place the child in a cane basket and push her out of sight down the current of the stream to a berceuse-like melody.

II

There is a flash of light on the darkened stage and Bluebeard appears, slim, dapper, mercurial.

With the aid of his alchemist, Popoloni—a withered old man who seems the spiritual counterpart of Count Oscar—Bluebeard kills his five wives in quick succession. The fourth, politely anticipating his wish, just lies down and stops breathing.

ACT ONE

Eighteen years later, King Bobiche still leads an unhappy life. Although he is rid of his daughter, Hermilia, the King knows no peace, for the Queen is constantly receiving lovers from all over the land. One evening, matters reach a head when five outsiders appear consecutively at the palace within half an hour. First there are Alvarez and Armando; then the little page, Angelo; and finally Alfonso and Orlando. They are all denounced by Count Oscar to the King, who orders them hanged. Grieving because he knows no domestic affection, the monarch suddenly thinks of the child he cast off some years before and is obsessed with the idea of finding her. Bidding Count Oscar set out on a quest, Bobiche stays behind to fulfill the demands of court life. First, for the sake of appearance, he seeks his Queen and takes her hand in a polonaise that is a masterful burlesque of kingly convention. Then, acknowledg-

ing the bows of his subjects with a sigh, the ruler leads his wife to their unhappy chamber.

FIRST INTERLUDE

Count Oscar, setting off on his quest for Hermilia but not yet out of the kingdom, meets the five condemned lovers of the Queen on their way to be hanged. He releases them all for a small consideration and goes happily on his way, tossing the newly won purse in the air, while the liberated suitors dance off in the other direction.

Photo: Maurice Seymour   MARKOVA, GIBSON, AND BARONOVA   *Courtesy Dance News*

ACT TWO

A pastoral scene is revealed, with peasant youths and maidens dancing a tarantella. Liveliest of the group is the Princess Hermilia (known
to the others as Floretta), who has been brought up as a country girl.
Unconscious of her royal origin, she is happy in the courtship of a
shepherd. But this youth, also ignorant of Hermilia's position and attracted only by her beauty, is really a prince in disguise, Sapphire by
name. Dressed in a herdsman's shaggy coat, he whirls with her in the
midst of the revelers.

Suddenly the peace of the countryside is shattered by the arrival of
the volcanic Boulotte, an attractive and extroverted peasant girl of the
neighborhood who is also in love with the shepherd. At first the two
women face each other, determined to fight out their differences; but
little Hermilia soon realizes she is no match for the bounding Boulotte
and retreats with the youth, her rival close on her trail.

Now the aged alchemist, Popoloni, appears and announces to the
maidens of the village that his master, Bluebeard, is coming to select a

new wife. Almost immediately, the debonair killer enters in a stately carriage. Looking over the girls who line up for inspection, he seems attracted by none of them—until Boulotte comes leaping in, fresh from the chase. Her salty vigor and roughness of manner greatly appeal to Bluebeard, who offers his hand in marriage. The girl accepts him without hesitation, takes her place beside him, and drives off to the acclaim of her fellow villagers. All of the crowd run after the couple, and only Popoloni remains.

Suddenly the alchemist stands rooted at the sight of his spiritual counterpart, Count Oscar, who has arrived in the village on a search for the missing Hermilia. Fascinated with each other, the men converse and, during their talk, notice the shepherd and his girl crossing the meadows. As the couple advances, Prince Sapphire—avoiding Count Oscar because of the disclosure of his rank that might follow—slips off and leaves Hermilia to face the chancellor alone.

Count Oscar identifies the lost princess at once by her royal bearing, as well as by the pendant attached to a ribbon about her neck. When he invites her to go back with him to the court of her father, Hermilia consents. She waves eagerly to the shepherd to come along . . . but he is nowhere to be seen.

SECOND INTERLUDE

Two magnificent vehicles cross the stage. One bears Hermilia on her way to Bobiche's court; the other carries Bluebeard and his lusty new bride toward their castle. At the sight of Hermilia, the murderer tires of Boulotte and can think only of the princess who passes.

ACT THREE

The withered Popoloni is seated at his desk in a vault of Bluebeard's castle, mixing philters and devising secret formulae. Six graves may be seen beside him, five of them with the names of Bluebeard's murdered wives, and the sixth freshly prepared. As the alchemist pursues his studies, Bluebeard appears and orders that Boulotte be dispatched. Almost at the same time, the bride enters the vault, sees the graves, and begs Bluebeard for mercy. He ignores her, glances commandingly at Popoloni, and strides off.

The time has come for the old man to obey his master. As Boulotte looks on, terrified, he brews a poisoned wine and bids her drink. Unable to refuse, she sips it and falls senseless to the floor of the dungeon. In a flash, Bluebeard returns and, satisfied that his latest wife has been disposed of, does a dance of limitless glee.

SIMON SEMENOFF BEFORE ONE OF THE CURTAINS DESIGNED BY MARCEL VERTÈS

There is nothing to detain him now. Leaving the details of the burial to Popoloni, he sets out to woo Hermilia. The old alchemist remains with the body . . . and suddenly turns benevolent. Through his own special formula—tickling her chin with a feather—Popoloni revives the girl and confesses that he has saved all of her predecessors by the same device. As proof of his word, he summons the five vanished brides, who come tripping from their hiding places to join the alchemist and Boulotte in a merry *pas de sept*.

THIRD INTERLUDE

Despite his constant bravado, Bluebeard is haunted by memories of the women he has slain. Their shades surround him in melancholy, accusing circles. Recoiling from the visions, he is overwhelmed by guilt.

ACT FOUR

With gilded pomp, Princess Hermilia is led to her father's court and received joyfully by the King and Queen. She is not quite the tractable child they have been expecting; and when the royal parents intimate that plans are in progress for her to marry a prince, the girl—always thinking of her shepherd—rebels. Her rage is quelled, however, by the appearance of Sapphire, who stands before her without his disguise. It is he whom the monarchs have chosen as their son-in-law.

An uproar at the castle gates puts an end to this family party—Bluebeard has come to claim the hand of Hermilia. His first request is couched respectfully enough; but when the King withholds consent, Bluebeard bids his mercenaries overrun the hall. Invading guards advance; the forces of the King retreat; and only Prince Sapphire has the courage to challenge Bluebeard to a duel. The murderer accepts, but treacherously stabs the Prince in the back. While her fiancé is carried off mortally wounded, Hermilia is forced to accept Bluebeard.

Now a strangely dressed troupe of dancers, led by a hobbling figure in red, enters the hall to celebrate the wedding. First the performers approach the dais where the bridal pair are enthroned; then, at a given moment, they tear the masks from their faces and confront Bluebeard. These are his wives, raised from the dead by Popoloni, who even now—for he is the figure in red—has performed a similar courtesy for Prince Sapphire.

Shocked into repentance by the reappearance of his wives, Bluebeard gives up all thought of Hermilia and decides on a lasting union with Boulotte. Hermilia is wed to Sapphire, and—with the approval of the King—Bluebeard's remaining wives are paired off with the Queen's ex-lovers. Thus, on a note of general reconciliation brought about by the genius of Popoloni, the ballet comes to its whimsical end.

Photo: Maurice Seymour   Courtesy Ballet Theatre
ANTON DOLIN AND IRINA BARONOVA AS
BLUEBEARD AND BOULOTTE

SCENE FROM THE FINALE *Courtesy Dance News*

Bogatyri

THIS FANTASY-BALLET in three scenes was given its world première by the Ballet Russe de Monte Carlo in October, 1938, at the Metropolitan Opera House, New York. The libretto by Léonide Massine—also responsible for the choreography—was based on old Russian folk tales; and the musical background was that of Borodin's Symphony No. 2 in B minor, played in its entirety. As originally produced, the ballet also had a prologue which was danced to the Nocturne from Borodin's String Quartet No. 2 in D major. In the 1941 revival, this scene and its accompanying music were cut.

Perhaps the most striking features of *Bogatyri* were the colorful settings and costumes by Nathalie Gontcharova, which at times engulfed the action. The scenario itself, a seeming blend of *The Fire Bird* and *Contes Russes,* with little of the freshness of either, was hardly among the clearest of ballet plots, nor did Massine's choreography—with the notable exception of the second scene and part of the finale—come up to this artist's usual standards. A strong cast was provided for the première, with Mia Slavenska as the heroine, Anastachiuska; Igor Youskevitch and Frederic Franklin as the heroes, Alyosha and Dobryna; Marc

75

Platoff as the Mourometz, and George Zoritch as the Tartar Youth. After the 1941 revision of *Bogatyri*, the role of the Tartar was completely eliminated, and the characters of Alyosha and Dobryna were combined.

The Bogatyri were legendary Russian heroes of the early Middle Ages, Lohengrinlike in impulse, dedicated to the furtherance of good and the crushing of evil, loyal servants of St. Vladimir (c. 956-1015), champion of Christianity in Russia. Several of their exploits are celebrated in this ballet by a series of dance tapestries.

The first of these takes place in the room of Princess Anastachiuska—beautiful maiden of Kiev—who lies dreaming of a Tartar youth. She rises from her couch and dances ecstatically with the vision, though the Tartars are traditional enemies of her people. Soon the youth disappears and Anastachiuska awakens—to receive her flesh-and-blood fiancé, the dashing Alyosha Popovich, one of the Bogatyri. She loves him no less than the vision, which she drives from her mind.

This is the prologue, charming in itself, which was cut out soon after the première.

FIRST MOVEMENT

In its revised version, *Bogatyri* begins under the walls of Kiev, to the heroic opening strains of Borodin's Second Symphony. The Bogatyri—

led by their general, the Mourometz—have assembled in Kiev preparatory to starting a military expedition against the Tartars. As they enter the principal square of the town in warlike dress, Princess Anastachiuska and her attendants join the heroes to wish them success. At this moment an enormous monster descends from the sky, grasps the Princess in its claws, and flies away with her. The Bogatyri, kneeling in prayer, invoke the help of an angel, who blesses their expedition to rescue the Princess.

SECOND MOVEMENT

In the barbaric *Scherzo* of this symphony, Massine has created the most persuasive dance patterns of the ballet. To its swift opening theme, the Tartar warriors are seen in their camp, dancing in light-footed cir-

Prestissimo

cles, waving their swords. The Bogatyri—led by the Mourometz and another noted hero, Dobryna Nikitytch—invade the camp and defeat

Photo: Alfredo Valente   *Courtesy Museum of Modern Art*

GEORGE ZORITCH AND MIA SLAVENSKA

the Tartars; but in a short while the victors themselves are trapped by
the wiles of the enemy women, who dance about them so seductively
that they forget their mission.

THIRD MOVEMENT

The focus of the action shifts to a dense forest through which Alyosha,
fiancé of the captive Anastachiuska, is making his way to find her. Then,
framed in the foliage of the monster's garden, Anastachiuska and four
ladies-in-waiting are seen expressing their loneliness in a slow, poignant
dance. As Alyosha and his friends appear, they are challenged by the

monster, who falls, however, at the sight of the Bogatyr's sword. Anastachiuska is rescued, and the scene changes without pause.

FOURTH MOVEMENT

The great banqueting hall of the castle in Kiev is seen. A feast is being
held in honor of the liberation of Anastachiuska and the victory over
the Tartars by Dobryna and the Mourometz, who have finally broken
the wiles of the Tartar women and brought them back to Kiev as cap-
tives. Jubilant music sounds, and all the heroes—together with the Prin-

cess—stand behind the great dining table as the Tartar women dance
for them. At last the Princess and Alyosha lead the revel themselves,
ending the ballet on a note of heroic joy.

Photo: Cosmo-Sileo
RADIO CITY MUSIC HALL PRODUCTION, WITH CHOREOGRAPHY BY FLORENCE ROGGE

Bolero

THIS FAMOUS score by Maurice Ravel was composed for Ida Rubinstein's Paris performances in 1928, in which the music was created as background for choreography by Bronislava Nijinska. Miss Rubinstein danced the leading role. Since that time *Bolero* *—in several different versions—has been performed extensively and produced in places as diverse as the Rome Opera and the New York Radio City Music Hall. Fascinated by Ravel's rhythms, many choreographers have tried their hand at his music. With the exception of Nijinska's original production, perhaps the most successful has been devised by the Hungarian choreographer Aurel Milloss, who staged the work in Rome.

Since *Bolero* is in essence a gigantic musical crescendo, every choreographic interpretation of the music—no matter how widely it differs from other versions in style and background—has had to follow the basic pattern of dynamic tension and growth. The score is based on the repetition of a single theme, over the pounding of a rhythmic ostinato, with

* It was introduced in concert form to the United States by Arturo Toscanini, conducting the New York Philharmonic-Symphony Orchestra in November, 1929.

mounting acoustical power until all of the instruments in the orchestra
—which have been introduced singly and then in choirs—roar out a brilliant climax on a sudden change of key. This unique musical construction inevitably shapes the form of the ballet itself.

A soft, persistent rhythm is heard as the curtain rises on the Nijinska
version—the lifeblood of the score, a rhythm which is to spin itself con-
tinuously through the fabric of the music until it becomes an irresistible

force. As the scene is revealed, a seductive Spanish woman is dancing

Photo: Cosmo-Sileo

GIL GALVAN AND MARGARET SANDE IN THE RADIO CITY MUSIC HALL PRODUCTION

on a table top in a café, under a circle of light, to the languid strain of a bolero.

Tempo di Bolero moderato assai

Twenty men surround her, fascinated by her movements, which grow constantly more voluptuous. The men themselves move in a sort of counterrhythm, equally intense. Their excitement mounts until passions are aroused which cannot be controlled and knives are brought into play. At last the men seize the dancing woman and raise her in their arms—the sacred elevation of Lust. It is at this moment that the music changes key and the ballet comes to a riotous close.

Le Bourgeois Gentilhomme

THIS COMIC ballet in two scenes ("The Would-Be Gentleman"), with
libretto by Boris Kochno and choreography by George Balanchine, was
first staged by Mr. Balanchine for the René Blum Ballets de Monte
Carlo in 1932. It was revived in its present form for the Ballet Russe de
Monte Carlo at the City Center in September, 1944. On this latter occasion, Nicolas Magallanes, Michel Katcharoff, Nathalie Krassovska,
Ruthanna Boris, Maria Tallchief, and Leon Danielian were seen in leading roles. The scenario is based on *Le Bourgeois Gentilhomme* of Molière, first given at Paris on October 23, 1670. Performed since then in almost every European language, the play enjoyed an especially sumptuous revival at Stuttgart in 1912. The German adaptation was made by
Hugo von Hofmannsthal, celebrated poet and librettist of the operas
Elektra and *Der Rosenkavalier*. The incidental music was composed by
Richard Strauss. Max Reinhardt was the stage director. Not long afterward, Strauss divided his score for this production into two separate
units. One—a vocal interlude—became, with added first act, the opera
Ariadne auf Naxos. The other grew into the difficult but rewarding concert suite called *Le Bourgeois Gentilhomme,* on which Balanchine has
based his ballet.

First comes an overture in which Strauss—ordinarily identified with
large musical canvases—shows his mastery in the handling of chamber

style and eighteenth-century idiom. Then the curtain rises to a slow
minuet.

Monsieur Jourdain, a good-natured but vain member of the middle
class suddenly come into great wealth, is preening himself in his new
home under the watchful eyes of his tailors, servants, and instructors in
music, dance, fencing, and philosophy. Ashamed of his origin, he has

Courtesy Museum of Modern Art
GROUP FROM LE BOURGEOIS GENTILHOMME

decided to do better for his daughter, Lucile, and marry her to a nobleman.

Jourdain has reckoned, however, without the opposition of Lucile's
admirer, the bourgeois youth, Cléonte, who is determined to wed the
girl himself. Unlike her father, Lucile has no social ambitions. In this
contest of wills, her sympathies go out wholly to Cléonte.

The youth, without Lucile's knowledge, vows to defeat Jourdain and
humiliate him. His entrance, in Strauss's score,* is tender and exalted;

* To a theme after music by the composer Jean Baptiste Lully, contemporary
of Molière.

but once Cléonte sets his ruse in motion, he is relentless. Dressed as a Moslem prince with several slaves in his retinue, he puts in an appearance at Jourdain's home and asks for the hand of Lucile. The pretentious old man, dazzled by the stranger's finery, consents. His joy increases when the prince offers him a patent of nobility.

Anxious to hold the Moslem's good will, Jourdain stages an elaborate divertissement in his ballroom. First there is a *pas de trois* for solo ballerina and two male dancers; then a *pas de deux*; and finally an acrobatic ensemble by three girls and a male dancer.

In the midst of the ceremonies, Lucile appears. On seeing the Turkish suitor, she is frightened and tries to escape. All ends amicably, however, when Cléonte—having been accepted by Jourdain as son-in-law—removes his disguise and claims the girl in marriage. Jourdain, who has no other choice, submits to the inevitable and calls for a celebration in honor of the engagement of Lucile and Cléonte. The ballet closes with a brilliant finale.

La Boutique Fantasque

SECOND IN popularity perhaps only to *Coppélia* in the repertoire of ballets that deal with animated toys, this work was first given by the Diaghilev company at the Alhambra Theatre, London, in June, 1919. The choreography was by Léonide Massine, with scenery and costumes by André Derain. Not until sixteen years later did America have a chance to see *La Boutique Fantasque.* It was presented at the Majestic Theatre, New York, in October, 1934, and at the Metropolitan Opera House in 1935.

Musically, the new ballet was of special interest. It had a score arranged and orchestrated by Ottorino Respighi from several short pieces by Gioacchino Rossini, composer of *The Barber of Seville* and *William Tell.* Rossini (1792–1868) had stopped writing for the operatic stage at the age of thirty-seven. It is said that general disillusionment with theatrical conditions in France and Italy prompted his retirement. He withdrew to his home at Bologna, settled later at Passy, and until his death, which came almost forty years after his retirement, meditated mostly on food and cookery. In this frame of mind, he produced the piano works (some of them bearing such whimsical titles as "Hors d'Oeuvre," "Castor Oil," and "Almonds") on which most of the music of *La Boutique Fantasque* is based. The balance of the score includes other Rossini miniatures, notably the famous tarantella—"Danza! Danza!"—beloved of tenors. All of the music, especially in Respighi's brilliant instrumentation, lends itself well to dance.

Massine, who prepared this ballet during the period of *The Three-Cornered Hat,* added further value to it in performance through his work as the cancan dancer, a part in which he still appears whenever *La Boutique Fantasque* is revived. His partner at the Alhambra première—equally acclaimed for her performance—was Lydia Lopokova. Alexandra Danilova ranks highest among the dancers who have followed Lopokova in the part.

The latest revival of *La Boutique Fantasque* was offered by Ballet Theatre in April, 1943, at the Metropolitan Opera House, with its name changed to *Fantastic Toyshop.* On this occasion, Karen Conrad was Massine's fellow cancan dancer. Inadequately rehearsed, the work did not win the favor of the public as in earlier years. The production was not a good one; nor was the mood of the audience, during this wartime era, in tune with the plush whimsy employed in *La Boutique.* A restudied version, suitably presented, might set at rest some basic doubts regarding the piece's durability. At its prewar best, this ballet was delightful.

After a witty overture, the curtain rises on a formalized inner drop and then, in turn, on a setting which depicts a toyshop of the mid-nineteenth century. A sunny atmosphere is established, suggesting—through a backdrop glimpsed from the windows of the shop—the tranquil harbor of a Mediterranean resort not too far from Nice. As the owner and his apprentice open the store for the day, their bustle is reflected in the chattering music of the orchestra.

Various types of people soon enter the place: a young shoplifter, who is quickly detected and put out; two elderly ladies, prim and strutting; an American family (a century-old European version of one) who have come to see the toys. Mother, father, and two children make up the entourage.

Under the guidance of the shopkeeper, various mechanical dolls are shown to the visitors: first, two Italian figures which perform a tarantella (the "Danza! Danza!"), and then, four others, dressed as playing

cards, that dance a courtly mazurka. The display is interrupted by the arrival of another foreign family—a rich Russian merchant, his wife, and their four small daughters. The two elderly ladies disapprove of the Russian customers and depart, but the Americans stay on, eager to see more of the toys.

Now comes an exhibition of two of the choicest items in the stock: a "snob" in pearl-gray hat, dashing clothes, insouciant manner, and the contrasting figure of a melon-hawker. The two toys, which complement each other in appearance and gesture, yet are so radically diverse, perform to the delight of the visitors. They are followed by a troupe of mechanical Cossacks and a team of dancing poodles.

At length the shopkeeper displays his greatest prize: a pair of cancan dancers. The male doll, a caricature of nineteenth-century elegance,

Photo: Sasha

DANILOVA AND MASSINE

wears mustache and side whiskers, and tight clothing of a fantastic cut. His partner is an adorable figurine, archetype of all soubrettes who have ever beguiled in the cancan. When the dolls have been wheeled before the customers, they break into their exhilarating dance.

All of the visitors are delighted with the show and eager to buy the cancan pair. After a brief conference, it is agreed that the dolls are to be divided—the Americans acquiring the male member of the team, and the Russians the female. Both parties pay a high price in advance and leave the shop, arranging to call on the following morning for the dolls, which are to be boxed separately and ready for delivery. Pleased with the upturn of business, the shopkeeper and his assistant put the place in order and lock up for the evening.

As the shadows take over, the deserted interior of the store is transformed. To the accompaniment of an ethereal waltz, the toys emerge

from their resting places, led by a graceful line of mechanical ballet dancers. As the music becomes sharper in accent, the Cossacks appear, then the snob, the poodles, the tarantella dancers. Finally the cancan couple are spirited from their separate crates and reunited under the sympathetic eyes of their toy companions. A poetic ensemble follows in which the pair, removed from the raciness of their customary dance, become the symbol of young love. The girl is borne away by her companions, and the male remains to lead a final revel. Then all the toys disappear.

In the morning, the shopkeeper and his assistant return to open the store. At first everything looks as they had left it; but at the moment that the customers arrive demanding delivery of the cancan figures, an unexpected impasse develops: the two dolls are not to be found.

The customers are irate and claim they have been cheated. Determined to smash all the stock in revenge, they invade the rear of the store, where the mechanical figures are kept; but the dolls suddenly come to life with terrifying militancy, beat and kick the clients, overwhelm them and drive them out. As the abject band of invaders peer into the shop from the street, they can see the toys thronging in triumph about the inseparable cancan dancers. Even the proprietor and his assistant—who have kept the two dolls and the purchase money—join happily in the celebration.

Capriccio Espagnol

DESIGNED AS closing number for an evening of traditional ballet (in the genre of *Beau Danube* and *Gaité Parisienne*), *Capriccio Espagnol* was first presented at the Théâtre de Monte Carlo in May, 1939. Léonide Massine constructed the formal outline and collaborated on the choreography with Argentinita. Nicholas Rimsky-Korsakov's score of the same name was used as musical background, with scenery and costumes by Mariano Andreù (whose *Capriccio* setting had been created originally for Fokine's *Jota Aragonesa* two years previously). The Monte Carlo cast included Argentinita and Massine—in one of his finest parts—as a pair of gypsies, with Alexandra Danilova and Michel Panaieff as a peasant couple. When the ballet was given its first American performances at the Metropolitan Opera House in October, 1939, Mia Slavenska was seen instead of Argentinita, and André Eglevsky replaced Panaieff. The work enjoyed an immediate success and is perhaps Massine's most effective coloristic ballet. Musically, it remains one of the few stage works which add fresh value to a well-known symphonic score. Rimsky-

Korsakov's *Capriccio Espagnol,* long taken for granted as a piece of somewhat faded tone painting, gains immeasurably in brilliance, in architectural and rhythmical interest when united to the imaginative choreography of Massine and Argentinita.

Rimsky-Korsakov's score is in five compact, connected movements. The ballet has been cast in a single scene and relies more upon atmosphere than plot. In fact, it is a series of divertissements intensified by their skillful interrelation and consistent use of Spanish atmosphere.

As the curtain rises, a group of boys armed with sticks and wearing peaked hats is seen in the square of an Iberian town on a festival day. They move with short, energetic steps to the measures of an alborada, typical of Spanish Galicia.

The second movement begins. Girls of the town enter and join the older men in a languid seguidilla suggestive of paintings by Goya. Here the music seems to take on new grace from the groupings of the dancers.

For a moment the boys—with their sticks and peaked hats—resume the prancing motion of the alborada. Then, to a flourish of trumpets, the fortuneteller enters: a gypsy woman of great beauty.

This section of the score is known as "Scena e canto gitano" ("Scene and gypsy song"). Technically, it consists of five successive cadenzas for brasses, violin, flute, clarinet, and harp, between whose entrances a pulsating gypsy tune is heard, gradually mounting in dynamic emphasis until it spills over into the colorful finale of the piece, "Fandango asturiano."

For those who saw early performances of *Capriccio Espagnol*, the entrance of Slavenska—vivid, and spectacularly blond in the midst of a swarthy ensemble—made a deep impression. But even more compelling, as this ballet moved masterfully from one pictorial climax to another, was the first appearance of her partner, Massine. Soft strokes of the timpani, imperceptible throbs of the cymbals, faintly reiterated rustlings of the tambourine; and, from the wings, insistent tapping of heels, flamenco style. At last Massine emerged: slim, dark, slightly sinister with his broad-brimmed hat pulled down over his face, whip in hand. From the moment of his entrance until the fall of the curtain, it was he who dominated the ballet.

Based on steps of the traditional buleria, panaderas, and bolero, the scene of the two gypsies gathers excitement, enkindling the townspeople and country folk who have gathered for the festival. In a supreme touch of theatre, two new leading characters are brought on stage at the moment that the gypsy dance plunges into the closing fandango.

A peasant girl and her beau come leaping forward at the head of a crowd to join the gypsies, boys, and townsfolk. The whole ensemble dances a jota, with the four principals flashing in a circle and leading the revel. As the curtain falls on a blaze of Spanish color, Massine demonstrates again, as in the twenty-year earlier *Three-Cornered Hat*, his complete mastery of Iberian style and his genius in using that idiom as the material of formalized ballet.

CASIMIR KOKITCH, TAMARA TOUMANOVA, AND LÉONIDE MASSINE

Le Carnaval

THIS ROMANTIC ballet in one act, with story and choreography by Michel Fokine, was first produced at Pavlova Hall, St. Petersburg, in 1910 as part of a charity entertainment. In final form, *Le Carnaval* had its première at the Paris Opéra in June, 1910, where it was given by the Diaghilev Ballet Russe during the company's second season in the French capital. Scenery and costumes were by Léon Bakst. Among the principal dancers at the Paris première were Vaslav Nijinsky and Thamar Karsavina as Harlequin and Columbine, Vera Fokina as Chiarina, Bronislava Nijinska as Papillon, Adolph Bolm as Pierrot, and Enrico Cecchetti as Pantalon—a fabulous cast. The first American performance of *Carnaval* took place under the auspices of the Diaghilev Ballet Russe at the Century Theatre, New York, in January, 1916.

Musically and atmospherically, Fokine's ballet was based on a celebrated suite of piano pieces by Robert Schumann—*Carnaval.*° Like several of his composer-contemporaries at the beginning of the nineteenth century, Schumann was interested in literature as well as music and had achieved a special sort of fame in Germany through his critical writings. Sometimes he cast these essays in semidramatic form, inventing whimsical characters such as Florestan and Eusebius, who represented the writer's own shifting moods and acted as mouthpieces for his opinions on the arts.

In *Carnaval*, Schumann the composer transformed these figures—along with others from his literary gallery—into musical miniatures, portraits of strollers in a passing throng. When Fokine brought them to the stage, against a *commedia dell' arte* background,† Schumann's original carnival folk—who had bordered on the philosophical—kept their warmth and poetry, lost their argumentative quality, and became a group of finely etched *élégants*.

As originally produced, this ballet was celebrated for the virtuosity of its dance patterns. In latter days, with standards of performance somewhat slackened, emphasis has been shifted to sentimental by-play, not always with fortunate results. During its most recent revival by the

° The orchestration of these pieces for ballet purposes was launched by the Russian composer Alexander Glazunov as a "collective" project. Among the distinguished musicians who scored the many separate sections of *Carnaval* were Glazunov himself, Klenovsky, Rimsky-Korsakov, Kalafti, N. Tcherepnin, Liadov, Winkler, Wintol, Arensky, and Sokolov. This edition was published by the firm of Belaieff.

† See a discussion of the *commedia dell' arte* in the section on *Pulcinella*.

Photo: Count Jean de Strelecky
LYDIA LOPOKOVA AND STANISLAW
IDZIKOWSKI

Photo: Maurice Seymour
Courtesy Museum of Modern Art
TATIANA RIABOUCHINSKA AND ADOLPH
BOLM

Ballet Russe de Monte Carlo at the New York City Center in March, 1949, *Carnaval* showed definite signs of age.

The curtain rises on a ballroom, to the strains of an animated introduction. Several couples cross the stage, interspersed with some of the

principal figures of the ballet, including the charming Chiarina and Estrella,* each of whom is attended by a gallant.

They go off, and the melancholy Pierrot slips timidly from behind a curtain. In sharp contrast to this lovelorn character, the leaping Harlequin appears, deriding Pierrot and bounding from sight while the sorrowful clown remains. More whirling couples pass, yielding to the romantic Florestan and Estrella, to Eusebius and Chiarina. Then Papillon enters, tempts Pierrot with delicate provocation, and quickly flies off, leaving the aroused dreamer to himself.

* More of Schumann's literary whimsy. Chiarina, in his vocabulary, was a pseudonym for Ernestine von Fricken, his early fiancée, and Estrella for Clara Wieck, later his wife.

Several varied episodes follow, among them a meditative number for Chiarina and two friends.*

At length the central episode of the ballet arrives, that of Harlequin and Columbine. In mischievous mood, the couple plays tricks on the elderly roué, Pantalon, who is led on by Columbine, denounced by Harlequin, and pardoned soon after by both lovers in a good-natured *pas de trois*.

Now the finale of the work is at hand. The ballroom is again crowded with dancers, this time offering congratulations to Harlequin and Columbine, who have just become engaged. For a moment, the revelry is interrupted by a march of smug-looking bourgeois, but these are soon

dispersed by the joyous throng of artists. The effervescent Harlequin joins with Columbine to play one last trick on the two characters of the ballet who have been so awkward in love: Pantalon and Pierrot. Deftly, he binds one disgruntled figure to the other so they cannot disentangle themselves and, on this appropriately whimsical note, brings *Le Carnaval* to a close.

* This section of the music is known as "Chopin"—a successful take-off by Schumann on his Polish colleague's nostalgic style.

IRINA BARONOVA AND PAUL PETROFF

Les Cent Baisers
(THE HUNDRED KISSES)

THIS BALLET in one act with libretto by Boris Kochno after the fairy tale "The Swineherd" by Hans Christian Andersen, was first given by the Ballet Russe de Monte Carlo at Covent Garden, London, in July, 1935. The American première took place three months later at the Metropolitan Opera House. Bronislava Nijinska was the choreographer; Frédéric d'Erlanger composed the score; and Jean Hugo designed the scenery and costumes. The principal performers in this work, which achieved a blend of attractive music and divertingly ironic dance, included Irina Baronova as the Princess, David Lichine as the Prince, and Roman Jasinsky and Yura Lazovsky as his two servants. Among the Princess' maids of honor were Nina Verchinina, Vera Zorina, and Sono Osato.

95

A Princess of legendary times has come through castle gates onto a meadow in order to meet the Prince of a near-by kingdom who has sought her hand in marriage. With her are several maids of honor. Perhaps the Princess has expected too much of her suitor, for when the young man arrives and offers two modest symbols of his love—a rose and a song-bird—she turns on him disdainfully, leads her maids back through the gates, and leaves the Prince standing humiliated in the meadow.

The youth dismisses his servants (those who had borne the luckless gifts) and remains alone. Grieving over his lost illusions, he is suddenly attracted by the music of a passing swineherd. This rustic is not filling the neighborhood with the traditional piping of legendary times, but with a special kind of music produced by scraping a bowl with a spoon. The result borders on the fantastic, producing such merriment that all who hear it are moved to dance. The Prince, cured at once of his melancholy, offers to buy the instrument. Since the swineherd has no interest in gold, he declines to sell the magic crock but, instead, agrees to exchange his peasant dress and the instrument itself for the Prince's courtly costume. Once the bargain has been struck, the swineherd goes off in his new clothes and the Prince remains with the musical toy.

Now disguised in the swineherd's outfit, he scrapes the bowl until a tune comes forth so brightly that it lures the Princess and her maids of honor from the castle. They dance to the music, crowd about him, and finally the Princess herself asks the supposed swineherd for the toy. He names his price: a hundred kisses. At first the Princess refuses, filled with repugnance at the thought of kissing a man of such low estate. Then desire for the toy overcomes her, and covetousness leads her to submit. Suddenly—as payment is being made—the King appears, roused by the sound of the music and by the excitement outside. When he sees his daughter kissing a lowly swineherd, he disowns her at once and orders her maids into the castle. At this point the Prince reveals his identity, bids the girl farewell, and goes back to his native land. The Princess sinks sorrowfully to the ground as night sets in.

GROUP FROM CHOPIN CONCERTO

Chopin Concerto

THIS WORK in three movements, with choreography by Bronislava Nijinska, was first produced in 1937 by the Polish Ballet at the International Exposition, Paris, and given its American première two years later by the same group at the Music Hall of the New York World's Fair. Based on the Concerto No. 1 in E minor for Piano and Orchestra, by Frédéric Chopin, it contains patterns of abstract dance which develop with the structure of the music. In October, 1942, the work was revived by Mme Nijinska, taken into the repertory of the Ballet Russe de Monte Carlo, and presented at the Metropolitan Opera House with a cast including Alexandra Danilova, Nathalie Krassovska, Igor Youskevitch, and Frederic Franklin. Mia Slavenska danced successfully in later performances.

FIRST MOVEMENT

Allegro Maestoso

To the martial opening strains of the E minor Concerto—one of Chopin's most splendid themes—two groups of men enter, one in gray

and the other in blue. They are followed by five female soloists and two principal ballerinas. This entire movement is based on the shifting of both male groups, the interplay of secondary soloists, and the entrances of the ballerinas, who dance sometimes as a pair, sometimes with the entire group, and on occasion as separate performers.

SECOND MOVEMENT

Larghetto *

The lights dim to blue, the music of the slow movement begins, and the cast of the Allegro leaves the stage. Eight new girls appear, in group formation. As one of the ballerinas re-enters, this time with a male part-

ner, the *corps* moves to the background and provides a fluid accompaniment—much in the manner of the ensemble in *Les Sylphides*—to a long, sustained adagio by the two principals. At the end of this interlude, the cavalier follows his ballerina from the stage.

THIRD MOVEMENT

Vivace

As the sprightly first theme of the finale is announced, all of the principals, with the exception of the male partner, return. There are brief

* Chopin wrote in a letter to his friend, Karasowsky: "The slow movement is in a romantic, quiet, and partially melancholy mood. The impression it leaves should be as if one's gaze rested on a favorite landscape which awakens beautiful recollections in the soul, as for example on a night in spring illumined by moonlight." It is this poetic scheme which Nijinska has carried over into her choreography.

solos for the two ballerinas, alternating with group dances for the five secondary girls. Finally the whole *corps* appears and carries the movement to an elegant and ingeniously spaced conclusion.

Photo: Maurice Seymour   *Courtesy Museum of Modern Art*

MIA SLAVENSKA AND DARIO THIMAR

GROUP WITH LICHINE AND TOUMANOVA

Chorearteum

CHOREARTEUM, the second of Léonide Massine's choreographic ballets
—unperformed now for years—remains the most abstract. It was a choreographic version of Brahms's Symphony No. 4, in E minor, with massed
groups and solo figures approximating, in terms of motion, the architecture of the symphony itself. Scenery and costumes were by Constan-
tine Terechkovitch and Eugene Lourie. The work was first produced at
the Alhambra Theatre, London, in October, 1933, and had its American
première two months later at the St. James Theatre, New York, with a
cast including Tamara Toumanova, Alexandra Danilova, Vera Zorina,
Tatiana Riabouchinska, and David Lichine. Its four structural subdivi-
sions grew out of the four individual movements of the Brahms symphony.

FIRST MOVEMENT

The autumnlike quality of the music, especially the melancholy first
theme, gives rise to a series of dance patterns that begin soberly and

then grow in color, intensity, and volume until the entire stage is filled with a noble panorama of dancers, one of them borne aloft.

SECOND MOVEMENT

To the pronouncement by horns and winds of an austere melody—almost antique in its starkness—long, chained lines of mourning women

enter, led by a tragic female figure. They break into solo groups, constantly reacting to the inflections of their leader—now passionately, now in resignation. At last they retrace their steps and disappear.

THIRD MOVEMENT

Musically, this Allegro Giocoso is perhaps the least successful of the four parts of the symphony, its bluff humor serving more as a foil to the melancholy of the other movements than as a landmark in itself. Consequently, it is no surprise that the third section of the ballet falls slightly below the others in artistic conviction. Clever use has been made, however, of folk-dance elements, which harmonize with the rustic nature of the music.

FOURTH MOVEMENT

The close of the E minor Symphony is ranked by many musicians among the finest pages in Brahms; and Massine's choreography—in relation to his own best works—does not fail it. Here, while the orchestra announces the eight-bar motive on which the entire movement is based,

Allegro energico e passionato

the choreographer has arranged a line of six male dancers, spinning in consecutive air-turns. As the fabric of the score grows increasingly complex, its atmosphere more somber, all of the performers (for there is little differentiation between principals and *corps*) form intensified patterns against a wintry-gray background until—uniting in one great mass—they merge sculpturally the currents of music and dance that have flowed through this finale.

Photo: Maurice Seymour   *Courtesy Museum of Modern Art*
LICHINE, DANILOVA, OSATO, AND ZORINA

*Chout**

THIS COMIC ballet in six scenes, based on an old Russian folk tale, was first produced by the Diaghilev company at the Théâtre de la Gaîté-Lyrique, Paris, May, 1921, with enormous success. The exotic settings and costumes were designed by Michel Larionov, who collaborated as well on the scenario and choreography of the ballet with Tadeo Slavinsky. Mr. Slavinsky was seen in the title role of the Buffoon, with Lydia Sokolova as the Buffoon's Wife. The outstanding musical score was by Sergei Prokofiev. Inexplicably, this ballet—so well received at its first performances—has not remained in the repertory. A revival in 1929, produced by the de Basil Ballet Russe de Monte Carlo, was choreographed by Boris Romanoff. Fantastic humor abounds in both the music and the action.

SCENE ONE

The Buffoon, a shrewd yet sympathetic figure, is sitting on the edge of a stove in his home. He is characterized by a musical motive which not only underlines the dramatic action but forms the basis of all five orchestral interludes that are played during the changes of scene.

The Buffoon's Wife is busy washing the floor but stops work at once as the Buffoon jumps from his perch and explains a magnificent plan he has in mind:

Seven other clowns are due shortly as guests of the Buffoon. When they arrive, he will order his wife to set the table, she will refuse, and he will pretend to murder her. As she falls, he will grasp hold of a whip. After he strikes it once, she is to revive; on the second stroke she is to open her eyes; and on the third, get up and set the table. The seven buffoons, impressed with the disciplinary powers of the whip, will undoubtedly buy it.

As the conniving pair chuckle in expectation, the seven clowns arrive

* French transliteration of the Russian word *shoot*—buffoon.

—a noisy band. At once the Buffoon orders his wife to set the table. She

refuses, he strikes her, and she falls according to plan. As she rises from
the ground and lays the plates on the table, the seven buffoons are overwhelmed. Holding counsel, they persuade the Buffoon to sell them his
magic whip for three hundred rubles. Then they go off merrily with
their purchase, while the Buffoon and his wife, left to themselves, laugh
uproariously.

SCENE TWO

The wives of the seven buffoons are waiting at seven dinner tables
for their husbands. At length the clowns come in triumphantly, slaughter
their wives, and are appalled—after cracking the whip three times—to
see that the women do not rise to set the table. The scene ends with a
funeral march.

SCENE THREE

The Buffoon, in terror, awaits the return of the clowns he has cheated.
Hiding his wife securely, he dresses as a woman (in order to be mistaken for his own sister), sits at the hearth, and spins. As he works, to
music which has suddenly become mincing, the clowns break in furi-

ously, search the house, fail to find the Buffoon, and, in his place, abduct
the supposed sister, whom they plan to use as their cook.

SCENE FOUR

A short time has passed, and the seven daughters of the seven buffoons are to be inspected—with an eye to marriage—by a rich merchant.

Preening themselves and lording it over their new cook, the girls dance about the parlor of their house.

Finally the merchant arrives with two matchmakers. The buffoons receive him with honor; their daughters pass before him in review . . . but he prefers the cook. With great ceremony he leads his bride away as the enraged buffoons beat the matchmakers.

SCENE FIVE

The bride-Buffoon, on his wedding night, tries as best he can to escape from the merchant. Pretending to be ill, he begs to be lowered by a sheet from the window in order to get some air. The merchant agrees, stipulating that when his bride feels better she will tug at the sheet from the ground and he will draw her back into the room.

The bride is let down; the merchant dozes but suddenly feels the sheet in motion. He hoists it as prearranged and finds, enmeshed in the linen, a goat. Terrified, he calls for help. The matchmakers and servants

come running, convinced that the bride has been dehumanized through magic. Invoking a counter-spell, they pull the poor animal in all directions—until, to their dismay, it bursts.

SCENE SIX

Grieving inconsolably, the merchant sets out to bury the goat, as the seven buffoons, still stung by his rejection of their daughters, leap through the hedges with joy and gloat over his misfortune.

Now, unexpectedly, the Buffoon arrives in male attire, accompanied by seven soldiers. First he demands the return of his sister. Then, when the seven buffoons wave helplessly in the direction of the dead goat, he orders the soldiers to arrest them and exacts three hundred rubles' indemnity from the merchant.

A celebration follows. The Buffoon's Wife arrives and joins her husband, who flourishes his newly gained purse. The seven daughters of the seven buffoons dance gaily with the seven soldiers, and the ballet ends on a jubilant note.

MARGOT FONTEYN   *Courtesy S. Hurok*

Cinderella

WITH THE successful production of *Cinderella* at Covent Garden by the
Sadler's Wells Company in the spring of 1949, it became apparent that
the lavish, three-act ballet form popular with nineteenth-century audiences, had returned, albeit with some modifications in style, to public
favor. Frederick Ashton's choreography rang modern, scintillating
changes on the fairy tale of the scullery maid and her slipper; and Sergei

Prokofiev's masterful score brought a full range of contemporary color to the accompanying orchestra. The title role was danced alternately by Margot Fonteyn and Moira Shearer; Mr. Ashton and Robert Helpmann appeared in amusing characterizations of the two wicked stepsisters; and Michael Somes was the Prince. *Cinderella* was given its American première by the Sadler's Wells troupe in October, 1949, at the Metropolitan Opera House.

ACT ONE

Two angular, unattractive and generally shrewish ladies—the stepsisters of Cinderella—have been invited to a ball at court and are busy embroidering the shawls they are to wear. Pursuing their work with acrid precision, they ignore the shabby but potentially beautiful Cinderella, who sits in a corner by the fire. When the sisters quarrel between themselves and leave the room in an access of fury, Cinderella embarks on a daydream, the memory of days when her mother was alive and on hand to bring her affection.

The girl's father still loves her, but is afraid—in the presence of the spiteful stepsisters—to show his devotion. Even now, as he enters the room and approaches the girl, the sisters return and pour abuses on him. As their anger mounts, the scene is suddenly interrupted by the appearance of a stranger, a mysterious old beggar-woman who asks for alms. She is driven off by the sisters; but just before she goes, Cinderella furtively gives her a crust of bread. The old woman looks gratefully at the girl and vanishes.

Now the sisters, their outburst of anger soon forgotten, preen actively for the ball. Dressmakers arrive; a hairdresser, jeweller. The two scrawny women practice the gavotte. Then, with their father, they set out for the palace and Cinderella is left alone.

Once more the mysterious beggar-woman appears; but this time she quickly throws off her sordid disguise and reveals herself as the girl's Fairy Godmother. Touched by the kindness that Cinderella has shown her, she summons the attendant sprites of Spring, Summer, Autumn, and Winter to dress the neglected maiden for the ball. As the girl, radiant in her new clothes, prepares to leave the house, the Fairy Godmother points to the clock, warning Cinderella that she must depart from the hall before the stroke of midnight, or else all of the charms which she has just acquired will vanish, reducing her to the obscurity from which she has come. Cinderella listens gravely; then, escorted by the Seasons and the Stars, she leaves in splendor for the ball.

MOIRA SHEARER

Courtesy S. Hurok

ACT TWO

In the midst of a gilded hall, courtiers are dancing ceremoniously. This is one of the great occasions of the kingdom, and the guests are dressed in their most sumptuous clothes. Among them are Cinderella's stepsisters and her father. The two women, now they have left their own hearth behind, are far less authoritative then they were at home. They seem overwhelmed by the brilliance of the company.

Now, to a fanfare of trumpets, the Prince appears. Just as he takes his place in the forefront of the splendid room, mysterious music is heard and Cinderella enters the ballroom. She is so beautiful that all of the guests take her for a princess. Even the malevolent stepsisters fail to recognize the scullery maid of their household.

All gaze at the girl with admiration; but it is the Prince who is most attracted to the stranger. He offers her three oranges, the rarest fruit in his land, which—with her characteristic kindness—she gives at once to her sisters. Then, as the scene empties, she stays to receive the Prince's declaration of love, forgetting time and place in the rapture of the moment. As the dancers return to the room and resume their grand waltz, the clock strikes twelve. At once, Cinderella—remembering her God-mother's warning—rushes from the palace, losing a slipper in her haste. The Prince, who is distraught, picks up the lost slipper and swears he will find the maiden.

ACT THREE

Once more Cinderella is at her fireside, waking as if from a dream. The remaining slipper, however, which she has hidden in her apron, convinces the girl that she was really in the palace, that she has actually danced with the Prince.

Now the stepsisters return, full of their triumph at the ball. More vainglorious than ever, they show Cinderella the oranges given them by a strange and beautiful princess. In the midst of their prattle, neighbors rush in to say that the Prince is looking everywhere for the girl who has lost the slipper. As the young ruler appears, the two argumentative step-sisters try on the shoe which is in the Prince's possession, and Cinderella modestly kneels to help them. As she does so, the second slipper falls from her apron; and the Prince recognizes in this obscure maiden the radiant princess of the ball. He takes her in his arms; they are formally united; and the Fairy Godmother appears to bless their betrothal.

RUTHANNA BORIS AND FRANK HOBI

Cirque de Deux

THIS INTIMATE comedy-ballet, with choreography by Ruthanna Boris, scenery and costumes by Robert Davison, and music drawn from the Walpurgis Night sequence of Gounod's opera *Faust,** was first performed by the Ballet Russe de Monte Carlo at the Hollywood Bowl in August, 1947. Miss Boris and Leon Danielian appeared in the leading roles, with Patricia Wilde and Frank Hobi as the two assisting pages. In the New York première, which took place at the City Center one month later, Mr. Hobi appeared as principal male dancer, with Stanley Zompakos replacing him as the page. The ingratiating little work, Miss Boris's first, won a decided success.

Cirque de Deux is a parody of a rock-ribbed institution of traditional ballet. The *pas de deux* is exposed here as a brassy piece of showmanship, a vehicle designed to dazzle the customers, glamourize the performers, and approximate the glitter of a well-upholstered circus. Not

---

* This is the famous ballet sequence interpolated into the last act of *Faust* by the composer ten years after its première at the Théâtre Lyrique in order to meet the requirements of the Paris Opéra, to which the work passed in 1869. The ballet is generally not included in performances of *Faust* given outside of France.

two performers grace the cast, as in the orthodox *pas de deux*, but four. Both the ballerina and her partner have pages who hold their trains and set them off in courtly panoply. The mechanism of the form, however, remains unchanged.

According to conventional plan, a meeting of two master dancers on common ground consists of an entry and adagio for both, a solo variation for each dancer, and a coda. These rules are followed faithfully and with outrageous irony in *Cirque de Deux*. Miss Boris has added to this scheme a brief interlude for the two pages.

As the curtains open without music, the stage is in darkness, shielded by a gauze. Then, to the first bars of the score, the pages run out, bow to the audience, and motion the gauze upward, revealing the two soloists, who stand in the midst of a pink and blue setting lighted like a tent. Streamers dangle from the rafters, touching two poles at either side which bear pennantlike flags and balloons. In the center is a blue revolving platform, reminiscent of those provided for elephants on display. At the rear, in side-show fashion, hangs a large placard reading: "Cirque de Deux."

The two soloists fling open their capes, march forward, and start the circus parade, with the pages emulating their every gesture. As the ballerina perches on her partner's shoulder, the girl page hops no less proudly onto that of her colleague. The cast makes its triumphal way in an introductory flight. At the end of this procession, which corresponds to the "entry" of the classical *pas de deux*, the principals remove their capes, hand them to the pages, and make ready for the exploits that lie ahead.

These begin with the adagio. First, as the ballerina sustains difficult poses atop the revolving platform, the pages dutifully wheel her around. Then, when she enters the intricacies of a formal duet, her partner holds her on a diagonal slant so that all the supporting mechanisms of an adagio, never revealed to the public by ordinary dancers, are here disclosed in full—and absurdly disillusioning—detail. After a romantic final pose, the principals separate majestically and walk off.

Now the pages have their moment. Snatching balloons from the poles at the sides of the stage, they glide about in a whimsical dance at the climax of which the male principal re-enters solemnly, to the rolling of drums and a pink spotlight. It is time for his solo variation.

Moderato maestoso

Seizing a jeweled stick from the boy page, he holds it parallel to his chest, weaving about—as though this baton represented an imaginary center of gravity—in great leaps alternating with mincing, close-knit footwork. At the end of his dance, the soloist lets the stick fly through the air, to be caught with one hand by the page. Then he makes a grave bow to the audience and is hidden by a blackout.

There is another drum roll, the lights come on, and the ballerina is revealed, set for her variation. Poised grandiosely, with her hands held

before her as if she were displaying precious stones, she takes a silver whip from the girl page, like those used by female bareback riders. Now she plunges into a virtuoso performance of fast turns, yielding the whip at the number's finish and preparing for the all-important coda, in which she is joined by her partner.

This closing section of *Cirque de Deux* employs most of the technical tricks known to standard ballet, none of them used too deferentially. The ballerina whirls in approved mechanical style. Every time her partner soars in a series of *entrechats six*,* the two pages sag, so that the spectator has the impression of a recalcitrant seesaw. Just as the soloists are reaching the heights of gymnastic prowess, the pages retrieve the capes, drape them augustly about the principals, and—together with their masters—make a deep bow to the audience, signifying that this holiday version of a classical *pas de deux* has ended.

* A movement in which the dancer crosses his legs repeatedly while in air. The number of crossings is said to indicate the extent of the dancer's technique, *entrechats dix* being considered a fabulous limit and *entrechats six* a very respectable attainment.

Photo: Maurice Seymour   *Courtesy Museum of Modern Art*
WILDE, BORIS, AND MAGALLANES

Concerto Barocco

THIS BALLET in three movements, with choreography by George Balanchine, set to the Concerto in D minor for Two Violins by J. S. Bach, was
first produced by the American Ballet on its South American tour of
1941. Eugene Berman designed the scenery and costumes. Two years
later (November, 1943), the work was offered by the American Concert
Ballet at the New York City Y.M.H.A., with Mary Jane Shea, Lillian
Lanese, and Francisco Moncion in the leading roles. A revival by the
Ballet Russe de Monte Carlo, with Berman's décor and costumes replaced by simple practice clothes, brought *Concerto Barocco* in April,
1945, to the New York City Center, with Marie-Jeanne, Patricia Wilde,

and Nicolas Magallanes in solo parts. Still another revival of the work was given in Europe (1948) by the Grand Ballet de Monte Carlo, featuring Marjorie Tallchief, Ethery Pagava, and George Skibine. The dance designs are clean-cut, abstract, and neoclassical in style.

FIRST MOVEMENT

Vivace

Eight girls and two female soloists enter to the vigorous opening theme. While the *corps de ballet* takes its place at the rear of the stage

in accompanying groups, a male partner appears, with no other purpose —according to the choreographer—than that of lifting the two ballerinas, one of whom represents the first violin in motion, and the other, the second. This casting is not literal, however, nor are there any immutable designs in the ballet arising from the distribution of the solo parts in Bach's score. As in all his abstract works, Balanchine is interested here in fashioning a work of art related to but not dependent on the music which forms its background.

SECOND MOVEMENT

Largo ma non Tanto

To a poetic accompaniment by the *corps*, the male partner and the girl who represents the first violin perform a *pas de deux* in strict classical style.

THIRD MOVEMENT

Allegro

The finale of *Concerto Barocco* is, as in the preceding movements, an imaginative expression in dance of the music's structural content. Dur-

ing the closing bars—when the solo instruments and orchestra, which have been running in counterpoint throughout, suddenly unite on a broad harmonic cadence—Balanchine groups his entire cast in a *toute ensemble* with everyone, principals and members of the *corps*, blending in the same mass design. It is on this large-scale unison that *Concerto Barocco* ends.

Photo: Bruno　　　　　　MARY JANE SHEA　　　*Courtesy Museum of Modern Art*

Contes Russes

THIS FANTASY in three episodes, with choreography by Léonide Massine, was produced by the Diaghilev company in its present form at the Coliseum Theatre, London, 1919. Previous versions of the work had been given in San Sebastian, Rome, and Paris over a span of three years. Massine himself appeared as Bova Korolevich in the final production, with Lubov Tchernicheva as the Swan-Princess. The scenery and costumes were designed by Michel Larionov.

Originally planned as a treatment in dance of the Russian fairy tale "*Kikimora, the Ogress*," the ballet was expanded—in its travels through Rome and Paris—to include the story of the Swan-Princess and her Knight, Bova, along with the tale of the Witch, Baba-Yaga. It is these three legendary episodes that form the body of *Contes Russes*. Music for the work was compiled from scores of the Russian composer Anatol Liadov, notably his orchestral rhapsody "Kikimora." The ballet has not been performed in the United States.

After a brief prologue in which a street vendor enters bearing two dolls—one of which represents Kikimora, personification of evil, and the other, the Cat, figure of malice—the curtain rises on the first scene. Kikimora, a woman of frightful ugliness, lies in a wooden cradle, with her protector, the Cat, close at hand. Waking from her slumbers, Kikimora perversely tortures the animal, beats it with straw, and finally bashes in its head with an ax. Then, thoroughly satisfied, Kikimora vanishes. The street vendor enters, and at the cracking of his whip the murdered Cat returns to life and prances out of the room.

The curtain falls and a peasant interlude follows on the apron of the stage. Groups of dancers pass in review, one of them bearing Kikimora in her cradle. As they disappear, the curtain rises on the second episode.

This chapter of the ballet is concerned with the Swan-Princess, who is enchanted by a dragon. She is permitted every night to keep watch, on a lake near the palace, for her rescuer. With the dawn, however, she must resume her own shape and return to the palace.

As this episode begins, the Swan-Princess dances on the banks of the lake; she looks about her imploringly, but no deliverer comes. The lake evaporates, and in its stead rises the palace of the dragon, with the mon-

117

ster himself at the summit of a great flight of steps. The Swan-Princess, attended by her sisters, mounts the staircase in the direction of the dragon, but is suddenly liberated by the gallant knight, Bova Korolevich, who arrives on a white steed. The champion does battle with the dragon, kills it, and then departs, while the Swan-Princess, in love with Bova, looks after him sorrowfully. The curtain falls again, and before it passes a mock funeral procession for the dragon. All the available forces of evil are present at this ceremony, including Kikimora and her ex-friend, the Cat. They are followed by a group of lively peasants.

Then the curtain rises on the last of the three Russian folk tales which make up *Contes Russes*. This one takes place in the hut of Baba-Yaga, a hideous witch who lives in a magic house supported on four hens' feet, which follows her wherever she goes. Baba-Yaga loves to feast on the bodies of children who have lost their way, and consequently it is no surprise when she and her attendant demons are revealed attacking a young girl who has strayed in the forest. Although the child begs for mercy, the witch beats her constantly and the hairy spirits stroke her dress with brutal humor. As a last resort, the girl makes the sign of the cross. Baba-Yaga and her demons are defeated; jubilant peasants arrive in the wood, and there is a general celebration. Among the participants are the Cat, who leaps high in the air, then the Knight, Bova, and finally the Swan-Princess, attended by Baba-Yaga's demons, who have reformed. The curtain falls on a colorful whirl of dance as nearly all of the characters in the three fairy tales—except the two ogresses, Kikimora and Baba-Yaga, who are conspicuously absent—join to celebrate the liberation of the girl who has wandered.

Courtesy Dance News

Coppélia

OR

THE GIRL WITH ENAMEL EYES

THIS BALLET in two acts and three scenes, with choreography by Arthur Saint-Léon, was first produced at the Paris Opéra in May, 1870. Charles Nuitter and Arthur Saint-Léon wrote the book, based on a tale by the German romanticist E. T. A. Hoffmann; and Léo Delibes composed the magnificent score—one of the outstanding examples of ballet music in any era.

The Russian ballerina Adele Grantsova had been chosen by the management of the Opéra to create the role of Swanilda; but owing to the length of the rehearsal period she was forced to return to Russia before the première, and the fifteen-year-old Giuseppina Bozacchi danced the part. This gifted child was to die shortly afterward from a fever contracted during the siege of Paris.

Her role passed the following year to the artist for whom it had been intended by the librettist, Nuitter: Léontine Beaugrand. Ever since Beaugrand's triumphs as Swanilda, the part has attracted a long line of stellar dancers, as it offers a performer full chance to display her talents

119

for wit, elegance, brilliance of movement, ingenuity of mime—everything but tragedy. Among the best-known exponents of the part have been Anna Pavlova, Adeline Genée, Lydia Lopokova, Vera Nemchinova, Ninette de Valois, Alexandra Danilova, Tamara Toumanova, Irina Baronova, and Mia Slavenska.

Coppélia was first produced in the United States as part of the repertory of a group called The American Opera, which appeared in 1887 at the Metropolitan Opera House. The resident Metropolitan company revived the ballet during the season of 1903–04; again in 1909–10, when Pavlova, supported by Mikhail Mordkin, was its star; and still later, in 1912 and 1913, for appearances by Katerina Geltzer and Miss Genée as Swanilda.

The first presentation of the work here by an independent troupe of dancers took place in October, 1938, when the Ballet Russe de Monte Carlo offered it at the Metropolitan Opera House in a version with certain revisions and additions—gathered over a course of years—by Marius Petipa, Enrico Cecchetti, and Léonide Massine. The basic outlines of Saint-Léon's choreography for the first two scenes, however, remained intact. On this occasion Miss Danilova was the Swanilda, establishing herself as the finest performer of the role in our time. A condensation of *Coppélia* into one act, with new choreography by Simon Semenoff, was attempted by Ballet Theatre in October, 1942, during its Metropolitan season; but, in this elided form, the ballet did not please, despite Miss Baronova's charming performance as Swanilda. It is essentially a full-length work, belonging to a period which stressed largeness of proportion.

Delibes's score, masterfully composed and orchestrated, symphonic in caliber yet serving the stage at all times, broke ground for the later achievements by Tchaikovsky in this field. The czardas of Act One is said to have been the first Hungarian folk dance of its type to enter serious ballet.

ACT ONE

After a brief prelude composed of many of the chief melodies of *Coppélia*, including the vivacious mazurka, the curtain rises on the public

Tempo di mazurka, animé

square of a small town in Galicia. The time is about two hundred years ago; the architecture, rustic.

One building stands out from the rest. It is the dwelling of an eccentric old man, Coppélius, who dabbles in all sorts of inventions. In an upper window of the house, exposed to the gaze of the town, sits a waxen-faced girl, Coppélia, said to be the old man's daughter. She has never spoken to anyone, nor ventured onto the streets, nor does she bow when greeted from below. She sits in the window all day long, reading.

On a certain late summer afternoon she is in her place as usual above the square when, suddenly, the window of an adjoining house is opened and Swanilda, a high-spirited maiden of the town, looks out. Seeing no one near, she steals from her dwelling and—to a delightful waltz—tiptoes into the square.

For some time past, Swanilda has suspected her fiancé, Frantz, of an undue interest in the girl who sits reading. Just as she slips toward the house of Coppélius to examine her rival more closely, she hears Frantz coming. Swanilda hides and watches him drawn as if by magic to Coppélius' dwelling. The old man stands in the window behind his daughter, his hand on her shoulder, looking down at the youth.

Frantz, with eyes only for Coppélia, tries to attract the girl's attention. He is successful . . . Coppélia nods to him, lays down her book with one hand and waves with the other. Her gestures are stiff and labored; they

are accompanied by a slight rasp; but to Frantz they seem heavenly. As he blows her a kiss, Coppélius indignantly draws the curtain, shielding his daughter from view.

Now Swanilda, thoroughly irritated, steps from her hiding place. Rather than admit to spying, she runs across the square apparently chasing a butterfly; but when Frantz catches the insect and pins it to his blouse, Swanilda's anger spills over as much at this offense against nature as at his faithlessness to her. She reproaches him bitterly.

Before Frantz can answer, a group of young people fills the square, dancing the joyous mazurka whose melody has been heard in the prelude (No. 1). The Burgomaster arrives with the happy announcement that on the following day the lord of the manor will present the town

with a new clock, and award dowries to all worthy young couples wish-
ing to be wed.

As the Burgomaster addresses the crowd, flames shoot up in the windows of Coppélius' house. First the villagers are frightened; then, mind-
ful of the old man's strange reputation, they shrug their shoulders—
Coppélius is probably at work on another of his experiments.

The excitement dies down; and, as the subject of the dowries is raised
again, the Burgomaster asks Swanilda if she too will be wed on the mor-
row. Looking significantly at Frantz, and miming to the music of an
exquisite ballade, the girl takes a sheaf of corn from one of her friends,

holds it to her ear, and listens. It seems to whisper that Frantz is untrue.
She pauses, then snaps the sheaf before her fiancé's eyes: their engagement has been broken.

As Frantz goes off indignantly, Swanilda dances a brilliant set of variations with the girls of the town, leading up to a dashing czardas in which

all of the men join the maidens. While they dance, the sunlight fades, and soon the crowd goes home, leaving the square deserted.

Now the door of the house at the right opens slowly and the sinister Coppélius hobbles out, muffled in a cloak and three-cornered hat. Locking the door carefully behind him, he looks up at the window where the shadow of Coppélia, seated in her chair, may still be seen outlined against the curtain, then crosses the square.

Suddenly he is surrounded by mischievous boys from the town who have been awaiting this chance to use the old inventor as a butt for their jokes. Hitting at them with his stick, Coppélius escapes but in the struggle drops the key to his house. As he runs off through the darkness that

Photo: *Maurice Seymour*   Courtesy *Museum of Modern Art*

MICHEL PANAIEFF AND TAMARA TOUMANOVA

123

has settled on the square, Swanilda appears, retrieves the key, and, curious about her rival, leads her friends inside the inventor's rooms.

No sooner has the door closed behind her than Frantz, also drawn to the mysterious dwelling, enters the street with a ladder. Rejected by Swanilda, all of his hopes center now in the studious young woman he has seen in the window. Just as he is about to climb toward his goal, Frantz is interrupted by Coppélius; the old man, discovering the loss of his key, has returned in a ferment. Frightened, the youth drops the ladder and escapes. Coppélius stares after him, then sees the door of his house wide open. Full of apprehension, he goes in.

ACT TWO

SCENE ONE: The workroom of Coppélius is revealed in a dim light, cluttered with tools and instruments of every kind. Fantastically dressed automatons are scattered about on pedestals. The studious Coppélia, still sitting in her window alcove, is shielded from the chamber by a heavy drape.

A group of figures may be seen making their way through the gloom: Swanilda and her friends. First they are frightened by the darkened laboratory; then, gathering courage, they look about inquisitively. Approaching the curtain that hides Coppélia, Swanilda pulls it aside and sees her rival seated in the chair, book in hand. She greets the girl, but there is no answer. Coming still nearer, Swanilda takes her rival's arm and finally puts her hand on Coppélia's heart. Feeling no beat, the girl realizes that she and her fiancé have been deceived by a mechanical doll.

Just at this moment, one of Swanilda's young friends stumbles over an automaton and sets the hidden spring in motion. The mechanism raises its arms, turns its head, plays a tinkling tune. Soon all the other toys, wound up by the girls, grow active. Life in the workroom has become enjoyable when, suddenly, the raging Coppélius enters. As the old man limps toward the window and draws the curtain shielding Coppélia, the girls escape by the staircase. Only Swanilda is left, concealed in the alcove with the doll.

Now a new intruder appears: Frantz has returned with his ladder. Coppélius sees him climbing through the window and, waiting until the youth is in the center of the musty room, demands an explanation for this visit. When Frantz confesses that he has dared everything for love of Coppélia, the old man—on the threshold of perfecting an invention at which he has been working for many years—feigns cordiality, invites the youth to be seated, and offers him a drink. The eccentric himself, raising his glass in a toast of friendship, takes care to throw away the contents, for the wine is drugged.

Soon Frantz is asleep; and Coppélius, peering into an enormous book, is about to embark on an experiment transferring the life matter of this doltish youth to the inanimate Coppélia. Confident of his success, he opens the curtain that hides the doll and rolls his masterpiece on its base to the center of the room. So perfectly has Swanilda disguised herself as the doll, wearing every last detail of its clothing and assuming the puppet's immobility, that not even the creator in his excitement notices the change.

As he goes through a series of incantations prescribed by the magic book, Coppélius notes with glee that the doll is coming alive. She rises, descends from the pedestal, looks about her with jerky movements. It seems to the old man that Coppélia has even shrugged her shoulders. Now he tries to make her dance, always with the thought of rendering her movements more flexible, less automatic. Under his ministrations, the imaginary Coppélia is gradually transformed; her eyes open wide; she smiles.

As Swanilda moves about the room, she sees the sleeping Frantz, notes the drink with which he has been drugged. Approaching the youth, she shakes him violently. To keep her quiet, Coppélius gives the doll a mantilla to play with; and Swanilda, full of life and grace, does a fiery Spanish dance. Still hoping to prevent her awakening Frantz and spoil-

ing the experiment, the inventor pins a Scotch plaid on the troublesome girl. Swanilda, diverted, performs a charming jig.

All these precautions, however, cannot hold her. She runs wild, overturning every automaton in the laboratory and finally rousing Frantz. When at last Coppélius succeeds in jamming the doll on her pedestal and wheeling her back into the alcove, Frantz is fully awake, Coppélius' work has been undone, and the enraged old man drives the youth from the house.

Unobserved, Swanilda slips down the stairs and joins her fiancé. When Coppélius, looking out after the retreating Frantz, sees the girl in the street below dressed as his masterpiece, he runs to the alcove, flings open the curtain, and there—mounted primly on her throne by the window—finds the real Coppélia, completely nude.

SCENE TWO: The night has passed and the promised holiday is taking place in full sunlight on a lawn before the manor house. First the clock donated by the lord to the community is blessed by the priests; then the young couples of the town who are to be wed advance for the nobleman's dowries. Among them are Frantz and Swanilda.

A furious noise interrupts the ceremonies. It is Coppélius, bemoaning the loss of his automatons, claiming that Swanilda has destroyed the lot. The girl is about to repay him with her dowry; but the lord of the manor stops her and himself reimburses the unhappy old man.

Coppélius hobbles off and the great festival of the clock begins as a chariot appears, symbolic of the flight of time. From the gilded cart descends a bell ringer who summons the hours of the morning: Dawn, Prayer, Work, Marriage, Discord, War, and Peace.

This entire scene, designed as a chain of *divertissements* with which to end the work, has—in its travels from one ballet capital to another—been cut or rearranged in every conceivable way; nor have the changes been without justification, for the tableau is long and not well knit organically. As presented today, a few of the solo and group dances of the festival remain, along with an interpolated *pas de deux* for Frantz and Swanilda based on music which, in the original score, was meant to accompany the variation for Peace.

At the close of this duo—an unusually severe test for the technique and staying power of the ballerina after the two rigorously demanding scenes that have just passed—the ending of the ballet is reached with a joyous finale for principals and *corps*. In these concluding moments, as throughout the whole of *Coppélia*, the music of Delibes is marked by its own special radiance.

Le Coq d'Or

This, the final opera by Nicholas Rimsky-Korsakov, was completed a year before the composer's death in 1908. Based on a tale by Pushkin, and adapted to the modern stage by the Russian poet Byelsky, the work has had a stormy career ever since its composition. Certain aspects of the libretto were considered politically taboo by the Czarist government. The opera was forbidden a performance unless cuts were made. Rimsky refused to make them, and consequently he never heard a performance of *Le Coq d'Or*. At length, by consent of the imperial censors, the work was given first privately in Moscow a year after his death (1909) and then one season later by the state company in St. Petersburg.

In 1914 another tempestuous element entered the picture. Diaghilev decided, for his Paris season, to present the work as a ballet-opera. The scenario was to be enacted by dancers, while the singers—in uniform, unobtrusive costumes—were to sit on the periphery of the setting in a kind of grandstand arrangement. The choreography for this historic Paris performance was by Michel Fokine. It should be noted that the family of Rimsky-Korsakov protested vigorously at what they described as a violation of the composer's intentions.

Nevertheless, it is this form of *Le Coq d'Or* that has been responsible for the music's international popularity. The work arrived at the Metropolitan Opera House as a ballet-opera (choreographed by Adolph Bolm) in 1918, and held the stage for many seasons in this form. Then it went into limbo for a long period.

Le Coq d'Or was revived at the Metropolitan in two radically different versions during the season of 1937. In February of that year, the Metropolitan Opera Association presented the work as pure lyric theatre, without the ballet. The principal singers—Ezio Pinza, Lily Pons, and their associates—mimed, as well as sang, their parts. Herbert Graf was the stage director. Much of this revival, especially the stunning interpretation by Mr. Pinza, reached real distinction. Then, in the following October, the Ballet Russe de Monte Carlo—headed at the time by Colonel de Basil—presented a new balletic synthesis of the opera.° Rimsky's music had been arranged for the occasion by Nicholas Tcherepnin; choreography, as in the days of Diaghilev, was devised by Michel Fokine. The principal dancers were Marc Platoff as King Dodon, Irina Baronova as the Queen of Shemakhan, and Tatiana Riabouchinska as the Golden Cockerel.

The 1937 ballet version was a great success. It disappeared from American stages when de Basil broke off relations with the Ballet Russe de Monte Carlo and took his own troupe of dancers and legally protected repertoire (including *Le Coq d'Or*) to South America. The operatic original had still another revival at the Metropolitan, in an English translation, in 1945. Poorly sung, it did not outlast the season.

The very first notes of *Le Coq d'Or* form the motive of the Golden Cockerel, from which the opera takes its name. They are played piercingly by the trumpets, like the crowing of the fabled bird.

In muted contrast, the cellos follow with the long-drawn, seductive theme of the Queen of Shemakhan.

An old Astrologer makes his way, at this point, through the curtains. Wearing a blue robe embroidered with stars, and a white astrakhan cap, he informs the spectators cryptically that—through his magic—they will see a panorama of ancient deeds and legends. The story they are to wit-

---

° Unlike the Diaghilev version, no voices at all were employed, and the score was abridged considerably. The opera is in three acts; the condensed ballet ar- relationship of Queen and Astrologer.

Courtesy Museum of Modern Art

TATIANA RIABOUCHINSKA AS THE GOLDEN COCKEREL

ness, he adds, may be less than true, but its moral is commendable. Then he sinks through a trap door and the curtain rises.

The Astrologer, one of the cardinal figures in the opera, has a musical theme that is especially commanding:

In the recent ballet version of *Le Coq d'Or*, this character—shorn of his opening speech—mimes the prologue. A touch of action is added by a magic telescope through which he glimpses the Queen of Shemakhan, daughter of the air, and decides to win her for himself. Invoking the aid of the Golden Cockerel, he sets out for the court of King Dodon, who will be used as his dupe in the conquest.*

* This mimed prologue is not so much a departure from the spirit of the opera as one might think, for Byelsky—the librettist—in his introduction to Rimsky's printed score, stressed the need of constantly emphasizing on stage the mysterious relationship of Queen and Astrologer.

SCENE ONE: Dodon is a proud, indolent South Russian monarch of the early Middle Ages. Seated on his throne at an extraordinary council of state, with his two sons—Aphron and Guidon—at his side, and the blunt old General Polkan (his chief of staff) near by, he makes an appeal to his people. War is imminent, he tells them. The country is besieged on all sides. How might the onslaught be stopped? As he speaks, cellos and basses play a motive characteristically associated with him.

Both of his sons advance nonsensical suggestions for defense of the realm. They quarrel with each other and with General Polkan, who denounces them. The King, defending his sons, harangues the honest old warrior and threatens him with violence. Tension at the palace increases when some of the courtiers suggest that the King's future may best be divined through beans, and others claim that his fortune can be told only by using fruit skins. As the two divergent parties are about to come to blows, the Astrologer appears. With him he bears the Golden Cockerel.*

The King is spellbound at the sight of the stranger. He listens eagerly as the Astrologer describes the magic powers of the bird. If the cockerel is mounted on a vane above the palace, it will shout an alarm when danger threatens from any point.

No time is lost by the monarch in acquiring the miraculous bird. Dodon has it placed on a perch, and offers the Astrologer whatever payment he might desire. To the King's surprise, the stranger asks nothing, preferring to name his price at some future time. As the Astrologer leaves, quiet descends on the palace. Dodon calls for his well-upholstered bed and dozes among the cushions, to the accompaniment of an exquisite lullaby.

Suddenly the cockerel crows of danger. Irritably, the King awakens long enough to send his two sons off to war with part of the army. Then he settles back to recapture, if possible, the dream of certain veiled beauties which affairs of state have interrupted. With the old palace nurse, Amelfa, conscientiously driving away the noonday insects, he

---

* In the opera and opera-ballet (Diaghilev) versions, the voice of the cockerel is taken by a dramatic soprano placed in the orchestra pit.

falls asleep again. Once more the cockerel screams; the invasion is growing serious. Resigned to the inevitable, the King rises from his bed, has his dust-covered armor brushed off, and with great difficulty climbs an inoffensive old nag on which he rides at the head of his army. A triumphal march accompanies his exit as the curtain falls.

SCENE TWO: The King, with his loyal General Polkan and a portion of the army, arrives in a forbidding gorge just before dawn. To his grief, Dodon finds the bodies of his two sons, each slain by the other in the darkness. In the midst of his lamentations, the sun rises. A brilliantly colored tent is seen; and Dodon's soldiers train their cannon on the tent, ready to fire when its occupants appear.

As the silken flaps open, they flee in terror. A ravishing woman emerges wearing a white turban and a sumptuous crimson garment trimmed with gold. She extends her arms in prayer to the East. It is at this moment of the opera that the famous "Hymn to the Sun" is heard. In the ballet, the music of the aria accompanies a beautifully choreographed solo for the ballerina.

The woman steps forward and faces Dodon. In answer to the King's questions, she tells him that she is the Queen of Shemakhan and has come to conquer his country. After this first bit of frankness, she resorts to guile and soon has the King under her spell. The old monarch orders the bodies removed; he makes love to the Queen; and finally, to the intense humiliation of Polkan and the soldiers, he allows himself to be drawn into an absurd dance before the Queen, with a kerchief covering his beard and tied about his gray head like a peasant girl's.

After the Queen has subjected him to every variety of public mortification—to which, blinded with love, he is oblivious—she accepts his offer of marriage. As her slaves gather up her jewels, carpets, and mirrors, she steps exultantly with the King into his golden chariot for the journey to his capital.

SCENE THREE: Although there is bright sunshine in the streets before the palace, a cloud can be seen over Dodon's chief city. The inhabitants seem worried as messengers keep arriving from the battlefield. At length Amelfa, the nurse, announces to the crowd that the King is bringing back a bride.

At that moment, distant trumpets are heard. The wedding march has begun.

Allegro alla marcia

Then, preceded by soldiers of the returning King, comes the Queen's weird procession. Freaks with one eye in the middle of their foreheads are seen. They are joined by other human monsters with horns and still others with the heads of dogs. Giants, dwarfs, slaves bearing caskets of precious jewels, march past the palace, while the exotic flavor of the procession on stage is matched by the pungent harmonies in the orchestra.

Allegro

Placated by the pomp and spectacle of the march, Dodon's troubled subjects hail him as he enters with his Queen. At the climax of their greeting, the Astrologer suddenly appears. He is welcomed warmly by the King, who asks if he has come to name his price for the Golden Cockerel.

The Astrologer nods, then abruptly claims as his reward the hand of

Photo: Maurice Seymour Courtesy Dance News
BARONOVA AS THE QUEEN OF SHEMAKHAN

the Queen. At first the King cannot believe his ears. When the Astrologer becomes insistent, Dodon orders him to leave. The stranger refuses. All this time the Queen looks at him fearfully. Finally the King, overcome with rage, raises his scepter and brings it down on the Astrologer's skull. The magician falls dead.

Darkness comes upon the scene. As the King turns to his bride, she repulses him. Suddenly the whirring of wings is heard, and the crowing of the cockerel. The bird has flown from its perch and is hovering above the crowd. While everyone tries to escape, the cockerel sinks its beak into the head of the King. The craven ruler is killed; his Queen, with quiet laughter, disappears; and, to the weeping of Dodon's people, the curtain is lowered.

As in the prologue, the Astrologer appears again. This time he tells the audience enigmatically not to be too upset over the outcome of the drama, since—of all of the characters—only he and the Queen of Shemakhan were real. Then, while the cockerel's theme surges to a piercing valedictory the Astrologer vanishes and the outer curtain falls.

In the Fokine version of 1937, this epilogue provided an unforgettable moment. As the Astrologer took his departure and the cockerel's motive was heard, Tatiana Riabouchinska—an overwhelming, golden vision as the bird—was the last to hold the audience's gaze, whirling to the music in a brilliant shaft of light.

Photo: Maurice Seymour
Courtesy Museum of Modern Art
URA LAZOVSKY AND HARCOURT ALGERANOFF

La Création du Monde

THIS STORY of the creation of the world in ballet form, as seen through the eyes of a savage, was choreographed by Jean Borlin for the Ballets Suédois and first produced at the Théâtre des Champs-Élysées, Paris, in October, 1923.* The book was by Blaise Cendrars, the scenery and costumes by Fernand Léger, and the music by Darius Milhaud. Mr. Borlin and Eban Strandin danced the leading roles of Man and Woman.

The ballet created a stir in Parisian circles through its use of Negroid and aboriginal art elements at a time when they were little known to the general public. For several years preparatory to this work, Borlin had made an intensive study of African civilizations. In the field of performance, he had created a solo dance at the Comédie des Champs-Élysées called *Sculpture Nègre* (1919). The dream of producing a large-scale Negro fantasy led him to visit Parisian museums of ethnography. *La Création du Monde,* haunting in its fusion of ballet and the jungle, was the result.

The chaos of pre-Creation is seen on a darkened stage as the curtain rises. Three aboriginal deities move among a tangled mass of bodies, muttering incantations. The mass responds to their charms. First a tree rises and lets fall one of its seeds, from which rises still another tree. Now animals appear, every one of them springing—as in the process of evolution—from a more primitive predecessor. Finally, as the three deities pronounce new spells, Man and Woman emerge. They perform a dance of desire, excited by the presence of primeval sorcerers and witch doctors. At last the frenzy of the celebrants subsides; the dancers disperse; and Man and Woman are left alone in a symbolic embrace which assures the fertility of human life.

* A revival of the work for the Carmago Society of London in 1931 (the year of Borlin's death) had new choreography by Ninette de Valois. This revised version appeared later at the Sadler's Wells Theatre. Still another edition based on Milhaud's score but with altered scenario was devised by Agnes de Mille for Ballet Theatre's 1940 season at the Center Theatre, New York: *Obeah* (*Black Ritual*).

The Creatures of Prometheus

THIS BALLET in two acts, first produced at the Imperial Court Theatre, Vienna, March 28, 1801, represents a fusion of two formidable creative minds. The score was composed by Ludwig van Beethoven; the choreography by Salvatore Viganò, famous for his pioneering work in the field of dance-drama * more than a hundred years before the similar but further-reaching activities of Michel Fokine. At the original Vienna performances the two statues—creatures of Prometheus—were danced by Viganò himself and Mlle Cassentini. The part of Prometheus was taken by a mime.

Like *Les Petits Riens* of Mozart, the scenario of Prometheus has been lost. Ample accounts of it exist, however, not only in journals of the day but in an elaborate analysis of the works of Viganò published in Milan in 1838; in the mansucript score with annotations owned by the Library of Vienna; and in Beethoven's own sketchbooks. The libretto, as described here, has been reconstructed from historical sources by Jean Chantavoine and Maurice Lena, and is contained in the Heugel edition of the Beethoven score.

The plot is of an allegorical type popular in Vienna at the end of the eighteenth century. Gods and demigods take part in the action, but as figures of pure reason rather than dramatic conviction. The moral lies in the benevolence of nature, the possibilities of man, and the loftiness of his destiny.

OVERTURE

The orchestral introduction to *Prometheus* is a formal one, with no direct relationship to the thematic material of the ballet. It achieves, however, a certain brilliance that fixes the attention of the audience on the work to follow.

* Viganò was one of the earliest choreographers after Jean Georges Noverre—credited with creating the *ballet d'action*—to lay stress on design and characterization in theatrical dance, as opposed to sheer technique.

ACT ONE

Prometheus appears during a raging tempest and crosses the summit of a hill. Brandishing a torch defiantly against the thunderbolts, he reaches a primitive shed which contains a pair of statues—male and female—on the verge of animation. In a supreme moment, Prometheus communicates the fire of his torch to the female statue. Then he passes the flame to the male and falls overcome before his own creation.

The male statue comes to life. Now its counterpart, the woman, begins

to move, and the two join in a symmetrical dance. When Prometheus tries to take control, they run off and then—caught by the creator—crash perversely beneath a tree.

Angered at their ingratitude, Prometheus thinks of destroying his work. At this moment the dawn comes up, and a ray of sunlight strikes the summit of the hill. Filled with a new inspiration, Prometheus relents

and plucks a morning flower. He shows it to the female statue, inducing in her a love of nature. Then he gathers fruits for the male, who becomes strangely docile at the sight of the products of the earth. Both statues, enchanted by the aura of the world about them, follow Prometheus gently.

ACT TWO

SCENE ONE: On the crown of Mount Parnassus, in the midst of a vast glade, stands the temple of Apollo. On its steps are grouped the god and his court—the Muses, Orpheus, Mars, Bacchus, and other deities. Now Prometheus approaches, followed by his creatures. As he presents them to Apollo, his gestures indicate that, as yet, the statues have neither reason nor heart. It is the hope of Prometheus that the gods will grant them these qualities.

Apollo makes a sign, and Euterpe produces music which charms the statues and awakens their sensibilities. Soon Orpheus plays his lyre, evoking sounds of such eloquence that the creatures give signs of emotion, agitation, sighing.

The climax of creation has been reached: the man and woman are mutually attracted. As Apollo himself joins the concert, they take timid steps toward each other; the woman indulges in some elementary coquetry; and at length they embrace. Prometheus cannot contain his pride at this fulfillment of his work.

The creatures salute him tenderly, first the woman and then the man. He takes them in his arms and bids them give thanks to Apollo. The god, who has remounted the steps of the temple, invites the creatures to stand at the foot of his throne and learn the arts of war and peace.

At once a procession of Mars fills the scene. Military music is heard, as three bellicose groups enter in an armed dance. The male statue wants

to join them; the female tries to hold him back. Drawn by the rhythms of the warriors, both take part for a moment in the general dance but soon withdraw, looking on in exaltation.

Suddenly the scene darkens. Death enters in the guise of Melpomene, muse of tragedy, with mask and dagger. Revealing the corpses of fallen warriors, she predicts an identical fate for the creatures of Prometheus and reproaches the master for having breathed fire into them. As she advances with her dagger, the creatures try to bar her way, but Death fells the creator. The two statues, now become man and woman, implore the help of the gods. Night falls on the temple.

SCENE TWO: In the light of the dawn, young couples—shepherds and shepherdesses—enter, and Death recoils before them. To the soft melody of a pastorale, Prometheus is raised from the ground by the couple he

has wrought. Now minor deities appear—fauns, nymphs, and Graces. Children of Love enter, binding the man to the woman. The couple, crowned with roses, lead a nuptial procession; and, at a sign from Apollo, the rites end in homage to Prometheus, who takes his place * at the feet of the gods.

* To a joyous theme which, three years later, was to reappear with even greater effect in the finale of Beethoven's "Eroica" Symphony.

Cydalise and the Faun

(CYDALISE ET LE CHÈVRE-PIED)

THIS BALLET in two acts and three scenes, with music by Gabriel Pierné, was first produced at the Paris Opéra in January, 1923. The choreography was prepared by Leo Staats from a scenario by G. A. de Caillavet and Robert de Flers. Carlotta Zambelli, as Cydalise, and Albert Aveline, as the Satyr, were the principal dancers. The ballet enjoyed a marked success; and much of its music—especially the "Entrance of the Little Fauns" (Act One)—has survived in concert form. The entire work, full of wit, elegance, and genuinely poetic feeling, ranks among the more distinguished ballets for the modern French theatre.

ACT ONE

It is night in the gardens of Versailles. Great marble vases gleam in the moonlight. The shining surface of a pond may be seen, with a grotto near by. Most prominent of all, in the rays of the moon is a statue of Cupid poising his ivy-covered shaft.

As the curtain rises on this nocturnal grove, the humming of an invisible chorus may be heard. Dryads and hamadryads rise from behind the trunks and branches. They are thirsty and raise their hands in supplication toward the grotto. At once the spring appears, bearing a vase, and travels among the dryads, pouring out water for them to drink. Suddenly the sound of a flute is heard . . . the dryads flee and the spring returns to its source.

Now, as the moonlight wanes, a strange procession makes its way through the garden: a group of little satyrs, paired off according to size,

Tempo di marcia (Tempo giusto)

led by an old faun in charge of their education. The aged teacher makes
the satyrs sit in a circle about him and gives them a lesson in playing
the flute of Pan. Whenever they miss, he corrects them.

All the pupils except one are co-operative. Only young Styrax is con-
spicuous for his lack of discipline. Constantly reprimanded by the in-
structor, he will not sit still but keeps bounding about.

Now a school of nymphs arrives, similarly arranged in pairs. They
are led by a governess. Soon the nymphs and satyrs, chaperoned by the
governess and the old faun, unite in a dancing lesson.

As before, Styrax offers the only discordant note, throwing the dance
into confusion with his gambols. The old faun decides to punish the
youngster; he rebukes him and boxes his ears. When Styrax tries to
escape, the old faun has the other pupils bind him to a tree with chains
of ivy. Only one of them—the little nymph Mnesilla—feels pity for Styrax.
As she sobs, the invisible chorus is heard again. Dawn is breaking, and
the old faun joins the governess in reassembling the pupils. Then all go
off, forgetting the prisoner.

The sky grows lighter; a bird sings; Styrax—his body bound to the
tree but his arms free—tries to imitate the bird on his flute. At this moment Mnesilla reappears. She has come to free Styrax; she undoes his
bonds and wants to take him away with her. Intoxicated by the odor of
the morning, Styrax refuses. As Mnesilla flees and Styrax is left alone,
the faun picks flowers and smells them, tastes the sweetness of the
fruits in the gardens, and looks ardently at the sun.

It is only a short while before the faun discovers the statue of Cupid.
First he is frightened, then inquisitive, and finally a bit contemptuous.
Snapping his fingers, he dances around the statue and pelts it with chest-
nuts. One of them touches the bow of love—the arrow leaves its resting
place and flies across the garden. Styrax retrieves it at once and does a
dance of triumph; but, while playing with the arrow, he wounds himself and feels an unknown pain.

At that moment, the noise of a coach, with little round bells on the
horses, is heard approching. Styrax looks about astonished as the carriage appears. Inside and on the roof are persons of the early eighteenth

century, some of them ill-clad and others overdressed. They are dancers and comedians in the employ of the King. Styrax stares at them admiringly, then darts forward, leaps to the trunk of the carriage, and hangs on. The coach disappears.

ACT TWO

SCENE ONE: The actors and dancers have assembled on the stage of an outdoor theatre at Versailles, where a performance of ballet is to take place that evening. At the right a platform prepared for the court is placed obliquely against the surrounding hedges. At the left may be seen a perspective of statues rising in tiers.

As the curtain rises, workers and guards are arranging the stage for the performance. A playbill has been set up: "*The Sultana of the Indies,* danced by Mlle Cydalise in honor of the betrothal of the Dauphin."

Now the ballet master arrives. Trunks are brought in, full of props and costumes. At a sign from the *maître de ballet,* the dancers go behind the pavilion to dress. The workmen saunter backstage for a drink . . . and, at this moment, Styrax appears on the empty scene.

The faun approaches, hiding among the trees; then he sees the costumes, handles them with curiosity, and ends by putting one on. As the actors return, he takes refuge in a trunk.

The entire company is uneasy, for the star dancer, Cydalise, has not arrived. At last she appears with a band of admirers, flings off her cloak, and stands ready to perform as the Sultana. Styrax, peering out of the trunk, opens and closes the lid several times. Meanwhile, two rival lovers of Cydalise arrive—the Farmer-General and the Captain of the Guards. Ironic bows and compliments are interchanged; then, when the ballet master strikes the platform three times with his stick, the performance begins.

The ballet is a short one, having to do with a Sultan of the Indies, who is ill and bored until a shipload of slaves arrives, including the beautiful Cydalise. He falls in love with the captive and ends by proposing to make her his Sultana. In the course of the action, the lovely Cydalise scores a great success with her audience, both through the charm of her dancing and through her personal beauty.

At length the ballet ends, and Cydalise motions to her admirers that she is cold. As the Farmer-General, looking for a heavy wrap, hurries toward the trunk and opens it, Styrax jumps out and leaps enthusiastically toward Cydalise to embrace her.

At first, everyone is too amazed to take action. Then the ballet master steps forward and asks the intruder who he is. Instead of answering, Styrax starts to dance—at first with restraint, then with increasing abandon. Spellbound at his movements, Cydalise joins in, and finally every-

one is seized by the frenzy of this bacchanale. In the passion of the moment, Cydalise and the faun are so closely interlocked that the Captain and the Farmer-General have to intervene and drag her away. Before departing, she throws Styrax the rose from her sash, and he gives her Cupid's arrow, which he has preserved and by whose sting he is possessed. Then, brandishing Cydalise's rose, he dances his joy.

SCENE TWO: The ballerina has been given a part of the granaries of Versailles as a cottage. A large window at the back opens on the park; there are knotholes in the wall, and there is a skylight.

After the performance, Cydalise enters the house escorted by her admirers. She is surrounded by flowers, adulation, a basket full of love letters. Dismissing her followers, she reads some of these notes but, with a gesture of boredom, tears them up and lets the pieces flutter out the window.

Then she draws from her sash the arrow that Styrax has given her. As she dreams over it, the faun himself appears. Now Cydalise plays the coquette. Showing Styrax the basket which still contains several billets-doux, she invites him to add his own; but Styrax does not write; neither does he read; and, with a sweep of the arm, the satyr indicates that his only talent lies in playing the flute of Pan. He strikes up a tune on the instrument, and Cydalise dances.

Styrax himself soon joins the dance, which becomes increasingly passionate. Moved by the faun's love, Cydalise makes him swear by the rose she has given him never to leave her. He promises. Still embracing, they go to the rear of the chamber and she opens the window to breathe the morning air. From the depths of the park mount the voices of the forest that is awakening. Styrax is moved as they call to him, "Return!"

Cydalise tries to draw him away from the window. He resists, spellbound by the sounds of nature. At the edges of the windows, in the growing daylight, appear the faces, then the figures, of nymphs and satyrs. Some of them leap into the room; little fauns and dryads fall from the skylight or tumble through the knotholes. They bear rose branches, rustic flowers, and leaves. Caressing Styrax, they make him breathe the scent. The invisible chorus sings, "Come, Styrax! The kiss of dawn is warming the forest. Woman is cruel and her heart is vain. Come, Styrax, come!"

Styrax, suddenly freed of the effects of Cupid's arrow, takes Cydalise in his arms, bears her to a couch, and receives from the hands of another faun a cluster of poppies which he presses to the face of the pleading girl. Following his comrades, he climbs toward the window and, as the others withdraw, lingers on the ledge to blow Cydalise a final kiss. Then he leaps out of sight.

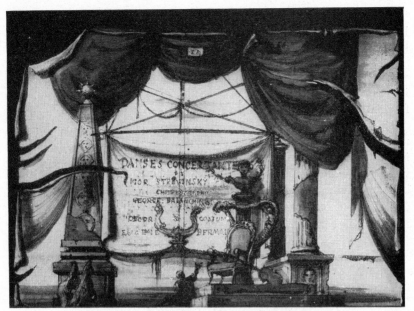

Danses Concertantes

THIS BALLET in six numbers, with choreography by George Balanchine, was first given by the Ballet Russe de Monte Carlo at the New York City Center in September, 1944, with Alexandra Danilova and Leon Danielian in the leading roles. Frederic Franklin later alternated with Mr. Danielian. The scenery and costumes were designed by Eugene Berman, and a special score was provided by Igor Stravinsky.

A brief orchestral march is heard. The ballerina and her partner come before a baroque inner curtain, together with four assisting groups—

145

each one composed of two girls and a boy. They perform brilliantly in prologue, bow, and go off. Now the curtain rises, and the concert dances are ready to begin.

The *corps de ballet* has taken its place on stage, with the ballerina presiding. It is she who starts the spectacle; then the groups of three join in. Four variations follow—a series of *pas de trois*—all of them differing fascinatingly in mood and construction.

The finale (a repetition of the opening march) has the same choreography and music as the prologue, save that it is presented on a full stage instead of before the footlights. At its conclusion, the dancers run forward to bow, the inner drop of the prologue falls behind them, and the ballet ends with the performers facing the audience in formal greeting.

Courtesy Museum of Modern Art

SASCHA YOUDOVICK, RUTHANNA BORIS, AND DOROTHY ETHERIDGE

146

Daphnis et Chloé

ALTHOUGH THIS "choreographic symphony" came into being during the Diaghilev Paris season of 1912 at the Théâtre du Châtelet, it was not the first time that the choreographer—Michel Fokine—had concerned himself with the legend of Daphnis and Chloë. In 1904, as a rising force in Russian dance, he had based a scenario on this subject—using the story as a vehicle for those artistic reforms he considered necessary to the survival of ballet—and submitted it to the Director of Imperial Theatres. The proposed work was in two acts and called for a completely integrated theatre piece, in which solo numbers gave way to an over-all dramatic scheme. One or two of the minor reforms suggested in Fokine's preface to the scenario were adopted by the Imperial Russian Ballet, but the work itself was not produced.

Eight years later the first act of the original Daphnis et Chloé, with major revisions, was created by Fokine for the Diaghilev Paris season, with Maurice Ravel as composer. Several practical difficulties arose in connection with the première. Ravel had hoped to finish the music a season earlier. Elaborate preparations had been made by Diaghilev for scenery and costumes in the Greek manner. When the composer was obliged to put the score aside because of other commitments, the properties intended for Daphnis were used in another Hellenic ballet devised by Fokine, Narcisse. By the time that Daphnis et Chloé finally came to production, some of its accessories were well worn. There was not enough rehearsal time (the finale was put together in only one session), and a company quarrel had developed over the resources then being lavished by Diaghilev on L'Après-Midi d'un Faune of Nijinsky—just turned choreographer—at the expense of Fokine's new work. Although Daphnis et Chloé enjoyed a public success, the result of this backstage conflict was the withdrawal by Fokine from the Diaghilev group for two years.

Today, Daphnis et Chloé has all but vanished from the stage. It has been given occasional performances in the United States by the Littlefield Ballet; but the material requirements of the piece keep it from the repertoire of the usual touring companies. Ravel's score calls for an instrumental ensemble of the size and technical excellence of the Boston, Philadelphia, or New York Philharmonic-Symphony orchestra. In addition, a large chorus is employed. One can realize from these indications how wonderfully equipped was the Diaghilev ensemble in every one

147

of its departments, and how different these early Paris performances were from the traveling kind of ballet known currently to dance lovers. At the Paris première of *Daphnis et Chloé*, the title roles were danced by Karsavina and Nijinsky, with Adolph Bolm as the shepherd, Dorcon. The décor was by Léon Bakst, and Pierre Monteux conducted.

Ravel's score, as theatre music, must be placed beside the finest works in this medium by Tchaikovsky, Stravinsky, and de Falla. In concert form (two suites have been extracted), it has outlived the ballet for which it was composed and is already one of the symphonic classics of our time.

SCENE ONE

As the curtain rises, vast meadows are seen, bordering on a sacred wood. At the right is a grotto whose entrance—used as an altar—has been chiseled from the natural stone in the form of three nymphs. In the background, just before the rise of the hills, stands a large rock in the shape of the god Pan. Sheep are grazing in the distance; the stage is empty.

Voices of invisible youths and maidens are heard. They are singing a wordless chant which recurs throughout the ballet—an invocation to the Nymphs.

Young Greeks enter. The chorus too appears, first in the background and then as part of the evolving stage picture. All of these rustic people have come bearing gifts for the Nymphs. They place wreaths and flowers before the altar of the grotto.

Then the shepherd youth Daphnis descends from the hills at the head of his flock. As he comes into view, the orchestra introduces his motif.

148

Soon the maiden Chloë, with whom he is in love, crosses the meadows to join him. The young couple go to the altar of the Nymphs to take their vows. At first the surrounding rustics look at them with solicitude and affection. Later, lightly jesting, they separate Daphnis from Chloë and draw the shepherd into a dance with the more attractive of the girls. Chloë sulks; but she, in her turn, is forced into a circle of the younger men. An admiring shepherd, Dorcon, makes crude advances to the maiden.

As Daphnis steps forward to drive him away, the theme of the youth's love for Chloë sounds in the orchestra.

The spirit of raillery persists, however, among the crowd. Someone

Photo: Teddy Piaz   *Courtesy Museum of Modern Art*

SERGE LIFAR AS DAPHNIS

proposes a dance contest between Daphnis and Dorcon for the favors of Chloë. The reward will be a kiss.

Both men accept. Dorcon performs a loutish number and is jeered at by the young Greeks. Daphnis launches a dance full of grace and poetry. He easily wins Chloë's kiss, together with the acclaim of the rustics. Then he sinks to the ground, motionless, in ecstasy. The crowd leads Chloë away.

As he lies on the grass, his chin resting in his hands, the youth does not see the temptress Lyceion, who approaches. She waits until he meets her glance, then allows several veils to fall; but when she notes in the youth only a sense of hostility and dark perturbation, Lyceion withdraws.

Daphnis looks after her with troubled thoughts; but his attention is shifted abruptly to the clanging of arms, the shouts of battle. Pirates have invaded the shore. Far above the grotto, on the portion of the meadow that borders the hills, the rustics may be seen in flight.

The youth runs toward the combat to protect Chloë. At the moment that he climbs the slope, the unfortunate girl appears on the plain below. She throws herself before the altar of the Nymphs, begging their aid, but a group of brigands carries her off.

No sooner has she gone than Daphnis reappears, still seeking her; then he finds her torn scarf, a sign of her struggle with the abductors. In despair, he curses the gods who have failed to protect Chloë, and falls exhausted at the entrance of the grotto.

A fantastic light envelops the landscape; a flame burns suddenly on the head of one of the Nymphs in the grotto. The figure comes to life and descends from her pedestal.* She is followed by her two sisters. And now the wordless theme which has been chanted by the chorus throughout this scene—the motive of the Nymphs—becomes a full-scale symphonic melody.

The Nymphs, in a slow mysterious dance, approach Daphnis and lead him toward the rock that is made in the image of the god Pan. They invoke that divinity; and gradually the rock takes on intensity of out-

---

* It is here that the Concert Suite No. 1 begins, including the nocturnal dance of the Nymphs, the following choral interlude, and the bacchanale of the pirates.

line until the spirit of the god himself seems to hover over the field. Daphnis prostrates himself in prayer, and blackness comes upon the scene.

INTERLUDE AND SCENE TWO

The voices of the chorus are heard in the distance, mournfully, unaccompanied save for a solo trumpet and cellos. Then the curtain rises again to reveal a jagged seacoast with orange-brown rocks. It is the hideaway of the pirates, who, loaded with booty, are running wild in jubilation. As torches are brought, the brigands take part in an orgiastic dance, at the end of which they fall in a stupor.

Rekindling their excitement, they stagger to their feet and drag in the captive Chloë, her hands bound. The pirate chief, Bryaxis, orders her to dance for him. At first, Chloë obeys; then she pleads with the chieftain to release her. As he refuses, a supernatural gleam of light is seen above the mountains. Little bursts of flame appear. Satyrs and other fantastic creatures of the god Pan invade the pirate camp, causing the brigands to flee in terror. And finally the shadow of the god himself is seen among the mountains, his arm extended threateningly. Chloë alone remains upon the beach, a shining crown on her head. The tableau dissolves and gives way to the opening scene of the pastures and hills.

SCENE THREE*

It is sunrise. As the orchestra suggests the murmurings of nature, Daphnis may be seen still prostrated before the grotto of the Nymphs.

Two shepherds pass with their flocks, calling and answering on their pipes. Then the ever-present chant of the chorus is heard behind the

---

* This whole scene is included in the Concert Suite No. 2—Daybreak, Pantomime, and General Dance.

scenes. A group of rustics appears, in search of Daphnis and Chloë. Finding the young man on the ground, they awaken him; and, almost in the next moment, Chloë appears miraculously among a group of shepherds, still wearing the luminous crown. She throws herself into the arms of her lover, who realizes that the god Pan has granted his prayers and intervened.

Here, the old shepherd Lammon explains to the youth that Pan has saved Chloë in memory of the nymph Syrinx, with whom he was once in love. As Lammon speaks, Daphnis and Chloë re-enact in gratitude the ancient tale of god and nymph: Syrinx (Chloë) appears through the foliage of the meadow. Pan (Daphnis) declares his love. The nymph rejects him. Desperately, the god snatches some reeds from the brush and fashions a flute on which he plays a melancholy air. Syrinx answers

Courtesy Museum of Modern Art
CATHERINE LITTLEFIELD IN HER PRODUCTION OF DAPHNIS ET CHLOÉ

his call and follows, in a graceful dance, the accents of his music. For this pantomime, Ravel has used the flute tone predominantly in the orchestra, bringing as an accompaniment to the solo instrument harmonies and rhythms suggestive of ancient Greece.

The dance of god and nymph becomes ever more animated. Finally, overwhelmed by her feeling for Daphnis, Chloë abandons her role as Syrinx and plunges into the shepherd's arms. The two lovers approach the altar of the Nymphs.

At this point a group of young girls enters, dressed as bacchantes, beating their tambourines. Daphnis and Chloë embrace tenderly. A band of young men invades the scene, and a joyous tumult follows. Musically, this is one of the most irresistible finales in ballet literature, building to a climax through steady intensification of dynamics, heightening of orchestral color, manipulation of rhythms. The theme of the general dance which concludes the work is in ⅘ time, and of a bold, striking pattern.

Daphnis, Chloë, the shepherds, and even the boorish Dorcon join the revel; and the massed voices of the chorus * (always wordless) ring above the closing moments of music and dance.

* Although indicated in the score, they are generally omitted in performances of Concert Suite No. 2.

Dark Elegies

THIS WORK in one act, with choreography by Antony Tudor, was first performed by the Rambert Ballet at the Duchess Theatre, London, in February, 1937. When it was produced in New York by Ballet Theatre at the Center Theatre in January, 1941, the principal dancers were Nina Stroganova, Miriam Golden, Lucia Chase, Hugh Laing, Mr. Tudor, and Dimitri Romanoff. The scenery and costumes for the American première were designed by Raymond Sovey, after those of the London production by Nadia Benois.

The novelty of *Dark Elegies* lay in its use of a complete song cycle by Gustav Mahler as musical background. In choosing this composer's *Kindertotenlieder* (*Songs of Childhood Death*) as accompaniment for the danced substance of his work—with the solo baritone in the orchestra pit—Tudor set himself a problem of balancing words, music, and dance which he surmounted successfully. The mood of the ballet stems entirely from the music; but at no point has Tudor attempted to duplicate the text. Rather have the words of Friedrich Rückert given new outlet to the choreographer's fantasy.

Rückert (1788–1866), a German romantic, wrote the five poems making up the *Kindertotenlieder* as an elegy for his two children, who had died in an epidemic of cholera in 1902. Mahler set these verses to music, little suspecting they were to mark the untimely death of his own daughter. The first of the songs deals with the disbelief of a parent in the brightness of nature and the sun, once his children have vanished; in the next, he recalls his children's eyes, with their flames that seemed to presage death; in the third, he thinks of the happy hours they spent at home; then he fancies the children are alive, have gone walking, only to know—with a new onrush of grief—that they will never return; and, in the last, he fears for the safety of these youngsters who, he imagines distractedly, have run out to play in a storm. His agitation ends when, realizing they are past earthly danger, he accepts his bereavement.

To this mournful set of lyrics, Mahler has composed a score uniquely moving in its spare use of voice and subdued orchestral tints. Although the music is communicative in itself, requiring no choreographic expression to clarify its meaning or heighten its effect, the work serves as an admirable background for Tudor's ballet.

Dark Elegies is meant to express a sense of grievous loss. Every one of the characters conveys his anguish in a subtly different way against a

LUCIA CHASE

scenic background of hard country with stormy lakes. The characters wear peasant dress, severe in cut and color, giving a massed effect of utter desolation.

When the curtain rises on the first song, one of the women soloists is on stage with a background of six girls. Her movements, suggesting a deeply felt sorrow, are thoroughly personal, while the girls—in contrast

—render the same patterns abstractly. Despair underlies this solo, ranging from sustained movements at the start to sudden breaks and passionate departures at the climax, after which the dance relapses into the dirgelike quality of its opening.

The next song begins. As the girls and their soloist withdraw to a corner of the stage, a new dancer and her partner enter. The man comforts the woman in a solacing *pas de deux*. She tries to restrain her grief; he

treats her with sympathetic reverence; and as the woman runs about despairingly, her companion catches her in a sweeping lift. The intimate movements of the heads, shoulders, and hands of the two performers only set off more strikingly the choreographic design of the whole, which is on a big scale.

The third song, in the nature of a folk dance for male soloist, is a conversation piece between the dancer and a surrounding peasant group of four girls and two boys. This number alone lightens the pre-

vailingly dark mood of the work, almost ritualistic in expression. As it ends, the remainder of the ensemble enters until there is a group of three dancers (two women and one man) at every corner of the stage.

Now, with the fourth song, a new soloist approaches all of these groups in a movement that yearns for reciprocity; but whenever this is

granted, she falls back in a fresh onrush of loneliness, fading at last into the somber peasant mass.

With the start of the final song, a group movement begins out of which bursts a single male figure. He is the only character who seems resentful of his loss; and, to the music in which Mahler treats of the

storm enveloping the children of the poem, the dancer seems to exclaim with passionate gestures of protest, "Why should this have befallen me?"

At the culminating point of his solo, the scene changes, revealing a softer landscape which gives indication of hope, or at least of calm resignation. Until now the dance patterns have been conceived in agitated, circular designs; but with this shift of mood and scene—corresponding to the transfigured closing pages of the music—the movements become square and sturdier in outline. For a moment, the grief-stricken community huddles together sympathetically. Then, with a gesture toward the inevitable, they face the course of their lives and go off in a stoic processional.

HUGH LAING AND NORA KAYE

Dim Lustre

THIS CHOREOGRAPHIC fantasy by Antony Tudor was first presented by Ballet Theatre at the Metropolitan Opera House in October, 1943. The principal dancers were Nora Kaye and Hugh Laing, with John Kriza, Janet Reed, Rosella Hightower, and Mr. Tudor in important supporting roles. Richard Strauss's *Burlesk,* for piano and orchestra, provided the musical background; Motley designed the décor.

Utilizing the technique of psychological flashback introduced by Marcel Proust in his *Remembrance of Things Past,* the ballet calls up vanished impressions through present sensations, binding the immediate moment—through the agency of touch, taste, or smell—to a ruling memory. Architecturally, *Dim Lustre* is tightly knit, one of Tudor's best ballets; but, owing to an enormously complicated lighting scheme, the work has been performed less often than it deserves to be. At all times, the choreography springs with a complete sense of naturalness from the music.

The percussive opening theme is sounded, an insistent motto to be repeated throughout the ballet, and the curtain rises on a blacked-out

Allegro vivace

stage. The lights come on immediately, revealing an elegant London ballroom with crystal chandeliers, at the turn of the century.

A first whirling couple passes, followed by another and then a third, until five pairs—in pale pink and dark maroon—are dancing exuberantly in the brilliantly lighted ballroom. It is then that the principal duo, in dead white, enter at the tremendous pace which marks this whole ballet. As they appear, the other dancers swirl off.

The man and the woman, left alone, swing into the first *pas de deux.* Life seems wonderful for them both; they are completely happy, fascinated with each other. As the music pauses, the woman turns to applaud. The man, filled with the joy of the moment, leans forward and kisses her on the neck. Immediately, everything on stage freezes. The other couples, who have returned, are immobile—there is a blackout.

Now as the lights come up, two parallel spotlights shoot from one set of wings to the other, establishing different planes of action and of time. The woman, standing at the rear of the ballroom, faces her own image (placed toward the front of the stage with her back to the audience) in mirror fashion. The kiss on the neck has caused this wrenching away of time, this searching into the past. Both the woman and her shadow seek the equivalent impression of long ago, which is stirring in their consciousness.

The woman's shadow disappears, the lights rise to pale blue, and a very young boy enters, dressed in flannels and a blazer. He was the first the woman ever met, and now—reunited in time—they dance together with tremendous ease and youthfulness. Just as the woman, flushed with pleasure, turns away, the boy leans over and kisses her on the neck. Suddenly the lights come up, the boy disappears, and—as before—the woman is standing in the center of the ballroom staring at her first partner. She seems to be saying, "It's not you, really. It was someone else who meant more to me."

The man, on whom this look is lost, swings her back into the dance, guides her among the other couples in the ballroom. As they pass, one of the guests touches him on the shoulder. He turns, there is a blackout, and again the parallel spotlights cross between the wings. This time, it is the man who remembers and sees his image standing before him. He, like the woman, goes through the same process of seeking in the past.

His image disappears. The lights cast a pale glow and three girls enter, dressed identically in grays and blues—juvenile in manner, like students on a holiday. The man is attracted to one of them; but, standing in the center of the group, this favored girl seems beyond his reach. Whenever he tries to dance with her, all three shift about him in a bewildering kaleidoscope. Just as he reaches out to kiss the girl of his choice, one of the others touches him mockingly on the shoulder. He turns, the three escape in a group, and the ballroom lights come up. Once more the man is in the present, facing his partner. He seems detached, looks at her quizzically.

The other couples keep moving about them; and they resume the dance, whirling ever faster until the woman brings a handkerchief to her brow. She drops it; the man, picking up this bit of lace, smells a certain perfume whose memory takes him far from the scene.

Once more the blackout, the parallel spotlights, the image. Now an elegantly dressed woman appears, wearing chiffons, pheasant feathers, a veil. She seems tossed about by the breeze on the deck of an ocean liner. The man, who stands looking at her, suddenly loses the poise that has marked his ballroom manner. He becomes a young college boy, fascinated by a woman older than himself; goes toward her, shelters her

Photo: Alfredo Valente   *Courtesy Ballet Theatre*
DIANA ADAMS

Courtesy Museum of Modern Art
ANTONY TUDOR AND NORA KAYE

from the wind. A flirtation follows, serious on his part, bantering on hers. At its close, she lets her handkerchief fall in a gesture of friendly farewell. He picks it up and smells it . . . the same perfume.

The lights come up once more, the ballroom is seen—and the strain between the partners has grown more acute. The man, as they dance, tries desperately to rise to the occasion. With a show of ardor, he bends the woman backward in a kiss. At once her powers of recollection set to work: once more the image, strange lights. Now a figure in faultless evening clothes comes out of the shadows, dances with her rhapsodically, leans over and pours kisses on her.

The lights come up. The woman is feeling as decided an emotional strain as her partner. They are, in reality, strangers; the enchantment they had known in the beginning is gone; but for the sake of appearance they keep dancing. As the music grows slower, they pull apart gradually at first, then with an ever-widening gulf, until both stand at opposite sides of the room. Their brief moment is over; they turn and go off. One of the other couples swirls by, stops in surprise, and looks each way after the departing pair . . . the curtain falls.

Photo: René Blum   Courtesy Dance News

INTERMEZZO BETWEEN ACTS I AND II IN THE BALLET RUSSE DE
MONTE CARLO PRODUCTION

Don Juan*

THIS HISTORIC work, with choreography by Gaspare Angiolini, was first given at the Burgtheater, Vienna, in 1761, to the music of Christoph Willibald von Gluck. It remains one of the earliest of dramatic ballets with a specially written score.†

* The legend of the audacious Spanish lover, Don Juan, has become so identified in the minds of theatre-goers with the opera of Mozart (*Don Giovanni*, 1787, libretto by Lorenzo da Ponte) that any departure from this version must seem a novelty. It should be remembered that there were many previous editions of the Don Juan story before Mozart set it to music—among them the Gluck ballet, which preceded *Don Giovanni* by twenty-six years and enjoyed an enormous popularity in the eighteenth century. The first dramatic form of Don Juan was created by a Spaniard, Tirso de Molina. Molière made a French adaptation (*Don Juan, or the Feast of Stone*), on which the Gluck-Angiolini ballet is based. In the Gluck work, unlike Mozart's opera, there is only one heroine, Elvira. Donna Anna is not present; the soubrette, Zerlina, does not as yet exist; and the leering servant, Leporello, is Sganarelle. The action moves with great swiftness, aided by Gluck's lovely score.

† Artur Michel, in his scholarly monograph, "The Ballet d'Action before Noverre" (*Dance Index*, Vol. VI, No. 3, April, 1947), claims that the first freely composed, coloristic score in the annals of theatrical dance was written by Karl Heinrich Graun for the Berlin production of Marie Sallé's pantomime-ballet, *Pygmalion* (as restaged by Jean-Barthélemy Lany) in December, 1745.

A reconstruction of Angiolini's scenario, employing the original Gluck music, was prepared in 1936 by Eric Allatini and Michel Fokine for a première in June of the same year at the Alhambra Theatre in London. Allatini traveled throughout Europe to piece together sections of the old Gluck score belonging to the libraries of widely separated cities. After much work, he was able to secure all of the numbers contained in the original ballet. This procedure seems a bit involved, as the full score of *Don Juan* had—previous to Mr. Allatini's quest—been published by the Vienna Universal Edition, edited by Robert Haas, in 1923.*

The choreography for the new version was by Fokine, and leading roles were danced by Anatole Vilzak as the Don, Jeanette Lauret as Elvira, and André Eglevsky as the Jester. Scenery and costumes were by Mariano Andreù. A student performance of *Don Juan*, with the Gluck music and staging by Charlotte MacEwan, was given at Wellesley in March, 1937, preceding the first American performance of the Fokine version at the Metropolitan Opera House in October, 1938.

There is a brief overture, brilliant in style, which sets the pace and

eighteenth-century atmosphere of the work: Then the curtain rises on an inner drop, fronted by a group of costumed musicians, who have assembled to play a serenade. As the inner drop parts, revealing a nocturnal square in Seville, the Don himself—handsome and dashing—enters.

Assisted by his lackey, Sganarelle, the Don prepares to serenade Elvira—daughter of the Commander—who can be seen dimly at the curtained window above. His serenade, in siciliana rhythm, is one of the most beautiful spots in the score, the nostalgic quality of the solo oboe lending additional color to the shifting harmonies below.

* Contained in the series of volumes known as "Denkmäler der Tonkunst in Österreich" ("Monuments of Tonal Art in Austria").

At length the Don enters the house, climbs to Elvira's room, and embraces her. Just as the couple descends to the street, Elvira's father enters. He knows the Don's reputation, is outraged at the seduction in progress, and orders his daughter into the house. Then he challenges the Don to a duel.

A brief struggle takes place, and the Commander is killed. Don Juan, Sganarelle, and their musicians escape, while Elvira and her duenna return to the square to find the Commander slain.

The inner drop is closed, and figures characteristic of the period and locale pass before it: a lord and lady of Seville, dancing torchbearers, Don Juan's lively jester. Then the curtain parts and the Don's banquet hall is seen. Against a brilliant and luxuriously appointed background, the guests take part in a festive dance, followed by a variation for the Don himself.

The banquet begins. Superintended by Sganarelle, servants bear lavish dishes to the Don and his friends. Suddenly there is a knocking at the door and a stony ghost—the spirit of the murdered Commander—appears. The guests turn pale; but Don Juan, with bravado, invites the shade to sup with him. Indignantly, the ghost vanishes.

Now, as Sganarelle sets off on an errand for the Don, gaiety returns to the hall. A number of solo and group dances are performed and, at their climax, Sganarelle returns—bringing with him a veiled woman. It is Elvira, abducted on the order of Don Juan. The Don forces her to sit with him at table, to join company with his profligate friends. Once more the ghost of her father appears, then vanishes just as abruptly.

The guests resume a festive dance, which is interrupted by renewed knocking of the phantom. This time the Commander enters the hall, refuses Don Juan's invitation to drink, and, instead, bids the Don visit him at his tomb. As the shade disappears for the last time, and Elvira faints, Don Juan sets out for the cemetery, and the inner curtain closes.

Then the last scene is revealed: a moonlit burial ground with the

Courtesy Museum of Modern Art

ANATOLE VILZAK AND JEANETTE LAURET

Commander's tomb, surmounted by his statue on a stone horse. Don Juan appears with his valet, but, terrified by the supernatural atmosphere of the place, Sganarelle flees. Don Juan is left alone. He confronts the statue defiantly, not weakening even when the Commander conjures up a train of his betrayed mistresses. Mockingly, the Don advances, only to be caught by the statue's stony arm. Now the spirits of Hell are unleashed upon him and Don Juan suffers the fate of the damned. For the impressive finale of this ballet, Gluck composed a wild, seething dance which, only a year later, was to be incorporated into his opera *Orfeo* as the Dance of the Furies. In *Don Juan,* it is at once the ballet's crown and climax.

L'Épreuve d'Amour

(THE PROOF OF LOVE)

THIS IS a minor but charming ballet with choreography by Michel Fokine, first produced at the Théâtre de Monte Carlo in April, 1936. The roles of the Chinese maiden, Chung-Yang, and her lover were danced by Vera Nemchinova and André Eglevsky, with Jean Yavzinsky as the Mandarin father. Scenery and costumes were by André Derain, who also collaborated with Fokine on the scenario. The work had its American première in October, 1938, at the Metropolitan Opera House, with Mr. Yavzinsky in his original role, but with the lovers now danced by Nathalie Krassovska and Michel Panaieff.

The music for *L'Épreuve d'Amour* consists of a short score by Mozart originally composed for a Chinese-style entertainment in the Vienna carnival of 1791 sponsored by the Imperial Court. This manuscript, subsequently lost, dropped out of sight for almost one hundred and forty years. It was found in the town of Graz a short time before Fokine set to work on the ballet. It is delicately pseudo-Oriental in feeling, as is the choreography.

The tenuous story of *L'Épreuve d'Amour* ("The Proof of Love") concerns itself with a disagreeable and materialistic mandarin. These qualities are symbolized by a flock of monkeys and a butterfly which persistently harass him. Thinking only of bettering his fortune, this man will not allow his daughter, Chung-Yang, to marry the youth who loves her but wants to pledge her instead to a foreign ambassador.

The youth, disguised as a dragon, and his friends, dressed as brigands, set upon the foreign suitor and rob him. At this point, seeing that the ambassador is penniless, the mandarin has no more use for him. When the youth and his friends—explaining the trick they have played—give the ambassador back his wealth, the mandarin veers again. Now that the money has been returned, the engagement of his daughter can go on as originally planned.

It is the ambassador's turn, however, to reject the greedy mandarin. Realizing that Chung-Yang has little use for him and that her father sees the marriage only through opportunistic eyes, he withdraws. The girl goes off to wed the youth she has always loved; and the mandarin, left alone, falls prey once more to the distracting flock of monkeys—representing his own misanthropy—and to the butterfly which seems never to leave him. Enraged, he hurls a stick at the insect.

Photo: "Anthony"   Courtesy Museum of Modern Art

FREDERICK ASHTON

Façade

THIS BALLET in one act with choreography by Frederick Ashton was first produced at the Cambridge Theatre, London, in April, 1931. John Armstrong designed the décor. The title of the work had been given originally to a group of poems by Edith Sitwell, recited to a musical accompaniment composed by William Walton and presented at Aeolian Hall, London, in June, 1923. Subsequently, Walton made his score into an orchestral suite. This was the edition used for Ashton's ballet.*

---

* Walton's suite had also served, in 1930, as background to a work by the German choreographer Guenter Hess offered at Hagen, Westphalia.

Among the dancers at the orginal Cambridge Theatre performance were Lydia Lopokova, Alicia Markova, Mr. Ashton, and Antony Tudor. The stage version was introduced to the United States during the Sadler's Wells Ballet season at the Metropolitan Opera House, October, 1949.

In line with the droll and often absurd characteristics of the score, intended to exploit the fantasy of Edith Sitwell's poems, the choreographic patterns of *Façade* are witty and occasionally pure burlesque. The outline consists of seven numbers without narrative connection, all adding up to the mood of a gay *divertissement*.

The first is a Scottish rhapsody for three dancers, followed by a yodel-

ing song, in which a milkmaid is depicted at work. In quick succession there come a polka for solo ballerina; waltz for four girls; popular song in the American soft-shoe manner of the old vaudeville days; *pas de deux* parody on a tango; and, as finale, a dashing tarantella. When the work was redone in 1935, a country dance for ballerina and two male partners was inserted before the tango.

The original version of *Façade*, with Miss Sitwell declaiming her own text to the accompaniment of chamber orchestra, enjoyed a succcessful revival at the Museum of Modern Art, New York, in January, 1949.

JEROME ROBBINS, JOHN KRIZA, AND NORA KAYE

Facsimile

THIS "choreographic observation" in one scene, conceived by Jerome Robbins, was first produced by Ballet Theatre at the Broadway Theatre, New York, in October, 1946, with Nora Kaye, John Kriza, and Mr. Robbins as the three protagonists. Leonard Bernstein provided the musical score, Oliver Smith the notably imaginative setting, and Irene Sharaff the costumes. After the first few performances, Hugh Laing replaced Mr. Robbins in the role, which the choreographer had originally designed for him.

Like several ballets by Antony Tudor, *Facsimile* deals with the psychological frustrations of our time; but where the works of Tudor offer some positive sign of hope, *Facsimile* remains inconclusive—which, perhaps, is just the point it wants to make about contemporary life. If Massine's lush *Bacchanale* mirrored prewar decadence, then *Facsimile* may certainly be identified with postwar bleakness and emotional insecurity. Masterfully constructed, it whips the emotions of both audience and dancers to the breaking point. Bernstein's music, consciously functional rather than independent, heightens the dramatic effect.

To a solitary theme in the oboe, like some far-off call, the curtain rises

Molto adagio

on a lonely place at night. This could be anywhere—a desert, a beach, or any other spot fixed by a restless mind. The Woman is there alone, at loose ends, too bored to create an interest for herself. She picks up a shuttlecock idly, twirls it. Finding no release, she draws a curtain between two shelter poles, forms an improvised screen, and lets her shadow fall on it. Now she dances to pass the time, making play with her own reflection.

In the midst of this halfhearted performance, she hears someone approaching and hides behind the screen. A Man who is as lonely, emotionally sterile, and restless as herself, enters, a red towel over his shoulder. Just as the Woman had played with the shuttlecock for distraction, the Man flicks the towel. He is disturbed, fighting against himself, unhappy. Suddenly, when he sees the shadow play on the screen, he stops; and, at the same moment, the Woman steps from behind the curtain. Their two personalities, half extinct when alone, change in each other's presence. They make grimaces, small talk. A flirtation starts.

Now they sit on the ground, working at a conversation that keeps fading into nothing. Whenever it lags, each of the solitary people pretends to be excited emotionally by the other. This courtship, to the strains of a waltz, culminates in physical fulfillment on stage. After the affair is over, both try to keep the same emotional tempo but find it impossible. Each is bored, though still outwardly charming: with a grim sense of duty he kisses her hand, she strokes his face.

These outward forms trail off. As the Woman sits by herself looking rather mournful and her companion stands aside, a Second Man passes. Immediately the two desolate souls who have lost interest in each other pull together at the sight of a third person. As they meet the newcomer, he reveals that he is of the same emotional type as they—a bit more carefree on the surface, but just as bitter and empty within.

The First Man, now that a rival has come, decides to maintain his rights over the Woman. For the moment, she consents. The Second

Man moves by himself, always followed by the eyes of the other two. Suddenly the situation is clarified: both men try for dominance.

To a biting orchestral scherzo, the Woman decides to play one against the other. Though interested in the newcomer, she has no intention of giving up the First Man. A futile conversation among the three follows in dance form. Then, losing interest, the Woman stands by herself and flirts with the Second Man over the First Man's shoulder. Angrily, the First Man detects her, claims her as his property. She demurs. There is an impasse. For a moment all three become charming again until the Woman shows her preference for the newcomer. The First Man, whose vanity is outraged, seems to scream with his hands and drags both the culprits across the lonely place. Soon all three, unnerved, are in a furious tangle on the ground, legs and arms interlocked. The Woman, unable to bear it, shouts, "Stop!" Both men rise and draw away.

Now the staccato music subsides, and the lonely opening theme of the ballet returns. The First Man leaves slowly, with a gesture of farewell as though his insides were seething. The Second Man withdraws in character, more flippantly, and the Woman is left alone. She looks after the two men, picks up her beach robe, throws it over her shoulders, and goes off, overwrought.

Photo: Alfredo Valente   *Courtesy Ballet Theatre*
HUGH LAING AND NORA KAYE

The Fair at Sorochinsk

THIS FANTASY in four scenes, with choreography by David Lichine, was first produced by Ballet Theatre at the Metropolitan Opera House in October, 1943. Its scenario is about equally indebted to the short stories of Nicholas Gogol and to Moussorgsky's unfinished opera, *The Fair at Sorochinsk,* which also provided much of the musical score for the ballet, in an arrangement by Antal Dorati. The same composer's tone poem, *A Night on Bald Mountain,* was incorporated into the final scene of Lichine's stage work. Nicholas Remisoff designed the scenery and costumes. Among the leading dancers at the first performance were Lucia Chase as Khivria, Anton Dolin as Red Coat (a virtuoso performance in which Mr. Dolin, emphasizing the diabolical attributes of the part, performed *sur les pointes*—a rare feat for a male dancer), and André Eglevsky as Gritzko.

Courtesy S. Hurok

ANTON DOLIN AND LUCIA CHASE

Courtesy Museum of Modern Art
ANDRÉ EGLEVSKY AND MARGARET BANKS

SCENE ONE

After a brief prologue in which a blind storyteller crosses the stage, led by a little boy, the curtain rises on an inn—first scene of the blind man's tale. The witch who runs it, Khivria, swoops down the chimney to greet a peasant group stopping off on their way to the fair at Sorochinsk. Among them is the youth Gritzko, who has been drawn to Khivria's attractive daughter, Parassia. This attachment—too dully respectable for Khivria's taste—irritates the witch; and, on seeing the girl return Gritzko's advances, she grows enraged, conjures up infernal visions, and drives the villagers from the inn. Parassia escapes with her suitor.

At this point, two secret admirers of Khivria arrive: the Mayor of Sorochinsk and the Sexton. Although they are rivals, both take refuge in the same sack which lies at the base of the chimney to make way for Khivria's real passion, the demon Red Coat. As her lover appears, Khivria gleefully shows him the sack containing the two officials. Red Coat slings it over his arm and, together with his mistress, rides off to the fair on a broomstick.

SCENE TWO

After a brief procession of peasants before the curtain, the second tableau is seen—the fair at Sorochinsk. All of the townspeople are strolling among the booths that have been set up, among them the young couple, Parassia and Gritzko.

At last, Khivria and Red Coat arrive with their bundle, which the demon flings to the ground, exposing both Mayor and Sexton to the ridicule of the crowd. Then he transforms the local drunkard into a goose. By this time the townspeople, who realize there is an evil spirit in their midst, attack the stranger and drive him off with pitchforks. As Red Coat retreats, the drunkard regains his original shape.

Now the healthier aspects of the fair come into play. To the music of a *hopak*, Gritzko and another youth engage in a dance competition. Evening comes on, the noise abates, the moon rises, and Parassia joins Gritzko in a romantic stroll. As the pair goes off, Khivria and Red Coat reappear. Up to more satanic intrigue, the fiend and his mistress prepare for the Witches' Sabbath, which they are about to celebrate, by plucking the moon from the sky and hiding it under Khivria's shawl.

SCENE THREE

The orgy of the Sabbath, led by Khivria and Red Coat, takes place on the haunted heights of Bald Mountain. As in a nightmare, all of the

principal persons of the ballet appear: Mayor, Sexton, drunkard, and even Gritzko and Parassia, who have been forced to attend the infernal rites.

Throughout the demons' rounds, the two young lovers stand firm; and at last the day dawns. The spirits of the damned disappear to the tolling of church bells; the lovers kneel in gratitude and make the sign of the cross.

As the curtain falls, the blind storyteller of the prologue once more crosses the stage as if to indicate that his tale has been completed.

SETTING BY OLIVER SMITH   *Courtesy Ballet Theatre*

Fall River Legend

THIS DRAMATIC commentary in seven scenes, prologue, and epilogue, with choreography by Agnes de Mille, was first produced by Ballet Theatre at the Metropolitan Opera House, in April, 1948. Nora Kaye, for whom the leading role was created, could not appear because of illness at the earliest performances, which were danced by Alicia Alonso and Dania Krupska. Miss Kaye later assumed the part with marked success. Others in the original cast were Diana Adams as the mother, Peter Gladke as the father, Muriel Bentley as the stepmother, Ruth Ann Koesun as the child, and John Kriza as the pastor. The musical score was specially composed by Morton Gould, the scenery designed by Oliver Smith, and the costumes by Miles White. These secondary elements were all of outstanding quality. Choreographically, the work proved strongest in moments of miming, weakest in organized dance.

The scenario of the ballet is based upon the famous Lizzie Borden murder case. On August 4, 1892, Miss Borden, who resided at 92 Second Street, Fall River, in the county of Bristol, Massachusetts, is alleged to have assaulted and killed her father and stepmother with an ax. Despite a widespread impression of her guilt, she was acquitted after a trial that lasted ten months, and passed the rest of her life in retirement. Part of her fame rests on the celebrated jingle:

> Lizzie Borden took an ax,
> And gave her mother forty whacks;
> And when she saw what she had done,
> She gave her father forty-one.

In Miss de Mille's ballet, the central character is called the Accused. Unlike her more fortunate counterpart in real life, she goes to the gallows.

PROLOGUE

There is an anguished outcry by the orchestra, suggestive of the ut-

most fear and terror, and the curtain rises to reveal the Accused standing at the foot of the gallows. With her are the Pastor and a few townspeople; facing her forbiddingly is the Speaker for the Jury. As the condemned girl looks fearfully at the rope that is about to hang her, the Speaker intones the details of the crime, the sentence, and as his words drone on in this harrowing place of execution—"A true bill . . . The house in which the murders were committed was the house in which you were born . . . You there with your father and mother lived happily"—the scene fades into the memory of the Accused when she was a little girl, establishing, as in Antony Tudor's *Undertow*, the psychological motive for her deed.

SCENE ONE

The house where the girl was born comes into view. Set against a bare stretch of sky, it has no exterior save for a door at one side. The old parlor is visible, with a table in the center surrounded by three rocking chairs. The doomed woman herself stands looking on at this evocation of her youth.

Townspeople of years before pass by, dancing. The Accused as a child is there with her father and mother, the object of real parental affection. Suddenly the dark spinster who will later become the child's

Photo: Louis Malançon   *Courtesy Ballet Theatre*
NORA KAYE AND DIANA ADAMS AS THE ACCUSED
AND HER MOTHER

stepmother crosses the scene. As she pats the girl on the head, the Accused herself—standing by—shudders with remembered dislike.

All of the child's love is bound up in her mother, and when, in the unrolling of the past, this woman suffers a heart attack in the street, the girl seems stricken too. At her frantic call, all the neighbors come running to help—even the spinster, who pushes the child aside.

The mother seems to recover. As the townspeople, reassured, go off, leaving the little family alone, she takes part in a tender *pas de trois* with father and child, the Accused standing in the background and following the steps as if she recalled them actively.

Then comes a second attack, which the mother cannot resist. She falls, the father carries her into the house, and the child is left outside, wondering. Ominously, the spinster pays a condolence call. The Accused, looking on, can barely repress an outcry.

Soon the widower comes from the house, in search of the child. The spinster is with him. Afraid and unhappy, the little girl tries to run inside, but the intruder bars her way. The struggle has been joined—and the father, in a torrent of indecision, falls at the feet of the woman who has mastered him.

It is at this point that the Accused breaks into lamentations and leaps on her father's back as if to keep him from the step he is taking. So much time stands between her and the past that the father feels nothing, and is aware only of the child he sees sulking in a corner. Raising the spinster in his arms, he carries her into the house as his bride. The Accused follows, the child disappears, and the scene changes to twenty-five years later.

SCENE TWO

Without a pause the house slides forward. Father, stepmother, and daughter (the Accused, who now takes full part in the action) are seated about the table in the parlor, rocking. This is evidently one in a series of interminable evenings passed by the trio. Bored and resentful, the Accused goes to the window and opens the curtains, which the stepmother promptly draws. Every so often the woman whispers something in the father's ear—then feels the Accused's forehead, as if to imply that the girl is insane and should be sent away. The Accused can only submit to these torments, but when the father picks up her dead mother's shawl and gives it to the torturer, she runs from the house. In the street before the dwelling she meets the young Pastor of the town, who consoles her.

Torn between affection for his daughter and love for the grim second wife, the father beckons to the girl impatiently to come back inside. As the Pastor strolls on, the girl obeys and sits in the middle rocking chair of the parlor. Then she suddenly rises, goes to a closet in the hall, and takes out an ax. The parents stop rocking, terrified. Strangely amused by their reaction, the girl saunters to the yard to chop wood, leaves the ax in the block, and returns with the sticks. Inviting the frightened family to be seated at table, she laughs hysterically, realizing what a horrible ending this episode might have had. There is a blackout and the house slides back.

SCENE THREE

Now the Accused sits on the doorstep, plunged in dreams. Illusory figures—like the happy young couples of Tudor's *Pillar of Fire*—pass her by and vanish. Suddenly she rises and bursts into a dance of lament which ends at the chopping block. She looks at the ax, grows frightened, and retreats.

As the girl stands desolate, the Pastor enters, bringing her flowers.

Photo: John Hugelmeyer   Courtesy Ballet Theatre
MURIEL BENTLEY

This one gesture of thoughtfulness gives new hope to the Accused; and when the young man invites her to the church social, she clings to him with a desperate longing for escape.

It is then that her parents come from the house. As the girl cringes, the stepmother advances, feels her head, and whispers to the Pastor. Then both these people—the father now only a pawn—order the girl inside. At first the Accused obeys; then, after a few steps forward, she tears the shawl from the stepmother's shoulder and, in the strongest of decisions, goes off with the Pastor. The scene is transformed: the house swings on its axis and becomes the brightly lighted church.

SCENE FOUR

Surrounded by his congregation, the Pastor is giving a sermon with intensity of gesture. The Accused stands quietly looking on, afraid of the people around her; but they welcome her with a kindness that she has never known. Soon the Pastor is at her side, and—as the others disappear—joins her in a duet of tenderness and elevated feeling.

Slowly moving

Now the worshipers return for the church social. They begin a joyful cotillion in which the Accused, to her own surprise, takes part. Suddenly, as the couples whirl, the stepmother appears.

The girl crumples at the sight of her, falling to the ground; and the stepmother is not long in reminding the Pastor that the Accused has lost her mind. With a new strength—the accumulated hatred of years—the girl rises and becomes a fury; but she is no match for the stepmother's insistent glare. As she subsides, the Pastor puts the shawl about her neck and sadly bids her good night. This time there is no escape for the Accused. Her family has won. The church turns about and again becomes the house.

SCENE FIVE

Striding ahead, the stepmother goes inside, but the girl does not follow. She lingers at the block, takes the ax that is embedded there, hides it under her shawl, and walks slowly into the parlor. As she takes her place in the center of the room, she moves her shoulders slightly and lets the scarf fall away, revealing the ax. The father and stepmother recoil, horrified, and she covers her eyes.

SCENE SIX

There is a blackout, and then an inner drop is seen representing, in distorted perspective, the parlor of the Accused's house. The three rocking chairs are overturned and on the floor is a pool of blood. As the orchestra plays a restless, whispering motive, the Accused glides forward as a figure in her own dream. Wearing a white dress with gory

stains, she is joined by another phantasm—her mother, to whom she confesses what she has done. Overwhelmed, the mother slaps her gently, as in the days of the girl's own childhood. Then, with a loving look at the Accused, she glides away, ending the strongest and most original scene of the ballet.

SCENE SEVEN

The curtain rises in silence on the exterior of the house. There is a livid, angry sky; and people come on one by one to watch the dwelling where the noise of murder has been heard. All this time, not a sound rises from the orchestra. Suddenly the Accused appears in the doorway. As she runs into the street as though screaming under the weight of her own tension, a cymbal crash is heard, followed by a violent fortissimo for full orchestra.

The terrible currents which have been raging inside her spill over; she tells the neighbors what has happened. They invade the parlor, bring out the bloodstained shawl and ax, and lay them at her feet. As the girl is formally accused of murder, the house where she was born is demolished; and one of its beams becomes the gallows.

EPILOGUE

Now, as in the Prologue, the girl faces the hangman's rope. Wild images flash across the background, thoughts of her mother, of herself as a little girl. The townspeople come on in a staring processional, with only one consoling figure among them: the Pastor, who remains when the others have gone. Then he, too, departs; and as the orchestra rises to a climactic roar, the Accused is alone with her doom.

Photo: Friedman-Engeler   *Courtesy Ballet Theatre*
OLIVER SMITH'S ORIGINAL SKETCH FOR THE OPENING SCENE

Photo: Baron of London   Courtesy Ballet Theatre

Fancy Free

THIS BALLET in one act, with choreography by Jerome Robbins, was given its première by Ballet Theatre at the Metropolitan Opera House in April, 1944. The work was an immediate success and, in the intervening years, has stood up so valiantly in every one of its departments as to suggest that *Fancy Free* is among the best-integrated products of American theatrical dance. Leonard Bernstein composed the exuberant score; Oliver Smith created the background of a New York summer night; and Kermit Love designed the costumes. The following season *On the Town*, a musical comedy involving the same collaborators and a similar theme, was a great hit on Broadway.

At the première of the ballet, Mr. Bernstein conducted the orchestra and Mr. Robbins danced as one of the gobs. Harold Lang and John Kriza played the other sailors, with Muriel Bentley, Janet Reed, and Shirley Eckl as the three girls. Since that evening, Miss Bentley and Miss Reed have reappeared steadily in their roles, as has Mr. Kriza. Of the many replacements for the other men, Paul Godkin—in the Robbins part—has been the most striking.

Architecturally the work is a gem, the perfection of its individual numbers matching the over-all skill with which they have been joined.

Fancy Free

The curtain rises on a deserted street in the lower part of New York—deserted not in a solitary or mournful sense, but pregnant with expectation. It is night, and the lighted towers of the city may be seen in the background. At one side of the stage is a street lamp; at the other, the interior of a barroom—with a stretch of pavement between. The orchestra is silent, only a recorded torch song wailing its way through the hot summer night, the empty street, and the sleepy bar.

Suddenly, four sharp drum beats are heard, followed by a noisily jubilant theme, and the heroes of this little piece—three sailors on shore

leave—burst onto the stage. They come around the corner like the wind, as if projected by a rocket from ship to shore. On the town, they swagger

ERIC BRAUN, JOHN KRIZA, PAUL GODKIN, JACQUELINE DODGE

along the deserted sidewalk, joke with each other, shoot off splinters of the energy they have been saving.

As soon as they reach the lamppost, their first excitement dies. A perplexéd restlessness follows . . . where to go from here? Finding the bar open, they enter, put their feet on the rail, and order three beers. One of them, constantly duped by the others, pays the bill; then they move out to the street again, scanning the asphalt horizon. A stick of chewing gum is divided three ways as they ponder their next move.

There is not much time for thinking. A good-looking, dark-haired girl has crossed the street. Her head is high, her walk proud. At once the boys go into action and decide to break down her resistance. They snatch her handbag and play ball with it, teasing the girl into a show of animation. The moment she gives ground, two of the sailors go off with her, leaving the third—the least aggressive—on his own.

The boy looks after them, and turns to re-enter the bar. Just then another girl appears—this one, an attractive redhead. She is less difficult than the brunette and readily accepts the sailor's invitation for a drink. As they perch on the stools in the barroom, he tells of his life aboard ship, of his heroism under fire. This is somewhat of a line, but the girl accepts it and dances with the boy. Their *pas de deux*, made up of ballroom steps and other patterns in the popular idiom, transcends all these sources in emotional inventiveness. Here are two young people in a nocturnal spell, on the verge of love. When the peak of intensity has been reached, the boy gently takes the girl's arm and draws her out into the city night.

Their romantic mood is shattered as the two other sailors reappear with the brunette, all in a huddle. The boys learn, not with too much surprise, that the girls are old friends. All five stroll back into the tavern —but with a sense of antagonism among the sailors, hidden at first but constantly rising. This ill will revolves around a problem in simple mathematics: Given two women to three men, how may they be divided in equal parts?

After much thought, the sailors decide on a contest as the best way out. All three are to dance; the girls will choose the two winners; and the loser must disappear.

The first of the contestants takes the floor. He is crude, boisterous, slap-happy. His dance culminates with a leap to the top of the bar, on

Galop tempo (very fast)

JOHN KRIZA AND JANET REED

which he balances momentarily, followed by a descent to earth and the snatching of a beer from the bartender.

The next sailor (he of the *pas de deux*) is less brash by nature. To the sound of a caressing woodwind tune, this boy moves poetically—free

for the moment of the fleet's rugged idiom.

In contrast to the brassy first and lyrical second comes the third sailor, intense, dancing with feline skill as the orchestra rolls out a Cuban rhythm.

Unfortunately, the contest solves nothing. The rivalry that has been brewing throughout this session reaches its height as all of the sailors try to take possession of the girls at once. Fists fly, brunette and redhead are forgotten in a free-for-all, and the sailors disappear behind the bar in a belligerent heap. Annoyed and frightened, the girls stalk out of the café, leaving the contestants to scramble to their feet and discover that the prizes are gone.

Anxiously, the boys run to the door and look down the street. There is no one to be seen; and suddenly the humor of the situation—their having slugged it out in vain—dawns on all of them. Friends again, they go back to the bar for a drink; the same dupe as before pays for the beers, and they stroll outside and divide another stick of gum three ways.

Once more the street is deserted, but with that pregnant feeling of something to come. Soon it arrives in the form of a flashily dressed blonde who swings past the boys. For a moment they pause, undecided. Then, as the girl saunters off, they put on speed and follow, vanishing in a joyous group among the city lights.

Les Femmes de Bonne Humeur

(THE GOOD-HUMORED LADIES)

THIS, THE first of Léonide Massine's successful ballets, was produced by the Diaghilev company at the Teatro Costanzi (now the Teatro dell' Opera), Rome, in April, 1917. Based on Goldoni's comedy, *Le Donne di Buon Umore* ("The Good-Humored Ladies"), the work has a witty musical score, consisting of eighteenth-century harpsichord pieces by Domenico Scarlatti adapted and arranged for modern orchestra by Vincenzo Tommasini. Scenery and costumes were by Léon Bakst. Its early performances were especially notable for the brilliance of Lydia Lopokova as Mariuccia, the superb clowning of Enrico and Giuseppina Cecchetti as two decaying members of the Venetian nobility, and the youthful dash of Massine himself as Leonarde. *Les Femmmes de Bonne Humeur* has been revived on occasion by the de Basil Ballet Russe, but is no longer in the standard repertoire.

The scene is Venice, in the pleasure-loving time of Louis XV of France. Before the curtain rises, there is a lively little overture, then a

typically Adriatic tableau is revealed: balconies, sloping roofs, and a café in the center of it all.

The aging Marquise Silvestra is making up for the evening, trying to hide her years under a lavish coat of powder and paint. As she sits on her balcony, applying cosmetics, a beggar who passes below tips his hat in admiration. Then she goes inside, and the square is empty.

Not for long, however. Count Rinaldo, a Venetian dandy—engaged to the old Marquise's niece, Constanza—appears and sits at one of the café tables. He drinks debonairly, looks around for signs of social activity, and seems unaware that he is the victim of a lighthearted plot in which the Marquise herself is involved. Count Rinaldo's fiancée, Constanza, in order to test his fidelity, has sent him an anonymous love letter (via her mischievous maid, Mariuccia) supposedly from a woman who has been ostensibly attracted by his good looks and wants to meet him. As a sign of her identity, she will wear a pink rose in her hair.

Three friends of Constanza—their names are Felicità, Dorotea, and Pasquina—are in league with the girl, having promised to test Rinaldo's constancy. The old Marquise, too, prompted by vanity, has joined forces with the conspirators. She and the three girls now appear in identical headdress—a pink rose in their hair, masks on their faces.

Rinaldo makes advances to all four, but the three young girls rebuff him. Finally, he falls victim to the elderly Marquise, who inadvertently drops her mask. The trap has been sprung, however, and—in spite of Rinaldo's protests—he is dragged off by the Marquise to the carnival as her escort. The forsaken Constanza has gone to look for her aunt at the very moment that the old schemer traps Rinaldo. The three young girls leave for the carnival. The square is empty; and Mariuccia, the saucy serving-maid of Constanza, seizes this opportunity to entertain her beau, Leonardo (who is the husband, incidentally, of one of Constanza's girl friends), and his companion, Battista (lover of another of the three ladies), at supper in front of the Marquise's house.

The jovial trio sits down to a choice meal, with laughter and clattering of plates. Soon an elderly but active nobleman, the Marquis di Luca —an admirer of Mariuccia *—asks to join them. In a moment he presides at their table, drinking far beyond his capacity. The exuberance of the young folk rises in proportion to the old Marquis's indiscretions. Mariuccia does a bewitching *pas seul*; Battista, a breath-taking solo; and finally all three—after the Marquis himself has tried to take a few steps but, retarded by age and wine, has fallen back in his café chair— join in a brilliant *pas de trois*:

Suddenly, two of Constanza's three girl friends arrive on the scene. (one of them being the wife of Leonardo, who flees immediately). The girls tell Battista, not without malice, that the third member of their party (Pasquina, with whom Battista is in love) has been flirting with

---

* Of all ballets, this is the most complicated in the who-loves-whom department.

Photo: Maurice Seymour   VERA ZORINA   Courtesy Museum of Modern Art

a certain Captain Faloppa. Even as they talk, Pasquina and her Faloppa pass by. Enraged, Battista pursues them, knocking over a table of the café and bringing the somnolent Marquis to his feet.

Now a fresh intrigue begins, of which the old roué is the central figure. Constanza's girl friends tie a mask over his eyes and hide in an archway. Constanza enters, portraying in an expressive solo her sorrow at Rinaldo's faithlessness. But this shadow on the good humor of the situation soon passes. The Marquise, returning from the carnival with Rinaldo, crosses the square in triumph, little knowing that she, together with the Marquis, will soon be a target for ridicule.

An elaborate double ruse now takes place. Leonardo and Battista, dressed as women, invite the old nobleman to join them at table. They lead him on with romantic advances until the Marquis is ready to enjoy the fruits of conquest. At the climactic moment, they lift their veils, reveal their identity, and the wretch collapses.

Almost simultaneously the girl friends of Constanza induce Niccolò, a lowly employee of the café, to appear as a glamorous prince and offer his hand in marriage to the Marquise. At this point, a street musician plays the famous "Cat's Fugue" of Scarlatti and the Marquise enters.

She falls for the trick, accepts the alleged prince, and—at the height of her pride in this royal alliance—sees the saucy Mariuccia rip off the mask that her suitor has been wearing. He stands revealed as Niccolò, long known to the Marquise for his expert juggling of trays. The old lady, infuriated, harangues the waiter, attacks him, and makes such an uproar that she awakens the Marquis, who, thoroughly miserable after his encounter with the two pretended ladies, has gone to bed.

The disgruntled nobleman enters, brandishing a stick, which he waves about him. It comes down by chance on the old lady's elegantly arranged coiffure and, making a clean sweep, reveals her as thoroughly bald. The young people, whose lives she has tried to disrupt, shout with laughter. They pair off happily, and Constanza's sorrows are forgotten.

Le Festin de l'Araignée

(THE SPIDER'S BANQUET)

THIS BALLET-PANTOMIME in one act, with choreography by Leo Staats, has a scenario by Gilbert de Voisins based on the *Souvenirs Entomologiques* of Henri Fabre. It is notable for its character dissection of the insect world in terms of human sensibilities. The excellent score was composed by Albert Roussel, with scenery and costumes by Maxime Dethomas. Principal dancers at the first performance, which took place at the Théâtre des Arts, Paris, in April, 1913, were Sahary Djell as the Spider, and Dimitria as the Dayfly.

After a short prelude the curtain rises on a garden, disclosing a spider in its web. As the insect looks around, scanning the neighborhood for prey, a group of ants enters, discovers a rose petal that has fallen, and—after a great struggle—bears it away.

The spider, alone, looks intently at the landscape. It tests the resistance of the threads in its net and makes some slight repairs. For a moment, it finds distraction in the entrance of several beetles; but these go off almost immediately, and the ants return. They are trying to carry off another rose petal when a butterfly arrives.

Here is the prey for which the spider has been waiting. First the insect watches the butterfly dance, then invites it nearer the edge of the garden, toward the web. Inevitably, the butterfly is caught, struggles, and dies. The spider rolls it up in a gray shroud, dancing for joy.

191

Suddenly a fruit falls noisily from a tree. The spider jumps backward, frightened. New insects appear: fruit-worms, who get ready to feast on the fallen morsel; two warlike praying mantises, who forbid anyone to approach the food. They are tricked by the worms, who draw together, pass between them, and bore rapidly into the fruit.

Now the mantises quarrel over their defeat. They challenge each other to a fierce battle, while the spider—dancing around them—stirs them on to greater excitement and finally traps them in the web.

Still the spider is not satisfied; it sees new prey—a dayfly, which hatches slowly. The little insect wriggles on the ground, rises, and moves with graceful motion.

Saluted by the beetles and ants, who have returned, the dayfly interrupts its flight. The ants withdraw; the two worms crawl out of the fruit (they have grown very stout) and, with friendly gestures, induce the dayfly to join them in a dance.

All this time the spider is standing by, waiting. At length its chance arrives . . . the dayfly is trapped and killed. Now the spider begins its banquet; as it feasts, one of the mantises—freed from the web by the beetles—glides behind the glutton in a frightful attack. The spider dies in agony.

No one mourns it, but there is a touching funeral procession for the dayfly, and the curtain falls on an empty garden.

Courtesy Dance News

Filling Station

THIS BALLET-DOCUMENTARY in one act, with scenario by Lincoln Kirstein and choreography by Lew Christensen, was first presented at the Avery Memorial Theatre of the Wadsworth Athenaeum, Hartford, in January, 1938, by Ballet Caravan. The cast included Mr. Christensen in the leading role of Mac, the filling station attendant; Douglas Coudy and Eugene Loring as Roy and Ray, two truck drivers; Todd Bolender as a State Trooper; Fred Danieli and Marie-Jeanne as the rich boy and girl; and Erick Hawkins as the gangster. Paul Cadmus provided the décor. In conjunction with the American Lyric Theatre, Filling Station was given at the Martin Beck Theatre, New York, in May, 1938, with substantially the same cast.*

The musical score by Virgil Thomson is witty, concise, and often

* Gisella Caccialanza replaced Marie-Jeanne as the rich girl, and Dwight Godwin took over the part of the gangster.

probing in its exploration of the American scene. Cast in twelve separate numbers, it has outlived the stage work in concert form; but the honesty of Mr. Christensen's choreography, his resourcefully direct presentation of life as seen almost anywhere along the highways of this country, is not to be underestimated.

After an orchestral prelude establishing the sturdy, almost national tone of the ballet, the curtain rises on a neatly kept filling station. In the center stands the attendant, Mac, his vigor and probity revealed in a strong opening solo.

Doppio movimento

Soon he is besieged by motorists who stop for information, help, or companionship. The first traveler has lost his way. The necessary road maps are furnished quickly and with courtesy. Then two truck drivers, Roy and Ray, boisterous friends of Mac, dash in, pursued by a State Trooper who threatens to book them for speeding.

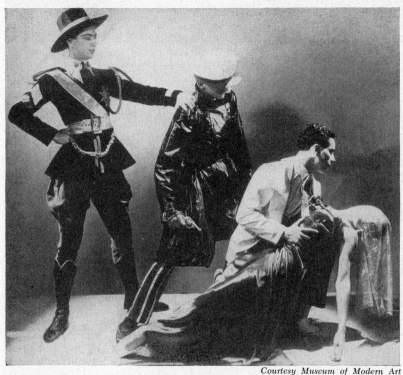

Courtesy Museum of Modern Art

TODD BOLENDER, DOUGLAS COUDY, FRED DANIELI, AND MARIE JEANNE

Now a whole family enters—a tourist, his wife, and child—seeking the comforts this well-appointed station can provide. They are followed by a spoiled couple from the country club, who stagger in drunkenly and perform a tango. Attracted by the stalwart Mac, the reeling pair invite him to join them in a *pas de trois*. The hilarity at the station increases when all the passers-by—the couple, the family, and the truck drivers—pool their efforts in a Big Apple.

At the height of the fun, a gangster enters, his revolver hot for a holdup. Mac and the truck drivers, aided by the State Trooper, advance on the criminal; but, in the chase that follows, his gun goes off and the rich girl is killed.

The finale of the ballet is at once a dirge, in which the body of the unfortunate girl is carried off by the motorists, and a restatement by the

orchestra of the broad, earthy theme of the introduction, while Mac, free for a moment, reads his newspaper, turns on his radio, and waits for the next car to drive up.

DEATH OF PAOLO IN THE ORIGINAL BALLET RUSSE PRODUCTION

Francesca da Rimini

THIS BALLET in two scenes, with book by David Lichine and Henry Clifford, was first produced by the Ballet Russe de Monte Carlo at Covent Garden in July, 1937. Mr. Lichine prepared the choreography, which was danced to the tone poem of the same name by Tchaikovsky; Oliver Messel designed the scenery and costumes. Among the principals were Lubov Tchernicheva as Francesca, Paul Petroff as Paolo, Marc Platoff as Gianciotto Malatesta, and Alexandra Danilova with Roman Jasinsky as the apparitions of Guinevere and Lancelot. The American première of *Francesca da Rimina* took place at the Metropolitan Opera House in October, 1937. The work has been revived since then in New York by the Original Ballet Russe in 1941 and again in 1946.

SCENE ONE

The music for this episode is drawn from the opening section of Tchaikovsky's tone poem, suggesting the cruel winds and lacerating tortures of the second circle of Hell to which Francesca da Rimini was condemned for breaking her marriage vow on earth.*

Lichine's choreography does not follow the implications of the music at this point but describes, instead, the stormy arrival of Francesca at the castle of Gianciotto Malatesta. As the deformed prince sits at his council table with his dwarfs and courtiers, the curtain rises.

In order to cement peace between his own province of Rimini and the neighboring terrain of Ravenna, Gianciotto has asked for the hand of Francesca—daughter of the Lord of Ravenna—in marriage. Fearing a refusal because of his ugliness, he has sent his handsome younger brother, Paolo, to marry her by proxy and bring her home.

Soon Francesca, accompanied by her old nurse, enters the castle. The deformed Gianciotto has learned through a spy that Francesca is already in love with Paolo. Seizing her roughly, he bears her from the room the moment that Paolo appears. When the girl returns in flight, Paolo tries to escape with her, but his way is barred by Gianciotto's malevolent spy.

SCENE TWO

This, the balance of Lichine's ballet, corresponds to the second and third portions of Tchaikovsky's *Francesca da Rimini*. As Paolo and Francesca are seated in the girl's bower, reading the love story of Lancelot and Guinevere—who appear in the background as the figures of a vision—the beautiful love motive of the tone poem, played first by the clarinet and then later by full winds and strings, appears in the or-

chestra. Carried away by the story and each other, they put down the book and read no more. Celestial figures fill the room in token of their love.

* Dante—*Inferno*, canto V: "*Nessun maggior dolore, che ricordarsi del tempo felice nella miseria!*" ("No greater pain than to remember one's joys in sorrow!")

Gianciotto suddenly approaches. Hearing his footsteps, Paolo hides on the terrace but is discovered there by his brother's dwarfs; he is forced into a duel and slain.

The closing pages of the tone poem, which reflect in Tchaikovsky's music the ultimate hopelessness and terror of the lovers in Hell, are here used as background for a scene of carnage. As the final chords of the piece are sounded, Francesca crawls the length of the room, offering her breast to Gianciotto's sword. It is on this pitch of climactic violence that Lichine's ballet comes to an end.

Courtesy Museum of Modern Art

LUBOV TCHERNICHEVA AND PAUL PETROFF IN SCENE TWO

THE CANCAN

Gaité Parisienne

THIS PERENNIAL closing ballet, which in the comparatively few years of its existence has become one of the most popular works in the repertoire, was first produced at the Théâtre de Monte Carlo in April, 1938. Its American première took place at the Metropolitan Opera House in October of the same year. The sense of brilliant design, of atmospheric color, flair for the comic, and superb use of massed groupings for theatrical effect—which had only been hinted at by Léonide Massine in his earlier but similar ballet, *Le Beau Danube*—was here brought to a climax. The racy décor by Count Étienne de Beaumont, who also provided the theme of the slender story, was of no small help in the success of the work.

The score, arranged and orchestrated by Manuel Rosenthal * from music by Jacques Offenbach, is among the most striking assets of *Gaité Parisienne*. Fresh, tuneful, and sophisticated in its harmonic idiom, Rosenthal's free adaptation of famous theatrical melodies rarely fails to put an audience in the mood for Massine's *divertissement* on stage. The role of the Peruvian, which the choreographer himself created, has been taken on more recent occasions by James Starbuck, Sviatoslav Toumine,

* In collaboration with Jacques Brindejonc-Offenbach.

and Leon Danielian. All have had their varying degrees of merit, especially Mr. Danielian, but none has approached the originator in his projection of a studied humor, an overripe elegance attuned to the background of the piece. Sharing honors with Massine at the American première,* and long after, were Alexandra Danilova, in her incomparable performance as the Glove Seller, and Frederic Franklin, equally successful as the Baron.

Individual artists aside, it is the expert pacing and canny sense of theatrical values exhibited in *Gaité Parisienne* that have made the work successful wherever it has been performed.

The setting is an elegant café of the Second Empire. Before the curtain rises, a brief overture, sparkling in content, sets the gay tone of the

piece, and then the action begins.

A number of waiters are busy tidying up the tables in the main salon. Since everything is rhythm and design in this ballet, the men move in

energetic patterns at their work. They take time off, however, to join in a lively dance with the scrubwomen, who are also preparing the room for the evening.

New arrivals brighten the scene. The Flower Girl, of considerable beauty, comes in to arrange her merchandise and display it to advantage. Then a group of billiard players (traditionally danced by the most talented of the younger soloists) enters in company with several *coco-dettes.†*

Last of these preliminary arrivals, as the café opens for business, is

---

* The part was originally danced at Monte Carlo by Nina Tarakanova.
† Girls of loose morals, but amateur standing.

the attractive Glove Seller, admired by waiters and students alike. More

reticent than the Flower Girl, she goes to her stand and awaits the first patrons.

One of them turns up immediately: the fabulous Peruvian, a motile, agitated flirt, who has just arrived in Paris from South America with two traveling bags full of riches. On the town, he is obviously looking for conquests; and at once the Glove Seller attracts him. Approaching

her stall, he goes through the motions of trying on a pair of gloves, but is so violently agitated by the girl's beauty that he can hardly slip his hands into the leather. As he stands there, looking at her lasciviously, the easygoing ladies who have come in with the billiard players escape with the Peruvian's bags. He runs after them, leaving the Glove Seller to herself.

LÉONIDE MASSINE AND FREDERIC FRANKLIN *Courtesy Dance News*

The moment is ripe for a romantic attachment. Waiters and guests have left the main room of the café; the Glove Seller is alone; and now the handsome young Baron enters in elegant uniform. For him and the

Glove Seller there can be no doubt, in this first encounter, of complete infatuation.

Their brief time together is interrupted by the arrival of several soldiers, led by a strutting Officer. The military, on the prowl, make friends

with the *cocodettes*, who are still hanging about. Their Officer cannot take his eyes off the Glove Seller; the Peruvian, his bags recovered, returns to the scene; and now, further to complicate this collection of highly charged personalities, the most famous beauty of Paris, La Lionne, arrives at the café. Magnificently dressed in red, she is accom-

panied by the Duke but immediately makes eyes at the Officer. At the same time, the Flower Girl—who has been neglected by the guests— tries her charms on the Baron. He ignores her, since his interest lies entirely with the Glove Seller.

It is at this point that the passions which have been generating in the café reach the point of explosion. The Peruvian, trying to arrange an after-hours rendezvous with the Glove Seller, becomes embroiled with the Baron. The Duke and the Officer start fighting over La Lionne, who plays one against the other. A general confusion ensues, and blows are exchanged by everyone—even the billiard players, who leap from one formation to another. Finally the angry guests disperse, and the Peruvian, hiding·under a table, is discovered by the waiters and driven off.

Once the troublemaker is gone, the atmosphere is cleared; and, in the deserted main room of the café, the Glove Seller and the Baron dance

SCENE FROM THE BALLET RUSSE DE MONTE CARLO PRODUCTION

a romantic *pas de deux*. Both in the choice of music—one of Offenbach's

finest waltzes—and in choreographic sweep, this duo marks the high
point of the ballet.

The room is not deserted for long. A burst of uproarious music heralds
the arrival of the cancan girls, preceded by their dancing master.

Soon all of the patrons who were involved in the brawl come back
peacefully, even the restless Peruvian, to watch the girls go through
their paces.

The spell of the dance and of the music is so intense that everyone joins in: the Glove Seller, the Flower Girl, La Lionne, and the Peruvian, among others.

Finally, the excitement of the evening has run its course and the time has come for the guests to leave. To the melting music of the Barcarolle from Offenbach's *Tales of Hoffman*, the soldiers pair off with the cancan

girls; La Lionne leaves with the Officer; the Flower Girl attaches herself to the Duke; and the Peruvian appears, bags in hand, hoping that perhaps the Glove Seller will keep her rendezvous with him after all. He sees the girl on the terrace, but in the arms of the Baron; and, as the lovers go off, bidding him farewell, he drops his bags in defeat and stands—a lonely but diverting figure—in the center of the darkened café.

Courtesy Museum of Modern Art

MIA SLAVENSKA AND LÉONIDE MASSINE

Gala Performance

This satirical ballet in two scenes, with choreography by Antony Tudor, was given its first performance by the London Ballet at Toynbee Hall Theatre, London, December, 1938. The cast on that occasion included Maud Lloyd, Peggy van Praagh, and Gerd Larson as the three ballerinas. When the American première of the work was offered by Ballet Theatre at the Majestic Theatre, New York, in February, 1941, Nora Kaye, Nana Gollner, and Karen Conrad assumed the leading women's parts. Décor and costumes were designed by Nicolas de Molas.

Possessed of a sparkle and pointed brilliance different in mood from the other major works of Mr. Tudor, which are given to tragic intensity and introspection, *Gala Performance* uses for its background the music of Sergei Prokofiev. During the first scene, representing the tense backstage preparations of a ballet company, large portions of the brooding first movement of Prokofiev's Piano Concerto No. 3 in C are employed. To depict the hilarious performance which follows out front, the composer's "Classical Symphony"—with its tongue-in-cheek treatment of a traditional form—provides a perfect foil.

SCENE ONE

A gala performance involving the participation of three internationally celebrated ballerinas is about to take place at the turn of the century. One of the divas comes from Moscow, the second from Milan, and the third from Paris. As the curtain rises, backstage life at the Theatre Royal is revealed, with the resident company anxiously awaiting the arrival of the distinguished guests. The stage is dimly lighted, the *corps de ballet* is practicing, dancers are applying last bits of costume and make-up. In the remote background, a tableau curtain—rope side toward the spectator—may be seen masking the company from the auditorium beyond.

The first of the visiting stars to come on stage is La Reine de la Danse, from Moscow. Adjusting her jewels, practicing her curtain calls, and giving the conductor—who is about to enter the pit—some brisk instructions on tempi, she is greeted with deference by the company. A few moments later, La Fille de Terpsichore, from Paris, arrives with her partner. Unlike the more pretentious Reine de la Danse, this one is on the fluttery side—an eternal ingénue.

Now the last of the three artists appears: La Déesse de la Danse, from Milan. Dressed entirely in black, her costume culminating in an enormous headdress, the ballerina strides forbiddingly to the center of the stage, which she marks as her spot for the coming performance. Keeping the company at arm's length, she turns—after a brief argument with the costumer—and goes off imperiously toward her dressing room.

At this point the "overheads" are turned on, the orchestra is heard in a rising flood of sound, and all the excitements of life backstage just before the rise of the curtain are in evidence. Suddenly there is a blackout, and when the lights come up again, the perspective has been reversed, with the Theatre Royal's proscenium in full view and the dancers in their places.

SCENE TWO

Four episodes—a variation for every one of the three visiting ballerinas and a joint finale for all of them—make up the gala performance, danced to the four brief movements of the "Classical Symphony." Against a setting which boasts all of the curlicues to be found in bad theatrical art of the 1890's, the Russian ballerina appears first for her

solo. She performs—assisted by the *corps* of girls—with a lush exaggeration designed to win over the least dance-minded member of any audience. Applause is her goal, and when it comes through, the ballerina leaves the stage reluctantly, milking her public for several additional bows.

In frozen contrast to the overanxious dancer from Moscow, the Milanese diva now advances. She has lost none of her hauteur and seems even more formidable in the presence of an audience. Surrounded by a

dutiful *corps de ballet*, she sustains adagio poses that are amazing in their repulsive authority, and, at the conclusion of her turn, strides from the stage like an empress dismissing her court.

Courtesy Ballet Theatre

NORA KAYE, ALICIA ALONSO, AND NORMA VASLAVINA

The time has come for the French ballerina to exhibit her skill. Turning on all the personality at her disposal, she leaps across the stage with

her cavalier, a bombshell of effervescence. Her curtain calls, no less buoyant, find her bounding from every conceivable side to acknowledge the applause.

Now the long-awaited finale arrives, in which—as might have been expected—the three ballerinas jockey desperately for the center of the stage. As they advance together to the footlights, the Milanese diva

holds with supreme resolution to the spot she has marked out for herself. Every one of the stars performs a tour de force in turn; and their gala appearance at the Theatre Royal concludes with all of them joining the *corps* in an overposed, ill-tempered celebrity group.

The curtain does not come down to the final bars of the music. Instead, the three divas receive a barrage of bouquets from the orchestra pit which they acknowledge with smiles to the audience and mounting antagonism toward one another, until the house curtain descends just in time to avert a public vendetta.

Gayne[*]

THIS "patriotic folk ballet," with music by the Soviet Armenian composer Aram Khatchaturian and choreography by the ballerina N. A. Anisimova, who also danced the title role, was first produced in the city of Molotov on a visit by the Kirov Theatre for Opera and Ballet of the Leningrad State Academy, in December, 1942. The libretto was by K. N. Derzhavin, and the scenic design by N. Altman. In February, 1945, *Gayne* was re-staged in Leningrad with new scenery by V. Ryndin.

For his score, charged with the musical folklore of his native province, Khatchaturian received the First Degree Stalin Prize. The ballet itself was named for the composer's wife. An orchestral suite from the work, arranged soon after the production in Molotov, contains thirteen separate dances, the best known of which is the "Saber Dance," given its American première by the Kansas City Philharmonic, directed by Efrem Kurtz, in the season of 1944–45.

Gayne, the young heroine of the story, lives in the midst of cotton pickers on a collective farm near Kolkhoz, southern Armenia. She is industrious and straightforward, but her husband, Giko, drinks and consorts with criminals. When Gayne, unable to bear his crimes against the community, denounces Giko to the workers, the man ignites the bales of cotton which have been stored in the village, seizes their child, Ripsik, as hostage, and threatens his wife with a dagger. Gayne is saved by the arrival of a Red Army Border Patrol, whose commander, Kozakov, rushes between Giko and his wife, but not before Gayne has been stabbed. The girl recovers; Giko is exiled, leaving her free to rewed; and Gayne realizes that she is in love with the young commander.

At their engagement party, with which the ballet ends, a number of dances of various parts of the Soviet Republic are performed, including characteristic numbers from Armenia, Georgia, the Ukraine, and a brilliant Saber Dance of the Kurds.

Allegro

[*] Also written *Gayaneh.*

PAVLOVA AS GISELLE

Giselle

OR

THE WILIS

THIS FANTASTIC ballet in two acts, which occupies one of the most important places in the annals of theatrical dance, was first performed at the Paris Opéra (Académie Royale de la Musique et de la Dance) on June 28, 1841. The book, by Théophile Gautier, written in collaboration with Vernoy de Saint-Georges, was based in part on a legend recounted by the German romantic poet Heinrich Heine, in a book known to French readers as *De l'Allemagne* ("The Lore of Germany"). Adolphe Adam composed the musical score, and Pierre Ciceri provided the décor.

The title role of *Giselle* was danced at the Paris première by Carlotta

Grisi, whose presence in the company brought about a number of cir-
cumstances directly affecting the birth of the ballet. Gautier, her admirer, designed the story as a vehicle for her dramatic and technical
talents; Jules Perrot, her husband, renowned choreographer, created
his wife's solo numbers, but anonymously, because of backstage ma-
chinations at the Opéra; and Jean Coralli, who was given full credit on
the programs for the staging of *Giselle*, designed the balance of the
work. The original cast, in addition to Mme Grisi, included Lucien
Petipa as Albrecht; Adèle Dumilâtre as the Queen of the Wilis; and
Coralli himself in the mimed role of Hilarion.

The scenes of peasant life in *Giselle* woven in tapestry about the noble
figures of the Prince of Courland and his court, and the earthy pathos
of Giselle's love for Albrecht juxtaposed with her ghostly appearance
beside the tomb, offered to perfection the types of dramatic contrast
favored by the romanticism reigning in the opera and ballet theatres of
the mid-nineteenth century. The architectural line that unified these
elements was the choreography, integrating the contrasts of the plot
in a smooth-textured, imaginative design.

Adam's score, too, brought its own cohesive strength to *Giselle*. The
composer's development in the orchestra of motives associated with
leading persons and events of the drama anticipated the same symphonic device used later so strikingly in the ballet music of Delibes and
Tchaikovsky. Unpretentious in texture and sweetly nostalgic in mood,
this score served as a mirror for the action as well as a cornerstone for
the structure of the work itself.

Giselle was the climax of French romantic ballet. Apparitions of
woodland spirits, of première danseuses who rose on their toes and
floated through space seemingly in defiance of natural laws, had been
introduced successfully to Parisian audiences in the two ballets *La
Sylphide* (1832) and *La Fille du Danube* (1836) which Filippo Taglioni choreographed for his famous daughter, Marie. Neither of these
works, however, is performed today; while *Giselle*, aside from a few
cuts and minor revisions, has survived as a classic constantly performed,
a pillar of the repertory.

Any list of ballerinas who have danced the title role, even though
partial, includes most of the great in the history of theatrical dance.
This is the coveted prize for all female soloists because of its expressive
range. Among the artists who have appeared in the part since Grisi's
first performance have been Marie Taglioni, Fanny Elssler, Lucille
Grahn, Fanny Cerito, Thamar Karsavina, Anna Pavlova, Olga Spessivtzeva, Vera Nemchinova, Tamara Toumanova, Mia Slavenska, Alexandra Danilova, Alicia Markova, Nana Gollner, Annabelle Lyon, Nora
Kaye, Margot Fonteyn, Yvette Chauviré, Galina Ulanova, and Marina
Semenova.

A majority of the prominent male dancers in ballet since 1841 have
essayed the companion role of Albrecht. Outstanding contemporary

interpreters are Anton Dolin, Igor Youskevitch, André Eglevsky, and Frederic Franklin.

The United States first saw *Giselle* when it was presented at Boston in January, 1846, with Mary Ann Lee, the American ballerina who had studied with Coralli, in the name part. Later in the same year, a French dancer, Mme Augusta, took over the role in New York. Further presentations of the ballet were given in New York in 1870, with Kathi Lanner as the heroine, and again in 1910, when Anna Pavlova and Mikhail Mordkin performed the work at the Metropolitan Opera House.

More recent revivals have been offered by the Mordkin Ballet (1937), the Ballet Russe de Monte Carlo (in a restaging by Serge Lifar, given at the Metropolitan in November, 1938, which introduced Alicia Markova, greatest of modern Giselles, to American audiences), and by Ballet Theatre, in the mounting of Anton Dolin, first presented at the Center Theatre, New York, in January, 1940. Mr. Dolin's version, based on a celebrated previous reconstruction by Marius Petipa,* was prepared with the assistance of Nicholas Sergeyev.† Still another edition was produced by George Balanchine for the Ballet Russe de Monte Carlo in October, 1946.

Although these adaptations vary in certain external respects, they are all bound in fundamental adherence to the original *Giselle*, a work still

---

* The Petipa revival of 1887, marking the debut of the French ballerina Emma Bessonet, at the Mariinsky Theatre, St. Petersburg, was a revision and integration of various performances of *Giselle* given in the Russian capital, including one presented by Perrot himself in 1851.

† Sergeyev, long associated with the Mariinsky as ballet master, was thoroughly familiar with traditions of the Petipa production.

Photo: Florian de Narde   *Courtesy Ballet Theatre*

EUGENE BERMAN'S SET MODEL FOR ACT I

theatrically valid. The Ballet Russe revival of 1938 offered scenery and costumes after designs by Alexandre Benois; Ballet Theatre brought décor by Lucinda Ballard; and the Balanchine edition provided pictorial backgrounds by Eugene Berman.

ACT ONE

A peaceful village near the Rhine is seen at vintage time in the Middle Ages, as the curtain rises after a brilliant prelude. At one side of a little clearing is a cottage where Giselle, a young peasant girl, lives with her mother, Berthe. At the other stands a hut of deceptively mean appearance which shelters Albrecht, the Duke of Silesia. Disguised as a peasant named Loys, he has come to live in the village to be near Giselle, whom he adores.

As sunlight beats down on the clearing and a sense of rustic peace

fills the air, a single disruptive element crosses the scene: Hilarion, gamekeeper from the near-by forest, who is also in love with Giselle. He glances angrily at the house of his rival, then withdraws.*

* This first entrance of Hilarion is usually omitted in present-day versions of the ballet.

Photo: Florian de Narde   *Courtesy Ballet Theatre*

EUGENE BERMAN'S SET MODEL FOR ACT II

Now the door of the hut is opened and Loys appears, accompanied by his squire, Wilfrid. The attendant, whose rich attire clashes with the peasant costume of his master, urges the noble to give up this unfitting disguise. He points reproachfully at the sword, sign of noble rank, that Loys carries when no villagers are about; but Loys, bidding the squire hide it inside the hut and begone, approaches the cottage of Giselle and knocks at the door softly.

In immediate answer, Giselle runs out to meet him. She is a slight girl, outwardly like a peasant, yet ethereal—a figure spiritually apart from the rest of the village. At the sight of Loys, she bounds toward him with an exaltation of feeling that has pure innocence as its root.

It is in this section of the ballet that a love theme arises which is to be used throughout the work with almost Wagnerian consistency—a tender, yearning phrase representing Giselle's devotion to Loys.

The girl tells her lover of a dream she has had the night before. He appeared in it as a prince, she relates, and was about to wed a great lady. Taken aback, the would-be peasant tries to reassure Giselle; but the girl, inwardly restless, plucks the petals of a flower one by one in the time-honored test of fidelity. Laughingly seizing the flower, Loys completes the augury, which is favorable; and, Giselle's fears at rest, the lovers dance together. (The motive that describes their happiness is repeated, like the love theme, during the course of the plot in varied form and with telling emotional results.)

At this moment, Hilarion returns. On seeing Giselle in the arms of his rival, he threatens Loys and the girl. They order him to go; and, as the gamekeeper withdraws, it is clear that he will seek revenge.

Now it is the turn of the villagers to interrupt the lovers, but benevo-

Photo: *Fred Fehl*

ALICIA MARKOVA AS GISELLE IN THE MAD SCENE

lently, as a group of girls and their escorts cross the clearing, carrying baskets to gather the autumn grapes. Invited by Giselle to linger, they put aside their work and join her in a waltz.

Aside from her love for Loys, dancing is Giselle's greatest passion. As she leads her friends in a joyful variation, her mother, Berthe, comes from the house and looks on in alarm. The superstitious old woman is thinking of the legend of the Wilis—ghostly maidens who, dying before their wedding day and inordinately fond of dancing during their life-time, are condemned to wander the forests at night, traveling through the mists and luring wayfarers to their doom by compelling them to join the dance. While these fears invade Berthe's mind, the motive of the Wilis—to be heard prominently in Act Two—first appears in the orchestra.

Suddenly a distant horn call is sounded; a hunting party is at hand. Disturbed by the thought that his noble fiancée, Bathilde, and her father, the Prince of Courland, may be riding in the neighborhood, Loys slips off to the vineyards with the party from the village. The clearing soon is empty; Giselle and her mother enter their cottage; and Hilarion, unobserved, steals inside the hut that stands opposite. Coming out with the sword, he runs off to await the moment for exposing his enemy.

Loys's escape has been well timed. A sumptuously dressed party of nobles appears, led by the Prince and his daughter. Tired from the chase, they approach the cottage in search of refreshment. At once the girl and her mother set up a table outside with food and drink. Giselle shyly welcomes Bathilde, looking raptly at the gown she is wearing. Touched by such admiration, the Princess removes a golden chain and places it about the maiden's neck. Then, attended by her father and his retinue, she enters the cottage to rest. Only the ducal huntsman remains outside, his horn poised for a signal to speed the party on its way.

Now that the visitors have disappeared, Loys returns and takes Giselle in his arms. At the same instant, the girls who have been working in the field come bearing vine leaves, prepared to crown the maiden as queen of the harvest. Just as the celebration is reaching its peak, Hilarion appears and denounces Loys as an impostor. Giselle indignantly tries to silence him, but the gamekeeper produces the sword that gives proof of her lover's rank. As Loys rushes at him enraged, Hilarion seizes the horn from the waiting huntsman and blows a call upon it. Immediately the Prince and his daughter hasten from the cottage.

Amazed at seeing Albrecht, Duke of Silesia, dressed as a peasant, they stare at him in consternation. Giselle, understanding the situation at last, recognizes Bathilde as the Princess of her dreams and tears the golden chain from her throat. Filled with a despair that borders on madness, she seizes Albrecht's sword, which the noble has hurled to the ground, and—after describing a frenzied arc with it—thrusts the blade into her body.

On the point of death, Giselle re-enacts with supreme pathos her former dance of joy. The music itself, a repetition of themes describing her happiness with Loys (Nos. 3 and 4), seems to falter with the girl, as she drags her feet listlessly through what was once an exuberant pattern. There are, in ballet, few equals of this scene for direct emotional appeal. With a last trembling gesture, Giselle falls dead at the feet of her lover; and Albrecht, torn between shame and fury, forces the gamekeeper whose jealousy has brought about this tragedy to kneel with him beside the body of Giselle.

Courtesy Ballet Theatre
ANTON DOLIN AND ALICIA MARKOVA IN ACT II

ACT TWO

The depths of the forest are seen at night, with tall, fantastic trees growing on the banks of a pool. Over the water hangs a strange, bluish mist; and beneath a great willow in a corner of this unhallowed ground is the suicide's grave, above which stands a cross bearing the name Giselle. The inscription is seen every so often as the moonlight plays upon the mound.

It is midnight. A hunting party led by Hilarion enters fearfully, seeking refuge from an approaching storm. Suddenly the men recognize the neighborhood—a part of the forest long haunted by the Wilis. As unearthly lights are seen moving through the trees, they flee.

Now a pallid figure floats across the scene: Myrtha, Queen of the Wilis.* She dances in the moonlight and calls her ghostly subjects

* The role of Myrtha, which demands a phenomenally sustained technique and imposing dramatic authority, is quite as exacting in its way as that of Gisella. Among its best-known modern interpreters have been Alexandra Danilova, Rosella Hightower, Nora Kaye, and Mary Ellen Moylan.

217

together to celebrate the admission of a new sister to their band.

Moderato

Waving her flowery scepter over the newly dug mound, Myrtha commands Giselle to arise. In obedience, a veiled phantom emerges from the grave. At another sign from the Queen, the veil vanishes in air, and the spirit of Giselle—become a Wili—advances submissively. Suddenly, filled with the dance madness that is the curse of these spirits, she springs through the glen with overpowering leaps.

Moderato   **Andante**

The girl, beautiful as in her lifetime, no longer wears the peasant garb that marked her days in the village. She is dressed in flowing, ankle-length white, the *tutu* of romantic ballet.

Hearing mortal footsteps, the Wilis vanish, drawing Giselle with them, and Albrecht appears, come to visit the grave of his loved one. Stirred by his remorse, Giselle returns; she reveals herself to the youth. Just as he is about to embrace her, the Wilis fly into the glen, in pursuit of a second wayfarer: Hilarion. Wandering through the forest in a brooding

Allegro molto

sense of guilt, the gamekeeper is confronted by the white-clad phantoms ranged in line. They surround him and force him to join them in a wild bacchanale until he whirls giddily into the pool, where he is

Allegro molto

drowned. Then, in a stroke of fantastic splendor, the Wilis dash from the scene in columns, like a spectral army.

One of them, strayed from the rest, discovers Albrecht, who has gone unmolested. Immediately the Queen, intent on the destructive work of her band, orders Giselle to draw him into a dance of death. The maiden pleads with the Queen, but to no avail . . . the order is repeated by the relentless Myrtha. Secretly Giselle signals to her lover to stay near the tomb, whose cross alone can protect him against evil. Even as the Queen draws near it, her scepter breaks before the holy symbol.

Still, Myrtha orders Giselle to dance. Albrecht, led by a longing to join the girl, forsakes his refuge and supports her in a *pas de deux* of notable lyricism, its long-drawn melody played by solo viola.

The Queen's plan is succeeding. As the dance progresses, Albrecht is overpowered by the madness that seizes all of the Wilis' victims before they die. In a solo variation celebrated for its frantic vigor, he darts through the air and, with the Wilis standing by, crashes to the ground, their prey. The Queen waits; the time has come to mark off another vic-

Photo: Maurice Seymour   *Courtesy Ballet Theatre*

ALICIA MARKOVA AS GISELLE

tim; but, at the moment of fulfillment, the dawn breaks and Albrecht is saved.

Now the Wilis vanish, their powers gone with the darkness; and Giselle, who lingers for a final glance at Albrecht, flits wanly toward her grave. Albrecht rises from the ground, looks at her tenderly, stands with

arms outstretched. But, with the tolling of the hour, Giselle disappears into the tomb, never again to be seen by her lover, who remains desolate on the banks of the pool as morning light invades the forest.

Photo: Lipnitzki   *Courtesy Museum of Modern Art*

SERGE LIFAR AS PRINCE ALBRECHT

The Golden Age

This "athletic ballet" in three acts and five scenes, with music by Dmitri Shostakovich, was first produced at the Bolshoi Theatre, Moscow, in 1931. The book was by A. I. Ivanovsky; choreography by E. I. Kaplan and V. I. Vainonen; scenery and costumes by V. M. Khodasevich. The score by Shostakovich, which had taken the prize during the preceding year in a contest for the best ballet on a Soviet subject, marked the composer's first music for theatrical dance. To date, Shostakovich's other works in this form have been *The Bolt* (Leningrad, 1931), on an industrial motive, and *The Limpid Stream* (Moscow, 1936), with an agricultural background. Despite its lack of subtlety—induced by an aggressively political theme—*The Golden Age* contains some amusing moments. Shostakovich has drawn a concert suite from the final section of the ballet, consisting of an Introduction, Adagio, Polka, and Dance. It is this Polka, danced during the music-hall scene of the last act, that brought fame to the work in America, where the full stage version has not been seen.

ACT ONE

SCENE ONE: The action begins in the main hall of a great capitalist advertising exhibit, known as "The Golden Age." Among the guests of honor are a group of Fascists, welcomed with great pomp, while the visiting Soviet football team—invited by local labor representatives—enters with painfully contrasting inconspicuousness. There follow a review of window displays, demonstrations of exhibits, and then a boxing match between a white man and a Negro. The Fascists in charge of the exhibit have rigged the match; and, just as the Negro is on the point of winning, the white man deals him a foul blow which is sustained by the referee. The workers are enraged at the verdict, and a woman of the local Communist Soviet Youth rushes out of the crowd and slaps the referee in the face.

SCENE TWO: A cabaret at "The Golden Age" is revealed, with a great many Fascist boys and girls dancing about. At the height of their revelry, various dignitaries of the exhibit appear, including the Director, the Chief of Police, and finally, Deva, the celebrated Fascist performer, beautifully gowned.

After Deva has glided through an adagio and received a round of applause, the Soviet football team enters. Deva is attracted by its captain, who resists her many invitations, first to dance and then to drink. As he refuses to join her in a Fascist toast, her comrades attack him, and he raises his football in defense. Certain that the pigskin is a bomb, the Fascists drop to the ground, expecting a detonation. In the confusion that follows, the captain and his comrades leave and the Fascists, once they have recovered their composure, take refuge in the decadent strains of a fox trot.

ACT TWO

SCENE ONE: The football captain, the Negro boxer, and the woman of the Communist Soviet Youth walk about the streets of the city, looking at the sights, and are followed by Fascist detectives. After slipping counterfeit notes into the captain's pocket, these hirelings manage to have him and his companions arrested. The Negro and the woman escape, but the captain is led off by the police.

SCENE TWO: The workers, engaged in a great variety of outdoor sports, are holding a festival at the exhibition stadium. Boxing, discus-throwing, tennis, fencing, and other activities are revealed to an enthusiastic crowd, which gives an especially warm reception to the Soviet football team. Films are shown, including one depicting the brutality of the police who control the very city in which the exhibit is taking place. Hearing of the danger in which the Negro boxer and the woman of the Communist Soviet Youth now find themselves, the workers rush to their aid in a United Red Front.

ACT THREE

A festival is in full swing at the music hall of the exhibit, with a varied bill for the entertainment of the crowd. First comes a tap dance to advertise "Superfine Boot Polish"; then a polka, "Once in Geneva," satirizing

the World Disarmament Conference. Other numbers follow, including a "Dance of Reconciliation of all Classes," performed ironically by Deva and a Fascist cavalier.

At the climax of this entertainment, the music hall is invaded by the Red Front. The bourgeois public retreats, and the ballet ends with a dance depicting the solidarity of the workers of Western Europe with the emissaries sent them by the Soviet Union.

Photo: Maurice Seymour THE CADETS MEET THE GIRLS Courtesy Dance News

Graduation Ball

THIS BALLET in one act, with book and choreography by David Lichine, was first performed by the Original Ballet Russe at the Theatre Royal, Sydney, Australia, in February, 1940. The American première, given by the same company, took place seven months later at the Fifty-first Street Theatre, New York. Alexandre Benois designed the scenery and costumes; Antal Dorati compiled, arranged, and orchestrated several unfamiliar pieces by Johann Strauss—found in the manuscript collection of the Vienna State Opera—and made them into an attractive musical score. After winning considerable success as a closing ballet, in the manner of *Gaité Parisienne* and *Beau Danube,* and then disappearing from the local scene together with the Original Ballet Russe, *Graduation Ball* was revived by Ballet Theatre at the Metropolitan Opera House in October, 1944, with new décor by Mstislav Dobujinsky. Mr. Lichine and Tatiana Riabouchinska, who had headed the cast in the early performances, were seen again in their accustomed roles. The strong supporting group in the revival included Alicia Alonso, Rosella Hightower, Mar-

223

jorie Tallchief, John Kriza, Harold Lang, and Richard Reed. As before, the dash and humor of the work commended it.

In the fall of 1949 the Ballet Russe de Monte Carlo acquired the scenery and costumes from S. Hurok, who owned them, and added the ballet, revived by Vladimir Dokoudovsky, to its repertoire.

The scene is the reception room of a girls' school in Vienna, where the pupils are preparing for a ball to be held in honor of the annual graduation. Divided into two groups, the older girls, poised and condescending, and the younger ones, visibly excited over the party at hand, are all awaiting the arrival of the cadets of a near-by military academy who are to be guests at the ball. At the last moment their headmistress (played for comedy by a male dancer) checks on the appearance and conduct of the pupils. Then, as the sound of military music announces the approach of the cadets, she goes to meet them.

Now the boys march in, headed by the General—an absurdly monumental figure—who takes at once to the headmistress. As the well-matched couple go off together, the young students dance, at first diffidently and then—to the strains of a brilliant waltz—with more enthusiasm. Prominent among the youngsters is a junior girl, exuberant in her behavior, and a rather bashful cadet who heads his group.

Soon the General and headmistress come back to the ballroom to preside over the entertainment of the evening. Several set dances are per-

Photo: Alfredo Valente   *Courtesy S. Hurok*
TATIANA RIABOUCHINSKA AS THE YOUNG GIRL

DAVID LICHINE AS THE BASHFUL CADET

formed, including a number called "The Drummer"; a romantic *pas de deux* with Scotch background; a dance-step competition, based on a whirling fouetté * contest; a diverting episode, "Mathematics and Natural History Lesson," which pokes fun at traditional ballet attitudes; and a final "Perpetuum Mobile," for the leading dancers of the group.

During the *divertissement,* the headmistress and the General have effected an even closer *rapprochement* than before. When the young people go off to the next room for supper, these two remain alone and are caught in an embrace by the returning students. A mood of abandon sets in on the part of everyone; the party spins along merrily until the moment when the two supervisors bid the students retire to their dormitories. Then the cadets march out after a farewell to the girls, and the lights in the hall are lowered.

The bashful young cadet, spurred on by the expansive turn the evening has taken, steals back for a farewell to his partner. He is discovered, however, by the watchful headmistress and routed. His defeat must not be taken to heart, for *Graduation Ball* in music and dance is a genial ballet.

* Undoubtedly the most spectacular technical feat in a ballerina's armory, consisting of a turn on one foot obtained in large part by a whipping motion of the other leg. The effect of fouettés in ballet is proportionate to the consecutive number obtained; and in the *Graduation Ball* contest, several aspirants try to reach the highest total.

Photo: Alfredo Valente   Courtesy Ballet Theatre
NORA KAYE AND ANDRÉ EGLEVSKY

Graziana

THIS BALLET in classical style, based on the music of Mozart's Concerto for Violin and Orchestra in G Major (No. 216 in the Köchel Catalogue), and with scenery and costumes by Alvin Colt, was first produced by Ballet Theatre at the Metropolitan Opera House in October, 1945. John Taras was the choreographer. The cast included Nora Kaye, Alicia Alonso, and André Eglevsky.

The ground plan of the work, in three episodes, grows out of and corresponds to the three-movement form of the concerto itself. The dancers are dressed in traditional classical style, the girls in short *tutus* and the men in tights and close-fitting jackets. They move against a fixed blue background.

226

FIRST MOVEMENT

Allegro

Three soloists and the *corps de ballet* take part in this, the most ambitious of the episodes, characterized by neatly drawn group patterns and elaborate solos for the principal dancers, notably the first ballerina.

SECOND MOVEMENT

Adagio

Here, a group of five secondary artists weaves the sustained designs that match the languid phrases of the Adagio.

THIRD MOVEMENT

Rondo

The finale brings the entire cast to the stage in a well-paced conclusion that approximates the sparkle of the music. This is formal ballet, clean, precise, and unpretentious, inspired perhaps by certain works of George Balanchine but possessing—along with the promise shown by its young choreographer—a marked personal style.

RUTH ANN KOESUN, DIANA ADAMS, AND JOHN KRIZA

Helen of Troy

THIS WORK, in a prologue and three scenes, was originally sketched in
Mexico City for Ballet Theatre by the late Michel Fokine during the
summer of 1942, just before his death. Completion of the ballet was
subsequently entrusted to David Lichine, and the first performance—
in Mr. Lichine's version—took place in November, 1942, during the company's Detroit season. Irina Baronova appeared in the title role, with
André Eglevsky as Paris and Jerome Robbins as Hermes. After much
revision, and with the restaging of a few numbers by George Balanchine,
Helen of Troy came to the Metropolitan Opera House in April, 1943,

228

with Vera Zorina in the name part. Later performances have brought
Maria Karnilova, Nana Gollner, and Diana Adams in the lead; John
Kriza as Hermes; and Igor Youskevitch as Paris.

Owing to a lack of unity in style, which seems to have been passed
over by Mr. Lichine in favor of sheer theatrical effectiveness, *Helen of
Troy* remains a variable ballet, active on the entertainment side but
weak as integrated dance. Its chief present appeal, aside from one fine
solo variation for Paris, lies in the musical score culled by Antal Dorati,
like that of *Bluebeard* before it, from the works of Offenbach. The
sparkle and opulence of the orchestral background do much to chart the
dancers through some rough choreographic moments. Good pictorial
backgrounds have been provided by Marcel Vertès.

PROLOGUE

On a certain afternoon the young shepherd Paris is standing on Mount
Ida tending his flock. Suddenly the god Hermes appears—a tough, gum-
chewing caricature of that legendary figure—with an invitation for Paris
to preside as judge at an Olympian beauty contest. The entrants are to
be Hera, Pallas Athena, and Aphrodite, all rival goddesses. Paris accepts,
the contest takes place, and Aphrodite wins—after first having promised
Paris to lead him to the most beautiful woman on earth if he awards her
the prize. Paris bestows the golden apple, as agreed; and Aphrodite,
keeping her part of the bargain, conducts him to the court of Helen of
Sparta, wife of Menelaus. The goddess and her protégé do not travel
alone. They are followed by Paris' pet lamb and the unpredictable
Hermes, who, despite his godlike wings, just slouches along.

SCENE ONE

When they have arrived at the gates of the court, Pallas leaves them;
and now Paris, Hermes, and the lamb enter the halls of the senile Menelaus. After a few initial difficulties, Paris succeeds in reaching the side
of the beautiful Helen, who is bored with her husband; and here he
performs a variation of tremendous surge and vitality that marks the one
moment of exciting dance in the ballet.

As Menelaus falls asleep on his throne under the ministrations of Hermes, Paris and Helen join in a romantic *pas de deux*. Then the conspirators, enlisting the aid of Calchas, the High Priest, awaken the poor old monarch and tell him that his kingdom has been invaded. Calling for the royal armor and chariot, they pack him off to war as Helen gives Paris the key to her room.

Allegro vivace

First Interlude

The youth Orestes, also in love with Helen, persuades the Queen's lady-in-waiting to disguise him as a maid so that he may slip into her chamber.

Photo: Alfredo Valente   Courtesy Ballet Theatre
RUTH ANN KOESUN AND IGOR YOUSKEVITCH

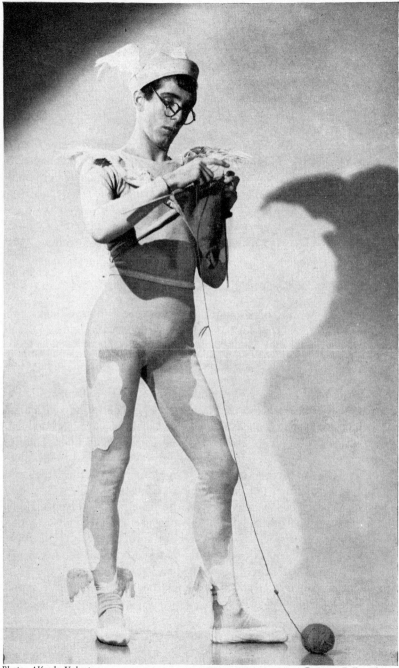

JEROME ROBBINS AS HERMES

SCENE TWO

As the Queen prepares for bed, the new maid appears, first causing Helen annoyance, through a too evident desire to please, and then embarrassment. Soon Orestes tears off his disguise and makes love to Helen; but with the help of Hermes, who strolls in at an opportune moment, the Queen gets rid of this youth who is spoiling her plans, and prepares to receive Paris.

At last the shepherd appears, and the lovers embrace; but their rendezvous is interrupted by the King, who has returned unexpectedly from the war. During the excitement, Paris' pet lamb has also managed to slip into the chamber. Now follows a scene in the standard tradition of bedroom farce as Helen, Paris, the lamb, Hermes, and Menelaus dash after one another in a circle around an intervening screen. Hermes, bored with this pursuit, takes a post in the center of it, blowing a whistle and directing traffic. As Menelaus, exhausted, gives up the chase, Paris escapes.

Second Interlude

The King, lamenting his domestic disgrace, stands before the curtain and weeps so bitterly that his tears cascade into the prompter's box.

SCENE THREE

The seashore of Sparta is seen, with some of Helen's attendant ladies taking their leisure on the beach. Among them is a court lady with a pet faun, which she leads on a leash. Here Mr. Lichine, long associated as a dancer with the title role of Nijinsky's *L'Après-Midi d'un Faune,* has interpolated in his choreography a fairly amusing travesty of that ballet's friezelike style. As the trained faun, overstimulated by the ladies surrounding him, becomes too passionate, he is hustled off.

Now a ship arrives—the last instrument in the plot to separate Helen from her witless husband. The King, Queen, and Hermes climb aboard, accompanied by Paris, who is disguised in the robes of the High Priest. Just as the ship pulls out, the conspirators toss Menelaus ashore, where he is caught in mid-air by his courtiers; and the two lovers, under the benevolent guidance of Hermes, sail onward to the hero's native Troy.

L'Histoire d'un Soldat

THIS WORK ("A Soldier's Tale"), to be read, acted, and danced, grew out of the financial strain experienced by Igor Stravinsky in Switzerland during the First World War, when royalties from his music were blocked off by the international situation. Together with a group of friends including C. F. Ramuz, the writer, and Ernest Ansermet, the conductor, who were also hard hit, Stravinsky developed the idea of a traveling theatre with small orchestra that could tour Switzerland and perhaps realize a profit. This project was to combine a narrator, actors, and orchestra in an unusual treatment of musical and dramatic values. Thus developed L'Histoire d'un Soldat. The poem was written by Ramuz, the music by Stravinsky, and the dance of the Princess was worked out by the composer together with Ludmila Pitoëff, who created the role. Others who took part in the première of L'Histoire d'un Soldat at the Lausanne Theatre in September, 1918, were George Pitoëff as the Devil and Gabriel Rossel as the Soldier. The scenery and costumes were by René Auberjonois. A London production followed, with Lydia Sokolova in the role of the Princess.

The first stage performance of this work in America was given under the auspices of the League of Composers at the Jolson Theatre (now the Century Theatre), New York, in 1928 with Jacques Cartier as the Devil, Tom Powers as the Reader, Lily Lubell as the Princess, and Blake Scott as the Soldier. Michio Ito directed the pantomine; Pierre Monteux conducted; the décor was by Donald Oenslager; and an English translation by Rosa Newmarch of the French text was used. On this occasion, L'Histoire d'un Soldat was presented on a double bill with Manuel de Falla's puppet opera, El Retablo de Maese Pedro. Since then, New York has seen it intermittently. An especially notable revival was presented at the Juilliard School of Music in May, 1948, under the direction of Dimitri Mitropoulos.

Stravinsky's treatment of the orchestral portion of L'Histoire d'un Soldat is a veritable tour de force in economy and resourcefulness. Only seven players make up the orchestra: violin, double bass, clarinet, bassoon, cornet, trombone, and percussion (the last-named handling a variety of instruments so expertly timed in their entrances that one virtuoso drummer can perform on all of them). The resulting sonorities are as elegant as chamber music, rowdy as a seven-piece street band, full as a symphony orchestra. The instrumental group is seated not in the traditional pit, but at one side of the stage, with the Reader—in evening dress—placed at the other side, and an inner stage, on which the action is seen, mounted in the center.

PART ONE

The little orchestra strikes up a marching tune and the Reader sets the scene of the action. He speaks of a soldier who is returning to his

native town on fifteen days' leave. The youth has already marched a long way and is impatient to get home.

SCENE ONE: The curtain of the inner stage rises and the Reader goes on with his story as the Soldier enters. (Often during the action, the youth—primarily a speaking part—carries out in pantomine the sense of the Reader's words.)

The Soldier stops at the edge of a stream, sits down, and opens his duffel bag. To the accompanying words of the Reader, he takes out a holy medal, a picture of his girl, and—after reaching into the depths of the bag—a little violin. He starts to play on it, remarking that the instrument, a cheap one, seems always out of tune.

As he performs, the Devil enters—a mild little man carrying a butter-fly net. He comes up quietly behind the Soldier, who stops playing at the sight of him. Anxiously, the Devil offers to buy the violin. The Soldier, puzzled, refuses to part with it, but, on being pressed by the Devil, agrees to exchange the instrument for a mysterious book. Although the youth protests he cannot read, the Devil claims that the book will be clear to him, that it is a strongbox which, on being opened, will bring securities, bank notes, gold.

The Soldier is persuaded, sells the Devil his violin, and begins to read the book. Suddenly the Devil asks the youth for a few lessons on the fiddle, inviting him to his home for two or three days. When the Soldier hesitates because of the shortness of his leave, the Devil promises him food and lodging of the finest quality, plenty of butter, wine, and cigars with gold bands.

The inner curtain falls and the Reader goes on with his tale. He relates how Joseph, the Soldier, stayed for two days at the home of the Devil and left on the third, after thanking his host for an enjoyable visit. Then the Soldier turned homeward again (here, the little orchestra resumes the strains of the opening march). He finally reached his native town; but no one recognized him—neither his mother, who, when she saw him, rushed away in terror, nor his girl, now married and the mother of two children. It was then that Joseph realized he had spent not three days but three years with the Devil.

SCENE TWO: In the distance can be seen the steeple of a village. In the center of this rustic scene stands the Devil, leaning on his cane, dressed as a cattle merchant. He remains there silently, as the Reader— intoning the thoughts of the Soldier—blames this malignant figure for the loss of the violin and the youth's present misfortunes. Music sounds, the curtain is lowered, and then it rises again. The scene is the same, the Devil in the identical position. Suddenly the voice of the Soldier is heard in the wings. He rushes onto the stage, sword in hand, ready to attack the Devil, who remains unruffled. Urging the youth to speak more politely, Satan orders him to throw away his sword and put on civilian clothes. The Soldier obeys. Then, at the prompting of the Devil, he searches in his bag for the magic book. At the same time the Fiend draws the violin from his pocket, observing that each of them holds the object which does him the most good, and leads the Soldier away. The stage is empty for a moment; the same music sounds that has been heard at the beginning of the scene; and the curtain falls.

Here the Reader takes up the story, relating how—through the power of the infernal book—Joseph became rich, possessed everything he wanted except the happiness which is enjoyed by common people and cannot be bought. Crying out (through the voice of the Reader) that he has been robbed by the Devil, the Soldier—now a stockbroker—is imagined to be doing business by telephone, jotting down orders from all over the world, powerful in everything except the regulation of his destiny.

SCENE THREE: The Soldier, prosperously dressed, is seated at his desk, reading the magic book. The Devil—disguised as a poor old woman

—calls him. Violently astonished, the Soldier drops the book and listens as the pretended beggar, who creeps onto the scene, offers to sell him odds and ends from her trinket bag. Among the filthy souvenirs that she produces are a holy medal, the picture of somebody's girl, and a little violin.

The Soldier rises, rushes toward the Devil, and asks the price of the fiddle. The Devil smilingly tells him to try it first and discuss the price later.

As he seizes the instrument, the youth tries to play but no sound comes out. He turns wildly, but the Devil has disappeared. Now, in an access of rage, the Soldier hurls the violin into the wings with all his strength. He goes back to his desk, takes the Devil's book, and tears it into a thousand pieces.

PART TWO

Music is sounded, the same march as was heard at the beginning of the play; and the Reader, too, resumes the cadence of his opening remarks. He speaks again of a soldier who once marched homeward on fifteen days' leave, but now travels through the world trying to shun the influence of the Devil. By tearing up the infernal book, he has escaped the riches that were corroding him and taken refuge in a foreign town, where the daughter of the reigning King is suffering from a strange malady. This Princess does not sleep, eat, or speak. She has been promised in marriage to anyone who may cure her. In the words of the Reader, Joseph decides to undertake the task.

As the royal march sounds, the Devil appears before the inner curtain

in full evening dress. Holding the little violin over his heart, he bows to the audience and goes off gaily.

SCENE FOUR: The curtain rises on a room in the palace. The Soldier is seated at a table with a deck of cards before him, a pitcher and a glass at his side. He suggests the Reader himself, who is also seated at a side table with the same kind of cards, the identical pitcher and glass. Thumbing through the deck to read his luck, the Soldier is sure he will win the

Princess. He feels, however, that the Devil is somewhere near and shows no surprise when the Fiend strikes up an air on the violin.

At this point the Reader intervenes, urging the Soldier to gamble with the Devil and lose everything. Satan is so greedy that he will seize the externals, ignore the soul within, and let the youth slip from his grasp. The Devil, who does not hear this aside, gloats over his approaching victory. He matches cards with the Soldier, wins every hand, and grows increasingly weak. At last the youth springs at him, forcing him to drink until his power has ebbed, and then snatches the violin. As the Soldier plays triumphantly, the curtain is lowered.

Music sounds, over which the Reader announces that the youth will cure the Princess. The curtain rises again and the royal bedroom is seen, with the girl lying motionless on her couch. Suddenly the Soldier enters. As he plays his violin, the Princess opens her eyes, turns to him, and smiles. She rises from her bed and dances first a tango, then a waltz, and finally a bit of ragtime.

The music ends; the Soldier takes the Princess in his arms; but they are interrupted by horrible cries from the wings. The Devil enters in traditional Satanic dress, leaping on all fours. The beast crawls about the Soldier, alternately begging for the violin and trying to snatch it. As the Soldier lashes out with the bow, the Princess takes refuge behind him. Furiously, the Devil increases his efforts until the youth has the presence of mind to play the fiddle. The Devil is forced to dance—a

grotesque, horrible performance, at the end of which he falls exhausted. At a sign from the Soldier, the Princess—no longer afraid—grasps the

Devil by one of his paws and helps the Soldier drag him off. Then the lovers return to the center of the room, absorbed in each other. As fantastic music sounds, the Devil peers through a doorway and whispers of revenge to come. So long as the Soldier remains within the limits of the kingdom, the Fiend implies, no harm can reach him; but once the youth sets foot outside, he will be Satan's prey. More music sounds, now slow and sustained. The curtain falls and the Reader takes up the burden of the tale.

He informs the audience of certain conversations between the Princess and her lover. The girl wants to know more of the Soldier's past, is anxious to see the village where he was born and where his mother still lives. The Soldier answers that such a trip would be forbidden; but, in the face of her pleading, he agrees to go, hoping that this time, unlike the last, his mother will recognize him and come back to the palace to live with him and his bride.

At this moment, as the Reader is narrating the Soldier's tale, the Devil passes before the lowered inner curtain in a magnificent red costume. He disappears, and the Reader goes on to reveal that the Soldier and the Princess have left the kingdom, that they are about to reach the youth's home town, where the Princess will await her lover at the frontier. Once more the Devil passes before the curtain, which now rises.

SCENE FIVE: The Soldier's native village is seen, as in the second tableau, with a steeple in the distance. The frontier is near by. As soon as the Soldier crosses it, the Devil falls upon him. Now it is Satan who holds the violin. He plays it and marches triumphantly. The Soldier follows with lowered head, stopping for a moment as someone calls to

him from the distance—but the Devil is adamant. The Fiend and his prey leave the stage, the inner curtain is lowered, and the music of *L'Histoire d'un Soldat* ends on a page of Satanic triumph during which only the drums are heard, with the solo percussion player—almost like the Devil himself—leaping from one instrument to another.

H.P.

THIS SYMBOLIC ballet in four scenes, with music by Carlos Chávez, scenery and costumes by Diego Rivera, and book by both these distinguished Mexicans, was given its world première by the Philadelphia Grand Opera Company at the Metropolitan Opera House, Philadelphia, in November, 1932. The choreography was by Catherine Littlefield. Leopold Stokowski conducted, and leading roles were danced by Dorothie Littlefield as the Siren and the Flapper, Alexis Dolinoff as H.P., and Douglas Coudy as King Banana. The project was intended as a medium for the diffusion of modern Mexican culture.

According to Diego Rivera, the theme of the ballet represented a cross section of the contemporary life and interests binding the two Americas. Its title and general idea were conceived by Carlos Chávez in 1926 and worked out subsequently with Mr. Rivera. Chávez composed the music during the following year, rescoring *H.P.* for large symphony orchestra in 1931.

In presenting the relationship of the tropics—producer of raw materials—with the northern regions, which use these products to manufacture various commodities, the ballet tries to establish one region's dependence on another, arguing—in terms of dance—that the North requires the lifeblood of the tropics just as the tropics seek the finished goods of the North.

SCENE ONE

Modern Man, personified by the name H.P. (significant not only of horsepower but of that dynamic energy which controls whole worlds), is at the height of his strength and inventiveness. He expresses the boundless potentialities contained within himself, his eagerness to conquer the unknown forces that surround him.

SCENE TWO

A cargo ship is seen at sea, symbolizing the commerce between North and South. A dance of the sailors on board denotes activity and physical force. Mermaids of the tropical seas come over the side of the ship, conveying their special brand of sensuality. An all-embracing rhythm joins the forces of the two regions—sailors and mermaids—in a syncopated bacchanale.

SCENE THREE

Here the abundance of the tropical earth is seen. The fruit trees sway in the breeze, the fruits themselves grow animated as the natives pass by, peddling their merchandise. Sailors from the northern ship come ashore to gather cargo, and the scene takes on increasing life as the men load the produce on board.

SCENE FOUR

In contrast to the serenity of the tropics, the northern city of industry is seen, with its skyscrapers and great machines. The raw materials of the world are assembled here to be manufactured for the needs of civilization. Economic forces keep the pattern going, but Man revolts against material values and returns to his longings for the products of earth. Human beings and raw materials then join in a final jubilant dance.

The Incredible Flutist

This BALLET in one act, with choreography by Hans Wiener, was first presented by Mr. Wiener's company of dancers at a "Pops" Concert, Symphony Hall, Boston, in May, 1938, with Arthur Fiedler conducting. Walter Piston composed the music. A concert suite from *The Incredible Flutist*, about one-half the length of the original score, was first performed by the Pittsburgh Symphony Orchestra under the direction of Fritz Reiner in November, 1940.

A slender story about a village in carnival time animates a work which has been designed chiefly for purposes of color. As the siesta hour in the market place of a small, unspecified village draws to a close, vendors appear, open their shops, and receive their customers. Suddenly a march is heard—the circus has come to town. Various characters enter, associated traditionally with the Big Show: jugglers, a snake dancer, a monkey trainer, a crystal gazer, and—as headliner—a flutist who is able to charm all of the circus animals with his playing. This star performer also dates a girl of the town for eight o'clock that evening in the square.

The hour arrives; but the flutist and the girl are not alone, for the dusk has brought out several other couples, including a wealthy widow of the town and a suitor who has been pursuing her unsuccessfully for some time past. In the charged atmosphere of the evening, the widow yields, only to be discovered in the arms of her admirer by the neighbors. The flutist, however, saves the situation, sets the widow to rights with the town, dances a lyrical measure with his girl, and—as the circus band strikes up again—joins the waiting procession of troupers and leaves the village.

Photo: Baron of London   *Courtesy Ballet Theatre*

SILHOUETTE FROM THE FIRST MOVEMENT OF INTERPLAY

Interplay

THIS BALLET in four movements, with choreography by Jerome Robbins, was first produced at the Ziegfeld Theatre, New York, in June, 1945, as part of Billy Rose's "Concert Varieties." The cast of eight dancers included Janet Reed, Muriel Bentley, John Kriza, Michael Kidd, and Mr. Robbins. Musically, the new work was based on Morton Gould's "American Concertette" * for piano and orchestra which had been given its première with José Iturbi as piano soloist and Mr. Gould conducting on the Cresta Blanca radio program of August 25, 1943. The décor for this production of *Interplay* as part of "Concert Varieties"—with a bluish gray backdrop, overalls for the boys, and play-clothes for the girls—was designed by Carl Kent.

The new work soon entered the repertory of Ballet Theatre and was given by that group for the first time at the Metropolitan Opera House in October, 1945, with Miss Reed, Miss Bentley, and Mr. Kriza in their original parts. On this occasion, Fernando Alonso, Harold Lang, and Tommy Rall were added to the ensemble. New scenery was designed by Oliver Smith, multicolored in nature, and new costumes by Irene Sharaff. As before, *Interplay* achieved an immediate success, Mr. Robbins' witty and resourceful choreography sharing honors with Mr. Gould's piquant music.

* The music is now known in concert form by the title of the ballet.

A program note for this work labels it "a short ballet in four movements in which there is a constant play between the classical ballet steps
and the contemporary spirit in which they are danced." In simpler language, this is a series of shifts between traditional dance and jive.

FIRST MOVEMENT

The opening number consists of salutations and greetings. First one
boy comes on stage, followed by three others; then a girl, another girl,
a couple—until all eight performers are in place and dancing together.
No footlights are used in this movement and there is a unique effect

Photo: Alfredo Valente   JOHN KRIZA AND JANET REED   Courtesy Ballet Theatre

of silhouette as, at one point, the dancers rush forward to the edge of the stage and are outlined by the lights from overhead.

SECOND MOVEMENT

Gavotte

Originally subtitled "Horseplay," when the ballet was first given at the Ziegfeld Theatre, this episode brings an amusing solo for one of the male dancers, following in its choreographic line the droll interplay of the score between old gavotte style and modern jazz. Most of its steps provide a burlesque on the hallowed solo number of ballet tradition.

THIRD MOVEMENT

Blues

The ideological content here is strictly boy-girl, to a background of modern "blues," although the style is that of a classical *pas de deux*. Mr. Robbins has kept his dancers' basic movements in harmony with ballet fundamentals; but the true character of this duo—as shaped by the nature of the music—is nostalgically modern.

FOURTH MOVEMENT

All eight performers share actively in the finale. As an energetic theme is announced by the solo piano, they compete one with the other in

dancing skill, each solo variation more difficult than the last. At the end of this team play, the girls run forward, stand with legs outstretched, and provide just enough space for the boys to slide under, along the floor, toward the footlights. There is a quick blackout.

Iron Foundry

THIS BALLET in one act, with choreography by Adolph Bolm, was originally prepared as an interlude for the film *The Mad Genius*, starring John Barrymore. With most of the dance eliminated in the final screen play, the work had its first complete performance at the Hollywood Bowl in August, 1932, with Elise Reiman and Robert Bell in the leading roles. The costumes were designed by Mr. Bolm and Nicholas Remisoff. Later known as *Ballet Mécanique*, the work was presented at the Center Theatre, New York, by Ballet Theatre in January, 1940.

Iron Foundry is based on a score of the same name * by the Soviet composer Alexander V. Mossolov. Composed in 1928 shortly after Mossolov was graduated from the Moscow Conservatory, the music contains a percussive quality ideal for suggesting the tempo of industry in dance.

On a stage that represents the glowing furnace of a metalworks, groups of dancers move as units of machinery. The solo ballerina, more lyrical than the others, suggests the fascination of electricity, while her male partner, dramatically vigorous, communicates its might. All of the individual groups unite in a rhythmic climax like the throbbing of some giant piston; and the ballet closes on the spectacle of every unit of machinery combining to produce molten iron from the fiery blast.

* Known originally as *Music of the Machines*.

Jardin aux Lilas

THIS BALLET ("Lilac Garden"), with choreography by Antony Tudor, was first performed by the Ballet Club at the Mercury Theatre, London, in January, 1938. Exactly two years later, it was given its American première at the Center Theatre, New York, as part of Ballet Theatre's repertory, with the part of Caroline danced by Viola Essen, the Other Woman by Karen Conrad, and the two men by Antony Tudor and Hugh Laing. Since that time, the principal interpreters of the role of Caroline have been Alicia Markova and Nora Kaye, while the most definitive performance of the Other Woman has been offered by Maria Tallchief. Messrs. Laing and Tudor have appeared in practically all presentations of the work. One minor part, that of a jealous and then forgiving female guest, was danced memorably by Sono Osato during her stay with Ballet Theatre. The settings and costumes were designed by Hugh Stevenson.

The all-pervading musical background of *Jardin aux Lilas* is the romantic *Poème*, for solo violin and orchestra, by the French composer Ernest Chausson. So perfectly has Tudor captured the mood of the music and even extended its imaginative scope that the listener who has once seen this ballet will find it hard to hear *Poème* in concert form without constant memories of action and lighting—for the choreography matches this score color for color, with fresh expressive power at every climax. The solo violin part—effective enough in symphonic performance—becomes, in the danced version, a kind of Greek chorus commenting on and enriching the tragic situation on stage. The first of Tudor's ballets to win popularity in America, *Jardin aux Lilas* remains a distinctive fusion of music and dance.

A formal evening party, in the style of the early 1900's, is taking place in a garden ringed with lilac bushes. One of the guests advances: Caroline, a beautiful young woman about to enter on a marriage of convenience. Although she has come to the party escorted by her fiancé—a stern, withdrawn man—she is driven to seek her real lover there and bid him farewell.

As Caroline steals through the garden in search of him, the solo violin introduces one of the principal motives of *Poème,* a theme which in the

NORA KAYE, HUGH LAING, AND MARIA TALLCHIEF

Lento e misterioso

ballet is made to speak of longing. The latter part of this melody is often used independently, telling of a resignation bitterly arrived at, of the renouncement of happiness.

Lento e misterioso

The entire ballet—an essay in frustration—takes form in a series of entrances and exits on the part of the two lovers, thwarted in their last farewell by the appearance of Caroline's fiancé and then by the intervention of the Other Woman, smoldering and passionate—the opposite of the gentle Caroline. This second woman has been in love with the fiancé and cannot bring herself to give him up. The man, outwardly conventional, is torn between desire for this ex-mistress and a sense of social urgency that drives him to marry Caroline. Intermittently, the two couples are approached by others who dance about them to a rythmic figure which might have been created expressly by Chausson—so

Animato

mp
(flottato)

strongly does Tudor's choreography stem from the music—to trace the patterns of the dancers as they move idly back and forth across the darkened garden.

Whenever these intruders disappear, a sustained and impassioned theme is heard in the orchestra and one or another of the pairs of lovers passes briefly before the gaze of the audience. As Caroline is about to

Allegro

p

fall into the arms of the young man whom she loves, one of the women guests dashes jealously through the garden, threatens to denounce her, but—reminded by another guest that this girl has been marked for their own unhappy group—makes an impulsive gesture of sympathy and runs off.

And still the lovers can snatch only the briefest kiss before they part. Caroline's lover offers her a spray of lilacs. She takes the flowers sadly, and her fiancé comes from the house bearing her wrap. While the Other Woman looks on in gloomy resignation, Caroline—glancing back wistfully—leaves with her future husband, and the cycle of unhappiness has run its course.

VASLAV NIJINSKY

Jeux

THIS BRIEF work was first given at the Théâtre des Champs-Élysées, Paris, by the Diaghilev company in May, 1913. It is notable chiefly for the score, which Claude Debussy composed for it, and for certain aspects of the scenario, which were to mirror modern life and its problems rather than the worlds of Russian fairy tale or abstract movement, which had dominated ballet up to that time.

With choreography by Nijinsky, setting by Bakst, and—as a revolutionary note—costumes by Paquin, *Jeux* was a bold break-away from stereotyped plots. It marked the beginning of a trend in Diaghilev's repertoire toward contemporary subjects which took firmer hold a decade later in the topical ballets by Nijinsky's sister, Bronislava, *Les Biches* and *Train Bleu*. It also anticipated, in the complex relationship of its three characters, a phase of that communal type of romance which was to blossom twenty years later in Noel Coward's *Design for Living* and in certain of the ballets of Balanchine.

Nijinsky took the part of the Young Man at the première of *Jeux*; Thamar Karsavina was the First Young Girl; and Ludmila Schollar, the Second. Pierre Monteux conducted a score that has not yet gained adequate recognition for its qualities of color and of communicative emotion. This music is performed occasionally in concert. The ballet was recently revived by Ballet Theatre, with Igor Youskevitch, Nora Kaye, and Norma Vance. The choreography was by William Dollar.

The curtain rises on an empty park at dusk. At first the orchestra is vague and restrained, then suddenly brilliant, as a tennis ball bounces on the scene and a young man in tennis outfit leaps across the park. He is gone in a flash.

Then two young girls appear, timid and curious. They seem to be looking for a spot in which to exchange confidences. First, one of the girls—moved by the atmosphere of the park at twilight and the emotional release that it brings—dances alone. When she has finished, the other takes up in turn. Debussy has underscored this episode with music of a very special charm.

Suddenly the two girls are startled by the rustling of leaves. The young man in the sports outfit has been standing behind the trees, following their movements. Now he comes out to face them.

The girls want to flee, but the youth catches them and leads them back gently. He begins to dance; and the first girl, caught in the spell of rhythm and dusk, runs toward him. They dance together in romantic mood.

He demands a kiss. She escapes and then rejoins him, yielding. Meanwhile, the second girl looks on spitefully, showing her jealousy in an ironic, mocking dance.

The young man follows her movements with curiosity; then he abandons the first girl, unable to resist the desire to dance with the second. She still mocks him as they start to the strains of a waltz, but soon their

dance grows tender. The girl runs off and hides behind a clump of trees. The youth, too, is lost to sight for a moment as he pursues the girl. Then both figures reappear, taking up their dance.

In their infatuation with each other, they have neglected the first girl, now restless and chagrined, who hides her face in her hands. It is only when she starts to leave that the dancing pair comes to her side. The second girl tries to hold her back, but she will listen to nothing. At last she falls into the arms of her friend. The young man intervenes, gently separating them.

They look about them. The beauty of the night, which has come on, puts them into a fantastic mood. The three of them dance; the music grows phosphorescent.

The young man, with a passionate gesture, unites their three heads; a triple kiss sends them into ecstasy. Abruptly, a tennis ball lands at their feet. Surprised and frightened, all three leap away and disappear in the depths of the park.

GROUP FROM JEUX D'ENFANTS

Jeux d'Enfants

THIS MINIATURE ballet in one act, with book by Boris Kochno and choreography by Léonide Massine, was first produced at the Théâtre de Monte Carlo in April, 1932, with Tatiana Riabouchinska in the principal role of the Child, David Lichine as the Traveler, and Tamara Toumanova as the Top. Its American première by the Ballet Russe de Monte Carlo took place at the St. James Theatre, New York, in April, 1934. Scenery and costumes were by Joan Miró. The music was based on the *Petite Suite d'Orchestre* of Georges Bizet.

Although the subject of *Jeux d'Enfants*—animated toys and their foibles—was hardly novel, Massine's dance patterns were fresh and inventive. The work derived special charm, too, from the fantastic scenery of Miró, which emphasized the bright, enameled surfaces of the toys as they might appear in the mind of a child.

A little girl enters her nursery late at night and sees the toys come to life, driven into motion by two governing spirits. A top spins about; then rocking horses, shuttlecock rackets, amazons, sportsmen, and a traveler begin to move. The traveler especially attracts the little girl, who dances with him. Soon afterward, the youngster is equally drawn to one of the sportsmen, who does magnificent setting-up exercises. The top, highly jealous, spins between the girl and her new lover, driving them apart. Suddenly the dawn appears, and the governing spirits restore peace to the nursery as the toys resume their state of immobility.

Labyrinth

LABYRINTH—the second of three collaborations by Léonide Massine with Salvador Dali (the first was *Bacchanale,* the third, *Mad Tristan*)—had its world première at the Metropolitan Opera House in October, 1941. The cast was a strong one, with André Eglevsky as Theseus, Tamara Toumanova as Ariadne, and Frederic Franklin as the Minotaur. George Zoritch and Chris Volkoff danced a memorable duo—the one outstanding bit of choreography in the work—as Castor and Pollux. The music employed was the great C Major Symphony of Schubert.

Photo: Maurice Seymour   *Courtesy Museum of Modern Art*
DOROTHY ETHERIDGE AND IGOR YOUSKEVITCH

ANDRÉ EGLEVSKY AND TAMARA TOUMANOVA

Short on choreographic inventiveness and swamped by Dali's massive scenery, *Labyrinth* represented, along with *Bacchanale,* one of the lower points in Massine's creative career. The perverse costumes, devitalized dance patterns, and overelaborate backdrops created an impression, as in *Bacchanale,* of decadence.

The program book of the Ballet Russe de Monte Carlo bore the following annotation at the première: "In *Labyrinth,* one revives the eternal myth of the aesthetic and ideologic confusion which characterizes romanticism, and especially, in the highest degree, that of our epoch. The 'thread of Ariadne,' by which Theseus succeeds in finding the exit from the Labyrinth, symbolizes the thread of the continuity of classicism —the saviour. All romanticism merely seeks more or less dramatically its 'thread of Ariadne,' of classicism."

Ironically enough, this ballet trapped the choreographer, Léonide Massine—a romanticist himself—in its own neoclassical labyrinth. Massine's collaborator, Dali—unlike the considerate Ariadne—had left no guiding thread.

In the first of this ballet's four scenes, which correspond to the four movements of the Schubert symphony, the three Fates (symbolizing Destiny) attempt to keep Theseus (symbol of History) from approaching the Labyrinth. Theseus, however, overpowers his destiny and enters. The second scene shows Theseus, led by Ariadne—who, from a remote height, unwinds the thread that guides him—in his battle with the Minotaur. He kills the monster (symbol of Revolution) and, thanks to the "thread of Ariadne" (Tradition), finds an exit from the cave. The third movement, a joyous scherzo, celebrates the liberation of the people. In the finale—which employs a striking backdrop of the sea—Theseus abandons Ariadne and departs for new adventures, borne along by the waves which symbolize the march of History.

Isolated moments of Massine's genius managed to filter through this mass of philosophic double-talk and scenic weightiness. Certain passages of the scene within the Labyrinth, the jovial cockfight of the scherzo, the excellent *pas de deux* for Castor and Pollux in the finale, indicated that the choreographer could rise above his scenario; but rarely did this ballet seem more than a grinning travesty on the music which formed its background, one of the noblest of symphonies.

Mother Goose

THIS SYMBOLIC ballet in one act, based on the orchestral suite *Ma Mère l'Oye* by Maurice Ravel, was first performed by the American Concert Ballet at the Central Needle Trades Auditorium, New York, in October, 1943. Todd Bolender designed the choreography. Among the principal dancers were Mary Jane Shea, Lillian Lanese, Zoya Leporsky, Yvonne Patterson, and Francisco Moncion. Subsequently Mr. Bolender revised the entire ballet, except for the episode of Beauty and the Beast. His new version was first presented by the New York City Ballet at the City Center in November, 1948, with Marie-Jeanne, Francisco Moncion, Mr. Bolender, Dick Beard, and Beatrice Tompkins in the leading roles.

Written by Ravel in 1908 as a set of four-hand piano pieces for the pleasure of two gifted children, Mimi and Jean Godebski, *Ma Mère l'Oye*—inspired by Charles Perrault's collection of fairy tales by the same name—was transcribed for orchestra by the composer two years later. Though given in choreographic form,* with book by Ravel, at the Théâtre des Arts, Paris, in January, 1912, the work is known chiefly as a concert suite. Its five movements, played without pause, are: "Pavane of the Sleeping Beauty"; "Hop O' My Thumb"; "Little Ugly One, Empress of the Pagodas"; "Beauty and the Beast"; and "The Enchanted Garden." The scoring for small orchestra—no brasses are used, except two horns which blend with the wind choir—conveys a marvelously varied sense of color.

Mr. Bolender, in adapting this suite to his needs, has used very little of Ravel's own program, nor has he kept the sequence of movements inviolate.† His purpose has been to create, on the same imaginative plane as Ravel's music, a ballet that is linked to the score through similarity of mood rather than of program.

---

* This early ballet version, an afterthought on the part of Ravel, disappeared from the stage almost at once. It was a choreographic translation of the Sleeping Beauty story and contained an added musical number at the opening, associated with the whirring of the spinning wheel and the accident to the princess as she pricks her finger. The maiden is laid to rest on her couch to the strains of the Pavane; she dreams of fantastic episodes from Fairyland, which are enacted during the next three movements; and, in the finale, she is awakened by Prince Charming.

† "The Enchanted Garden" is played second, instead of last, in Bolender's version, while the action is brought to an end with "Beauty and the Beast."

The choreographer's thesis for *Mother Goose* is: "In dreams, one is haunted by images that take many forms to mask a single reality."

FIRST MOVEMENT

Pavane of the Sleeping Beauty

A young girl enters, dreaming, her head in the clouds. Presently a grown woman appears, to the same arched line of music, grave and

wistful, bearing a mask and a fan. She walks to a seat at the side of the stage as if to take her place in a box and watch the panorama of her youth. For the first time, the woman notices the young girl—her previous self. The two people glance at each other, turn away, and the woman's memories begin.

FINALE

The Enchanted Garden

The young girl, dancing the years that are gone, keeps trying to find someone who will fill a void in her life. She wants to join the other couples passing by, but they ignore her. Pulsing with loneliness, she falls to the ground and the couples disappear.

SECOND MOVEMENT

Hop o' My Thumb *

A sensitive young man enters with a bird that dominates him. This creature—danced by a ballerina with long, enmeshing hair—alternately possessive and disdainful, is a symbol of the young man's weakness, his dependence on outside values instead of his own spiritual resources. The youth is in love with the bird.

As the young girl, still seeking companionship, tries to win the young

---

* Ravel's own program note for this movement contains a quotation from a fairy tale by Charles Perrault: "He believed he would easily find his way back by means of his bread crumbs, which he had scattered as he passed along, but to his surprise he could not find a single crumb, for the birds had come and eaten them up."

man's friendship, the bird leaves him abruptly. He goes after it, searching, and forsakes the girl, who again stands alone.

THIRD MOVEMENT

Little Ugly One, Empress of the Pagodas *

To the sound of exotic music, a Chinese Prince, surrounded by a

group of maidens, is playing in a garden. The young girl suddenly appears, masked, and the Prince goes toward her. As the maidens lift the
mask from her face, she dances with the boy; but this friendship—like the
others—knows no fulfillment. The Prince is led away by the maidens,
and the girl leaps desperately into the arms of the oncoming Beast.

FOURTH MOVEMENT

Beauty and the Beast

After the first embrace, she is repelled by the Beast and leaves him.
The animal is filled with love for the girl; he almost dies when she has
gone. As if in a vision, the girl sees him from afar, turns to the seated
woman for guidance, and accepts from her a ring, symbol of constancy.
Now she returns to the Beast and, in a reversal of the first embrace, takes
him in her arms. He rises, and she accepts him as her lover. In a miraculous transformation, the Beast removes his mask, places it on the
ground, and is revealed as a handsome young prince.

Clouds, denoting the thickening of memory, start moving across the
scene. The seated woman rises sadly, moves toward the Beast's mask for
a final glance; then, as if the recollection were too painful, turns and
goes off in the opposite direction from that in which the girl and her
lover have disappeared.

* From "The Green Serpent," by Marie Catherine d'Aulnoy, in which a princess
—rendered ugly through a witch's spell—marries a reptile who has also been cursed,
and goes with him to rule over a land of living pagodas made of precious stones.

FROM THE BALLET CARAVAN PRODUCTION

Mozartiana

THIS BALLET-DIVERTISSEMENT, with choreography by George Balanchine, was first produced by Mr. Balanchine's own company, Les Ballets 1933, during their season at the Théâtre des Champs-Élysées, Paris. Its American première was offered by the American Ballet at the Avery Memorial Theatre, Hartford, Connecticut, in December, 1934. The same group presented *Mozartiana* at the Adelphi Theatre, New York, in March, 1935, and the work went over into the repertory of the Ballet Russe de Monte Carlo exactly ten years later at the New York City Center. In the Ballet Russe performances, the principal parts were danced by

Alexandra Danilova, Frederic Franklin, Dorothy Etheridge, and Yura Lazovsky. Christian Bérard provided the original décor.

The choreography for *Mozartiana* was inspired by Tchaikovsky's orchestral work of the same name. In 1887 the Russian composer, who revered the music of Mozart, finished a suite for small orchestra based on lesser-known melodies by that master. The first two movements, "Gigue" and "Menuet," came from a set of twelve piano pieces. The "Preghiera," which follows, was derived—indirectly through a piano transcription by Franz Liszt—from Mozart's motet, "Ave Verum Corpus." The finale of the suite was based on a set of variations written by Mozart to a tune from Gluck's comic opera, *The Pilgrim from Mecca.* In line with the affinity of Balanchine for the music of Tchaikovsky—whose rhythms, lines, and sonorities accord so readily with the needs of classical dance —his use of this score for ballet was both logical and desirable. The result was ingratiating.

The curtain rises on a sunlit plaza, rococo in its architectural mood. Two men and a girl are seen dancing a gigue.

Photo: *Maurice Seymour*   Courtesy *Museum of Modern Art*
GISELLA CACCIALANZA

Now eight girls in red enter to the music of a court minuet. After an elaborate ensemble, four of them leave the scene and the others remain to greet a white-robed figure borne in on a litter topped by black plumes. The sacred music of the "Ave Verum Corpus" follows, as the dancer in white moves solemnly to its measures.

The climax of the ballet arrives with a closing adagio, containing a magnificent *pas de deux* for the two principals, and a final set of variations on a folk theme, during which gypsies in green and lavender—

their skirts sewn with coins—flash across the stage. At the end, the mass of dancers disappears, leaving—with a kind of inevitable and poetic symmetry—the three performers of the opening gigue posed as at the beginning.

Namouna

This ballet in two acts and three scenes, with choreography by Lucien Petipa and book by M. Petipa in collaboration with Charles Nuitter, was first produced at the Paris Opéra in February, 1882. The musical score was composed by Édouard Lalo. Rita Sangalli appeared in the title role, with Louis Mérante as Don Ottavio. Like *La Source*, whose book was also written by Nuitter, *Namouna* more often suggests opera than dance in the complexity of its plot.

PROLOGUE

Count Ottavio, dashing gallant of the seventeenth century, is playing at dice in a great hall on the island of Corfu. His opponent is Adriani, a shipowner of glowering appearance and dubious background. On losing round after round with Ottavio, Adriani stakes his ship and then his most beautiful captive, Namouna—who enters the hall heavily veiled— against a final victory. Ill luck stays with him, and he loses everything, including the slave.

The chivalrous Ottavio not only sets Namouna free but offers her the ship and other property lost by Adriani. In gratitude, the veiled woman divides a flower with Ottavio—symbolizing a bond between them—and departs.

ACT ONE

A large public square may be seen on the island, with a palace at one side and the sea in the background. It is dawn; Ottavio is serenading his fiancée, Hélène. Just as she appears at the window, Adriani enters the square. Still brooding over his losses, he begins a quarrel by striking the musicians in Ottavio's employ. Their master challenges him to a duel. As both men draw their swords, they are interrupted by a veiled figure dancing between them with unceasing vigilance. It is Namouna, whose interruption of the duel, cast in adroit choreographic form, marks the high point of the ballet.

Allegro vivace

At last the fighters are separated, the veiled woman disappears, and Hélène—her jealousy roused by this strange figure—goes to meet her lover. Ottavio reassures the girl of his affection and, after a tender duet, escorts her to the entrance of her palace, when suddenly he is set upon by cutthroats.

Namouna is no longer there to intervene; but, having learned of Adriani's plans, she has ordered the men from her ship to Ottavio's rescue. They arrive in time to save the Count and insist that he follow them abroad. Curious to know who has sent them, Ottavio agrees—just in time to escape a last attack by Adriani as the vessel leaves the port.

ACT TWO

Namouna, still veiled, arrives with Ottavio on an island belonging to Ali, a slave-dealer. Finding the women whose captivity she once shared still held in bondage, she buys their freedom. Then she raises her veil, reveals herself to her comrades, and, for the first time, enables Ottavio to admire her beauty. When the Count asks Namouna why she has saved him, the half-flower in her hand provides the answer.

Suddenly, Adriani's ruffians land on the island and take Ottavio captive. Instead of doing battle, Namouna has a more inventive idea: to sap the morale of these pirates through charm. Always willing to help, her women friends disarm the intruders with beguiling dances. Namouna herself waits on Adriani and fills his cup with wine until his strength and senses disappear.

The ruse is at an end, and Namouna dashes with her lover for the shore. Just as they reach it, Adriani regains his self-control sufficiently to aim with his pistol; but he is stabbed by a retainer of Namouna and falls dead. The boat containing Ottavio and the beauty who has saved him puts out safely to sea.

Les Noces

(THE WEDDING)

THIS SERIES of Russian choreographic scenes, with text and music by Igor Stravinsky, was first presented in June, 1923, at the Théâtre de la Gaîté-Lyrique, Paris, by the Diaghilev company. Bronislava Nijinska was the choreographer; Nathalie Gontcharova created the scenery and costumes; and Ernest Ansermet conducted. The work itself had been started in Switzerland during the First World War, when Stravinsky's patriotic feeling, roused at being distant from his country, led him to a deep study of Russian folk poems. During this period, he wrote three shorter pieces in old Slavic style, and worked at *Les Noces* ("The Wedding") in the winter of 1914–15. The score was dedicated to Sergei Diaghilev.

The completion of *Les Noces* was held up for some time by the problem of a suitable orchestration. Stravinsky's ballet represented a Russian folk wedding with implications of racial memory, starkness as well as gaiety. To evoke the unchanging, ageless ritual, the composer thought at first of using a pianola, electrically driven harmonium, and two Hungarian cymbalons, among other instruments. He gave up this plan because of difficulties in synchronization, finally deciding on a vocal quartet, chorus, four pianists, and percussion orchestra including four timpani, xylophone, cymbals, tambourine, triangle, bell, and various types of drums.* The effect of this orchestra is unique in its sense of timelessness, of color without deliberate "atmosphere."

Musically, *Les Noces* belongs to the line of *L'Oiseau de Feu, Petrouchka,* and *Le Sacre du Printemps,* being Stravinsky's last work whose roots sprang from the old Russian romantic traditions. Here, as in *Le Sacre,* the composer indulged in great metrical freedom, in revolutionary and sometimes arbitrary rhythmical construction; but the idiom was none the less personal, the approach as intensely subjective as in his earliest ballets. It was after this score—marking the climax of the "dynamic" period in his career—that Stravinsky turned to classicism and objectivity.

Although the choreography remains a vital part of *Les Noces,* the piece is in essence a dramatic cantata. Stravinsky had intended to mount it in the same manner as *L'Histoire d'un Soldat*: that is, with the instrumental apparatus on the stage side by side with singers and dancers;

---

* "Such a sound combination . . . was the necessary outcome of the music itself, and it was in no wise suggested by a desire to imitate the sounds of popular fetes of this kind. . . ."—Stravinsky: *Autobiography.*

but Diaghilev disapproved and banished the orchestra to the obscurity of the pit.

A fine French version of the composer's text, by C. F. Ramuz, was commissioned for the published score, in which the translator faithfully reproduced the word patterns of the original. The style of the text is not too unlike certain passages in the poetry of Gertrude Stein, with its insistence on repeated rhythms and acoustical imagery.

The American première of *Les Noces,* in concert form, took place in February, 1926, under the auspices of the International Composers' Guild at Aeolian Hall, New York. In April, 1929, the League of Composers presented the work in a stage version at the Metropolitan Opera House, with Leopold Stokowski conducting and with choreography by Elizaveta Anderson-Ivantzoff. Among the solo singers were Nina Koshetz and Sophie Braslau. All four pianists at this performance have since become famous as composers: Aaron Copland, Louis Gruenberg, Marc Blitzstein, and Frederick Jacobi. Among the dancers were Valentina Koshuba, Jacques Cartier, and Don Oscar Becque. Sergei Soudeikine designed the settings and costumes. Another production of *Les Noces,* offered by the Ballet Russe de Monte Carlo, was given at the Metropolitan seven years later. This time the original choreography of Nijinska and settings by Gontcharova were used. Among the dancers were Irina Baronova and Yurek Shabelevsky.

In all of its performances here, the music commanded the utmost admiration. Nijinska's choreography, however, has aroused an unusual amount of controversy.

SCENE ONE

Even before the curtain rises, the chant of the bride is heard, elemental and forceful. A primitive peasant house is revealed, with the

bride, her mother, and her friends assembled in a group of simple severity. The bride bids her friends bind her hair; her mother helps in the preparations for the wedding.

SCENE TWO

At the home of the groom, the young man's father and friends help him dress, shine the buckles on his shoes, wish him well.

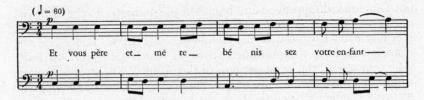

Et vous père et mé re bé nis sez votre en-fant

SCENE THREE

The bride is about to leave her house, and her mother, father and friends bid her farewell. Everyone goes off; then the mothers of the bride and groom return from opposite sides of the room, mourning the loss of their children. As they depart, the empty stage is eloquent of the void that has overtaken both families.

SCENE FOUR

There is boisterous revelry at the wedding festival. The bride's mother leads her to the groom. A friend of the young married couple chooses a man and wife among the guests to warm the bridal bed. The newlyweds embrace. Then they are conducted to the bed, and left alone. The door of the house is closed from the outside, while the two fathers and mothers install themselves on a bench before the door, the center of the neighbors' attention. The curtain falls slowly as the ritual reaches its climax, a primitive mixture of rejoicing and solemnity.

Photo: Fred Fehl

MARKOVA AND DOLIN AS THE SUGAR-PLUM FAIRY AND THE PRINCE

The Nutcracker

(CASSE-NOISETTE)

THIS GRAND ballet in two acts and three scenes, with choreography by Lev Ivanov, was first produced at the Mariinsky Theatre, St. Petersburg, in December, 1892. The book, also by Ivanov, stems from "The Nutcracker and the King of the Mice," one of the collection of fantastic tales by E. T. A. Hoffmann, German romanticist of the early nineteenth century. Dramatically, the story lines have not been strictly maintained but serve rather as pretext for an elaborate scenic spectacle, semiabstract in feeling. At the first performances in St. Petersburg, Antonietta dell' Era appeared in the leading role of the Sugar-Plum Fairy, and Paul Gerdt danced the part of the Prince. The work was given its first full presentation in the United States by the Ballet Russe de Monte Carlo at the Fifty-first Street Theatre, New York, in October, 1940, with Alicia Markova and André Eglevsky as the principals. Since then it has become an audience favorite, especially on tour, sharing with *Scheherazade* and *Gaité Parisienne* a standard place on popular programs.

There are two attractive *pas de deux* in *The Nutcracker*, and several charming solos. The ultimate worth of the ballet, however, lies not in its choreography, which is scarcely of the most imaginative sort, but in the remarkable musical score with which Tchaikovsky has colored this slight subject, investing it with a sweep and beauty more outstanding in the orchestra pit than on the stage. A concert suite has been drawn by the composer from three episodes in the ballet: (1) the overture; (2) a number of characteristic dances from the scene in the Kingdom of Sweets; (3) the Waltz of the Flowers. These in themselves, all well known, are rewarding musically; but the large balance of the score, most of which is unfamiliar to the concert listener, deserves to be heard both as pure sound and as ingenious support for dancing. It represents theatrical craftsmanship of a high quality.

ACT ONE

SCENE ONE: At the start of this fairy tale, the orchestra plays a scintillating "Overture Miniature," which sets the once-upon-a-time mood of the piece. Those who have heard the prelude in the concert

suite alone can have little idea of the heightened effect induced by the glow of the footlights, the darkened theatre. This is music written in terms of the stage. Then, as the curtain rises, the interior of a wealthy bourgeois home is revealed in the Europe of over a hundred years ago.

It is Christmas Eve. A gaily ornamented tree * stands in the center of the room, and a prosperous government official—described in the scenario as President of the Council—is welcoming his friends to a party which he and his wife are giving for their children and a group of playmates. The clock strikes nine, and a band of youngsters—the guests of honor—advance in a spirited march.

The adults look on approvingly and then turn to greet Counselor Drosselmayer, an eccentric but kindly old man, who enters bringing toys for Claire and Fritz, the President's two children. He is their godfather.

---

* In the drabness of certain current productions of *The Nutcracker,* seasonal festivities at a Bowery mission are suggested.

Photo: Alfredo Valente   Courtesy Museum of Modern Art
ALICIA ALONSO AND IGOR YOUSKEVITCH

First he offers the little girl a doll embedded in an ornamental cabbage; then he gives the boy a soldier mounted on a pie. Claire and Fritz want to carry off their toys to bed with them, for the retiring hour—ten o'clock —has struck, but their parents are adamant; it is time for them to sleep. As Claire weeps, old Drosselmayer draws still another gift from his pocket. It is in the nature of a prize to cheer the little girl: a nutcracker.

The toy is not especially handsome or valuable, yet Claire seems attracted to it at once. Her brother Fritz seizes the bauble enviously and, after handling it roughly, breaks the mechanism. Not at all concerned, he turns away and joins his friends in a noisy game. By this time, the uproar of the children has become deafening; to break it off, the President and his wife lead their older guests in a formal dance.

Before long, the time has come to say good night. Waving affectionately to the children, Drosselmayer departs, followed by the other guests. Claire and Fritz go off to bed; the President and his wife retire, and the big, old-fashioned room is left in darkness, save for the glow of the ornaments on the Christmas tree.

Suddenly, Claire tiptoes into the parlor, drawn to her broken toy. Frightened by the dark, she imagines that the glint of the doll embedded in its cabbage is the mocking smile of Drosselmayer. Then, with growing fear, she hears the scratching of mice, but is powerless to flee. The Christmas tree rises, becoming immense, and at its base an angry battle takes place between the mice and an army of gingerbread soldiers commanded by the nutcracker. Claire looks on breathlessly. At the height of the battle, she throws her shoe at the Mouse King, destroying him.

The victory which Claire has brought about breaks the spell binding the nutcracker and transforms the toy into a gallant Prince. Turning gratefully to the girl who has freed him, he invites her to follow him to the enchanted Palace of Confiturenbourg (The Fortress of Sweets). Claire consents, and the young pair set out together.

SCENE TWO: On their way to the palace, Claire and the Prince pass through a wintry landscape. The Snow King and Snow Queen appear, as flakes begin to fall, and dance a *pas de deux* of notable fantasy. (In

most modern productions of *The Nutcracker*, Claire and her escort are not brought on stage at this point. The entire scene is taken, instead, to be a projection of the little girl's imagination.) When the ice monarchs are completely surrounded by their subjects in a white, dazzling swirl, the curtain falls.

ACT TWO

The glowing interior of the Palace of Sweets may be seen, with the open sky above the terrace walls. Claire and the Prince alight from the skiff which has brought them down a rosewater stream and are hailed by the Sugar-Plum Fairy, who is ruler of the kingdom. Led by two diminutive pages with torches, the Prince comes forward to tell the Fairy how Claire saved his life. When he has done, the entire court turns to the girl and greets her with acclaim. She is ushered to a miniature throne and from there looks on at a spectacle given in her honor.

The *divertissements* which follow are the heart of the ballet, although some of them are cut or rearranged in modern performance. First there

DANILOVA AND FRANKLIN

is a number called "Chocolate," suggesting the confectionary nature of the palace itself; then "Coffee," designated in Tchaikovsky's score as

"Danse Arabe." Now comes a fantastic dance, "Tea," offered by a group

of jumping Chinese, followed by a vigorous, swinging Cossack number (trepak). The mood of the performance grows more lyrical as a little

cluster of animated reed pipes appears. Then follows a group of Merry

271

Photo: Maurice Seymour   TAMARA TOUMANOVA   Courtesy Museum of Modern Art

Andrews, and finally the spacious moment for the ensemble, which is known as the Waltz of the Flowers.

The time has come architecturally for the great *pas de deux,* danced by the Sugar-Plum Fairy and her cavalier (the same artists who appeared previously as the Ice King and Ice Queen, although no dramatic or psychological relationships are involved). The adagio, based on a

solid, well-knit musical theme and strongly contrived lifts, is followed by the usual solo variations for the dancers—of which that for the Sugar-Plum Fairy, whose melody is intoned in the orchestra by a celesta, has

become one of the best-known pages of the score.

At the climax of this *pas de deux,* the courtiers of the Kingdom of Sweets kneel in homage to the little girl who has rescued their Prince, and the ballet ends with a brilliant waltz.

L'Oiseau de Feu

(THE FIREBIRD)

PRODUCED at the Paris Opéra in June, 1910, this fairy-tale ballet in one act served as a transition in the development of Michel Fokine, the choreographer, between the overripe *Scheherazade* of that same season and the lithe *Petrouchka* which was to come a year later. Fokine himself danced the role of Ivan Tsarevich at the Paris première, with his wife, Vera Fokina, as the Princess, Karsavina as the Firebird, and Enrico Cecchetti in the part of Kastcheï. The first American performance took place at the Century Theatre, New York, in January, 1916.

The Fokine design for *The Firebird* was based on a patchwork combination of several Russian legends. Though picturesque and often imaginative, it did not represent one of this master's more lasting efforts for the stage; and indeed the work has disappeared from the active repertoire, save for an occasional revival.

The Firebird's real importance is musical, for it marked the theatrical debut of Igor Stravinsky—one of the two or three greatest composers of our century. A pupil of Rimsky-Korsakov, Stravinsky had first come to the attention of the Russian public with a performance of his brief and colorful fantasy for orchestra, *Fireworks*, in 1909. When the composer Liadov, who had been commissioned by Diaghilev to write the score for *The Firebird*, delayed his work too long, the impresario chose Stravinsky instead (the young man's only previous ballet experience had been the orchestration of a pair of Chopin piano pieces for *Les Sylphides*).

His choice made history. The new work, though outwardly close to the scores of Rimsky-Korsakov, was Stravinsky's final link with the past. Along with a certain conformity to nineteenth-century technique, there were also manifest in *The Firebird* a fresh use of dissonance, a striking freedom in the handling of rhythmic patterns and orchestral sonorities. With his next big work, *Petrouchka*, in which the nineteenth-century mold fell away, Stravinsky was to emerge as a composer of world stature. Ballet, his laboratory and sounding board, had brought him to maturity.

Stravinsky has carved three concert suites from *The Firebird*, all of them reworkings of the same excerpts. The first suite, with a huge instrumentation, soon gave way to the second, in which—using the iden-

Photo: White Studio   *Courtesy Dance News*

LÉONIDE MASSINE AND LUBOV TCHERNICHOVA

tical materials, minus two numbers—Stravinsky reduced the size of the orchestra. Then, in 1945, years after he had laid aside the style and idiom of this music, the composer rescored the two suppressed numbers of Suite No. 1, added them to Suite No. 2, and thus begot a Suite No. 3. This expanded version has not found favor with concert audiences accustomed to the brevity and conciseness of the second suite, which consists of five sections: Introduction and Appearance of the Firebird; Round of the Princesses; Infernal Dance of King Kastcheï and his Court; Berceuse; and Finale. The excerpts are performed without pause.

In 1945, S. Hurok commissioned Adolph Bolm to stage a shortened version for Ballet Theatre. The décor and costumes were by Marc Chagall. In 1949, the New York City Ballet acquired the costumes from Mr. Hurok, and George Balanchine staged his own version with Maria Tallchief as the Firebird, Francisco Moncion as the Prince, and Pat McBride as his bride-to-be.

The orchestra plays a sinister prelude, filled with vague harmonies and recurrent rhythms that appear in the depths of the string section.

Then, at the rise of the curtain, a shadowy grove is revealed, in the center of which grows an enchanted tree. The Firebird (danced by the leading ballerina), a wonderful vision in orange, crosses the stage, wings gleaming in the sultry light, to its flashing theme given out by winds and strings.

Young Prince Ivan, in hunting dress, climbs an outer wall into the grove, sees the strange bird, and immediately draws his bow. He misses as the creature, startled by his movement, flies away. Soon the bird returns to frolic at the base of the magic tree. This time Ivan, who has lain in wait, seizes it. The captive begs the Prince for its freedom; and on receiving a golden feather as ransom, Ivan relents. Then the bird disappears.

The scene grows lighter. Twelve maidens, led by a richly dressed Princess, descend a rustic staircase to the grove. As they play at the foot of the tree, scattering its fruit, the Prince reveals himself and the orchestra plays the delicately sensuous "Round of the Princesses." At

this point Ivan makes love to the chief maiden, although he is seeing her for the first time. She warns him to flee, for he is in the gardens of the demon Kastcheï, who holds the grove and its occupants under his spell.

A harsh dissonance is heard. As the Prince turns to escape, a horde of imps cuts off his path; and finally Kastcheï the Terrible enters. The ogre tries to enchant Ivan, but the young Prince, remembering the pledge of the Firebird, waves the golden feather. At once the magic bird comes to his aid. Forcing the attendant demons of Kastcheï to follow her, she leads them in a dance which so exhausts them that they fall in slumber. The music of this dance, perhaps more than any other section of the score, abounds in the dissonant and percussive elements which were to become major factors in Stravinsky's *Petrouchka* and *Le Sacre du Printemps*.

Photo: White Studio   XENIA MACLEZOVA   *Courtesy Dance News*

The Firebird conducts Ivan to the safety of a tree; and one of the finest melodies in the score—the folklike Berceuse—is heard.

At the prompting of the bird, Ivan extracts a metal chest from the trunk of the tree. Within the chest is a gigantic egg—the soul of Kastcheï. As the Prince throws this prize into the air, Kastcheï tries frantically to get hold of it; but Ivan hurls the egg to the ground and smashes it. The demon and his court disappear, their spell forever broken. Once they have gone, the grove is transformed. The Princess, radiantly dressed, comes to meet Ivan. Following her is a procession of nobles, all of them former victims of Kastcheï. They are prepared to crown Ivan as their deliverer.

At the beginning of the procession, a soft theme for solo horn is heard.

Then the music grows in grandeur until the full orchestra mirrors all of the brilliance on stage.

This closing tableau has its special effectiveness. More appealing, however, than any of the massed pictures in the ballet is the figure of the Firebird. The fantasy surrounding it marks the one striking choreographic note in a work that is more often pageantry than dance.

On Stage!

THIS BALLET in one act, with choreography by Michael Kidd, was first presented by Ballet Theatre at the Boston Opera House in October, 1945. A New York production took place a few days later during the company's Metropolitan season. Norman Dello Joio provided the specially composed musical score; Oliver Smith designed the scenery, and Alvin Colt the costumes. The scenario was the work of Michael and Mary Kidd. At the première, Mr. Kidd created his appealing portrait of the Handyman, with Janet Reed as the Girl, Nora Kaye as the Ballerina, and John Kriza as the Hero. Subsequent changes of cast have brought Alicia Alonso and Ruth Ann Koesun as the Girl, Diana Adams as the Ballerina, Peter Gladke as the Hero, and Mr. Kriza in a winning performance of the choreographer's original role.

On Stage! was Mr. Kidd's first choreographic work. Its characters were well drawn, its story projected with touching humor. The quality of the dance, especially in the satirical ballet-within-a-ballet running parallel to the plot, came off with less notable invention than that of the miming, but Kidd's later numbers for *Finian's Rainbow* (1947) — brilliantly planned — showed striking growth in the mastery of formal design.

There is a sparkling little overture to this comedy of life in the theatre, based on a waltz theme to be heard during the ballet. Then the

curtain rises on a bare stage, with chairs and packing boxes scattered about. An upright rehearsal piano stands to the fore; the only illumination comes from dull white working lights.

Two stage hands are discovered tying a backdrop to a batten. Once the drop is raised, they go off; and the Handyman, a sentimental figure lost in dreamy thoughts, enters pushing a broom. Intent on an inner life of his own, he gets entangled in a bit of rope as he works, singes his

hand on a safety lamp, stumbles over a chair. Brimming with an urge
to create, he approaches the piano and picks out a nostalgic tune with

one finger. Then he plays the magician, doing tricks as he sweeps, balancing his broom on its handle, standing a chair on one leg.

At the climax of this make-believe, the regal Ballerina of the company
steps in from the street and crosses the stage to her dressing room.
Vaguely in love with her, the Handyman puts his poetic fancies to work,
imagines himself taking her out for the evening, dancing beside her.
But she walks right past him, stopping only for a moment to adjust her
shoe. As she straightens up, a scarf slips unnoticed from her shoulder.
The Handyman pockets it, sighs romantically, and goes back to sweeping the stage as the lights come on and other members of the company
trickle in for rehearsal.

Some of them read their morning papers; others lie down and sleep,
converse, knit, finish eating breakfast. One or two warm up perfunc-
torily. Stage hands wander across the platform carrying set pieces.
During the lull before the start of the rehearsal, one of the dancers plays
some jazz at the piano. Two of his colleagues jitterbug while the company, suddenly come to life, claps an accompaniment. Just as the pair
are in full swing, the director enters and the dancers disperse. After a
few instructions to the *corps de ballet*, he starts the rehearsal.

No sooner has it begun than the Handyman returns with two girls
who have asked for an audition. One of them, the taller, is dressed in
blue. She is easygoing, smiling, and unbothered. The other, a little girl
in a new pink practice costume, is intensely shy. She seems frightened,
ill at ease. The girl in blue has friends in the company who wish her
luck; the little girl in pink knows no one.

After clearing up a few preliminary details with the company, the
director turns to the applicants. He is ready to see them dance. The big
girl, still easygoing, waves to her friends; the little one, more nervous
than ever, twists her music sheet and looks at the ground. She is watched
closely by the Handyman.

Now the audition begins. The girl in blue calmly hands her music to
the pianist and performs a big, jumpy waltz. There can be no doubt
when it ends that she has made the company. The *corps* applauds her
and the director indicates his approval. Then he motions to the other
girl, who has been standing apart from the group. Slowly, she untwists
her music, hands it to the pianist, and gets ready to dance. She tries a

<table>
<tr><td>Photo: Alfredo Valente</td><td>Courtesy Ballet Theatre</td></tr>
</table>

RUTH ANN KOESUN AND MICHAEL KIDD

few faltering steps and then, unequal to the strain, breaks down. The Handyman has waved encouragingly, but the little girl in pink does not see him. Unable to go on, she runs sobbing to a corner of the stage.

With the audition at an end, the company is ready for a full rehearsal of its new ballet, *The Captive Princess and Her Hero.* The Ballerina enters in practice clothes, and the director goes to greet her. At the same moment, the Handyman gallantly returns her scarf. As she accepts it without a word of thanks, he walks away crestfallen and mounts a ladder at the rear of the stage—his private point of vantage. The director claps his hands for the beginning of the rehearsal.

A large platform at the rear of the stage represents the tower of a castle, the space in front of it a courtyard. The Ballerina, who plays the

Princess, is seen high in her tower, a prisoner. Six handmaidens surround her; guards are stationed near by. Meanwhile, the little girl in pink—who is sitting at the opposite side of the stage from the Handyman—looks on with fascination.

The handmaidens dance a mournful step, lamenting their captivity, until one of them spies the Hero in the distance. He is approaching with a rescue party. The good news travels quickly, and the castle guards—who are the last to hear it—run to head him off. A violent fight takes place, with all of the liberators, except their leader, slain in the courtyard. Only the Hero stands against the guards. They have him trapped and are just about to close in on him when the lights fade and a "spot" illumines the Handyman in his corner on top of the ladder. The rest of the stage is in darkness.

Now the Handyman's daydreams take form. *He* is the Hero. Wielding his feather duster like a sword, he runs up and down the ladder going through an imaginary battle with the guards, lunging at them, running them through, bracing his foot against somebody's chest to extricate his sword. Then, shoving the imaginary bodies contemptuously out of his way, he struts forward and lights a cigarette in satisfaction.

At this moment the Princess comes down from her tower. She approaches the Handyman admiringly, but the incident of the scarf still rankles in his mind. He spurns her. The Princess beseeches, but to no avail . . . the Handyman is adamant. Finally his natural generosity overcomes him and he decides to be kind. As he turns to take her hand, there is a yell, "Watch out!" and—while the lights flare up—the guards come charging across the stage after the Hero. The Handyman jumps back on his ladder, his dream at an end. By this time, the real Hero is in an awkward spot. The guards are about to finish him off when he turns for a last look at the Princess. She blows him a kiss. This so inspires him that, with one sweep of his sword, he mows down his enemies and concludes the battle.

Now the couple celebrate their reunion with a formal *pas de deux*. The lights dim as before, and it is the girl in pink who is released in dreams. She imagines herself to be the Princess; and as the Hero comes forth and extends his hand, she steps forward to dance with all the confidence in the world. Her shyness is gone; her movements are large, open, free in spirit.

The Hero kneels before her. Taking a flower from her dress, she kisses it and lets it fall. But the lights come on, the Hero is in the midst of his *pas de deux* with the Ballerina, and the little girl in pink sadly realizes that she has been dreaming.

At length the rehearsal ends with a general dance by the *corps de ballet.* The director calls, "Thank you. That's all!," and the performers, gathering up their belongings, leave the stage. Only the Ballerina—in a bad mood—stays on with her partner, trying over some of the movements from the *pas de deux.* As they finish, the Hero lifts her in his arms and carries her off, in the grand romantic tradition. Again the Ballerina unwittingly lets her scarf fall; but this time the Handyman, who picks it up, makes no effort to return it.

He stands alone on the stage, following the Ballerina and her partner with his eyes. Then, balancing a broom in his arms in much the same way as the Hero has borne the Princess, he walks toward the wings. Suddenly he collides with the little girl in pink, who has lingered after the others. Still feeling bad over the results of her audition, she tries to slip past him; but the Handyman detains her and, in his own clumsy way, decides to help.

His job is to raise her spirits. Tearing a page from a magazine, he balances it on his nose; she laughs, takes heart. Then he sees the Hero's cape lying in a corner and puts it on. Remembering the Ballerina's scarf in his pocket, he ties it around the little girl's neck. Now *she* is the Princess, and he her partner. The girl starts to dance, performing as never

Photo: Fred Fehl
MICHAEL KIDD AS THE HANDYMAN

before, with a fire and ability that have been waiting for release. At first the Handyman does his best to keep up with her. Then he edges offstage and, a few moments later, returns with the director. A group gathers quietly at the back. The girl is still dancing, unaware of anyone's presence.

Suddenly she sees the onlookers and stops, frightened; the borrowed scarf falls to the floor; but the director comes forward and embraces her. The dancers, too, gather about the little girl and welcome her into the company. Just before she leaves with them, she turns—as if in afterthought—and waves to the Handyman.

He is standing on the opposite side of the stage watching her go, and waves back. Once she has left, his arm falls slowly. He takes up the broom and drags it across the stage, picks out the same nostalgic little tune on the piano (No. 2), stoops over for the scarf, looks at it for a moment, stuffs it into his pocket. The curtain falls as he pushes the broom offstage.

ORPHEUS AND THE BACCHANTES

Orpheus

THIS CHOREOGRAPHIC drama in one act was first presented by Ballet Society at the New York City Center in April, 1948. George Balanchine was the choreographer, and Igor Stravinsky composed the music. The cast included Nicolas Magallanes in the name part, Maria Tallchief as Eurydice, Francisco Moncion as the Dark Angel, and Herbert Bliss as Apollo. The strikingly imaginative scenery and costumes were the work of Isamu Noguchi. The ballet won an instantaneous success, with both composer and choreographer adding new luster to their careers.

This was not the first time that Mr. Balanchine had treated the Orpheus legend in terms of the dance. When attached, with the American Ballet, to the staff of the Metropolitan Opera House, he produced a choreographed version there of Gluck's *Orfeo ed Euridice* in the spring season of 1936, with singers and chorus in the orchestra pit. Pavel Tchelitcheff did the settings for this production, which aroused considerable controversy at the time. The new *Orpheus* of Balanchine and Stravinsky was necessarily more unified in concept, since the idea took form in the minds of both creators at once; and Balanchine's own choreographic style had grown simpler and more eloquent over the years. This classical and starkly moving account of the myth, with Stravinsky's music, must be ranked among the impressive additions to modern ballet.

SCENE ONE

After a short overture which represents Orpheus in mourning for his

lost wife, Eurydice, the curtain rises, revealing the minstrel surrounded by his friends, who offer him sympathy. He wears a mask, symbol of his musical gift, his creative genius. In the midst of his desolation, he dances —an expression of grief for the departed. Drawn by his song (in the idiom of this ballet, minstrelsy and dance are as one), little trees and fauns appear. They greet him with affection. Once more, Orpheus takes up his lyre. Now the Angel of Death approaches.

This figure, as drawn by the choreographer, is infinitely noble. Bidding Orpheus follow, the angel leads him toward the gates of Hades, through which he must pass to seek the shade of his wife.

SCENE TWO

After a short interlude, the angel and Orpheus are seen in the eternal night of Tartarus. At once they are set upon by the Furies, but the wild

band of spirits is soon calmed by Orpheus' music. Souls in torment, bearing enormous burdens, listen gravely as the minstrel exhorts them to let him pass. He is encouraged by the Angel of Death, who dances with him to the accompaniment of two oboes.

MARIA TALLCHIEF AS EURYDICE

287

Calmed by Orpheus' song, the Furies surrender Eurydice, with Pluto's injunction that he is not to look at her until they have returned to earth. Orpheus consents, and as a veiled curtain falls behind them, he dances a *pas de deux* with his wife, uniquely affecting because at no time does either of the dancers see the other. Their desire for unity, for mutual vision, grows always stronger until Orpheus is driven to tear the mask from his face. But in casting off this symbol, he denies himself, his art. Eurydice dies at once. Creatures from Hades move the veiled curtain forward until it envelops her body.

SCENE THREE

After another orchestral interlude, the gauze rises on the same setting as that of the first scene: Orpheus' abode on earth. Wild Bacchantes—creatures of infernal vengeance—appear, seize Orpheus, and tear him to pieces. Here, where Stravinsky has introduced spasmodic and dis-

jointed accents in his score, Balanchine has kept the Bacchantes dancing against them on the regular beats of the music to add a further sense of inevitability and terror to this episode.

The minstrel is destroyed. Apollo, god of the arts, appears, takes up the rejected mask, and places it in the earth, where, like a seed, it will bear fruit—the music of Orpheus living on after he has died. As a tree arises from this symbol embedded in the soil, the orchestra plays a solemn apotheosis and the god looks long at the plant through which

Orpheus' art will flourish.

SCENE FROM THE ORIGINAL BALLET RUSSE PRODUCTION

Paganini

THIS FANTASY in three scenes, with scenario by Sergei Rachmaninoff and Michel Fokine, had its world première in June, 1939, at Covent Garden, London. Its first American performance took place at the Fifty-first Street Theatre, New York, in November, 1940. Rachmaninoff's noted *Rhapsody for Piano and Orchestra on a Theme by Paganini* —with a new ending composed especially for the ballet—was used as musical background. The choreography was devised by Mr. Fokine. Sergei Soudeikine designed the scenery and costumes.

The ballet, built around freely imagined incidents in the life of the great Italian violinist Nicolò Paganini (1782–1840), was enthusiastically received by press and public; but as part of the repertoire of the Original Ballet Russe, whose activities have—since the New York première of *Paganini*—been confined largely to Central and South America, the work has not been seen again in the United States except on the infrequent visits of this company.

In its first American performance, Dimitri Rostoff mimed the title role, while Tatiana Riabouchinska was responsible for the unforgettable solo of the Florentine Maiden. With the exception of her dance, *Paganini* was cast largely in pantomimic form, not too divergent from the style of Fokine's earliest narrative ballets.

SCENE ONE

In the choreographic plan of this work, every one of the variations on Paganini's theme mirrors a different facet of Paganini's life. The famous violinist, though highly successful, is supposed to have enjoyed little happiness. His extraordinary powers with the bow, his dazzling virtuosity, added to his forbidding appearance, were associated by the more superstitious among the public of his time with diabolical powers, derived from Satan himself. Sometimes this resulted in persecution. It is with this phase of the violinist's career that the Fokine ballet is concerned. First, there is a statement from the piano and orchestra of the

Allegro vivace

original theme by Paganini, and then the Master is seen on the concert platform—tall, cadaverous, fantastic—surrounded by an audience that seems more preoccupied with his outward appearance than with his art. They gape at Paganini as he plays, and see in him the Devil's apprentice. Abstractions of Envy, Scandal, and Gossip dart about the great performer, and Guile takes its place beside him; but Paganini—ignoring these visions of the public which seeks to destroy him while paying him homage—stands resolute, producing divine music.

SCENE TWO

In contrast to the oppressive atmosphere of the concert hall, the next tableau—expansive and airy—takes place on a hilltop above Florence. Youths and maidens dance together. Suddenly Paganini enters on a solitary walk, carrying with him a guitar which he plays as beautifully as the violin. He strums the instrument, hoping to share its sounds with the people about him. A handsome girl, leader of the festive group, starts to dance to his music. As Paganini's pace grows faster, the girl whirls in ecstasy until she falls. Her indignant friends drive off the stranger who has brought about this ill fortune through the unconscious power of his art.

SCENE THREE

The concluding episode reveals Paganini at his loneliest, improvising in the solitude of his study. The Divine Genius stands above him but is rebuffed by hordes of demons—imitators dressed like Paganini. Satan himself leads them on. The violinist, overwhelmed by these visions, retreats before them, but the Divine Genius returns and, in one of the great moments of the ballet, guides his bow arm gently across the strings as the tenderest of the variations of the original theme sounds in the

orchestra. The legions of Satan fall back. Now the Divine Genius leads Paganini, whose soul has been released from his body, into Immortality.

Photo: *Alfredo Valente*   *Courtesy Museum of Modern Art*
DIMITRI ROSTOFF AS PAGANINI

Parade

THIS CUBIST ballet (it was labeled "realist" by its creators) had its first performance at the Théâtre du Châtelet, Paris, in May, 1917. Several distinguished figures in the world of music, theatre, painting, and the dance collaborated in its preparation, which took place in Rome during the winter preceding the première. Jean Cocteau wrote the scenario; Erik Satie composed the score; Pablo Picasso designed the scenery, costumes, and drop curtain; Léonide Massine provided the choreography. This fusion of the finest contemporary minds in theatrical dance was one of the ideals of Sergei Diaghilev, who supervised the production.

The work was frankly experimental in its use of cubist décor and side-show atmosphere. It drew mixed audience reactions. During the intermission following the première, Cocteau was threatened with a hatpin by an angered lady in the audience. The sound and fury of the première have long since disappeared, like the ballet itself. Satie's score, amusing and piquant, has survived and is played occasionally in concert version.

Among the principal dancers at the first performance of *Parade* were Mr. Massine as the Chinese Conjurer, Lydia Lopokova as one of the two acrobats, and Galina Chabelska as the Little American Girl.

The scene of *Parade* is a street theatre on a Sunday, a Parisian phenomenon celebrated by Seurat in his painting *La Parade*. As the curtain rises, a magnificent drop curtain is seen representing the interior of a carnival booth in which the performers are resting before their entrance on stage. The sight of this drop is accompanied by a short, fugue-like overture representing the bustle of the carnival. Then the inner curtain rises and the action of the ballet begins.

The scenario takes root in what Cocteau himself has called "rehabilitating the commonplace." Two circus managers appear outside a neighborhood carnival tent, exhibiting their performers in a sample routine to drum up business for the attractions inside.

First the French manager, an enormous cubist creation mounted on human legs, strides in. The figure moves across the stage, faces the audience, and reveals his particular client: a Chinese Conjurer who advances from inside the booth and regales the prospective public with various tricks, including an egg-disappearing act and the swallowing of fire.

Despite his best efforts, the Conjurer does not attract the public. As he disappears inside the booth, no customers come forward.

The manager from New York now enters from the other side of the stage. His cowboy riding boots and the skyscraper on his back are designed to suggest America. Bearing a card which prominently displays the word "Parade," he approaches his colleague and listens with sympathy as the Parisian manager complains about business. Then the New Yorker prepares for the appearance of his own performer.

The curtains of the booth open, and the Little American Girl appears; she is a 1917 version of United States mores, as seen through European eyes. She mimes the mounting of a race horse, riding a bicycle, quivering like movies on the screen, imitating Charlie Chaplin, chasing a thief with a revolver, boxing, dancing to ragtime, going to sleep, being shipwrecked, rolling on the grass on an April morning, buying a Kodak. Despite all her exertions, no customers come forward for the show inside.

Both managers give vent to their rage at this lack of appreciation on the part of the public. Now a third barker, suggested by a dummy in evening dress, appears, mounted on a prancing cubist horse which trots along at a haughty gait. He represents two acrobats who are about to perform.* After the usual fanfare, the acrobats emerge, go through their paces, and are met with complete indifference by the public.

Now comes the finale of this pathetic *Parade*. The two managers and the American Girl appear jointly to ragtime accompaniment, followed by the capering horse. The Chinese Conjurer follows with the acrobats in feats of skill and daring. Still, no reaction from the public.

The company lines up indignantly, the Little American Girl leading the horse, the managers gesticulating that the turns presented are only a sample of what can be seen inside. But no contact is established with the vast, paying audience; the managers wilt, their artists pine, and the horse collapses from exhaustion.

The music, which has included in its course such bizarre effects as the use of a typewriter to suggest—with its clicking—the American background of the Little Girl—now returns to the fugue of the overture while the curtain falls on this real-life tragedy of little people and their inability to communicate their talents to those who might be in a position to encourage and sustain them. The theme of *Parade* was valid; its treatment perhaps too bizarre and mannered, too strictly *avant-garde*, to keep it in the repertoire once its novelty had passed.

* This, according to Cocteau's scenario. Actually, at the dress rehearsal, the dummy fell off the horse and was suppressed thereafter. The steed itself, of commanding appearance, embodied at all subsequent performances the idea of horse and rider combined, a sort of equine manager of the acrobats.

Le Pas d'Acier

THIS WORK, whose title may be translated roughly as "The March of Steel," was a product of Sergei Diaghilev's last period. Although identified with Czarist Russia, in this ballet Diaghilev employed, for the purposes of theatrical effectiveness, certain left-wing subjects that lent themselves well to mass ensembles on stage and to controversy in the audience. *Le Pas d'Acier*, with choreography by Léonide Massine and stage design by the Soviet artist Georges Jakouloff—who had worked under Meyerhold in Moscow—was first given by the Diaghilev company at the Paris Opéra in June, 1927. Lubov Tchernicheva, Alexandra Danilova, Serge Lifar, and Mr. Massine were the leading dancers.

The score was composed by Sergei Prokofiev and played no little part in drawing public attention to the work. Hard, steely as the driving of pistons, and yet possessed of great imagination, the music proved the most durable element of the production.

In April, 1931, Prokofiev's score came to America when a ballet of the same name, with scenario by Lee Simonson and choreography by Edwin Strawbridge, had its première at the Metropolitan Opera House under the auspices of the League of Composers. Aside from the music and certain features of *ballet-mécanique* style, this production had little in common with the Diaghilev mounting. Yeichi Nimura was the principal dancer. Neither the Massine nor the Simonson edition has survived in the repertory.

The original *Pas d'Acier* was divided into twelve successive sections: entrance of the cast; march of the peasants; the commissars; the newsboys; the orator; the sailor and the working woman; change of scene (during which the orchestra plays an interlude); the sailor becomes a worker; the factory; the hammers; finale.

Various effects, some of them powerful, sprang from the use of a factory as theatrical background. Bare walls and heavy timber formed the scene; and, as the hammers smashed away toward the end of the

Moderato pesantissimo

ballet, revolving green, red, and white lights flashed on the grease-stained, half-nude bodies of the workers.

The Simonson production in New York was more of a political tract. Its scenario dealt with the crowning of labor by the bourgeoisie and the subsequent fight between the two elements; glorification of the rural worker; capital's attempt to speed the production of iron, coal, and steel; the revolt of the proletariat, finally quelled by soldiers; and the ironic triumph of capital as the curtain falls, with the rhythm of steel intact. Conception and performance were heavy-handed. This version has never been revived.

NORA KAYE, ALICIA MARKOVA, ANNABELLE LYON, AND KAREN CONRAD
AS THE FOUR BALLERINAS

Pas de Quatre

THIS DIVERTISSEMENT in one scene was originally created by the famous
French choreographer and dancer Jules Perrot (1810–1892) for a series
of performances at Her Majesty's Theatre, London, in the month of
July, 1845. Four reigning ballerinas—Fanny Cerito, Marie Taglioni,
Carlotta Grisi, and Lucile Grahn—among the greatest in the history of
theatrical dance, took part. The work displayed their skills individually
and in combination with such mastery as to have been hailed without
reserve by all who saw it. In 1847, *Pas de Quatre* was revived at the
same theatre with Cerito, Taglioni, and Grisi, as before, and with Car-
olina Rosati replacing Lucile Grahn. Again, the piece achieved a great
success.

The contemporary artist A. E. Chalon made lithographs of the cast
in action. Almost a hundred years later, these were to provide—at the
prompting of Cyril W. Beaumont, English authority on ballet—both the
inspiration and the source material for a revival of *Pas de Quatre*. Mr.
Beaumont's associate, Keith Lester, reconstructed the dances from a

296

close study of the drawings and accounts of the period. Leighton Lucas edited the original musical score by Cesare Pugni, which was discovered in the British Museum.

The restored work was first presented in London by the company of Alicia Markova and Anton Dolin in 1936, with Mollie Lake, Diana Gould, Kathleen Crawfton, and Prudence Hyman as the four ballerinas. Ballet Theatre produced it in 1941 at the Majestic Theatre, New York, in a special staging by Mr. Dolin. The cast included Nana Gollner (Taglioni), Nina Stroganova (Grahn), Alicia Alonso (Grisi), and Katharine Sergava (Cerito).

Perrot's production of 1845 was aimed not only at assembling the four greatest living ballerinas of the time on a single stage but at pitting one against another in well-bred rivalry. The first modern performances of *Pas de Quatre* overlooked this fundamental, concentrating instead on a restudy of the choreography. It was only when Alicia Markova, an artist in the great tradition, took over the part of Taglioni that the competitive idea at the core of the work was again spurred into being.

In presentations by Ballet Theatre which followed, Miss Markova was surrounded by artists of such stature as Nora Kaye or Rosella Hightower (Grisi), Irina Baronova (Grahn), and Annabelle Lyon (Cerito). Still another star cast was seen in a revival of the work by the Ballet Russe de Monte Carlo at the Metropolitan Opera House in September, 1948: Alexandra Danilova (Cerito), Miss Markova * (Taglioni), Mia Slavenska (Grisi), and Nathalie Krassovska (Grahn). Here, unfortunately, the humor of the Dolin restaging—with its hints of backbiting among the four distinguished performers—was projected too broadly by the dancers. When played with a proper balance of taste, solo and ensemble virtuosity, the modern *Pas de Quatre* can conjure up certain glamorous moments from another age.

As the curtain rises, the four ballerinas are seen in a pose inspired by the best-known of Chalon's lithographs: Taglioni, her arms gracefully flexed, stands in the center of the group like the pistil of a flower, surrounded by Grisi, Cerito, and Grahn. Soon the divas emerge from the past and, after a gravely formal beginning, move in an animated group —always ruled by the poise and suppleness that are keynotes of the ballet.

Moderato

The time has come for the first variation; and Taglioni, Grisi, and

* Alternating with Ruthanna Boris.

Cerito, with a deferential bow to their colleague, leave the stage. Grahn, who remains, performs an athletic solo with clean, strong movements, free of affectation. Vigor is her forte.

Her variation at an end, she salutes the audience and withdraws after a welcome to the next diva, Grisi. This artist, the creator of *Giselle*, favors a lyrical style, intricate footwork, multiple turns.

When Grisi, too, has bowed her acknowledgments, Taglioni and Grahn reappear to present the next dancer. Balancing on points, both ballerinas join hands so as to frame the little kneeling Cerito between them. (Even in modern performances, the girls are not above knocking each other off balance at this point by a subtle pressure of the wrist.) Then they smile amiably and vanish.

Cerito's variation, a gracious waltz, breathes lightness and youth.

This artist, most juvenile of the four, relies perhaps as much on personal magnetism as on dance; but her solo is irresistible in its charm.

After Cerito's bows and departure, the stage is set for the greatest ballerina of all—her supremacy admitted even by the rival goddesses—Marie Taglioni.* This artist's special gifts, aside from her noble bearing, lie in balance and elevation. She hovers in air with no apparent effort, remains poised *sur les pointes* with the greatest of skill.

Now that the conventions have been satisfied and every ballerina has come forward at her solo best, the four join hands in a concluding ensemble.

At its culmination, the dancers resume the pose they held at the start of the ballet, withdrawing from reality into the lines of a lithograph, and the curtain falls.

* The famous creator of *La Sylphide*, in which she introduced the ankle-length *tutu* that has become the symbol of romantic ballet.

La Péri

THIS DANCE drama, with choreography by Leo Staats and music by Paul Dukas, was first produced at the Paris Opéra in 1921. The comparative merits of music and dance were decidedly uneven, with the scales tipped in the direction of Dukas, whose splendid score is still played at symphony concerts. Staats's stage piece was presented in a revised version by Serge Lifar during a visit of the Paris Opéra Ballet to the United States in the autumn of 1948, on which occasion Mlle Bourgeois and M. Bozzoni danced the leading roles. Its old-fashioned symbolism met with little success, but the accompanying music commanded much admiration.

A legendary Peri,* holding in her hand the lotus flower of immortality, is awakened by a King who seizes it. She is characterized in the orchestra by a flowing theme of great beauty.

The Peri is not disturbed at losing the flower, for she knows the King will return it. First, she dances and charms him. Then, just as she has thought, the King's longing for her overcomes his thirst for immortality, and he surrenders the lotus. The Peri disappears at once and the King's life fades.

* In Persian mythology, an imaginary being, like an elf or fairy, represented as a descendant of fallen angels excluded from Paradise till their penance is accomplished. (Webster.)

Courtesy Dance News

DAVID NILLO (WOLF), SONO OSATO (CAT), NORA KAYE (BIRD), JEAN HUNT (DUCK),
EUGENE LORING (PETER)

Peter and the Wolf

THIS BALLET for children, with choreography by Adolph Bolm, was first produced by Ballet Theatre at the Center Theatre, New York, on January 13, 1940. It follows the story of Sergei Prokofiev's symphonic tale of the same name for narrator and orchestra. Eugene Loring created the role of Peter, in which he has been succeeded by Yura Lazovsky and Fernando Alonso.

Peter and the Wolf had its first orchestral performance at a Moscow children's concert in 1936. Soon afterward it was introduced to the United States by Serge Koussevitzky and the Boston Symphony, with Richard Hale as narrator. This is a delightful score in its own right, amusing to an adult audience and exciting for children. When heard in the concert hall, *Peter* conjures up for listeners of all ages the fragile, laughable world of its hero and his enemy, the Wolf.

The reading of the text by the narrator (in which he not only tells the story but describes the musical themes of the score) is a droll and diverting preparation for the tonal effects that follow. As for the plot, it is really a prop on which to rest the music.

In the ballet adaptation by Mr. Bolm, Prokofiev's story has been faithfully retained. While symphonic wit and color stream from the orchestra pit, the stage pictures are an acted-out replica of a secondary tale. Although Mr. Bolm's choreography has several ingratiating moments, such as the fanciful treatment of Bird and Cat, his ballet lacks the lightness and elasticity of the score itself.

As the lights in the theatre go down, an offstage voice describes through a loud-speaker the characters of the ballet and identifies the musical themes as they are played. The curtains part and reveal the characters in turn, each one rising successively from behind a screen to face the audience as his motive is heard. First comes the Bird, played by the flute,

then the Duck, by the oboe,

the Cat, by the clarinet,

the Grandfather, by the bassoon,

the Wolf, by the horns,

and finally Peter himself, by the strings.

These themes, as named and presented, offer the children an interesting picture of some of the solo instruments of the orchestra. Part of Prokofiev's over-all plan for *Peter and the Wolf* is a subtle blend of music appreciation with a parody of its own pretentious workings.

Once the characters have been established, the action gets under way, and the narrator is no longer required. The story can best be given by directly quoting Prokofiev's own story, read in the original version by the narrator:

"Early one morning Peter opened the gate and went out into the big green meadow. On a branch of a big tree sat a little Bird, Peter's friend. 'All is quiet,' chirped the Bird gaily.

"Just then a Duck came waddling round. She was glad that Peter had not closed the gate, and decided to take a nice swim in the deep pond in the meadow.

"Seeing the Duck, the little Bird flew down upon the grass, settled next to her, and shrugged his shoulders: 'What kind of a bird are you, if you can't fly?' said he. To this the Duck replied: 'What kind of a bird are you, if you can't swim?' and dived into the pond. They argued and argued, the Duck swimming in the pond, the little Bird hopping along the shore.

"Suddenly, something caught Peter's attention. He noticed a Cat crawling through the grass. The Cat thought: 'The Bird is busy arguing, I will just grab him.' Stealthily she crept toward him on her velvet paws. 'Look out!' shouted Peter, and the Bird immediately flew up into the tree while the Duck quacked angrily at the Cat from the middle of the pond. The Cat walked around the tree and thought: 'Is it worth climbing up so high? By the time I get there the Bird will have flown away.'

"Grandfather came out. He was angry because Peter had gone into the meadow. 'It is a dangerous place. If a Wolf should come out of the forest, then what would you do?' Peter paid no attention to Grandfather's words. Boys like him are not afraid of Wolves, but Grandfather took Peter by the hand, locked the gate, and led him home.

"No sooner had Peter gone than a big gray Wolf came out of the forest. In a twinkling the Cat climbed up the tree. The Duck quacked, and in her excitement jumped out of the pond. But no matter how hard the Duck tried to run, she couldn't escape the Wolf. He was getting nearer . . . nearer . . . catching up with her . . . and then he got her and, with one gulp, swallowed her.

"And now, this is how things stand: the Cat was sitting on one branch, the Bird on another—not too close to the Cat—and the Wolf walked round and round the tree looking at them with greedy eyes.

"In the meantime, Peter, without the slightest fear, stood behind the

Photo: *André Kertesz*   *Courtesy Dance News*
PETER AND THE HUNTERS (EUGENE LORING IN THE AIR)

closed gate watching all that was going on. He ran home, got a strong rope, and climbed up the high stone wall. One of the branches of the tree, round which the Wolf was walking, stretched out over the wall. Grabbing hold of the branch, Peter lightly climbed over onto the tree.

"Peter said to the Bird: 'Fly down and circle round the Wolf's head; only take care that he doesn't catch you.' The Bird almost touched the Wolf's head with his wings while the Wolf snapped angrily at him from this side and that. How the Bird did worry the wolf! How he wanted to catch him! But the Bird was cleverer, and the Wolf simply couldn't do anything about it.

"Meanwhile, Peter made a lasso and, carefully letting it down, caught the Wolf by the tail and pulled with all his might. Feeling himself caught, the Wolf began to jump wildly, trying to get loose. But Peter tied the other end of the rope to the tree, and the Wolf's jumping only made the rope around his tail tighter.

"Just then, the hunters came out of the woods following the Wolf's trail and shooting as they went. But Peter, sitting in the tree, said: 'Don't shoot! Birdie and I have caught the Wolf. Now help us to take him to the zoo.'

"And there . . . imagine the procession: Peter at the head; after him the hunters leading the Wolf; and winding up the procession, Grandfather and the Cat. Grandfather tossed his head discontentedly: 'Well, and if Peter hadn't caught the Wolf? What then?'

"Above them flew Birdie chirping merrily: 'My, what brave fellows we are, Peter and I! Look what we have caught!' And if one would listen very carefully he could hear the Duck quacking inside the Wolf; because the Wolf in his hurry had swallowed her alive."

As the final page of music sounds, the lights go down again and—matching the opening of the work—all of the characters bob up rapidly from behind the screen and take their bows.

Les Petits Riens*

THIS BALLET-PANTOMIME, with music by Wolfgang Amadeus Mozart and choreography by Jean Georges Noverre, exists more in tradition than in actuality. The score survives—it was written by Mozart in the spring of 1778, during his third stay in Paris—but Noverre's scenario has disappeared, with only a small account of the action extant.† In June of 1778, the ballet had its Parisian première on a double bill with Nicola Piccinni's opera, *Le Finte Gemelle* ("The Bogus Twins"), and on that occasion, according to the custom then in vogue, only the name of Noverre appeared on the announcements. Mozart contributed thirteen numbers, including the overture, six or seven other sections of the work being written by a colleague whose identity has not since been established. Mozart's music, lost for almost a hundred years, was rediscovered in 1872 by a German musicologist named Viktor Wilder, in the library of the Paris Opéra. It is played often now in concert, while the libretto of Noverre—its creative source—has gone into limbo.

New versions of *Les Petits Riens* have been staged for the Old Vic Theatre, London, by Ninette de Valois (1928); for Ballet Rambert at the Mercury Theatre, London, by Frederick Ashton (1928); and for Ballet for America by Ruth Page (1946).

As described by musical historians, the work began with a sprightly overture.

Three pastoral scenes followed. In the first, Amor—mischievous God of Love—falls into a trap and is imprisoned. The second episode depicts a game of blindman's buff, that aimless sport so popular with the court of Versailles at the time the ballet was planned. The final scene portrays the knavery of Amor in presenting a couple of lovesick shepherdesses

---

* A literal translation of *Les Petits Riens* ("The Little Nothings") would belie, through its heavy-footed quality, the mercurial grace of the score. The title of this *divertissement* might best be rendered in English: "As You Like It."

† This was printed in the *Journal de Paris* of June 12, 1778.

to a third one, disguised as a shepherd. Here there occurs a charming musette.

The two shepherdesses fall in love with the supposed stalwart, who finally uncovers her breast to prove the deception.

THE DEATH OF PETROUCHKA

Petrouchka

THERE CAN be no doubt that *Petrouchka* is one of the most important
works in the dance repertoire. With its first performance by the Diaghilev troupe at the Théâtre du Châtelet, Paris, in June, 1911, Michel
Fokine—the choreographer—introduced a theatrical elasticity and freedom of movement hitherto unknown to ballet. Through its startlingly
vivid décor by Alexandre Benois—who was also responsible for the
costumes—the work brought to Western audiences a still stronger taste
of Russian color than had come out of St. Petersburg previously with
Scheherazade and *The Firebird*. With his historic score for *Petrouchka*,
Igor Stravinsky made modern music come of age.

There are some who hold that, despite the many outstanding later
compositions of Stravinsky, this score is the composer's finest. Whatever
the final verdict—and it seems not too necessary that one should be arrived at in view of the diversity of creative periods in Stravinsky's
career and the special excellence that every period has brought—there
can be no denying the tremendous influence that *Petrouchka* has exerted
on all music since that time through its insistence on rhythm as an element of equal importance with melody and formal structure, and

through its radical innovations in harmonic usage which have become a part of every composer's vocabulary.

Originally, *Petrouchka* was an interim project on the part of the composer. Sergei Diaghilev had approached Stravinsky with the idea of a score for a projected ballet, *Le Sacre du Printemps*. Instead of carrying out his work on schedule, Stravinsky found himself constantly drawn toward the execution of an idea which had come to him some time earlier: the composition of an orchestral piece, with piano obbligato, in which the solo instrument might take on the qualities of an obstinate puppet, quarreling with the orchestra amid noisy showers of keyboard arpeggios and retaliatory trumpet blasts. At the end, the puppet was to give way under the strain. Diaghilev, on visiting Stravinsky to inspect sketch material for *Le Sacre* and finding him at work instead on *Petrouchka*, took a great interest in the score as a basis for a new stage piece. He, Stravinsky, and Benois worked out the story of the ballet as it now stands, and Michel Fokine provided the choreography.

The première in Paris created a furor. Not only was the quality of the music new and strange to audiences of the time, but the choreography —with its accent on characterization rather than formalized dance— was also novel. Vaslav Nijinsky danced the title role with overwhelming success, and Thamar Karsavina won equal praise as the Ballerina. The Moor was interpreted by Alexander Orlov, and the role of the Charlatan by the famous mime Enrico Cecchetti. Pierre Monteux conducted the orchestra. The first performance of *Petrouchka* in the United States took place in January, 1916, at the Century Theatre, New York. Léonide Massine, who was to appear in the name part on many future occasions in America, danced the role, with Lydia Lopokova as the Ballerina and Adolph Bolm as the Moor. Since that time *Petrouchka* has had a varied career in this country, passing from the repertoire of one organization to another. It has been performed by the Metropolitan Opera Association, the de Basil Ballet Russe, and Ballet Theatre. In 1940, Fokine restaged *Petrouchka* for the de Basil company, cleaning off the accumulated grime and restoring the ballet—so far as physical conditions allowed—to its original condition. Later performances of *Petrouchka*, with Mr. Fokine officiating in their preparation, were given by Ballet Theatre.

It is interesting to note that Stravinsky, in his autobiography, was none too enthusiastic about Fokine's choreography. He seems to have felt that, although the big lines of the work came off well, the choreographer left unrealized—especially in his handling of the opening crowd scene—many of the music's rhythmical subtleties.[*] A revised *Petrouchka*, following the original story line but handling the crowd episode in more detail, was produced some three decades after the

---

[*] "It was a pity that the movements of the crowd had been neglected. I mean that they were left to the arbitrary improvisations of the performers instead of being choreographically regulated in accordance with the clearly defined exigencies of the music." (*Stravinsky: An Autobigraphy.*)

NIJINSKY AS PETROUCHKA *Courtesy Museum of Modern Art*

work's Paris première, at the Teatro dell' Opera in Rome, by the Hungarian choreographer Aurel Milloss. This edition did some further justice to Stravinsky's score, but complete fulfillment in dance of the music's extraordinary power is still awaited.

Among the more distinguished interpreters of the title role in *Petrouchka*, seen in America, have been Massine, Vaslav Nijinsky (who appeared here for the first time in this part at the Metropolitan Opera House in 1916 and was called incomparable), Adolph Bolm, Yurek Shabelevsky, Yura Lazovsky, Jerome Robbins, Michael Kidd, and Hugh Laing. Practically every major ballerina since Karsavina has appeared as the Dancer, notably Lydia Lopokova, Alexandra Danilova, Alicia Markova, Irina Baronova, and Tamara Toumanova. Outstanding among those performers who have been seen as the Moor are David Lichine, Frederic Franklin, and André Eglevsky.

The score of *Petrouchka* is one of the few which can be heard with equal profit either in the concert hall or in the theatre. Stravinsky himself drew a symphonic suite from the ballet, retaining several major episodes and cutting others. In recent years, public interest in *Petrouchka* has been so great that its complete score is often played at concert performances and on records.

SCENE ONE

As the curtain rises on the opening scene, a carnival is in progress at St. Petersburg. Part of the city skyline can be seen in the background, especially the famous golden spire of the Admiralty. The square itself, where the carnival takes place, is filled with low wooden buildings with a maze of overhanging balconies and gaudy banners. At the rear of the square stands the puppet theatre, its stage curtained off, silent and deserted.

Elsewhere there is constant activity, for this is "Butter Week"—the last days before the advent of Lent, when the citizens of St. Petersburg can still have their feasting and revelry. They pass in ceaseless motion

across the square, looking for entertainment. The background, the appearance of the strollers suggest St. Petersburg's prosperous days of the last century when it was a capital city.

There is constant activity in the square. Members of the crowd jostle each other, laugh crudely, surge toward the carnival booths and side

shows. An old man with a long white beard—"come-on" for a fortune-telling concession—is leaning over a makeshift balcony to attract the attention of the people below. Hopping back and forth along its wooden

planks, he waves his beard at the crowd in invitation. Two gypsy girls, part of the establishment inside, join him briefly and urge the crowd to enter.

The old man and his beard soon lose their hold on the strollers. The drone of a passing street organ catches the people's fancy; then the wheeze of a rival hurdy-gurdy. A third element enters in the person of a street dancer who moves in clocklike rhythm, beating time for herself on a small metal bar. As the girl finishes and the two rival organs

trail into silence, a moment of idleness comes over the crowd. It is broken by two barkers who come out of the deserted theatre, beating a tattoo on drums. Then, through the shabby curtains of the playhouse, emerges the head of the Charlatan. A shudder runs through the crowd as the

owner of the puppet show is seen. Known only as the Charlatan, he wears a richly woven robe, a conical hat with stars on it. Long gray hair covers his shoulders. Looking fixedly at the crowd, he produces a flute from inside his cloak and plays a melody that brings silence to the square.

Then he waves his arms and, in response, the curtains of the theatre part.

Three inanimate puppets are seen resting on the bars of their cells: Petrouchka, the most human-looking of the lot, with narrow slits for eyes and a pale wasted face; the Moor—a large, swarthy marionette with a malign expression; and, in the center, the Ballerina, conventionally attractive, with painted face and delicately turned figure.

At a sign from the Charlatan, the puppets start to dance. Perched on their stools, they extend their hands and feet in quick mechanical motion. Soon they leave the platform, as the dance grows livelier, and jig their

way into the square. The theme of their performance is simple: the Moor courts the Ballerina, and jealous Petrouchka attacks him with a club. As they keep dancing, people gather breathlessly about them. But the Charlatan lifts his flute, the three toy figures collapse, and blackness descends on the square.

SCENE TWO

There is no formal music between the scenes of *Petrouchka*, only a protracted drum roll, as an inner curtain—with fantastic night-figures, symbolizing evil and approaching doom—is lowered. After the first interval, the interior of Petrouchka's cell is seen. This secret place behind the puppet theatre is really a prison. The walls—with a design of stars, like the Charlatan's hat—slope sharply toward the floor. The ceiling hangs low. Into this miserable den, a huge boot—that of the Charlatan—thrusts Petrouchka.

The puppet, dazed and unhappy, tries to rise from the ground. He is

confused by an onrush of near-human thoughts; he is capable of love and of hatred, tortured by his own wasted, sawdust physique.

Suddenly the door of the cell opens and the Ballerina appears. She stares at him inquisitively but, frightened by Petrouchka's wild ad-

Photo: White Studio   Courtesy Museum of Modern Art

LYDIA LOPOKOVA AS THE BALLERINA

vances, withdraws almost at once. Petrouchka beats against the door—but it will not yield to him. He pounds on the walls of his cell. One of them gives way, only to bring him the sounds of the carnival outside, from which he can never escape. Finally, the despairing puppet throws himself to the ground defeated.

SCENE THREE

A complete contrast to Petrouchka's miserable quarters may be found in the luxurious cell of the Moor. The sensuous, self-indulgent puppet is sprawled on a plum-colored divan, as the curtain rises. Lazily balancing a coconut on the tips of his toes, the marionette soon tires of this sport.

He lets the shell fall, jumps to his feet, draws a sword with curving blade, and tries to split the coconut in two. His brute strength fails; the coconut stands firm; and the Moor bows before it, assuming that any object which resists his own force must be far superior to him, perhaps even a god.

The door of the cell is opened from the outside and the Ballerina appears, fresh from her visit to Petrouchka. Crossing the room *sur les pointes*, she carries a small trumpet on which she plays a lively tune—

symbol of the commonplace.

The Moor looks at her with admiration as she begins to dance an old-fashioned waltz.

Physical longing takes hold of him. Rising heavily, he goes toward the Ballerina, grasps her by the waist, and engineers a brutish *pas de deux.* Here Stravinsky's music, with its jangling blend of the Moor's coconut theme and the Ballerina's waltz in rhythmic counterpoint, sardonically underlines the situation on stage.

At the climax of this duo, the Moor draws the Ballerina toward the divan. They embrace; but a small hand thrusts itself through the doorway. It is Petrouchka, who has escaped from his cell.

Springing from the couch, the infuriated Moor reaches for his sword,

lunges at Petrouchka, and drives him from the room. Then the marionette seizes the Ballerina once more, falling with her onto the divan. She
does not resist.

SCENE FOUR

The carnival square is seen again in a winter sunset. Throughout the
day the merriment of the crowd has been increasing, and now it is at its
height. All kinds of figures keep thronging the square: rich merchants

from the provinces, nursemaids on a holiday, idle coachmen, and wan-
derers of the city. Above them looms the spire of the Admiralty, still
gleaming in the last rays of the afternoon. Slanting shafts of dusk have
already begun to play on the carnival booths, giving them a threatening
appearance.

A boisterous party begins. Several nursemaids have banded together
to the strain of an old Russian folk tune, and, with measured steps, they
dance in the gathering darkness.

The color and confusion of the scene are heightened by a group of
swaggering coachmen, by the antics of a trained bear that frightens the
crowd at first and then amuses them, by the reeling of a tipsy merchant
who, crossing the square with two gypsy girls, pays them to dance for
him.

The swaying of the trained bear, the rhythms of the gypsy girls rouse
the coachmen to a frenzy. Stamping on the ground, they begin a dance
almost overpowering in its force. Then they approach the nursemaids

and try to draw them into the revel. At first the women refuse, but finally
they yield to the joy and savagery of the men.

Photo: Baron of London *Courtesy Museum of Modern Art*
DONALD SADDLER, DIMITRI ROMANOFF, LUCIA CHASE, MICHAEL KIDD IN THE FIRST
SCENE OF PETROUCHKA

Snow begins to fall. To the pounding of vibrant orchestral rhythms
reinforced by the throbbing of the bass drum, the entire square is alive
with a blaze of motion. Kerchiefs are waved in the air, excited groups are
formed, complete in themselves yet bearing an inviolate relationship to
the picture as a whole. For many ballet lovers, this moment in *Petrouchka*
is perhaps the most exciting in the repertoire—a perfect combination of
sight, sound, and motion. Certainly, it represents the peak of Fokine's
creative activity, the investing of theatrical dance with maximum communicative power.

Night now veils the spire of the Admiralty. A group of maskers
dressed as demons with grotesque forms and evil heads join the company. The revel is split into little bands scurrying about the square like
phantoms.

As the maskers prance through the crowd, filling the onlookers with
terror and bringing a grisly touch to the end of the carnival, the curtains
of the deserted puppet theatre are suddenly agitated. A wailing cry is
heard in the orchestra. Now the drapes are torn apart, and Petrouchka
dashes into the square pursued by the Moor. The Ballerina ineffectually
tries to stop her lover, who has decided to put an end to his whining
rival.

The marionettes dart wildly through the crowd. With a leap, the Moor catches hold of Petrouchka, brings down his curved sword, and fatally wounds the puppet. The Moor and Ballerina disappear. Petrouchka, surrounded by the crowd, is left to twitch out his death agonies in the square.

All thoughts of revelry have left the carnival strollers. They stand appalled by the crime that has been committed, then hurry off in search of the police. An officer soon appears, and in his custody is the Charlatan, no longer dressed in starry robe and cap, but in a shabby overcoat and plug hat. Angrily, the crowd forces him toward the body of the murdered puppet; but the Charlatan, facing his accusers, lifts up the corpse and demonstrates that it has never lived but is only a thing of rags and sawdust.

Complete darkness has fallen. The crowd gradually leaves the square. With a sigh, the Charlatan stoops over, grasps the ruined marionette, and drags it toward the theatre.

A solo trumpet suddenly shrieks out the Petrouchka motive (No. 8). The Charlatan, hearing a thin cry in the night, looks up and sees, on the roof of the theatre, the body of a clown that swings maliciously toward him. It is the spirit of Petrouchka, set free at last, jeering at his former master. Frightened, the Charlatan fumbles with his load of rags, drops it, and flees into the night. The curtain falls on the deserted square to the sound of strings plucked softly in the orchestra.

Pillar of Fire

THIS BALLET with choreography by Antony Tudor, one of the most significant works in the repertory of theatrical dance, was given its world première by Ballet Theatre at the Metropolitan Opera House in April, 1942, with Nora Kaye creating her now historic interpretation of the role of Hagar, Mr. Tudor as the Friend, Hugh Laing as the Evil Young Man, Lucia Chase as the Eldest Sister, and Anabelle Lyon as the Youngest Sister (a role later taken with fine effect by Norma Vance).

The *corps de ballet* at this memorable performance included such dancers now risen to first rank as Rosella Hightower, Sono Osato, Muriel Bentley, Jerome Robbins, and John Kriza. The superlative settings and costumes, designed to reflect the oppressive atmosphere of a Victorian community toward the close of the last century, were the work of Jo Mielziner.

The musical background to *Pillar of Fire*, eloquent and suggestive, is contained in Arnold Schönberg's score for string orchestra, *Verklärte Nacht* ("Transfigured Night"). This romantic work, so unlike the later, uncompromisingly dissonant compositions of Schönberg, was written when the composer was only twenty-five (in 1899). Cast originally for string sextet, *Verklärte Nacht*, with some revisions, has been performed most frequently since its première by the full string sections of large symphonic groups. Its effect, always communicative and moving in the concert hall, actually gains in power when the score is heard with *Pillar of Fire*, for this music, according to the composer, follows a plot of its own which has been realized visually in Tudor's ballet.

The inspiration for *Verklärte Nacht* comes from a poem by Richard Dehmel, *Weib und die Welt* ("Woman and the World"), treating of the redemption of a woman who has given herself to a stranger for the sake of experience. Now with child, she walks beside another who really awakens her love. As they go through the night together, she confesses her past; and the man answers gently, in the grove where they have paused, that the moon which is enveloping them both will also cast its spell on the child to come, and make it part of their lives. They embrace, and the woman, her soul purged through confession, is forgiven. With certain departures and elaborations in the story line, the dramatic plan of *Pillar of Fire* is essentially that of *Verklärte Nacht*.

Although Tudor had already shown in *Lilac Garden* much of the plastic freedom to be found in this later work, he had not prepared his audi-

Photo: *Alfredo Valente*   *Courtesy Dance News*
ANNABELLE LYON, LUCIA CHASE, AND NORA KAYE AS THE THREE SISTERS

ence for the full fusion of ballet technique and modern concert dance that was to mark *Pillar of Fire*. Every gesture, every lift, no matter how apparently unorthodox or revolutionary, retained its classical basis yet carried a new kinetic strength, an ability to transmit psychological states of feeling with shattering directness.

As originally planned, the ballet was to close with the lovers receding through four consecutive curtains of gauze—the full depth of the Metropolitan stage. This ending was abandoned for reasons of economy and the present one substituted, with its two figures, hand in hand, strolling in a conventional moonlight apotheosis—a small flaw, however, beside the choreography's major dramatic power.

The curtain rises at once to the repressed, smoldering first pages of the music, and a bleak town at the turn of the century is revealed with

overhanging roofs and a mood of spiritual oppression.

Hagar, central figure of the work, is sitting alone on her doorstep, watching life go by. She is filled with longing as she sees happy young couples walk past her in the dusk.

The passions surging within this girl rise to the surface as the youth with whom she is in love crosses the street and approaches her house.

He has come to pay a call on her family; and, a model of kindliness and gentility, he does not divine the malicious motives that govern Hagar's younger sister, a precocious little girl—her hair tied with a bow,

her juvenile dress worn seductively over a growing body—as she coaxes him away from the frustrated woman on the doorstep and, together with the eldest of the three sisters—a prim spinster—invites him into the house.

Now Hagar is left alone, and her distracted thoughts are drawn to the building across the street, suddenly lighted up from within. It is an abode of sin as conceived by the puritanical mind, full of disheveled women and lustful men. As she gazes intently at this house, which symbolizes her own secret desire, the Evil Young Man steps from its doorway. Dark, slight, dressed in exotic colors, he stares at Hagar, bends his knee suggestively, removes his jacket. Then, glancing back at her, he re-enters the house. At this moment, Hagar's friend returns with the younger sister. The little girl, who has alternately pushed Hagar toward the kindly youth and then stepped between them, now takes possession of the suitor completely and goes off with him for a stroll. The strings sound a violent tremolo in the orchestra. Hagar, in a frenzy of jealousy and loneliness, clutches her womb.

Once more, the Evil Young Man appears in the doorway of the building across the street. This time he comes toward Hagar and engages her in a passionate *pas de deux*.

Overwhelmed with a desire for companionship, she surrenders herself to him and allows herself to be drawn inside the house of ill repute; and, across the back of the stage, flees a dimly lighted figure *sur les pointes,* perhaps the only animated symbol in all ballet of innocence on the run.

Now, as Hagar returns from her experience, the shameful house itself slides into the wings, leaving a void, and she crosses the street to face her older sister. Doubled over with a sense of debasement, she barely notices the younger sister coming home from her stroll with the friend.

The whole community soon appears, quick at detecting a scandal in its midst. Hagar's elder sister cuts through the crowd, moving toward a pair of prim, elderly gossips with whom she has never lost sympathy. Significantly, the youngest sister coquets with a group of men from the house of ill fame; but her movements are already so artful, so brazenly deceptive, that she will never experience the guilt and isolation that are Hagar's.

As the gapers finally move off, the two sisters take Hagar inside the house and bid the friend good evening.

The lights are lowered, and when they come up again the house where Hagar lives has disappeared. She and her sisters are huddled against a dim background, the collective object of censure in the community, since one of them has sinned.

It is not long before the two other women leave Hagar. She finds herself alone in a world fringed by distant trees, through which she is followed by figures from her past. The young man she really loves approaches her, but she turns from him in shame. Innocent boys and girls, whom Hagar had once seen walking before her doorstep in the evening, now appear in chaste procession. Whores and panders from the vanished house across the street return to haunt her memory.

Desperately, Hagar tries to cling to one group or the other. The respectable circles of the town will have none of her; the bawds and their consorts pass her by; and when she turns to the Evil Young Man, who has reappeared among them, he ignores her for a new conquest.

When it seems that Hagar's suffering at the hands of both worlds cannot be more intense, her original lover—the gentle young man—suddenly enters and confronts her. Here, to a transfiguration by the orchestra of

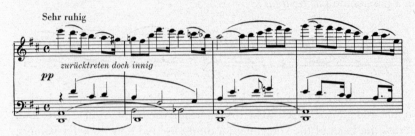

the opening theme, he offers the girl at last that strength of understanding she has needed. After an infinitely moving *pas de deux*, he takes Hagar in his arms and, together, they pass beneath the distant fringe of trees, dimly outlined in the moonlight.

Photo: Cecil Beaton   NORMA VANCE   *Courtesy Ballet Theatre*

KING, QUEENS, AND JACKS IN THE BALLETS DES CHAMPS-ÉLYSÉES PRODUCTION

Poker Game

(JEU DE CARTES)
(CARD PARTY)

THIS COMEDY in "three deals" (episodes) was first performed by the American Ballet at the Metropolitan Opera House in April, 1937, in an evening of music by Igor Stravinsky, with the composer conducting. It was then known as *Card Party.** Mr. Stravinsky collaborated with M. Malaieff on the book; Irene Sharaff designed the scenery and costumes; and George Balanchine contributed the choreography.

At its first performance, the ballet aroused enthusiasm through the stunning décor (representing a huge green felt card table with the hand of the croupier at the back), its trenchant score (in which Stravinsky wittily quoted thematic material from the music of Rossini), and resourceful production. It was not, however, until a revival by the Ballet Russe de Monte Carlo in 1940, when it became known as *Poker Game*, that the full choreographic merit of the piece was revealed through a

* The score is published as *Jeu de Cartes*.

MILADA MLADOVA

first-class dancing ensemble. Among the playing cards who passed across the stage with superb precision were Frederic Franklin as the Joker, Alexandra Danilova, Alicia Markova, André Eglevsky, and Igor Youskevitch. The ballet achieved such popularity in revival that it is hard to understand why *Poker Game* is not now performed, except perhaps for the impossibility of assembling a cast equal in collective sparkle to that of 1940. The work was given in a special edition by Janine Charrat (as *Jeu de Cartes*) for the Ballets des Champs-Élysées in Paris, 1945, with décor and costumes by Pierre Roy.

The following summary of the plot—which, in itself, is secondary, since the three "deals" are in essence three abstract designs—is quoted from the introduction to Stravinsky's published score:

"The characters in this ballet are the face cards in a game of poker, distributed among several players on the green cloth of a card room. At every deal the situation is complicated by the endless guiles of the perfidious Joker, who believes himself invincible because of his ability to become any desired card.

"During the first deal, one of the players is beaten, but the other two remain with even 'straights,' although one of them holds the Joker. In the second deal, the hand that holds the Joker is victorious, thanks to four Aces who easily beat four Queens.

"Now comes the third deal. The action becomes more and more acute. This time it is a struggle among three 'flushes.' Although at first victorious over one adversary, the Joker, strutting at the head of a sequence of Spades, is beaten by a 'royal flush' in Hearts. This puts an end to his malice and knavery."

Every one of the three deals is announced by the same musical motive,

played again at the close of the work as the cards are swept away by the croupier's giant hand.

Balanchine's choreography brought vivid detail to the single episodes of *Jeu de Cartes* yet kept building along large lines toward the finale, in which the humbling of the Joker and the annihilation of the entire pack were accomplished with a virtuoso sense of timing. The Stravinsky music for this denouement added the right dash of bitter brilliance.

Courtesy Dance News

LUBOV ROUDENKO AND IGOR YOUSKEVITCH AS THE TEN AND
JACK OF HEARTS

Polovtsian Dances

FROM PRINCE IGOR

THIS EXCERPT from the second act of Alexander Borodin's *Prince Igor* (the complete opera had its première at St. Petersburg in 1890) was first presented in its present form by the Diaghilev company at the Théâtre du Châtelet, Paris, in the season of 1909. Michel Fokine devised the choreography. The barbaric thrust of the music, the frenzied quality of the dancing, and the authentically Asiatic décor by Nicholas Roerich won an immediate success for the work. Adolph Bolm created the role of the Tartar Chieftain, which has been danced more recently by Yurek Shabelevsky and Frederic Franklin. Leon Woizikowsky has also been notable in the part.

Five years later the entire opera was done in the Russian season at Covent Garden, under the direction of Sir Thomas Beecham, and Western audiences had the opportunity of seeing the ballet in its proper framework. The opera itself provides the ideal setting for the Polovtsian dances. Not only are an immense chorus (used in the original Diaghilev performances) and band of supernumeraries called for in this scene— far beyond the financial capacities of any contemporary ballet troupe— but the dances themselves gain when put to the forefront of a crowded stage, linked to the dramatic action of the opera.

In the story of Borodin's work, these dances are arranged by Khan Kontchak, leader of the Tartar horde known as the Polovtsy, in order to divert his royal captive—Prince Igor—who has led a Russian expedition against the Khan and failed. Kontchak commands his warriors and their women to sing and dance for Igor, hoping that the prisoner will give up his hostility and cement an alliance between Russia and Tartary. Igor, however, refuses to swear friendship. Ultimately, in the final acts of the opera, he escapes to his own country.

With the Diaghilev excerpt, we find no Kontchak or Igor looking on from a primitive outdoor throne. The Polovtsy are merely assembled in a camp on the steppes to go through a number of tribal dances. The ballet is now generally offered without chorus, which mars its full effect, for Borodin's score needs the impact of massed voices above the boiling orchestral rhythms. Fokine's choreography has kept much of the barbaric vitality that once led audiences to cheer it; but contemporary performances of the work, reduced in scale and sluggish in execution, are at odds with the electric qualities implicit in music and dance.

As the smoke rises lazily from the campfires of a Tartar village, the women of the Polovtsy tribe engage in a graceful dance with veils. A soft, swaying chant is heard in the orchestra.

Now come the warriors with their bows and arrows, in battle formation. The vigorous theme that accompanies their entrance is to be heard later and simultaneously with the music of the women's dance, when both elements unite in the finale.

The women sway again, arousing the passions of the warriors. And there begins, with the throbbing of the timpani, one of the most exciting crescendi in all music. Through every one of its four bars, the drumbeat gains overwhelmingly in volume.

At its climax, the men leap forward and surround the women. This brilliant passage, dazzling in its orchestration, full of movement on the stage, is the climax of the scene.

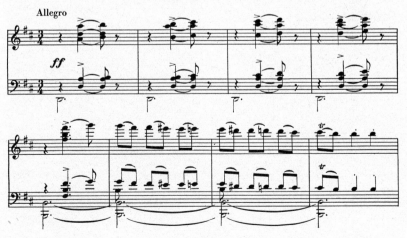

Then, to a wild call in the orchestra, four youths of the tribe spring forward and whirl about. The maidens join them, arms outstretched, feet dragging beneath.

The dance grows in fury. Led by their chieftain, who spins dizzily in the air, all of the warriors and women of the Polovtsy move with growing intensity until—with a kind of symmetrical abandon—the whole camp is plunged into the violence of a tribal orgy.

THE BALLET RUSSE PRODUCTION OF LES PRÉSAGES

Les Présages

THIS BALLET in four parts, corresponding to the four movements of Tchai-kovsky's Symphony No. 5, in E minor, was first produced at the Théâtre de Monte Carlo in April, 1933. The American première at the St. James Theatre, New York, occurred seven months later. Costumes and scenery were by André Masson. *Les Présages* began the series of essays in sym-phonic dance by Léonide Massine which was to reach a climax three years later in his version of Berlioz' *Symphonie Fantastique*. The princi-pal performers in this earlier work were Nina Verchinina, Irina Baron-ova, David Lichine, and Tatiana Riabouchinska. Dance patterns flowed from the music and were conceived in broad philosophical terms rather than in terms of plot.

FIRST MOVEMENT

The theme of *Les Présages* is that of Man's conflict with Destiny. As in the Fifth Symphony of Tchaikovsky, it is the dramatic embodiment of fate—alternately mysterious and militant—which dominates. As the first movement of the symphony opens with a motto theme expressing the

implacable forces of the universe, the curtain rises on the opening scene, showing Action—embodied by a solo female dancer—who speaks the case for Man and his right to freedom. For the moment, Action is successful.

SECOND MOVEMENT

In the following episode—danced to the celebrated Andante Can-

Courtesy Museum of Modern Art

TAMARA GRIGORIEVA IN LES PRÉSAGES

tabile—two lovers, symbolizing human dreams, are united and then driven apart by Destiny.

THIRD MOVEMENT

Here is Man in repose. A waltz theme is introduced by orchestra. Mas-

sine has designed the choreography so as to bring a moment of relief from the conflict.

FOURTH MOVEMENT

Now Destiny becomes a force for evil, driving humanity into war. Battle scenes follow, showing the chaos that arises from one nation's will to destroy another; but Reason prevails and changes Destiny through human effort. As in the symphony of Tchaikovsky, where the Fate motto is transfigured at the end, *Les Présages* closes on a note of strength and hope.

SCENE TWO   *Courtesy Museum of Modern Art*

The Prodigal Son

THIS NARRATIVE ballet in three scenes, with book by Boris Kochno—based on the Biblical parable—and music by Sergei Prokofiev, was first produced by the Diaghilev company at the Théâtre Sarah Bernhardt, Paris, in May, 1929, with scenery and costumes by the distinguished French artist Georges Rouault. George Balanchine was the choreographer. The cast included Serge Lifar in the title role, Felia Dubrovska as the Siren, Anton Dolin and Leon Woizikowsky as the Two Friends. In 1939 *The Prodigal Son* was revived for the Original Ballet Russe, using new choreography by David Lichine, who danced the name part. Sono Osato appeared as the Siren of this production, first given in Sydney, Australia, and offered later during the company's American season at the Fifty-first Street Theatre, New York, in November, 1940. The powerful score by Prokofiev remains the work's strongest and most consistently rewarding attribute.

SCENE ONE

After a vigorous orchestral introduction, the outside of the Prodigal

Son's home is seen. The youth enters to a wistful, searching theme. With

him are two evil companions who have turned him against his family. Under their influence, the young man quarrels with his father and leaves home in search of adventure.

SCENE TWO

In his travels through the world, the Prodigal Son falls in with a band of profligates and goes with them to a banquet. There he sees a magnificent Siren. As she draws him into an erotic dance, the two friends, who are always at his side, consort with the guests.

Drunkenness comes upon the youth—indicated in Prokofiev's score by a shrill fortissimo for woodwinds—followed by robbery in which, as the Prodigal Son lies in a stupor beside the banquet table, the Siren, his false friends, and the guests take all his belongings. Their thievery is echoed in the strings of the orchestra by soft, rapid passages like the scampering of rats.

At length the Prodigal Son awakens, laments his ill fortune, and sets out for home. On his departure, the Siren returns triumphantly with her accomplices to divide the loot in a full-scale orgy.

SCENE THREE

Once more the Prodigal's house is seen, as the youth drags himself toward the door. He falls exhausted, but his family—who have awaited his return—come from the dwelling and, in a fond greeting of joy and forgiveness, welcome him to their midst.

Photo: Alfredo Valente   *Courtesy Museum of Modern Art*

DAVID LICHINE AND SONO OSATO AS THE SON AND THE SIREN

The Prospect Before Us

THIS COMIC ballet, in seven scenes, is based on actual events in English theatrical history as related in John Eber's chronicle *Seven Years of the King's Theatre*, published in 1828. First produced in London—July, 1940—by the Sadler's Wells Company, the work has choreography by Ninette de Valois and a score arranged by Constant Lambert from music by the eighteenth-century British composer William Boyce. Scenery and costumes are by Roger Furse, and many of the settings are inspired by old theatrical drawings of the artist Thomas Rowlandson—notably the burning of the King's Theatre, and a *pas de deux* by Mlle Theodore and M. Didelot in the ballet *Amphion and Thalia* before a crowded audience at the Pantheon Theatre.* The racy atmosphere of backstage life in the 1700's pervades Miss de Valois's amusing choreographic patterns. At the première, Robert Helpmann appeared as the theatrical manager, Mr. O'Reilly, with Claude Newman as the rival impresario, Mr. Taylor. Frederick Ashton was seen in the historical role of Jean Georges Noverre, famous ballet master, with Ursula Moreton as Mme Noverre.

SCENE ONE

A rehearsal is taking place on the stage of the King's Theatre, London, in 1789. As Mr. Taylor, the manager, presides, and Mr. Noverre, the ballet master, tries to separate two incompatible dancers, the manager of the rival Pantheon Theatre—Mr. O'Reilly—comes in, with several friends, on a visit.

SCENE TWO

The King's Theatre burns to the ground in the midst of a performance (this is represented by a drop-curtain reproducing Rowlandson's drawing of the event). A woman jumps from the gallery; the audience rushes to the exits. Mr. Taylor is ruined; his dancers abandon him at the invitation of Mr. O'Reilly.

* This latter engraving is called "The Prospect Before Us," from which the ballet takes its name.

SCENE THREE

In an attempt to raise money for ballet at the Pantheon, Mr. O'Reilly has his artists perform in the streets of London, accepting all contributions. They carry a cardboard model of the theatre, inscribed: "Pray Remember the Poor Dancers."

SCENE FOUR

The big season at the Pantheon Theatre finally opens. Mr. O'Reilly takes his place proudly in the stage box at the left, accompanied by M. and Mme Noverre. In the opposite loge sits Mr. Taylor—invited by his rival—furious at the success that his former dancers are bringing to the redoubtable O'Reilly.

SCENE FIVE

With the help of friends, Mr. Taylor has been able to build a new King's Theatre on the site of the old. Meanwhile, Mr. O'Reilly's business affairs have gone badly; he is now in conference with Mr. Taylor, eager to be rid of his dancers and outstanding bills. Since the patent granted to the Pantheon Theatre cannot be transferred to the King's, the conference is ended and the despondent O'Reilly returns with his artists to their home base.

SCENE SIX

Now it is the turn of the Pantheon Theatre to burn to the ground. Mr. O'Reilly, however, does not grieve. Instead, he is delighted, since the fire releases him from all responsibility. Urging his dancers on Mr. Taylor, who has come to watch the blaze, the former manager cheers the dissolution of his troupe.

SCENE SEVEN

The company of the King's Theatre is assembled, as of old, under the direction of Mr. Taylor, with the ballet master Noverre rehearsing a new work on stage. Matters are going splendidly until Mr. O'Reilly enters, drunk and disheveled. He dances fantastically, mimics his one-time artists until they walk out. Then O'Reilly is left alone with Mr. Taylor, who courteously helps him to a table and offers him some wine. The drunkard spills most of the bottle, clutches the rest, and lurches from the hall. His adventures in ballet management are over.

Pulcinella

THE CREATION of this diverting one-act ballet for the Diaghilev Ballet Russe came about through the success of another work of the same kind —*Les Femmes de Bonne Humeur,* Léonide Massine's choreographic version of a Venetian comedy by Goldoni—which the company had produced three years earlier. The setting for *Pulcinella* was Naples, in place of Venice. The plot—instead of an extract from Goldoni—was taken from a South Italian manuscript comedy of the early eighteenth century, called *The Four Pulcinellas Who Look Alike.* The score was based on music by the celebrated Neapolitan composer of that period, Giambattista Pergolesi, in a modern adaptation by Igor Stravinsky. The entire production, in Massine's choreography, lay within the framework of the traditional *commedia dell' arte,** with Pulcinella as its sprightly hero.

Such a joining of creative minds as Stravinsky, Picasso, Massine, and Diaghilev could not but bring forth an important work. *Pulcinella* was first produced at the Paris Opéra in May, 1920, with Massine in the title role, Thamar Karsavina as Pimpinella, and Enrico Cecchetti as the Doctor. It has not been seen in America, though revived by Leon Woizikowsky's company (with Woizikowsky dancing the name part) in London, 1935. Part of the Stravinsky score was used as background for Todd Bolender's ballet *Musical Chairs,* presented at Jacob's Pillow, Massachusetts, in August, 1945, and offered, under the title of *Commedia Balletica,* by the Ballet Russe de Monte Carlo at the New York City Center in the following month. Bolender's work, excellent in itself, has no choreographic relationship to the *Pulcinella* of Massine.

The action of the ballet is preceded by a short overture which recreates the spirit of somewhat formalized gaiety to be found in the music of Pergolesi and the whole period of the *commedia dell' arte.*

---

* *Commedia dell' arte,* a form of theatre popular in Italy from the sixteenth to the beginning of the nineteenth century, means literally "comedy of the profession"— various skits performed by career players, who replaced the amateur actors of earlier days and appeared before a paying audience. The performers usually improvised these comedies, built around stock characters well known for their droll names, traits, masks, and make-up. Most famous of the *commedia dell' arte* personages, about whom these little plays clustered, were Harlequin (originally a French creation) and Pulcinella, sometimes known to English-speaking audiences as Punchinello. It is from the latter that the humorous magazine *Punch* derives its name.

Then the curtain rises on a nocturnal scene in Naples, showing a narrow street that leads down to the bay, with the lighted crater of Vesuvius in the distance. Two houses at the head of the street are to figure prominently in the action.

Although the stage is empty, a fanciful atmosphere is set at once by an old Neapolitan tune, sung in the distance.

Two gallants of the town, Caviello and Florinda, enter on the tide of this music to serenade their ladies, who live across the street from each other in the two front houses. As the gallants sing, Rosetta and Prudenza —the objects of their attention—appear at the upper windows and throw water on the serenaders. Then the pompous Doctor, Prudenza's father, strides from his house, attacks the two gallants with a stick, and drives them away. The street is again deserted.

Now the chief character of the piece appears: Pulcinella, in conventionalized white blouse, red tie, and oafish cap. He wears a mask and enters from an obscure doorway at the left, where he lives with his mistress, Pimpinella. Alone in the space before the houses, Pulcinella leaps about in a merry dance and plays a miniature violin.

His music has results. At once Prudenza appears. In love with him, she makes advances, but he drives her away. Then Rosetta enters, equally infatuated. She is accompanied by her father, Tartaglia, a silly old man with a turned-up nose, who scolds his daughter for favoring someone so base as Pulcinella. The girl disregards his warnings, makes the same advances to Pulcinella as had her friend Prudenza, and is received somewhat more cordially, but inconclusively. At length Rosetta goes off with her father.

Now it is the turn of Pulcinella's mistress, Pimpinella, to enter. She has noted his attentions to Rosetta and rebukes him; but when the masker swears his innocence, Pimpinella relents and joins Pulcinella in a charming dance.

Absorbed in each other, they do not see the entrance of the two disappointed gallants, Caviello and Florindo. These men, who hate the masker for the attentions shown him by their ladies, tear Pulcinella away from Pimpinella and force him to his knees. The masker at once calls for help. Prudenza and Rosetta rush in, force the gallants off, but make life miserable for the fallen Pulcinella by quarreling over him and pulling his tired body in all directions. The street fight between the women is stopped only by the appearance of the Doctor and Tartaglia, who drive their daughters indoors.

Pulcinella rises, glad to be alone with Pimpinella; but his joy does not last long, for the two marauders have returned, hidden in long black cloaks and bearing swords. Pulcinella sees them, grabs hold of his mistress, and tries to flee with her into the house. The doorway is so small, however, that only Pimpinella can pass through it in time. As Pulcinella follows, Florindo lunges at him with a sword. The masker falls to the ground dramatically, and the two gallants—satisfied that the interloper has been punished—go off. After they have left, Pulcinella rises blithely and walks away.

Now a curious procession appears in the street. Four little masked Pulcinellas in white enter, carrying on their shoulders another Pulcinella—apparently a corpse. They set the body down before the left-hand house and dance around it with simulated grief. Hearing the commotion, the Doctor and Tartaglia come into the little square with their daughters. Even the two old men are moved at seeing the alleged remains of Pulcinella, and there is general mourning.

In the midst of all this grief, a magician enters (Pulcinella in disguise). Balancing himself on a long pole, the would-be wizard leaps around the body, beats it, and finally bids the corpse arise—which it does obligingly, since it is no corpse at all, but only his friend Fourbo, made up to resemble one. The four little Pulcinellas, on witnessing this resurrection, go off happily; and the two girls dance joyously with Fourbo (a mischievous accomplice of Pulcinella), believing him to be the masker they both adore. At length the girls depart; their interfering fathers also leave the scene; and the two friends, Pulcinella and Fourbo, are left alone. Pimpinella appears for a moment, but—terrified at the sight of Pulcinella brought back to life (he has thrown away the magician's disguise)—she vanishes. The masker sends Fourbo in pursuit of her.

Now—after the advent of the four little Pulcinellas and of Fourbo disguised as Pulcinella—the ultimate compliment to the masker and his popularity is paid when the two murderous gallants, Florindo and Caviello, enter with their faces adorned by Pulcinellalike masks. They have come to renew their advances to Prudenza and Rosetta, sure of their success this time by aping the most sought-after lover in that part of Naples. Just as they appear, Fourbo returns with Pimpinella. Forgetting his vows of friendship, he is beginning to make love to her; and the poor girl, believing him—in his disguise—to be Pulcinella, responds. Rosetta and Prudenza, emerging from their houses, fall into the same trap with the two masked gallants. Each believes she is embracing the real Pulcinella.

Infuriated, Pulcinella—who has been watching—leaps among the three couples and reveals himself. At once, all of the women break away from their escorts and run toward him. Soothed by their attentions, he dances with the girls but then turns angrily on the men who have been imitating him, and unmasks them. The two gallants stand revealed in their own dull identity; the crafty Fourbo—much quicker than they—grasps the magician's robes that Pulcinella has left on the ground and climbs into them.

Once in this new disguise, Fourbo becomes benign and resolves the conflict. When he sees the fathers of the two girls returning, he suggests to them—in his capacity as magician—that Rosetta and Prudenza finally marry Florindo and Caviello. Both old men consent, as do their daughters. While the vows are being pronounced, Pulcinella and Pimpinella—completely reconciled—inform the magician that they, too, wish to be wed.

A delightful finale follows. The three couples dance by themselves, while Fourbo joins the Doctor and Tartaglia in a lively measure. When the four little Pulcinellas return to the scene, the picture is complete and the ballet ends with a gay celebration.

FRANK HOBI, MARY ELLEN MOYLAN, LEON DANIELIAN AS THE ALCHEMIST, THE
CONTESSA ILARIA, AND ZENOBIO BONAVENTURI

Quelques Fleurs

THIS BALLET in one act, with book and choreography by Ruthanna Boris,
was given its first performance by the Ballet Russe de Monte Carlo at
the Metropolitan Opera House in September, 1948. Scenery and costumes were designed by Robert Davison. The musical score, compiled
by Harry G. Schumer from several works of the French *opéra bouffe*
composer, Daniel François Auber (1782–1871), including excerpts from
the overtures to *The Bronze Horse, Fra Diavolo, Masaniello,* and *The
Crown Diamonds,* is pieced together in a continuity appropriate to the
action of the ballet. The 1830 Parisian atmosphere of this orchestral
background, deliberately selected as a contrast to the Italian Renaissance setting on stage, came off with graceful wit.

The work was planned and mounted on a financial grant from Houbi-
gant, Inc., as part of a promotional campaign for that firm's perfume:
Quelques Fleurs. While the product became better known through the
success of the ballet (and a national advertising tie-up), there is some
doubt as to whether it became better loved—for the plot is anticosmetic,

preaching the moral that woman should attract through natural beauty alone or, failing this, turn to other interests. At the première of the work, Mary Ellen Moylan appeared in the role of the Contessa who resorts to perfumes as a decoy, with Leon Danielian as her victim, Zenobio Bonaventuri, and Frank Hobi as the Alchemist.

To the brilliant opening measures of the overture to *The Bronze Horse*, the curtain rises on an inner drop, revealing two young girls with torches who dance briefly in greeting to the audience, place their torches

in holders at either side of the stage, and motion for the blue inner curtain to part. Now the locale of the ballet, the gardens of the Villa Carretto at the height of the Renaissance come into sight.

The first character to appear is the Alchemist, a nobleman in the employ of the Contessa Ilaria—proprietess of the villa—who acts as her majordomo, adviser, and friend. He is on hand in the gardens to receive several guests invited by the Contessa.

Soon they arrive, all elegants of the period: women wearing great, sweeping gowns; men in rich attire; and at last by himself, in an almost operatic entrance, Zenobio Bonaventuri, young man of fashion. It is he for whom the Contessa has set her cap and is giving this party. Until now he has parried her advances, but tonight must yield a definite result.

As the guests take their places, the Contessa advances. Fairly mature—somewhat over thirty-five—she is beautiful, powerful, and spoiled. Not more so, however, than Zenobio, who, completely wrapped up in himself, buffs his nails, fixes his cuffs, and ignores the Contessa. Terribly bored, he pays no attention to her; and, as the guests start to dance, he joins them without looking back.

Fuming, the Contessa claps her hands and stops the music. Now she summons the two little girls of the prologue, who come running with archaic instruments and strike up a new dance based on the changing of partners. Using this pattern as a pretext, the Contessa tries every possible means of snaring Zenobio, but with no success. Instead, she draws the Alchemist while Zenobio dances blissfully by himself. At the end of his little exhibition, he strolls off, and the guests follow him. The garden is deserted, except for the Contessa and her Alchemist.

Now, to the fierce opening of the *Fra Diavolo* overture, the Contessa

pours out her fury. The Alchemist tries to quiet her, for every now and then a group of guests passes through the garden; but she is too upset to control herself. At the height of her passion, Zenobio comes flying by with a bunch of flowers. Unaware of the two who are watching him, he leaps off, pursued by the Contessa.

The Alchemist detains the unhappy woman forcibly. Taking her by the shoulders, he leads her to a bush at the rear of the garden, waves his hands, and mutters mysterious incantations. Remote gong beats are sounded. Suddenly the bush opens, revealing three perfumed spirits of seduction—Rose, Violet, and Carnation—irresistible in their fragrance. Each of them dances a solo variation; then, in a band, they approach the Contessa and offer to help her win Zenobio.

For the only time that evening, the Contessa seems happy; the Alchemist is really a friend. She smiles as the nobleman summons the guests, proposes a game of blindman's buff, and arranges for Zenobio to be "it." When the handkerchief has been tied over the young man's eyes, all the ladies dance around him, followed by the Contessa and her three live flowers. No sooner do they pass than the sensitive youth swoons at their fragrance. Reviving, he seeks them out. The guests, piloted by the Alchemist, withdraw to another part of the garden; and the Contessa, relying on her perfumed allies, is left alone with Zenobio.

The young man is entranced with the odors; the Contessa sighs romantically, thinking she has captured her prey. At the end of an ingenious *pas de cinq*, during which the three flowers weave constantly between them, the Contessa—with a grand flourish—tears the bandage from his eyes and reveals herself as the object of his search.

Zenobio stares at her incredulously; then, overwhelmed with shock, he lets her fall. The flowers, badly frightened, desert the lady, rush toward the Alchemist, who is looking on cynically, and take refuge behind him.

Now Zenobio, a trifle more composed, faces the Contessa and tries to end an embarrassing situation as best he can. Apologizing for his rudeness, he suggests they both forget the whole affair.

At this crowning rebuff, the Contessa abandons all pretense of courtly behavior. She chases the young man angrily, tries to beat him. The flowers, drawn into the battle as if hypnotized, encircle Zenobio, with whom they flee; and the Contessa is left behind, holding only the bandage from the game of blindman's buff.

Now the guests return to bid her good night. Desolate, she can hardly look at them. Her friend the Alchemist stands by, telling her that life is not too hopeless, but the Contessa ignores him. As he goes off, she stands thinking only of Zenobio and of the scents which have failed her.

Suddenly the giddy youth bounds through the garden once more, still following the flowers. For a moment, the Contessa thinks of renewing the chase but, as the spirits run tantalizingly between them, she gives up. Instead, she leans against a balustrade, looking despairingly at Zenobio. The young man gazes past her, at the flowers who have been eluding him. As both these figures, the core of a perfect misunderstanding, seem to turn to marble in the Renaissance garden, the two girls of the prologue come forward and summon the curtain to fall. As it does, the three heady but unreliable perfumes flash across the stage to the final bars of the music.

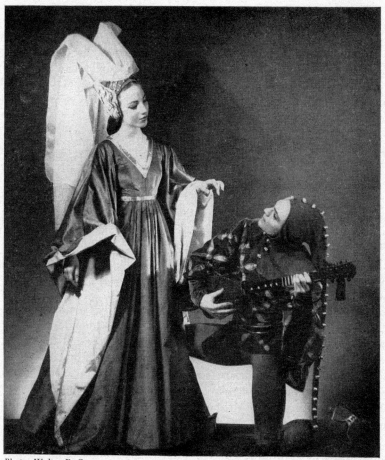

NATALIE KRASSOVSKA AND FRANK HOBI

Raymonda

THIS BALLET in three acts and four scenes, with choreography by Marius Petipa, and book by Petipa in collaboration with Lydia Pashkova, was first produced at the Mariinsky Theatre, St. Petersburg, in January, 1898. Alexander Glazunov composed a specially written score for the work, and Pierina Legnani danced the title role at the première. *Raymonda* was revived successfully by Alexandra Danilova and George Balanchine for the Ballet Russe de Monte Carlo in March, 1946, at the New York City Center with Danilova in the name part.

ACT ONE

SCENE ONE: Nobles, maids of honor, and troubadours are lounging in the great hall of a castle in medieval Hungary as the curtain rises, planning a birthday celebration for Raymonda, daughter of the family in residence. Roused to animation by the prospect, Raymonda's friends join in a brilliant waltz and ignore the elderly Countess Sybille—the

Tempo di valse

girl's aunt—who rebukes them for their indolence. Pointing to the statue of the White Lady, one of the family forebears, which dominates the hall, the Countess reminds the company that this ancestress is supposed to punish those who flaunt the noble traditions of her house.

As if in direct defiance, the dancing goes on until it is interrupted by trumpet blasts: a herald approaches, followed by a messenger from Raymonda's fiancé, Jean de Brienne, away at the wars. The courier bears news that de Brienne is to arrive at the castle on the following day.

No sooner has this messenger withdrawn than the herald announces another visitor: the Saracen knight, Abderam. Surprised at the strange warrior's visit, Raymonda and her aunt make him welcome; but when the knight offers Raymonda precious gifts to win her favor, the girl rejects them. Abderam is not discouraged. Secretly deciding to carry off Raymonda by force, he secures an invitation from the Countess to the birthday festival.

As dusk approaches, most of the guests withdraw and Raymonda remains in the hall with a few of her friends. They dance, play the lute. Then—drowsy at the close of day—they fall into a slumber. Only Raymonda remains awake. Suddenly, filled with terror, she sees the statue of the White Lady descending from its niche. The statue beckons to Raymonda, who follows it to the terrace as clouds hide the room in a scenic transformation.

SCENE TWO: Now the White Lady leads Raymonda from the terrace of the castle to a misty garden below. The clouds clear away and the girl sees a vision of her fiancé, Jean de Brienne, surrounded by his knights. Raymonda runs to join him in an elaborate *pas de deux;* but as their duet reaches its height, the White Lady makes another gesture, the apparition fades, and Raymonda discovers the figure of Abderam at her side, renewing his advances. When she rejects him, the knight threatens to take her life. Fantastic elves appear on the scene, terrifying

Photo: Walter E. Owen NIKITA TALLIN *Courtesy Dance News*

specters. Raymonda faints, the evil vision vanishes, and a party from the castle—in search of the missing girl—arrives to carry her back to safety.

ACT TWO

The birthday festival of Raymonda is taking place in the castle. As the guests enter, announced by the herald, Abderam may be seen among them. Haunted by thoughts of her vision, which she interprets as a warning, Raymonda begs the Countess to drive the knight from the castle; but the old woman insists on following the rules of family hospitality. Abderam has been invited to the ceremony, and he must remain.

Again, the Saracen pays court to Raymonda. This time he has members of his suite on hand to entertain her. There are performances by jugglers, Arab boys, and Moorish dancers. Then he orders wine to be distributed; and, in the midst of the bacchanale that follows, Abderam orders his slaves to bear the girl from the castle.

Providentially, Jean de Brienne arrives at this moment with the King of Hungary. Rescuing Raymonda, he is about to strike down the Saracen when the King orders the enemies to settle their differences in formal combat. Both men battle furiously, and at the climax of the contest the White Lady appears, bringing death to the Saracen. As she vanishes, the King solemnly unites Raymonda and de Brienne.

ACT THREE

The concluding scene of the ballet consists of a series of *divertissements* celebrating Raymonda's wedding. Opening with a processional

that suggests the pomp of Hungary's medieval kings, the tableau reaches its culmination in a pageant depicting the glory of knightly combat.

Photo: *Larry Colwell*
Courtesy Museum of Modern Art
NATALIE KRASSOVSKA AS RAYMONDA

The Red Poppy

THIS BALLET in three acts and six scenes, with book and décor by Michael Kurilko, choreography by L. A. Larchiune and Vassily Tikhomiroff, and music by Reinhold Glière, was first produced at Leningrad in 1926 and, during the following year, at the Bolshoi Theatre, Moscow. The American première, in a shortened choreographic version by Igor Schwezoff, took place at the New York City Center in April, 1944, with the company of the Ballet Russe de Monte Carlo. Alexandra Danilova was seen in the role of Tai-Hoa, with Ruthanna Boris, Igor Youskevitch, Frederic Franklin, and Leon Danielian in supporting parts.

The music of the ballet, cast in popular style, has melodies of broad appeal. Dramatically, *The Red Poppy* bears the exaggerated brush strokes of nineteenth-century melodrama applied to a political theme at its core.

ACT ONE

One of the few attractions of a sordid American treaty port of China, where coolies are flogged and foreigners pampered, is the beautiful Tai-Hoa, performer at a waterfront bar. One evening, while dancing for sailors and officers of all nationalities, she sees a young Soviet Captain come to the aid of a group of coolies who have been brutally treated by the port command. Tai-Hoa admiringly gives him a bouquet of flowers—among them red poppies, the symbol of liberty. Then she goes off with her manager, Li-Shan-Fu, a shadowy character already jealous of the Captain.

Now the coolies join with their women in a dance of freedom. The sailors who have been lolling on the waterfront add their own national flavors to the celebration. There are set numbers by a German, Englishman, American Negress, Chinese, Indian, and finally a joyous ensemble by a group of Soviet sailors, whose rousing tune has become the most popular excerpt from the score.

ACT TWO

SCENE ONE: Most of the leading characters now arrive at an opium den on errands of their own devising. Tai-Hoa has come to dance and smoke; Li-Shan-Fu to watch her; the Soviet Captain to see the girl once more; and the sinister commander of the treaty port, Sir Hips, to keep an eye on the political situation. He has heard of the Soviet Captain's support of the coolies, and plots with Li-Shan-Fu to do away with the troublemaker. As they attempt to seize the Russian, however, he summons his men and is rescued. Sir Hips disappears ignominiously; the clients leave; and Tai-Hoa remains alone. Her jealous manager has vowed to separate her from the Soviet Captain. In order to escape from Li-Shan-Fu and the realities of life, she takes up an opium pipe, smokes it, and falls asleep.

SCENES TWO AND THREE: First, Tai-Hoa dreams of the China of her ancestors: dragons, soldiers, gods, and priests. Then, as the scene changes, poppies, lotuses, and butterflies—all in dance form—crowd into her feverish mind. At the height of the vision, in which she herself moves ardently, the Soviet Captain appears. As she runs to his side, he vanishes, and all the grief which she has tried to escape in opium returns to overwhelm her.

ACT THREE

SCENE ONE: The enemies of the Soviet Captain have not given up their plans to be rid of him. Now they plan an elaborate dinner at which he is to be poisoned. Without revealing his purpose, Li-Shan-Fu persuades Tai-Hoa to perform with her troupe at the banquet. In this way he can be sure of the Captain's presence.

After she has danced for the guests, Tai-Hoa suddenly discovers the attempt against the Captain's life. She succeeds in warning him, but the Soviet officer refuses to leave. Instead, he reminds Tai-Hoa of the red poppy she once gave him, and makes her promise to work with him for the liberty of the oppressed.

As the conspiracy against the Captain reaches its climax, Li-Shan-Fu orders Tai-Hoa to hand the Russian a glass of wine which she knows to be poisoned. Pretending the stem has slipped through her fingers, she lets the glass fall to the ground and smash. Li-Shan-Fu immediately draws his gun and fires at the Captain. Unnerved, he misses, and the officer escapes.

Photo: Maurice Seymour Courtesy Dance News

ALEXANDRA DANILOVA AND FREDERIC FRANKLIN

SCENE TWO: As Tai-Hoa stands on the waterfront, waving farewell to the steamer that is taking the Captain back to his own country, Li-Shan-Fu enters. With jealousy at fever pitch, he plunges a knife into the girl. Tai-Hoa falls; and, surrounded by a group of children who have been playing on the wharves, she hands them a red poppy in this final moment of her life, urging them always to fight for freedom. She dies, and in an epilogue which reflects the spirit of her sacrifice, the Chinese proletariat emerges triumphant.

Rodeo

OR

THE COURTING AT BURNT RANCH

THIS WORK, with scenario and choreography by Agnes de Mille, was first performed by the Ballet Russe de Monte Carlo at the Metropolitan Opera House in October, 1942. Because of its skillful handling of American folk elements and contagious gusto, *Rodeo* was an instantaneous success.

The attractive score * was specially composed by Aaron Copland, with scenery by Oliver Smith and costumes by Kermit Love. Miss de Mille created the part of the Cowgirl at the première, with Milada Mladova as the Rancher's Daughter, Frederic Franklin as the Champion Roper, and Casimir Kokitch as the Head Wrangler. Later replacements have included Lubov Roudenko and Dorothy Etheridge as the Cowgirl, Herbert Bliss as the Roper, and Nicolas Magallanes as the Wrangler.

SCENE ONE

After a joyous outburst of music, Western and wide-open in feeling,

the curtain rises on the corral of a ranch, about fifty years ago. It is Saturday afternoon, time for the weekly rodeo.

Three figures may be seen leaning against a fence at the back: the Cowgirl, dressed in breeches, mistakenly hoping through competitive skill in riding and other sports to attract her man; the tall, dark Head Wrangler, whom she secretly admires; and the good-natured Champion Roper. They stand lazily, watching the horizon.

* Four symphonic episodes were later extracted from *Rodeo* for concert performance. They are: "Buckaroo Holiday" and "Corral Nocturne" from the first scene; "Saturday Night Waltz" and "Hoe Down" from the second. This suite was first performed in concert form at the Lewisohn Stadium in July, 1943.

One of the cowboys enters and circles vigorously as if he were on a horse.° In a moment he is gone, but the opening mood has been broken. The two men stroll away from the Cowgirl, move across the field with hardly a backward glance.

Lonely and stung by their indifference, the girl swings onto her saddle, galloping along in an attempt to keep up her spirits. Throughout the scene, an old American song, "If He'd Be a Buckaroo by Trade," is treated symphonically by Copland to underline the jogging motions of the dancers.

Never has the Cowgirl, plain in any event, shown to such disadvantage, for that afternoon, to the delight of the Wrangler, Roper, and other hands on the ranch, several well-dressed young ladies from Kansas City have arrived on a visit to the Rancher's Daughter. As the men turn out to greet them, the Cowgirl—finished with her ride—avails herself of the crowd to squeeze wistfully between the Wrangler and the Roper. The Roper moves away. The Wrangler pays no attention. He is concentrating on the Rancher's Daughter.

Late afternoon gives way to twilight; and as soft brasses in the orchestra, against plucked strings, evoke the feeling of dusk, a strange pensiveness settles on the ranch. The men and their visitors move in

hushed groups. Suddenly the Roper shatters their reverie with a tap dance—time to get ready for the evening at the ranch house. He and the rest stroll off. Only the Cowgirl, utterly ignored, stays behind in the corral.

Interlude

There is a blackout; and, when the lights come up, a curtain of prancing horses has fallen, shielding the scene. Four couples are revealed down front in a running square dance, with a Caller shouting the movements: "Ladies to the center, form a star. Gentlemen forward, and back to the bar." There is no music at this point, only a series of handclaps from the musicians in the orchestra and the performers themselves.

° Similar to the imaginary cavalcade of Eugene Loring's *Billy the Kid* (1938). An independent arrival at this same device, during the year of the Loring première, has been claimed for Miss de Mille's early *American Suites* by George Amberg in his survey *Ballet in America*.

Photo: Maurice Seymour   *Courtesy Ballet Theatre*
AGNES DE MILLE AS THE COWGIRL IN HER OWN RODEO

After a number of formations, each more vigorous than the last, the dancers form a circle which opens out; they run off stage in line, and the inner curtain rises.

SCENE TWO

The Saturday night party in front of the ranch house is going at full tilt. The Cowgirl, still not recovered from her melancholy of the afternoon, sits alone on a bench at the side. As always, she has eyes only for the Head Wrangler; and when the Roper, who feels sorry for her, strolls toward the bench, she ignores him. The Roper and the Wrangler —neither of whom understands the girl—look at each other puzzled, then fix their eyes on the doorway, for the Rancher's Daughter, whom they both are courting, has come out of the house. The young lady favors the Wrangler, and the Roper gallantly leaves the field to his rival.

Now the guests join in a period waltz, one of the most haunting passages in the score, related to the old American folk tune, "Old Paint."

Four couples take the floor, with the Wrangler and Rancher's Daughter forming a fifth, to the despair of the Cowgirl. As the dancers start to spin, one of the girls gets sick and has to be taken out; another is kissed and runs into the house. Her partner, in a state of remorse, sits next to the Cowgirl, who befriends him; but their alliance lasts only a moment. Another belle saunters by, flips her skirt, and moves on. The cowhand follows.

It is time for a new number; and the Roper, in good spirits, kicks high and leads the party in a second waltz. Suddenly he notices the Cowgirl, still isolated from the others. She has been crying. Determined to cheer her up, he takes her in his arms and they dance. Just as the pair reaches the center of the floor, the Cowgirl stops dead, her face goes white with jealousy—for she has spotted the Wrangler with the Rancher's Daughter. The Roper, thoroughly annoyed, smacks the ingrate on the flanks; and the girl, who has reached the limit of her humiliation, runs into the house.

In a moment, this ugly duckling is forgotten. The party has been going at a lively pace; and, as it reaches a peak of excitement, the Roper steps forward to clap the rhythms of a Hoedown.*

During the dance that follows, he chases the Rancher's Daughter— again unsuccessfully. He is about to give up and leave when a vision in yellow comes through the center door—the Cowgirl, wearing a dress. She looks so different, so attractive, that the boys and their guests are spellbound, most of all the Roper. Making up for his past obtuseness, he goes after the girl and courts her. As she accepts—not without one last wistful glance at the Wrangler—the ballet ends on a vigorous general dance.

* Based by Copland on an old American tune called "Bonyparte."

KAREN CONRAD

Romantic Age

THIS *divertissement* in one act, with choreography by Anton Dolin and décor by Carlos Mérida, was given its world première by Ballet Theatre at the Metropolitan Opera House in October, 1942. A wistful and sometimes ironic re-creation of mid-nineteenth-century dance, it derives its plot from an old ballet of Filippo Taglioni, *Aglaë, or Cupid's Pupil,** produced for Marie Taglioni by her father during the ballerina's Rus-

---

* In *Romantic Age*, the heroine's name has been changed from Aglaë to Elora.

sian tour of 1841. In his reanimation of this work, Dolin has followed the same procedure as in his earlier and more successful *Pas de Quatre*— the evocation of a vanished era with a nostalgic sigh and indulgent smile. The principal roles at the Ballet Theatre première were taken by Alicia Markova, who scored one of her great successes in the part of Elora; Mr. Dolin as the Youth; Karen Conrad as an athletic Cupid; John Kriza as the Faun; and Miriam Golden, Maria Karnilova, and Sono Osato as the three Muses.

One of the more distinguished features of *Romantic Age* was its exquisite score, based by Antal Dorati on excerpts from the operas of Vincenzo Bellini. This mating of Taglioni's libretto and Bellini's music —each, in itself, as romantic as the ballet's title—made for a work which had moments of special charm.

Elora, a bashful nymph, would like to dance but does not know how. Cupid takes an interest in her plight and, shooting a golden arrow at her feet, soon teaches the girl to surpass all the other nymphs in grace and agility.

Two figures now enter: a youth in love with Elora, and a faun, drawn by the beauty of her dancing. Jealous of the youth, the faun tries to attack him; but the friends of Elora bind the satyr in wreaths of flowers so that he cannot move and is compelled to seek forgiveness. The ballet ends with the union of the youth and Elora, who, as Cupid's only pupil, has become the most expert performer of all.

Romeo and Juliet

(PROKOFIEV)

THIS BALLET in four acts and nine scenes, with choreography by L. M. Lavrovsky, was first produced at the Kirov State Theatre for Opera and Ballet, Leningrad, in 1940. Peter Williams designed the costumes and scenery; the title roles were danced by Constantin Sergeyev and Galina Ulanova. A. V. Lopukhov was the Mercutio and S. G. Karen the Tybalt.

The work's outstanding feature is the music by Sergei Prokofiev which, independently of the ballet, has already become a classic. First given at Moscow as a concert piece in October, 1935, the score aroused much criticism at the time, especially in view of the composer's plan to add a happy ending to Shakespeare's tragedy: Juliet resurrected in her tomb, and a joyous final dance of the lovers. This modification was soon abandoned, and the ballet, musically and dramatically, remained faithful to the play. In answering criticisms concerning the music itself, Prokofiev remarked: "I have taken special pains to achieve a simplicity which will, I hope, reach the hearts of all listeners. If people find no melody or no emotion in this work of mine, I shall feel very sorry; but I am sure that they will sooner or later."

Two orchestral suites have been derived from the ballet. Suite No. 1, first heard at the Bolshoi Theatre in November, 1936, and given its American première two months later by the Chicago Symphony Orchestra under the direction of Prokofiev himself, consists of: (1) Folk Dance; (2) Scene (The Street Awakens); (3) Madrigal; (4) Minuet (Arrival of the Guests); (5) Masks (Romeo and Mercutio Masked); (6) Romeo and Juliet (The Balcony Scene); (7) The Death of Tybalt.

The second suite, first played at Moscow in December, 1936, and introduced to the United States by the Boston Symphony Orchestra under the composer's direction in March, 1938, includes: (1) Montagues and Capulets; (2) Juliet—The Little Girl; (3) Friar Laurence; (4) Dance of the Five Couples; (5) Romeo and Juliet Before Parting (Romeo and Juliet's Leave-Taking, and Juliet's Resolve to Take the Sleeping Potion); (6) Dance of the Maids from the Antilles; (7) Romeo at Juliet's tomb.

The scenario of Lavrovsky follows the Shakespearean drama almost exactly, the flow of the dance developing in harmony with the poetic text. Among the outstanding tableaux are the quarrel between the Mon-

tagues and Capulets, the tenderly composed Balcony Scene, which

occupies an extended portion of the score, and the final episode, more elegiac than outwardly dramatic, at Juliet's tomb.

Photo: Baron of London   Courtesy Ballet Theatre

THE MEETING OF ROMEO AND JULIET, WITH NORA KAYE AND HUGH LAING

Romeo and Juliet

(TUDOR)

THIS BALLET in one act, with choreography by Antony Tudor, was first presented by Ballet Theatre at the Metropolitan Opera House in April, 1942. The title roles were danced by Hugh Laing and Alicia Markova. Mr. Tudor appeared as Tybalt; Nicholas Orloff was the Mercutio; Dimitri Romanoff the Friar Laurence. Sono Osato and Richard Reed performed with distinction the minor roles of Rosaline and Paris.

Translating the text of Shakespeare's *Romeo and Juliet* into the idiom of ballet is a signally difficult task, but on the whole Tudor has accomplished it successfully. Here the lyrical side of the choreographer's nature has been active, devoid of the tensions to be found in his works with contemporary themes and moving instead on a plane of serenity. Though faithfully following the outlines of the play, he has created a form of independent worth, with subtlety of miming integrated in a large-scale dance design. The décor by Eugene Berman, evoking the spirit of Renaissance Italy, remains one of the splendors of the ballet.

For the musical background, Tudor has gone to the neutrally tinted scores of Frederick Delius, preferring to combine several pieces by this composer and shape them to his own artistic ends, rather than mold his ideas to a predigested *Romeo and Juliet* by another—which would have been the case had he worked with symphonic treatments of the theme by such strongly creative personalities as Berlioz and Tchaikovsky.

The scores of Delius which the choreographer has selected are: "Over the Hills and Far Away," "The Walk to the Paradise Garden" (from the opera, *A Village Romeo and Juliet*), "Eventyr," prelude to the opera *Irmelin*, and "Brigg Fair." They are played during the ballet in this order, uncut. A majority of them—notably "Over the Hills and Far Away," used with brilliant effect for the opening street fight and ballroom episodes; the "Paradise Garden" intermezzo, adding lyrical warmth to the balcony scene; and "Eventyr," pointing up the bitterness of the brawl in which Tybalt is killed—offer a choice background for ballet. The score of "Brigg Fair," however, which forms the final quarter of Tudor's work, beginning with the moment that Juliet takes the sleeping potion until the two lovers die in the tomb, is too intimate in its orchestration to sustain the weight and impact of the tragedy, nor do its Celtic harmonies and rhythms go well with the Italian scenery of Berman. If the closing moments of the ballet fail somewhat in effectiveness, the lapse can be ascribed to the choice of music at this point instead of to shortcomings in the choreography.

Much of the first impact of *Romeo and Juliet* came from the extraordinary performances by Miss Markova and Mr. Laing as the lovers, with Mr. Tudor a compelling Tybalt. Nora Kaye has danced the heroine more recently, bringing her own expressive powers to the part.

The action begins on a street in Verona. A large Renaissance palace with arched doorway is set near the footlights, masking the full-stage picture to follow. As the orchestra plays the first soft strains of "Over the Hills and Far Away," Romeo steps sulkily through the palace doorway.

He is followed by the dark and handsome Rosaline, with whom he is infatuated. For a moment, the youth remonstrates with the girl because of her indifference; then both go within, leaving the street deserted as before.

Two rival factions of the city suddenly appear. On one side are the Capulets, led by Tybalt, and on the other the Montagues—Romeo's family—commanded by Mercutio. The violence with which they meet head-on is admirably depicted in the choreography, which grows in dramatic intensity until the fight is quelled by the appearance of Montague and Capulet themselves with their wives. The rioters are dis-

Photo: Alfredo Valente

Courtesy Ballet Theatre

NORA KAYE AND HUGH LAING AS JULIET AND ROMEO

persed; Romeo, still under the spell of Rosaline, returns and joins Mercutio on his way to a ball at the house of the Capulets, which they plan to attend in disguise.

The lights dim, the palace is lifted, and now the great unit set appears —one of the dominant factors of the ballet. It is a series of colonnades, surmounted by Renaissance statuary against the bluest of Italian skies. Through the use of painted curtains which can be drawn so as to block off the archways and suggest, through their ingenious design, all possible changes of locale, this setting communicates every development of the drama.

As the lights come up, a great ball is taking place in the house of the Capulets. Young Juliet appears—a virginal, almost illusory figure—to the strains of a quiet melody which builds until it becomes the dominant motive of the scene. She is accompanied by her nurse. At once Romeo

falls in love with her, ignoring the fact that two enemies are standing by: Tybalt, militant leader of the Capulet clan, and young Paris, to whom Juliet is to be wed. When Tybalt discovers Romeo's presence in the hall, a furious fight breaks out. Only the intervention of Capulet, who forbids the use of force in his household, allows Romeo to depart in safety.

The next scene follows at once. With a magical change of lighting, the colonnades of the ballroom become the balconies of the Capulet palace in the moonlight. From the orchestra, the languorous curve of the "Paradise Garden" intermezzo bring a perfumed atmosphere to the action on stage. Solitary figures appear, torchbearers, then Romeo and Mercutio, one lost in a new love and the other exultant at the beauties of life as he has known them. This counterpoint of mood offers the most rewarding moment of the ballet. As Romeo stands by, all but oblivious to the sights and sounds about him, Mercutio performs—with an incredible wealth of gesture—a choreographic translation of the "Queen Mab" speech of the Shakespearean play. Then he goes his way, leaving Romeo alone. After a moment of solitude, Juliet appears. The great central motive of the intermezzo rises from the orchestra, and Romeo, moving

beneath the colonnades, expresses his love in rhapsodic dance. Juliet, on the balcony above, hardly stirs yet radiates equal intensity of feeling. After two interruptions, one by Juliet's nurse, and the other by Tybalt and Paris, who are walking nearby, the lovers conclude their duet. The inner curtains masking the colonnades are drawn and the stage becomes the cell of Friar Laurence, who receives Romeo gravely. The young man has come to ask the Friar's blessing. Soon Juliet arrives and the pair are secretly united in marriage by the holy man.

Now the inner curtains are drawn back and Berman's setting stands out in its full glory. A street scene is revealed, with the beggars, idlers,

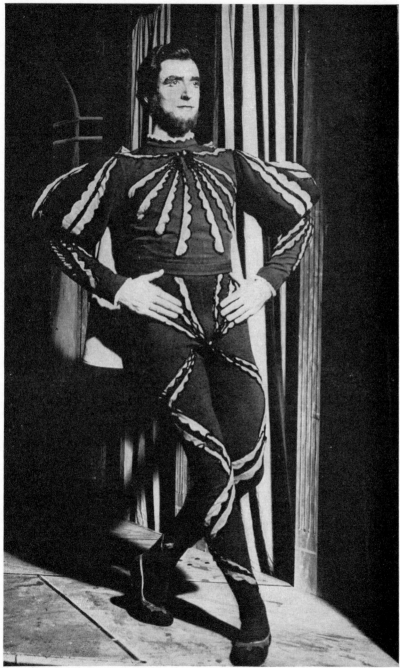

Photo: Hurrell   Courtesy Ballet Theatre

ANTONY TUDOR AS TYBALT IN HIS OWN ROMEO AND JULIET

Courtesy Dance News
ALICIA MARKOVA, DIMITRI ROMANOFF, AND HUGH LAING

and townspeople to be encountered in an Italian square at noon. Ominously, the orchestra plays the slow opening music of "Eventyr." Single

Slow and mysteriously

pp

members and then organized groups of the two rival clans trickle in, and the inevitable quarrel develops. Insults and derision between the factions bring violence; and, to an agitated fortissimo in the orchestra, a savage battle starts, culminating in the death of Mercutio at the hands

Quickly

ff

of Tybalt. Romeo, on his way back from the Friar's cell, is enraged at the sight, leaps at Tybalt and slays him. Fearing not so much the revenge of the Capulets as banishment from the city and from his bride, the youth flees. Then Juliet, returning home by another road, comes upon the body of her kinsman. As she runs off agitatedly, normal life in the square is resumed; the beggars reappear, idlers cross the scene, and, with the removal of the bodies, life in Verona goes on as before.

Through still another shifting of the painted curtains which decorate the archway—performed by two maids who remain at the side of the stage almost throughout the later portions of the ballet—Juliet's bed-chamber is seen at dawn. Here, to a tender *pas de deux*, Romeo, who has been exiled for the death of Tybalt, bids his wife farewell. No sooner has he left than Lady Capulet and Juliet's nurse come to awaken the girl on the morning of her long-projected marriage to young Paris. Juliet rises, resigns herself to wearing the heavy saffron wedding dress, and listens as Friar Laurence, who has appeared with her parents, whispers of a potion which will render her apparently lifeless but revive her in the tomb itself, where she can be rescued by Romeo. Throughout this episode, the rhythms of "Brigg Fair" have been at work, culminating in a

dirge as the bride, swallowing the potion, falls to the ground.

A procession of disconsolate figures hides the scene. Then a catafalque

Photo: Baron of London   ROMEO KILLS TYBALT   *Courtesy Ballet Theatre*

bearing the lifeless girl appears—Paris, his head bowed in grief, at its side. When the mourners have vanished, the family vault of the Capulets is revealed, with Juliet slumbering in the tomb. Romeo, who has learned of the tragedy in his place of exile and missed a guiding message from Friar Laurence, enters distractedly. He has come to join Juliet in death; but no sooner has he drained a flask of poison than his bride awakens. All of the couple's longing for each other, their pent-up emotions, are released here in a wonderful flood of communicative dance. At its climax Romeo falls; and Juliet, realizing there is no solution except to follow him, turns away from her lover and stabs herself.

As the pair lie at rest, the Renaissance palace of the prologue is lowered, masking the entire scene except—through the portal—a final vision of the lovers in the tomb. Their two families, shocked by these needless deaths, appear on either side of the archway in contrite reconciliation.

Photo: Baron of London   *Courtesy Ballet Theatre*

THE TOMB SCENE WITH LAING AND KAYE

Le Rossignol

(THE NIGHTINGALE)

THIS FAMOUS work by Igor Stravinsky has appeared in many incarnations: opera, ballet, symphonic poem. Originally a three-act opera, *Le Rossignol* ("The Nightingale") was begun in 1909, with the first act completed that year. Its libretto was based on Hans Christian Andersen's fairy tale of the same name, adapted to the stage by S. Mitoussov.

Composition of the ballets *L'Oiseau de Feu, Petrouchka,* and *Le Sacre du Printemps* interrupted Stravinsky in his writing of *Le Rossignol.* It was laid aside and then resumed in 1913 at the request of the Théâtre Libre of Moscow. Stravinsky, doubtful that his newer style—evolved through continuous writing for the theatre—would fit harmoniously with the music he had composed four years earlier, suggested at first that the Théâtre Libre present the opening act by itself. When the management replied by pressing him for completion of the score, Stravinsky agreed. Soon after, the Théâtre Libre collapsed, and Sergei Diaghilev decided to present the finished *Rossignol* at the Paris Opéra in May, 1914. The scenery and costumes were by Alexandre Benois; Pierre Monteux conducted.

The result was beguiling. The song of the Nightingale—like the voice of the Cockerel in Rimsky-Korsakov's *Le Coq d'Or*—was heard from the orchestra pit, with the rest of the characters singing and acting on stage. This opera achieved great popularity and was produced later in America at the Metropolitan Opera House (March, 1926) with Marion Talley in the title role, Adamo Didur as the Emperor of China, and Tullio Serafin conducting.

Still, Stravinsky was not satisfied. He decided to drop the romantic first act—so typical of his earlier style—and unite the second and third acts, after necessary revisions, into a symphonic poem for orchestra, eliminating voices and stage action. This was to be called *Le Chant du Rossignol* ("The Song of the Nightingale").

Always on the alert for novelties in connection with his Paris seasons, Diaghilev persuaded Stravinsky that the symphonic poem should be produced in ballet form. Stravinsky consented, but he had his reservations: "I had destined *Le Chant du Rossignol* for the concert platform, and a choreographic rendering seemed to me to be quite unnecessary. Its subtle and meticulous writing and its somewhat static character would not have lent themselves to stage action and the movements of dancing. . . . I reached the conclusion—very regretfully, since I was the author of many works for the theatre—that a perfect rendering can only be achieved in the concert hall." *

The new stage piece, given at the Opéra in February, 1920, won a moderate success. The singing Nightingale was supplanted by a silent dancer—as in Fokine's final version of *Le Coq d'Or*—and the song of the bird itself transferred to the solo flute by Stravinsky. Léonide Massine was the choreographer. In 1927 the Diaghilev company had another try at the *Chant du Rossignol*, this time with new staging by George Balanchine. The work, however, has never caught on as a ballet, yielding in public favor either to the symphonic poem or to the original opera, one of Stravinsky's most delightful works.

ACT ONE

This portion of the opera, omitted in the later ballet version and its related symphonic poem, evokes a picture of the solitary lake at the borders of the wood near the Emperor of China's palace. It is here that the Nightingale resides. Before the curtain rises, there is a dreamy orchestral introduction. Then the lake is revealed, with a solitary fisherman on its shore. His chant, simple and melancholy, is heard again through the interludes of the opera † and in its closing pages.

Por-té au   vent, tom-bant__ au loin, prends, mon fi - let,____ de beaux pois-sons,

As the fisherman moves off slowly, a beautiful, disembodied sound is heard within the wood—the song of the Nightingale. The timbre of the human voice, rising from the orchestra pit at this point, goes perhaps nearer to the heart of the Andersen fairy tale than the purely instrumental version of *Le Rossignol* which Stravinsky was to write later.

As the Nightingale finishes its song, various personages of the Chinese Imperial Court—Chamberlain, Bonze, and nobles—appear in the wood. They are looking for the bird, sent by their Emperor, who has never heard the Nightingale but has been told of its wonderful song. A little scullery maid leads them. Through frequent trips to the lake region where her humble family lives, she is the only one in the palace to know the whereabouts of the bird.

As the courtiers search throughout the glen, they hear first the lowing of a cow and then the croaking of some frogs. They grow ecstatic, believ-

* *Stravinsky: An Autobiography.*

† Also in the ballet version (always excluding the suppressed first act), where the fisherman's music is played instead of sung.

ing these sounds to be the song of the Nightingale. Finally, when the kitchen maid shows them the bird itself, small, gray, and unimpressive, sitting on the branch of a tree, the Chamberlain and his assistants are disillusioned; but when the Nightingale starts to sing, it wins the hearts of all. The Chamberlain invites the bird to perform that evening at the court of the Emperor of China, and the Nightingale accepts. While the courtiers go off jubilantly to announce the news to the Emperor, the melancholy song of the fisherman is heard once more, and a gauze descends on the scene. The orchestra continues with an interlude that leads into the next act.*

ACT TWO

It is at this point that the symphonic poem, *Le Chant du Rossignol*—a completely instrumental reworking of the opera score—begins; and it is here that the ballet version, based on this symphonic poem, has its dramatic opening.

Flickering lights are seen behind the gauze curtain. Torchbearers and courtiers come running by—some to tie little silver bells to the flowers in the Emperor's garden, others to prepare the great hall of the palace for the Nightingale's appearance. Voices are heard (in the operatic version) proclaiming that the scullery maid who found the bird in the woods will now become First Cook of the empire. As the Chamberlain announces the arrival of the Emperor of China, the gauze curtain rises slowly, revealing the Imperial Palace, which is made entirely of porcelain and built in fantastic style. Everywhere there are lights, banners. To the strains of an exotic triumphal march—Oriental in style—the

Nightingale is borne to the throne room on a lofty perch. The Emperor himself follows, carried in on a gilded throne surmounted by a baldachin. He gazes at the bird, makes a gesture, and the Nightingale begins to sing. In the opera, its song is a wordless vocalise—interspersed with

---

* Although labeled "acts" by the composer, the three dramatic episodes that make up the opera are, properly speaking, scenes and are played without interruption, bound by a continuous musical thread.

a few finely polished poetic verses—for coloratura soprano; in the symphonic poem and ballet, a solo flute plays the melody.

The Emperor, deeply moved by the song, offers the bird any favor it might ask. The Nightingale replies that a fair reward has already been granted, for it has seen tears in the eyes of the Emperor. At this point, the ladies of the court fill their mouths with water and gargle in an attempt to imitate the Nightingale's trill. As they work away, three envoys arrive from the Emperor of Japan, bearing a large golden box on which is mounted a mechanical nightingale, gift of the Japanese monarch to the Emperor of China. The sight of the artificial bird, studded with precious stones, fascinates the court, and, as its springs are set in motion and its song begins to sound, the courtiers and the

Emperor himself express their delight. Stravinsky's orchestral tone painting of the whirring mechanism of this artificial bird—identical in opera and ballet—is a stroke of instrumental genius.

At length the Emperor makes a sign that he has had enough of this mechanical creation. He turns to the real bird in order to hear its song again, but, during the music of its rival, the Nightingale has flown away. Angered at what he considers ingratitude, the Emperor banishes the Nightingale from his realm and orders the mechanical bird to be mounted in the place of honor next to his Imperial bed.

The monarch signals for the procession to begin; he is raised aloft on his throne, and the courtiers bear him slowly from the great hall as the curtain falls.

During the following interlude, the melancholy song of the fisherman is heard again in the distance.

ACT THREE

The Emperor lies dying in his vast bedroom. The night outside is clear; rays of moonlight penetrate the room. At the side of the gigantic bed sits Death, who has adorned herself with the Imperial crown, the

Emperor's sword and banner. A filmy curtain which separates the Imperial bed from the rest of the chamber is open. Specters are hovering about, peering in at the Emperor.

The monarch lies helpless, unwilling to see these ghosts, who represent his past deeds, good and bad. He calls for his musicians to drown out the noise of the accusing voices, but they do not come. Just as his life is ebbing, the voice of the real Nightingale is heard outside the window. It sings so ravishingly that even Death herself begs the bird to go on with its music.

The Nightingale agrees, on condition that Death restore the crown to the Emperor. Enchanted by the sound, Death consents; and then the bird sings lyrically of the silent cemetery where the dead sleep in peace, the dew falls from the flowers like human tears, and the moon gleams sadly on the tombs. Under the spell of this music, Death succumbs and disappears.

The Emperor, miraculously freed from his illness, turns to the bird and gratefully offers it first place in his heart. As once before, the Nightingale answers that the tears in the monarch's eyes have been all the reward it can hope for. Gently, it goes on to tell him that every night it will nest in the shadows and sing to him until morning. Then the bird disappears.

A solemn march is heard. The courtiers, thinking the Emperor is dead, enter the chamber gravely. Two pages draw the curtains of the bedchamber. But suddenly the curtains are reopened from within. To the accompaniment of a great glissando for harp, the bedchamber is bathed in sunlight, and the Emperor—in crown and full regalia—stands in the center of the room. As the courtiers, astounded, prostrate themselves, he greets them all and says, "Good morning!"

The curtain falls slowly and, in the distance, there sounds for the last time the solitary song of the fisherman which frames the work, ending it as it had begun.

GROUP FROM ROUGE ET NOIR

Rouge et Noir

THIS BALLET, in four episodes with one scenic background, must be accounted as one of Massine's finest. First produced by the Ballet Russe de Monte Carlo at its home theatre in the spring of 1939 and given at the Metropolitan in New York the following autumn, it ranks with *The Three-Cornered Hat, Symphonie Fantastique*, and *St. Francis* among the choreographer's most valid large-scale works.

Although Massine has provided a philosophic program, *Rouge et Noir* is—as its title implies—an abstract play of color and line which may be enjoyed without any recourse to a deeper meaning. Massine's patterns are self-sufficient; and in few other ballets by any master is emotional content so compellingly wedded to formal design.

The noble setting by Henri Matisse (who also created the costumes) sets the point of departure for the choreography. Within its monumental arches are painted vast panels of red, white, black, blue, and yellow. The costumes, which depersonalize the dancers so that they form part of the structural scheme, are of the same colors. It was Massine's problem to create a dramatic composition of this material, moving the dancers in architecturally and emotionally shifting groups.

As music, he chose the First Symphony of the contemporary Russian composer, Dmitri Shostakovich. No better selection could have been made. Its long melodic lines, with their neoromantic feeling, call for sustained dance patterns; its sharply etched contrasting sections help intensify the choreographic outlines. The symphony, though satisfying as music in any concert performance, seems to take on new luminosity when used in collaboration with the stage pictures of *Rogue et Noir*.

This ballet was revived most recently by the Ballet Russe de Monte Carlo at the Metrolopitan Opera House in September, 1948, when Alicia Markova and Frederic Franklin—admirable exponents of the Massine work—were again seen in their original roles, with Mr. Franklin adding the Figure in Black to his familiar Figure in Red. The ballet's printed program follows: "First movement: Man, symbolizing the poetic spirit, is pursued and overtaken by brutal forces. . . . Second movement: The men of the city encounter the men of the field and bear them off. . . . Third movement: Woman parted from man is tormented in her solitude by an evil spirit. . . . Fourth movement: Man eludes the brutal forces and finds woman again. But joy is short-lived, for in freeing himself from his worldly enemies he is conquered by destiny."

The four movements of the Shostakovitch symphony correspond to the four episodes of the ballet. There is no change of scene, only on lights.

FIRST MOVEMENT

A brief trumpet motive provides the orchestral introduction, then

dancers in yellow appear. They are Activity, the forces of everyday life, and they advance to the brisk, trenchant first theme of the symphony.

There follows one of those superb blends of music, movement, and internal mood that are hallmarks of the greater Massine. The bustle in the orchestra has subsided; faint pizzicati are heard; and as the solo flute—above plucked strings—plays the long, lyrical melody that is the second theme of this movement, two solo dancers representing the poetic forces of White make their appearance in a tender *pas de deux.*

Just as the leading motives of the music are developed symphonically by Shostakovich, so Massine plays upon and expands the basic elements of color. The forces in Black, ruthless and nihilistic, separate the man and woman in White. At the end of the chapter they bear the man away . . . and, in his despair, he has movement patterns that are an ingenious fusion of ballet with modern dance.

SECOND MOVEMENT

This is a satanic festival, in which the forces of Red—allied with Black, but more impish than destructive—race across the horizon, turn somersaults, play at nasty little games. Their dance is underlined by a brittle, staccato subject in the orchestra.

Pensive groups of Blue, Yellow, and White enter to a contrasting theme of great poignancy; but their static lyricism is no match for the dynamic malevolence of the Red. They are carried off by their adversaries.

THIRD MOVEMENT

In one of the most beautifully composed episodes of modern ballet, the solo woman in White appears upstage *sur les pointes,* framed in the mysterious dimness of Matisse's huge arches. The mournful sag of the knee and the listlessness of the hands are combined with the sorrow-

Photo: Maurice Seymour

IGOR YOUSKEVITCH AND ALICIA MARKOVA

ful oboe theme in the orchestra to give an impression of ultimate solitude.

The chief male dancer in Black appears. He is half evil spirit, half lover. Desiring the woman in White, supporting her in a magnificent adagio, he dominates her with dark, disturbing thoughts. Finally he withdraws into the shadows from which he has come.

FOURTH MOVEMENT

There is a furious onslaught by the forces of Black and Red, while the orchestra plays the first theme of the finale.

The figure in White is seen: he has escaped his captors and come to rejoin the woman. As they are reunited, one of the most poetic motives in the symphony soars from the orchestra.

They are not together long before the struggle recommences. The leader of the Black emerges, taking on a nobly tragic stature, his longing for the woman in White coupled with the destructive urge that is his element. All forces of the drama join battle until they are stilled by a bolt from above. To the pounding of the timpani, the man and woman in White are separated, this time irrevocably; and the forces of Black and Red which drive them apart act no longer as voluntary agents of evil but as the servants of an impersonal destiny.*

* According to the printed synopsis, which, at this point, belies—in its elaborate prose—the simplicity of the ballet itself.

Ruses d'Amour

(LOVE'S TRICKERY)

THIS BALLET, in one act, cast in the aristocratic, eighteenth-century outdoor spirit of Watteau's paintings, with book and choreography by Marius Petipa, was first produced at the Hermitage Theatre, St. Petersburg, in January, 1900. Pierina Legnani and Paul Gerdt danced the principal roles. The charming musical score, which is not the least of the work's merits, was provided by Alexander Glazunov.

The rise of the curtain is preceded by a jovial prelude, and then a

shady lawn is revealed with a formal staircase leading to the castle of the Duchess Lucinde.

A festival is being given by the Duchess in honor of her daughter, Isabel, about to be wed to a young noble whom the girl has never met. All the bride knows about this suitor, chosen by her mother, is that he is handsome, of excellent family, but not wealthy.

As the Duchess and her friends await the arrival of the groom, they take part in various old court dances—gavotte, sarabande, and farandole. Then they are entertained with a puppet show by a band of strolling players. All this time, the girl is waiting anxiously to see her future husband.

At last the fiancé is announced—he has reached the outer gates of the castle. In this final moment before his entrance, Isabel decides to test the good intentions of her suitor by changing places with her maid, Marinnette. If the young Marquis pays homage to the richly dressed servant, it will be clear that he has courted Isabel for reasons of wealth; but if he passes her by for the plainly gowned mistress, then true discernment and ultimate love are his.

The conspiracy completed—Isabel clothed as the maid, Marinnette as the lady—the Marquis appears. As the Duchess has prophesied, he is of fine appearance and gentle bearing. No sooner does he cross the lawn than the false maid runs to welcome him and lead him to her mistress.

Isabel's hopes are realized at once. The young Marquis is so much interested in the supposed maid that he shows little desire to meet the lady of the castle. In an apparent show of loyalty, the "maid" deflects the Marquis' advances, tells him how beautifully her lady dresses, how gracefully she can dance, and, by way of illustration, turns a few exquisite steps of her own in praise of her mistress' skill.

The Marquis looks so ardently at the girl that he does not see the Duchess descending the staircase from the castle. With her is a formal group including the real maid, Marinnette, dressed as Isabel. When at length the Marquis is presented to the lady he is supposed to wed, his reaction seems one of marked indifference.

A dance is proposed; and Isabel, still masquerading as the maid, shows her innate gracefulness in a waltz, while the false mistress reaches heights of gaucherie.

The young Marquis is so deeply discouraged by this performance that he decides to break off the match. Escaping from his hostess, he whispers hurriedly to the maid and begs her to run off with him. She consents—but the ruse grows more involved, for this time the maid *is* Marinnette, heavily veiled, who has changed places with her mistress.

Just as the pair is about to elope, the Duchess and her guests appear on the terrace. Isabel, veiled like Marinnette, stands among them. The Marquis is so embarrassed that he does not even attempt an explanation; but his dismay changes to joy when Isabel, lifting her veil, reveals that it is she with whom he has been in love all along.

The trick has worked; it is clear that the young mistress is desired not for her rank but for herself; and the ballet ends with a celebration by the Duchess, the happy couple, and their courtly friends.

FIRST SCENE WITH YURA LAZOVSKY AS THE SOLDIER

Russian Soldier

THIS WORK, in a prologue and four scenes, with choreography by Michel Fokine and scenery and costumes by Mstislav Dobujinsky, was first presented by Ballet Theatre at the Metropolitan Opera House in October, 1942. Its musical background is the suite, *Lieutenant Kije*, drawn by the composer Sergei Prokofiev from a film score of the same name that he had written in 1933. The suite's first performance in America took place at Tanglewood, Massachusetts, in the summer of 1938 by the Boston Symphony, under the direction of Serge Koussevitzky.

The music, satirical in nature, was intended as background to a Soviet comedy about Czar Nicholas I. One of his clerks—a half-literate fellow—misread an official military roster, managing to run the last syllable, *Ki*, of somebody's name together with the Russian expletive, *Je*, and thus created a brand-new officer of his own—Kije. The Czar's courtiers were so afraid to tell their ruler of this mistake that they invented a live Lieutenant Kije at once.

Out of this idea in the film arose many amusing complications and adventures. Five of them are depicted in Prokofiev's concert suite: the birth of Kije in the Czar's brain; a romance; Kije's wedding; scene in a troika; and the mock burial of Kije.

To this intensely whimsical score, Fokine has evolved one of the most lugubrious stage works on record, dealing with the life and death of a Russian soldier on the battlefield. The title role was danced at the work's première by Yura Lazovsky and later briefly by Léonide Massine and by George Skibine. Launched at a time when the war effort was at its height, the work could not fail of a certain effectiveness. Stalingrad and the heroism it represented were in all minds. Choreographically, however, and from the standpoint of musical adaptation, *Russian Soldier* marked a low point in Fokine's career. By now, this tragic ballet to a comic score has disappeared; but the music of *Lieutenant Kije* remains—as delightfully witty as ever—to be heard in the concert hall.

To the sound of a distant cornet a solitary soldier stands on a battlefield. His forehead is bound with war-stained bandages, his walk is un-

steady, the moment of his doom at hand. As he leans on his rifle, pictures from his past life flash before him.

First he sees the great parade ground where he drilled in the days of

his youth. The sound of fifes is heard, the beating of a military drum. Soldiers pass in strict formation, performing the manual of arms.

The martial picture dissolves into a field of wheat in which the girls of the ballet wave back and forth as vegetation. Death—a stalking figure with a scythe—appears abruptly but soon withdraws. The music for this episode is flowing and romantic in spirit, perhaps the only section of the suite that lends itself to the ballet's elegiac mood.

As the solitary soldier stands in the foreground, still brooding on his

Photo: *Maurice Seymour*   Courtesy *Dance News*

THE DEATH OF THE RUSSIAN SOLDIER

past, the scene changes again and memories of his wedding day are evoked with the appearance of a festive group in a crowded room. The

music becomes boisterous, as if for a celebration. From the standpoint of dance, this episode is the most successful in the ballet, with effective choreography for the wedding guests.

The revelry dissolves into the image of the battlefield once more, and now Death comes for the soldier. A doctor, stretcher-bearer, weeping

maidens are seen; and they surround the dying man in a ghoulish processional. As the soldier yields his last breath, the sound of the distant cornet is heard as at the opening, and the curtain falls.

Le Sacre du Printemps

(THE RITE OF SPRING)

THIS MOMENTOUS stage picture of ancient Russia has probably influenced the course of modern music more than any other single work of the century. The conception from start to finish is primarily tonal and pictorial rather than balletic, though—with unlimited rehearsals under a choreographer capable of grasping the complexities of the score—it offers possibilities for magnificent expression in dance.

Igor Stravinsky, who composed the music, was responsible for the fundamental idea of *Le Sacre du Printemps*: the evocation of pagan rites of Spring in primitive Russia, of games and sacrificial ceremonies to propitiate the gods. He took this scheme to Sergei Diaghilev, who, excited over its possibilities for ballet, entrusted the choreography to Vaslav Nijinsky. For the scenery and costumes Diaghilev turned to the noted artist and archaeologist, Nicholas Roerich. The finished work was given for the first time at the Théâtre des Champs-Élysées, Paris, in May, 1913, with Marie Piltz as the Chosen One and Pierre Monteux conducting.

The choice of Nijinsky as choreographer did not please Stravinsky. This young man, the most extraordinary dancer of his time, had only two ballets to his credit when Diaghilev turned over to him *Le Sacre*: *L'Après-Midi d'un Faune* and *Jeux*. In his new work, Nijinsky went further in the direction of creative achievement than might have been expected. His use of modern turned-in movement instead of the classical positions of ballet, his evocation of barbaric rites through repetitive, pounding rhythms on stage excited a certain admiration when the work was produced. Stravinsky, however, was dissatisfied: "[Nijinsky's] ignorance of the most elementary notions of music was flagrant. . . . As one was unable to discover any individual impressions, one began to doubt whether he had any." *

The saga of the work's première in Paris is celebrated. Audience reaction was so hostile, because of the unprecedented violence of music and dance, that the orchestra could not be heard through the din. Nijinsky—standing in the wings—was forced to beat time for the dancers with his fists. At one point, Diaghilev had to rise in his box to implore

---

* *Stravinsky: An Autobiography.*

the audience to let the spectacle go on. After the first night, public indignation subsided. But not all of the audience had been adverse in its reaction: indeed, many of the leading intellectuals of Paris and their followers hailed the new ballet for its bold and striking qualities. Five more performances were given, two of them in London. The work had required 120 rehearsals.

Seven years later, *Le Sacre du Printemps* was revived with new choreography by Léonide Massine, more to the taste of Stravinsky. On this occasion, the part of the Chosen One was danced by Lydia Sokolova. The new version remained in the Diaghilev repertoire for some time and was later given an independent American première, under Massine's direction, at the Philadelphia Academy of Music in April, 1930. Martha Graham, as the Chosen One, headed the cast. The performance, made possible through the auspices of the League of Composers, was repeated in the same month at the Metropolitan Opera House, New York. Playing in the pit was the entire Philadelphia Orchestra, conducted by Leopold Stokowski, who had been responsible for the first concert performance in America of *Le Sacre du Printemps* in 1922.

Le Sacre du Printemps has not been seen here in ballet form since the League of Composers' production, nor has it remained standard fare in Europe. Undoubtedly, the complexities of the dance patterns, which require innumerable rehearsals for even a semi-adequate realization, the size and virtuosity of the orchestra required, are stumbling blocks in the production of this work by any but a heavily endowed organization. Stravinsky's score, on its own, has become one of the concert masterpieces of our time, expressing in its restless rhythmic urge, its volcanic rhythms, the vanished barbarism of an entire era. Its freedom from conventional melodic line, traditional harmonies, rigid metrical scheme—preserving, withal, a classic mastery of design—its tightness of structure and economy of color at a time when elaborate post-Wagnerian tendencies were entrenched in symphonic music, has helped free almost every composer of initiative from the limitations of nineteenth-century technique.

The plot of *Le Sacre du Printemps* is of the simplest. Dealing with archaic Russian tribes and their worship of the gods of the harvest and fertility, it falls into two separate yet mutually interdependent parts—the Adoration of the Earth and the Sacrifice. These primitive peoples assemble for their yearly ceremonies, play their traditional games, and finally select a virgin to be sacrificed to the gods of Spring so that the crops and tribes may flourish.

Stravinsky's score serves at once as accompaniment and excitant for the pagan rites. Before the curtain rises, there is a prelude in which the composer evokes the primitive past when man was in intimate contact with nature. A soft bassoon solo, played high on the instrument with a strange tone quality, opens the work—like an immemorial chant heard from far off.

Other instruments enter, seemingly improvised against the solo melody of the opening which still flows on; then the curtain rises on a savage daylight picture of an ancient land. Insistent, barbaric rhythms are heard in the orchestra, shifting accent with almost every bar. The

first rites of Spring are being celebrated, and a group of adolescents appears. They dance until other members of the tribe enter. Then the

full round of ceremonies gets under way: a mock abduction—performed with much solemnity—games of the rival tribes, the procession of the

Sage, and the thunderous dance of the Earth.

The curtain falls, and the orchestra plays an interlude—soft and sustained—representing, in its shifting planes of instrumental color, the pagan night.

Soon the tribal meeting place is seen again. This time, it is dark and the adolescents circle mysteriously in preparation for the choice of the virgin who will be sacrificed to the gods. Suddenly their dance is interrupted, and one of the girls who has taken part is marked for the tribal offering. The others begin a wild orgy glorifying the Chosen One and—in a barbaric ritual—call on the shades of their ancestors.

Finally the supreme moment of the ceremony arrives: the ordeal of the Chosen One, perhaps the longest and most complicated solo in the annals of ballet. It is the maiden's duty to dance until she perishes from exhaustion. The rhythms of her sacrificial round move relentlessly forward, while a short, stabbing motive is repeated insistently in brasses and winds.

Throughout the dance the music keeps gathering power through the element of frenzied repetition until finally it spins like a top on its own axis, and ends with a crash as the Maiden dies.

St. Francis

ONE OF the finest of modern ballets, this work was given its première in July, 1938, at the Drury Lane Theatre, London, under the name of *Nobilissima Visione*. The book was by Léonide Massine—who devised the choreography and created the title role—in collaboration with the distinguished composer of the score, Paul Hindemith. Pavel Tchelicheff created the scenery and costumes. Among the principal dancers were Simon Semenoff as Pietro Bernadone, Frederic Franklin as the Knight, and Nini Theilade as Poverty.

In October of the same year, *Nobilissima Visione* was presented at the Metropolitan Opera House as *St. Francis*. The choreographer, who in the past had demonstrated his command of almost every traditional ballet idiom, now turned actively to the problems of contemporary dance. His new work was pronounced an artistic success and, in its mastery of modern design, led Massine logically to his *Rouge et Noir* of the following year. It also served, in the same season, as a startling contrast to his *Gaité Parisienne*, which was almost the twin of *St. Francis* in point of birth (April, 1938). Few men in the history of the theatre have turned out two prime works, so dissimilar, in the space of four months.

Unfortunately, *St. Francis* is not a repertory piece. A stark, mystical work, dominated by neo-Italian "primitive" décor and straight-line movement, it needs repeated performances by a company that believes in it so that a general public might be created and retained. The customary Ballet Russe audience, attuned to romantic stage design and rich orchestral harmonies, was puzzled by *St. Francis* at the outset; the management took no long-range steps to repeat the work until its style could become more familiar; and so the ballet has disappeared. Someday, when the greater works of Massine are restaged by their choreographer, it is to be hoped that *St. Francis* will be among them. In the meanwhile, one can hear Hindemith's score played in concert version under the title of *Nobilissima Visione*.

The music, as austere in design as the décor and the corresponding dance patterns, is composed of eleven separate numbers, all played without pause: introduction and march of the troubadours; buyers and beggars; the Knight; march; the Three Apparitions; festal music; close of the feast; meditation; the Wolf; wedding to Poverty; finale ("Incipi-

unt laudes creaturarum"). Its prevailing style is an evocation of the
Middle Ages, especially in the composer's use of an old troubadour melody, "Ce fut en Mai," which weaves its way through the score like the
thread of a tapestry, and in the Latin hymn character of the closing
pages. The whole score, archaic in feeling, has a color not unlike that
of Hindemith's opera, *Mathis der Maler* (written in 1934 and based on
the life of the ecclesiastical painter Mathias Grünewald), but its texture
is less impassioned and more chaste.

Photo: Maurice Seymour   *Courtesy Museum of Modern Art*
GROUP WITH FREDERIC FRANKLIN AS THE KNIGHT

There is a short prelude for orchestra, based on the medieval tune "Ce fut en Mai," and then the opening tableau is revealed.

SCENE ONE

In the house of his father, Pietro Bernadone, at Assisi, young Francis (Francesco) is passing the time with three comrades, watching the foreign buyers of Pietro's precious silks. Their presence evokes a world he has not known, the lands beyond the Umbrian hills. Eager to travel, he asks many questions of these merchants from abroad.

A beggar enters the luxurious shop, and Francis drives him away. Yet, on seeing the man's pitiful glance, the youth runs after him and spontaneously bestows a gift. This kinship with the poor lasts only for a moment. Francis' thoughts are deflected by the arrival of a young knight, who has stopped in at Pietro's to renew his wardrobe. The warrior is represented by a vigorous musical phrase.

Francis, stirred by military longings, wants to show the knight his strength. He challenges the newcomer to a contest and is defeated. Convinced that this is the master from whom he must learn the art of life, he takes service with the warrior and sets out from his father's house.

SCENE TWO

The youth, on finding himself near a country road with the knight and his soldiers, suffers a change of heart—for the splendid warrior, no more scrupulous than other powerful men of the time, orders his band to attack and rob a group of travelers, seize the women, and cut down the men. Francis, appalled at this carnage, casts off his armor, leaves the knight, and prays for guidance. In answer, three apparitions approach: Poverty, Chastity, and Obedience. Although Chastity and Obedience are to be his kin, they withdraw, leaving Poverty—his destined bride—to watch over him. In a most affecting scene, Francis confronts her with the new humility that is to become the root of his life.

SCENE THREE

It is evening and a feast is in progress at the house of Pietro Bernadone, who is overjoyed at his son's return. All the friends of the youth take part in celebrating his homecoming. Francis, too, dances, but without heart. In the midst of the feasting, a group of wretched beggars enters—men in rags, women disfigured by suffering—and they seek the crusts of bread left by the guests. Here the mystic identification with the poor that Francis had felt at an earlier moment comes to the surface and remains. On an impulse, Francis rewards the beggars with golden vessels from his father's table. When the merchant discovers this gift, he rebukes his son and strikes him. It is then that Francis takes off his rich clothes, lays them at his father's feet, and departs from the house to follow an inward call. As enacted by Massine, this was one of the great moments in danced theatre.

SCENE FOUR

Francis, clad in humble garments, has settled in the countryside, passing his days in meditation. As the scene opens, the orchestra calls up and sustains this meditative mood. The youth hears celestial music

inside himself; taking a pair of branches which he shapes into a cross, he dances to it exaltedly.

His reverie is broken by the people of near-by farms, fleeing from a wolf that is ravaging the countryside. Soon the beast appears, but its fury wavers before the serenity of Francis. This episode, which has drawn some criticism for its jovial treatment of the wolf, actually parallels in dance the spirit of much medieval art, with its blend of fervor and childlike fantasy.

The grateful folk lead the animal away and Francis is joined by the

Photo: Maurice Seymour   *Courtesy Museum of Modern Art*
NATHALIE KELEPOVSKA, NINI THEILADE, AND JEANNETTE LAURET

three companions who once shared the feasts with him at his father's house. Now they, like him, have renounced their former lives and are seeking truth through privation. In excessive regard for Francis, they prepare him a couch; but he refuses it and sleeps on the ground.

During his rest, the chaste figure of Poverty approaches. The three companions—again with mistaken zeal—forbid her to disturb their friend. Intuitively, Francis awakens and hails Poverty as his bride. They solemnly exchange vows and, with the three comrades, share a wedding feast of bread and water.

SCENE FIVE

Before a backdrop which Tchelicheff, the designer, has made memorable through the dominance of human hands—painted pleadingly, in the Byzantine style—a group of monks and nuns assembles to celebrate the union of Francis to Poverty. The nuns, crossing their hands, wave them gently like the wings of the birds so well loved by this saint. Then Poverty, guiding Francis, leads him to the summit of a great rock. There, above all human pride, the two figures stand outlined against the sky as the monks and nuns look on reverently.

El Salon Mexico

THIS BALLET in one act, with choreography by Doris Humphrey, was first performed at the Studio Theatre, New York City, in March, 1943, with José Limón and Florence Lessing as the featured dancers. The costumes and lighting were devised by Elizabeth Parsons.

Based on Aaron Copland's colorful score of the same name, which evokes impressions—at once nostalgic and strident—of a famous dance hall in Mexico City, the work consists of several episodes blending into one continuous line. A raised square platform, curved runway leading from it, two small blocks, and screens set at varying angles make up the scene, suggesting—as the occasion demands—a garden, a winding street, a ballroom, an amusement park.

As produced at the Studio Theatre, where formal-style scenery yields to the inventive use of platforms and lights, El Salon Mexico emerged as one of the most vital and dramatically integrated of American ballets. Miss Humphrey's strength of design was nobly sustained by Mr. Limón in his performance of the leading role.

As the lights come up, the central figure of the ballet—a Mexican peon—is seen alone, moving in a dreamlike step toward the center of the platform, where he meets the first figure of the fantasy: a peasant girl, slender and exquisite. She is characterized by a lyrical motive—a Mexican folk song entitled "The Mosquito"—which runs throughout the score.

Suddenly the secluded garden that gives the illusion of surrounding them disappears. The peasant herself is lost to sight, and now a cluster of girls approaches the peon in the middle of a noisy street. He dances with them as though in a ballroom, as if he were their only partner and lover; but sounds of a festival procession, with new erotic interests for the peon, interrupt the dance.

Two women with play sticks appear, weaving their way toward him. Forgetting the others, he goes with them to a fiesta, making sport with them in crude horseplay.

These comrades, too, vanish in the course of a dream flowing amorously onward, and the slender peasant girl—still dominant in the peon's mind—returns in a vision. Then all of the women he has desired appear together, merged in a confused mass.

Intuitively, the man realizes the close of his dream is at hand. Retreating to his original position in the center of the platform, while the women withdraw in groups, he is left clinging to his first love; but as the last notes of the music sound, she slips from his arms, is swallowed in the depths of fantasy from which she came—a striking climax, achieved by the girl's plunging directly into a gulf between the raised platform and the runway on which the dancers move—and the peon stands alone once more, his dream at an end.

Scènes de Ballet

THIS *divertissement* in one act was originally composed by Igor Stravinsky for Billy Rose's revue, *The Seven Lively Arts*, which opened at the Ziegfeld Theatre, New York, in December, 1944, and ran into the spring of the following year. The choreography was by Anton Dolin, who appeared in the work with Alicia Markova.

More than three years later, Stravinsky's music served as background to a new ballet of the same name with choreography by Frederick Ashton, produced in February, 1948, at Covent Garden, London, by the Sadler's Wells Ballet. Margot Fonteyn was the leading dancer in this production; and André Beaurepaire provided the décor.

Stravinsky's score, learned rather than theatrical, brought forth in the Dolin version of *Scènes de Ballet* a romantic interlude with *pas de deux* and solo dances set against a background of cloudland. Although the musical show which it graced, *The Seven Lively Arts*, was not an unqualified success, the little Dolin ballet won a fair measure of praise from the public.

The choreography of Frederick Ashton, eminently classical in nature, was designed chiefly as a vehicle for the splendid dancing of Margot Fonteyn. An essay in pure dance, it contained several numbers of note, especially Miss Fonteyn's turn with four partners, a waltz, and the dance of the four young men. Somewhat lacking in warmth, this London production compensated for that through its ingenious development of new technical possibilities within old ballet forms. Michael Somes was the brilliant collaborating dancer with Miss Fonteyn.

SCENE FROM THE BALLET RUSSE DE MONTE CARLO PRODUCTION

Scheherazade

THIS MOST famous of pseudo-Oriental ballets was devised by Michel Fokine for the second season (1910) of Diaghilev's Russian Ballet in Paris. The challenging décor—said, at the time, to be the last word in theatrical effectiveness—was by Léon Bakst. As music for this spectacle, the producers freely adapted the symphonic suite *Scheherazade*, by Nicholas Rimsky-Korsakov, to their requirements.

It will be remembered that Rimsky, in composing his four-movement suite, built his musical plan around the character of Scheherazade herself—the astute Sultana who, to distract her violent husband and save her own life, spun out for him in the course of a thousand and one evenings those tales which have become known as the Arabian Nights. The recurring violin figure in Rimsky's music, which appears in all four movements, is the voice of the Sultana, recounting and linking together her various stories. Four separate tone pictures make up the symphonic suite: 1. The Sea and Sinbad's Ship; 2. Tale of the Kalendar Prince;

3. The Young Prince and Young Princess; 4. Festival at Bagdad and Destruction of Sinbad's Ship on a Rock Surmounted by a Bronze Warrior.

Fokine's *Scheherazade* has no plot relationship to the pictures that inspired Rimsky's music—except for an over-all Arabian Nights atmosphere. The first movement of the symphonic suite is played in the ballet before the curtain rises; the second and fourth are fused as one dramatic unit; the third movement (except in occasional performances where it is inserted as a *pas de deux* for Zobeide and her lover) is omitted.

The use of the first movement as an overture has not proved satisfactory. It is too long, and too exacting for performance by the customary ballet orchestra. Undoubtedly in Diaghilev's early Paris seasons, when budget was no consideration, the instruments of the Russian Ballet orchestra must have played this music marvelously. But times have changed, and it is something of a trial for the music-lover to hear this mass of gorgeous, swirling tone cut down to the size of a traveling pit band; the dance-goer, on his part, can justifiably resent an eight- or nine-minute span of music with lowered curtain.

Those who were fortunate enough to see this ballet in première were thrilled by its abandon, its voluptuousness. The choreography was pronounced revolutionary, Bakst's setting unprecedented in its riotous use of color. Today, perhaps no other work in the whole repertoire has paled so perceptibly. The ingredients which once induced a *succès de scandale* are now common fare. An adequate restudy of the original, in terms of modern theatre, has never been made. The sweeping gestures of the Shah and his brother—in present performances—seem more archaic than the most frankly rhetorical flourishes out of *Swan Lake*; and throughout the ballet there is a constant shift between miming and dance that saps the work's foundations. This has come about in part because Fokine designed the central female role, Zobeide, for Ida Rubinstein—more mime than ballerina—while he created the part of the Favorite Slave for the fabulous dancer Vaslav Nijinsky, with a resulting conflict of styles that has come down through the years. Only one season after the première, the same choreographer's *Petrouchka* was to realize at once the theatrical unity, the fusion of all the arts for which *Scheherazade* strove without achievement.

Nearly every Russian ballerina since 1910 has assumed, at one time or another, the role of Zobeide, content to sacrifice her powers of motion to the absorbing problems of miming. Alexandra Danilova has been the most distinguished of recent Zobeides, Mia Slavenska the most lush. Yurek Shabelevsky and Léonide Massine have emphasized the sensuousness of the Favorite Slave, Frederic Franklin his vigor. It is generally agreed by those who attended early performances that Enrico Cecchetti has never been equaled for insidious subtlety in the part of the Chief Eunuch.

NIJINSKY AS THE FAVORITE SLAVE

FIRST MOVEMENT

A stern, symphonic motto which seems to swing open the doors of the East is heard at the start of *Scheherazade*. This theme returns constantly through the score, sometimes altered in shape or color, until the music's final page.

After the motto's first statement, there come a few soft chords in the woodwinds and then the melody of Scheherazade herself—a wheedling, storytelling passage for solo violin that prefaces, comments on, and concludes almost all of the tone pictures in the suite.

In the original program of Rimsky-Korsakov, the Sea is protagonist of the first movement. One hears the undulation of the waves in the violas and cellos; and, in the woodwinds, their full, rolling harmonies, suggesting an Oriental ocean touching on perfumed shores.

In ballet performances, this music—given out before a lowered curtain—is meant to imbue the audience with the feeling not only of Eastern seas but of the entire Orient.

SECOND MOVEMENT

To those ballet-goers with an aural memory, the languorous bassoon solo which is heard at the rise of the curtain will always suggest the gliding of the Chief Eunuch about the harem, the keys to the inner chambers jangling on a belt around his paunch.

MARY ELLEN MOYLAN AND ROBERT LINDGREN AS SCHEHERAZADE AND THE
FAVORITE SLAVE

Andantino

The boredom of an Oriental midday seems to be hanging over the
richly furnished chamber where the ruler Shahriar keeps his wives.
Shahriar himself is seated on a divan with his brother, Shah Zeman,
and with his chief concubine, Zobeide. Beneath this outward stagnance
run currents of suspicion and antagonism. Even as three dancing girls
perform to distract the brothers, Zeman mutely conveys to Shahriar his
doubts about the wives' fidelity.

Abruptly, Shahriar rises and commands that armor be brought for a hunting expedition. Trombone and trumpet calls, in different keys, are heard in the orchestra as the expedition assembles, finally blending into a glittering march as the ruler and his brother depart.

As soon as Shahriar has gone, the boredom is lifted. His troupe of wives, who, up to this point, have clustered in lazy groups, make for two of three blue doors at the rear of the chamber. They beg, and finally bribe, the Chief Eunuch to unlock these entrances to the inner rooms. The Eunuch consents, opens the doors, and two groups of male Negro slaves enter the harem—secret lovers of the wives.

Now it is the turn of the imperious Zobeide. She orders, pleads with, threatens the Chief Eunuch; and, finally at the price of a rope of pearls, her desire prevails. The Eunuch unlocks the third blue door, and a young Negro—the Favorite Slave—comes to embrace Zobeide.

THIRD MOVEMENT

This section of Rimsky's symphonic suite was omitted from the original stage production by Fokine. Minor companies, however, interpolate it now and then in the form of a long *pas de deux* for Zobeide (when the performer is a fully equipped dancer, not a mime) and her Favorite Slave.

A long-lined, sentimental melody gives a point of repose to this move-

ment in contrast to the other, more animated sections of the suite. When used as a musical basis for the *pas de deux*, it offers an ideal passage of the "adagio" variety, replete with opportunities for lifts, but totally out of keeping with Fokine's dramatic approach to the subject. The choreographer was right, from the standpoint of his theatrical scheme, to omit this tender, pointedly naïve piece.

FOURTH MOVEMENT

The orgy in the harem has got under way. First there is a feast, and then an organized dance led by the Favorite Slave. The music of the

Photo: Maurice Seymour   *Courtesy Museum of Modern Art*
ANDRÉ EGLEVSKY AS THE FAVORITE SLAVE

dance starts on a subdued dynamic level, but rises in the course of sev-

eral pages to a large-scale climax.

The Favorite Slave, in an erotic frenzy, travels between Zobeide's couch and the dancers, whom he leads with great leaps into the air. A group of the Eunuch's underlings steals out to bring Shahriar news of the orgy; and, at the climax of this perfidy in the harem, the ruler and his brother—with their armed guard—appear on the threshold.

It is at this point in the symphonic suite that the music of the Sea— played so vibrantly by the strings in the first movement—returns in the trombones as an overwhelming force, made even more terrifying by the whistling of the woodwinds above. Here, in Rimsky-Korsakov's conception, Sinbad's ship is dashed against the rocks. In Fokine's scheme the revenge of the two brothers is enacted. All of the faithless wives and their lovers are slain; the Favorite Slave gives a final leap on the threshold of death as in life; the venal Eunuch is dispatched; and Zobeide stands alone, awaiting her sentence.

For a moment Shahriar hesitates, still under the spell of her beauty; but when his brother Zeman contemptuously prods the corpse of the Favorite Slave, Shahriar thinks of his own dishonor. He gives the signal for Zobeide's death. His wife, thwarting the guards who are about to kill her, plunges her own dagger into her heart. As she dies, Shahriar is bowed with sorrow; and, in the orchestra, the final whisperings of the violin—representing the voice of Scheherazade—are heard above the brooding motive that is the motto of this suite.

The Seasons

THIS *divertissement* in one act and four scenes (*Les Saisons*), with book and choreography by Marius Petipa, was first produced at the Hermitage Theatre, St. Petersburg, in February, 1900. The scenery was designed by Lambini, and the costumes by Ponomarev. Alexander Glazunov composed the score, which is frequently played in concert form. Parts of the music have also been used as background for the ballet *Snow Maiden*, choreographed by Bronislava Nijinska and with book by Sergei J. Denham, first given by the Ballet Russe de Monte Carlo in October, 1942, at the Metropolitan Opera House.

SCENE ONE

A Field in Winter

As the curtain rises, the Spirit of Winter, together with his attendant sprites of Frost, Ice, Hail, and Snow, may be seen amid the snowflakes. Each of them has a solo variation. Suddenly, two gnomes enter and set fire to some kindling wood. Unable to resist the warmth, Winter and his glacial band disappear.

SCENE TWO

The Same Field in Bloom

As flowers raise their heads in the sunshine, Spring enters in a joyful dance with Zephyr. At the height of their revelry, the celebrants run off, giving way to the next change in this cycle of nature.

SCENE THREE

A Field of Wheat

Now, in the summer heat, the Spirit of the Corn appears; and the flowers, wilted, let their petals droop. Almost at once a group of Naiads enters, carrying veils which symbolize the coolness of the streams. The flowers revive and dance gratefully with the Naiads. Suddenly, satyrs invade the grove. Playing their pipes, they attempt to carry off the

Spirit of the Corn, but in vain. The Spirit remains, bound to its companion flowers through the magic of summer.

SCENE FOUR

The Field in Autumn

Now, as the grapes are on the vine, all of the seasons take part, in a stirring bacchanale, with solo variations for Winter, Spring, and Zephyr.

The dance grows wilder until a deluge of autumnal leaves puts an end to the revel. A starlit sky is revealed, with its reminder that beyond the seasonal changes on earth is the constancy of the universe.

Photo: Vandamm   *Courtesy Museum of Modern Art*

KATHRYN MULLOWNEY, HOLLY HOWARD, CHARLES LASKEY, AND ELENA DE RIVAS

Serenade

THIS WORK in four movements, with choreography by George Balanchine, was first produced by the American Ballet at the Adelphi Theatre, New York, in March, 1935, with Kathryn Mullowney and Heidi Vosseler in leading parts. The décor was by Jean Lurçat. Later *Serenade* was given by the American Ballet on its South American tour in 1941, with Marie-Jeanne in the featured role, and costumes by Alvin Colt. A revival by the Ballet Russe de Monte Carlo at the Metropolitan Opera House in October, 1940, found Marie-Jeanne as guest, supported by Igor Youskevitch and Frederic Franklin. The costumes were again by Lurçat. Since that time, Alexandra Danilova has danced the leading role at several performances by the Ballet Russe de Monte Carlo. The work was restaged by Mr. Balanchine for the Paris Opéra in the summer of 1947.

Set to the music of Tchaikovsky's *Serenade for Strings*, the ballet combines formal design with an intensely lyrical feeling. Its title, *Serenade*, carries no romantic connotation but has been used by Balanchine—as by Tchaikovsky before him—to denote a classical type of suite, relevant to the eighteenth century, usually played at evening in the ballroom or the courtyard of a palace.

FIRST MOVEMENT

Andante non troppo Allegro

A nocturnal mood dominates the opening section of the ballet as the dancers are revealed on a bare stage flanked by drapes. Seventeen girls,

arranged in diagonal cross-patterns, hold up their arms and turn away from the light of the moon. Then, led by a solo ballerina, they begin a flowing, beautifully molded ensemble.

SECOND MOVEMENT

Tempo di Valse

Here the soloist engages a cavalier in a waltz, with animated background by the *corps de ballet*.

FOURTH MOVEMENT

Allegro con Spirito

For the sake of choreographic unity and of building toward a poetic climax, Balanchine has taken one of his few liberties with Tchaikovsky's score by reversing the order of the third and fourth movements. This license is slight and readily admissible.

As a Russian folk theme is sounded in the orchestra, five girls who

NATALIE KRASSOVSKA AND MARC PLATOFF

Allegro con spirito

have been left on stage from the preceding number move to its measures. The soloists of the waltz return; and a lively group dance follows.
In these two middle episodes of *Serenade*, the cavalier is an impersonal

force, cast only to lend technical support to his lady.* With the end of the Allegro con Spirito, he departs.

THIRD MOVEMENT

Larghetto Elegiaco

The ballerina remains; and it is here that the more lyrical aspects of the ballet take form. The haunting music of the Larghetto presents in

itself a certain poignancy. Then, the principal male soloist enters for the first time, accompanied by another ballerina. What follows is an idealized struggle between the two women for the man, in which the first dancer loses. As the male and his consort go off, the chief woman stands alone, a figure of solitude in harmony with the bitter-sweet spirit of Tchaikovsky's score.

* As in Balanchine's similarly planned *Concerto Barocco* and *Ballet Imperial*.

SCENE WITH BACKDROP BY CHRISTIAN BÉRARD

Seventh Symphony

ONE OF the most ambitious of Léonide Massine's ballets, using as its musical background the Seventh Symphony of Ludwig van Beethoven, this work was given a first performance at the Théâtre de Monte Carlo in May, 1938. In the following October its American première took place at the Metropolitan Opera House.

There are notable episodes in the ballet as well as others which indicate a slackening in Massine's powers of self-criticism. It is hard to understand how a choreographer who arrived at the amplitude of the first scene in *Seventh Symphony* and the airy fantasy of the third should have allowed his finale to bog down in a morass of allegory at the expense of design; and how an artist with the generally good taste of Massine could introduce into the second tableau—which begins with the impression of a golden pagan afternoon—the idea of the Descent from the Cross, in a startlingly literal re-enactment. These flaws have worked against a critical acceptance of *Seventh Symphony*; but there is too much of the imaginative about the composition, along with the beautiful scenery and costumes by Christian Bérard, to warrant its being shelved. A major revision would seem in order.

411

'Massine's program—the creation and destruction of the earth, in four scenes *—is certainly on the pretentious side. But, in essence, this remains an abstract ballet built on the ebb and flow of massed groups, with edges of narrative cutting across an essay in pure motion. The first three scenes approximate Beethoven's structural designs through ingenious use of mood, color, rhythm, and line; the last movement misses fire, in its disparity between the jubilant sound of the music and the agitated dance patterns on stage.

Seventh Symphony was revived by the Ballet Russe de Monte Carlo in September, 1948, at the Metropolitan Opera House, with Frederic Franklin in his original role of the Spirit of Creation, and with Alicia Markova as the Sky. Her partner in the Olympian *pas de deux* was Anton Dolin, and in later performances, Leon Danielian.

SCENE ONE

The curtain rises in silence. Primeval chaos is revealed, and the slow introductory theme of the first movement sounds in the orchestra.

Just as this portion of the score is intensified rhythmically over several pages, so do the groupings on stage gradually acquire focus and animation.

A commanding figure in white—the Spirit of Creation—bids recumbent green forms, suggestive of seaweed and lower plant life, to arise. At a lyrical turn in the music, the Sky (danced by the prima ballerina) appears above the water. And when the sprightly allegro of the first movement emerges, the gloom dissolves and the arches of ancient

Greece may be seen. Two deer (charmingly characterized by Massine in the manner of William Blake's religious drawings) cross the scene.

* Corresponding to the four movements of Beethoven's A major Symphony.

Birds, Man, Woman, Serpent, the Sun take part in the process of creation. Their entries result inevitably from the patterns of the music,
choreographed with an acute feeling for structure. At the climax of the
movement, the world has progressed from a formless mass to the light
of Aegean culture.

SCENE TWO

Massine's official program for this next episode reads, "Humanity is
plunged into the depths of despair after the first crime has been committed."

To the somber strains of the second movement's principal theme,

a procession of mourners appears. The men are bearing on their shoulders the body of a slain youth known as the Adolescent; but the pictorial
implications of this group, its resemblance to countless religious paint-

Photo: Fred Fehl   GROUP FROM SEVENTH SYMPHONY

ings, are clearly New Testament. As a matter of fundamental taste, the presence of the Deity on the stage of a theatre—even though otherwise designated in the program—is most questionable; in the field of pure reason, Massine's superimposition of a Christian experience on an early Greek background is wild. This lapse seems especially unfortunate because of the exquisite dance patterns he has arranged for the groups of women who are onlookers at the tragedy. Their movements are noble, sustained, and musical in the extreme, particularly toward the end of the scene, when—as the individual voices of the orchestra enter in a fugato on the main theme—the women follow Beethoven's structural design at first singly, then in groups.

SCENE THREE

The scherzo of the symphony has provided the happiest choreography in this ballet. Far from the earth and its cares, the gods are frolicking on Olympus; and here Massine has used his dancers in a formal design of singular grace and inventiveness. A small solo group enters festively with the opening measures of the scherzo, and, in contrast, the Sky God-

dess and her mate glide in to the lyrical strains of the movement's second theme.*

Classic simplicity and sharpness of outline dominate the whole scene, in tune with the spirit of Beethoven's score.

SCENE FOUR

To the opening of the celebrated finale of the Seventh, which once caused Wagner to refer to this symphony as "the apotheosis of the

---

* In a formal analysis, this section of the scherzo would be called the *trio.*

dance," a mass of bacchantes enters, equipped with long trumpets, bowls

of flowers, and other conventional accessories of good times in ancient
Greece. Massine has taken a long chance here in relying entirely on mass
movement without soloists. Unfortunately, the motivation and the execution of the scene are pallid, and the bacchanale does not reach a true
climax. At a given moment, other dancers dressed in modishly trimmed
red rags representing Fire rush in to overwhelm their colleagues. As the
curtain falls, they flutter their hands like flames.

Shadow of the Wind

THIS BALLET in six episodes, with choreography by Antony Tudor, was first produced by Ballet Theatre at the Metropolitan Opera House in April, 1948. Like its predecessor of twelve years before, *Dark Elegies*—also designed by Tudor—the work was based on a song cycle of Gustav Mahler, this time *Das Lied von der Erde* ("The Song of the Earth").* The scenery and costumes were by Jo Mielziner.

Whereas the *Kindertotenlieder* cycle, from which *Dark Elegies* sprang, gives the possibility of a compact and homogeneous theatrical work, *Das Lied von der Erde*—undoubtedly the composer's masterpiece —is too complex to support the added element of dance. The text, Asiatic in origin (the work of the eighth-century philosopher, Li Po), breathes a Rhenish *Weltschmerz* in translation; † the music, though it moves in a facsimile of Oriental contemplative art, is actually romantic in feeling. This mixture of styles can be fascinating in a concert performance; but Tudor's attempt to provide a danced equivalent, notably in its filtering out of all coloristic ingredients except the Chinese, has fallen short of the dramatic concentration that marks his other works. The production was essentially a failure despite the co-operation of such fine dancers as Hugh Laing, Igor Youskevitch, Alicia Alonso, Nana Gollner, and John Kriza.

The sequence of songs in *Das Lied von der Erde* opens with a tenor solo, "Das Trinklied vom Jammer der Erde" ("The Drinking Song of Earthly Woe"), a dark, reeling serenade to death. Next, for alto voice, comes "Der Einsame im Herbst" ("The Lonely One in Autumn"), a poem of solitude when the leaves of the lotus flowers have withered and are scattered on the waters. A third lyric, for tenor, "Von der Jugend" ("Of Youth"), brings a more buoyant mood, with gleaming pavilions and bridges of jade, neighbors handsomely gowned drinking tea and gossiping. The fourth solo, for alto, "Von der Schönheit" ("Of Beauty"), offers scenes of an idyllic countryside, of maidens plucking flowers at the edge of the shore. Then comes a serenade for tenor, "Der Trunkene im Frühling" ("The Drunken One in Springtime"), differing from the stormy opening of the cycle in that here is no thought of lurking death, but only joy in living.

* Symphony for alto and tenor soloists with orchestra.
† Mahler drew the lyrics for these songs from Hans Bethge's anthology, *Die Chinesische Flöte*.

NANA GOLLNER

All of these individual songs pale in effect before the finale, "Der Abschied" ("The Farewell"), a solo for contralto which, in its monumental span, represents a full-scale symphonic poem. The text and music treat of the loneliness born of the loss of friends, the solace that comes from casting aside personal griefs in a contemplation of nature, its passing seasons, its wheel that turns the earth to spring. *"Ewig, ewig!"* sings the alto voice of the comforting flow of time . . . "Endless, endless!"

Completed by Mahler in the summer of 1908, *Das Lied von der Erde* was given for the first time at Munich in November, 1911, six months after the composer's death, under the direction of Bruno Walter. Its American première was conducted by Leopold Stokowski at a concert by the Philadelphia Orchestra in December, 1916. Among the famous altos who have sung the solo part in this country are Mme Charles Cahier, Margaret Matzenauer, Maria Olszewska, Kerstin Thorborg, and Kathleen Ferrier. The tenors have included Orville Harrold, Richard Crooks, Frederick Jagel, and Charles Kullman.

In the words of the choreographer, *Shadow of the Wind* symbolizes the impermanence of existence, the Chinese philosophy of accepting the mutations of life and bowing before them. Here human experience has no sudden beginning or ending but, like the recurrence of the seasons, is cyclical.

A single setting is used for the entire ballet, with changes of lighting to indicate differences in time and mood. As the curtain rises to the passionate opening bars of the score, a group of meditative men * is revealed

against a closed-in, Oriental landscape. Some stand poised on hillocks, others near the arched bridge that crosses the scene. Among them are figures who will appear throughout the ballet, chiefly an old poet and a young warrior, binding its separate chapters with some slight connecting tissue. This first picture is entirely in the nature of a scenic overture, establishing the archaic color and locale of the work.

The next episode, "The Abandoned Wife," has more intensity. A vignette of life in the valley, it reveals a young husband and wife in a duet of mounting pathos. The man is tired of his bride; but the more harshly he tries to thrust her aside, the greater are her submissiveness and loyalty. At length, he goes off to a newer love, and the bride stands alone, deserted.

A bit of chinoiserie follows (called in the program "My Lord Summons Me") with a bustling mandarin in willow-plate pursuit of an attractive maiden. The over-all spirit of the scene is whimsical, as is its pastel-shaded music.

This lighter side of life in the valley is continued under another phase in the next chapter, "The Lotus Gatherers." As one of a group of maidens

* Protagonists of the first episode: "Six Idlers of the Bamboo Valley."

leads her friends in plucking flowers, a cluster of young soldiers enters. These youths will return in the finale with tragic implications; now they are lively and on the loose. A brief flirtation follows between them and the girls, cut short by a call to duty.

Now the group tableau yields to an engaging solo, "Conversation with Wine Pot and Bird," based on the fifth song of the cycle. One of the best episodes in the ballet, treating with affectionate humor the benevolence of an old Chinese poet in love with Nature, its intimacy suffered in performance from a bird of too ample size suspended on wires.

The epic finale of *Shadow of the Wind* corresponds to the "Abschied" of Mahler's score. It is called "Poem of the Guitar." To the music's mournful beginning, an aged woman bearing a guitar in hand recalls the sad course of her life. As she dreams and lives the past, the tale is acted out. A young girl is seen whose lover bids her farewell and sets out to war with three comrades. In a long and tragic interlude, the girl awaits his return; but when the soldiers come back to the valley, her loved one is not among them. This vision of the woman in her youth dissolves into the lonely figure of the guitarist, who, strumming her instrument, sings of the many springs that have passed since the death of her warrior, and of how she longs to lie beside him.

To the wonderful closing pages of Mahler's score, with their repeated notes for deep harp, mandolin, and the murmuring of the alto voice on "*Ewig!*," the ballet brings no sense of outward climax, but rather that blend of resignation and timelessness which Tudor has taken as the essence of *Das Lied von der Erde*.

Skyscrapers

THIS BALLET of modern city life, in one act and five scenes, was given its world première by the Metropolitan Opera Association in February, 1926, on a triple bill with *Gianni Schicchi* and *Pagliacci*. John Alden Carpenter wrote the score, which, in its command of rhythmic variety and dynamic color, proved a perfect expression of contemporary mores. Sammy Lee, dance director from Broadway, was the choreographer, capturing in his designs the vitality and brashness of the period. Robert Edmond Jones created the settings and costumes. *Skyscrapers* remains one of the really important novelties to have been produced by the Metropolitan, a pathbreaker that focused attention on the rich ballet material to be found in the American scene. At its first performances, leading roles were danced by Albert Troy as the Strutter, Rita de Leporte as Herself, and Roger Dodge as White Wings. A German production, with choreography by Heinrich Kröller, was presented at the Munich Opera in 1929.

A vital, pounding rhythm is heard, the force of machinery in action,

of human energy at work. The curtains part and a dazzling black and white inner drop is revealed, with lights blinking at either side of the proscenium. Then, to clanging sounds in the orchestra, the drop rises, giving way to the panorama of a big city, skyscrapers, gangs of laborers and riveters at the feet and in the hearts of the towering buildings. Their garments glint, suggesting steel.

The scene changes to reveal a factory entrance and a time clock. Workers and girls appear, punch the clock, and disappear in the dark interior of the building. A few of them linger outside to chat and cut jazz rhythms but—like the rest—are soon swallowed up by the all-enveloping machine.

The city itself and its dour working habits have been disclosed. Now the scene shifts to a seaside resort, suggestive of Coney Island. The workers are at play in the midst of a carnival: bands, carrousels, all the attractions to be found on a midway. Here, as they relax, the solo dances of the people evolve from the steps of the musical comedy stage and cabaret. The Strutter, reminiscent of vaudeville days, with a black silk hat and springy walk, offers his own sly variation. An attractive girl, known only

as Herself, performs with gusto; and White Wings, a street-cleaner, adds a sentimental note to the hilarity at the shore.

The hours of the early dawn arrive, and White Wings falls asleep. As the seaside is cloaked in shadows, a chorus of invisible Negro voices sings a wordless chant. But this lull in the metabolism of a great city is

soon over. The jazz rhythms of earlier scenes sound in the orchestra once more; the tableau of the beach surrenders to the factory doors, the winking lights, the clanging of the opening; and the persistent rhythm of the first bars of *Skyscrapers* is heard again.

The laborers, too, are seen. Behind them appear shadows of other workers, swinging their sledges in a rhythm which becomes insistent, almost threatening. As some of them open their arms in supplication, the curtain falls.

ACT I, SCENE ONE, FROM THE SADLER'S WELLS PRODUCTION

The Sleeping Beauty

THIS MOST famous of nineteenth-century ballets, in three acts and five scenes, based on Charles Perrault's fairy tale, "La Belle au Bois Dormant," with book and choreography by Marius Petipa and music by Tchaikovsky, was first performed at the Mariinsky Theatre, St. Petersburg, in January, 1890. The cast included Carlotta Brianza as Princess Aurora, Paul Gerdt as Prince Charming, and Enrico Cecchetti doubling in the roles of the wicked fairy, Carabosse, and the Bluebird.

Although the production was staged with great magnificence, it did not make the immediate impression which might have been expected. Only with growing familiarity did *The Sleeping Beauty* establish a firm hold on Russian audiences. Misfortune followed it abroad, where the opulence of its scope stood in the way of the theatres of Western Europe and America, less richly endowed than the Mariinsky. With the exception of a historic revival prepared by Nicholas Sergeyev and designed by Léon Bakst for the Diaghilev company during that troupe's London season of 1921–22, and less elaborate presentations of the ballet in the

United States by Anna Pavlova (1916), Mikhail Mordkin (1936), and Catherine Littlefield (1937), the full-length version of the work seemed destined to remain a rarity. It was not until Sergeyev, with décor by Nadia Benois, again revived *The Sleeping Beauty*, a shade less spectacularly this time, for the Sadler's Wells Company at their London theatre in February, 1939, with Margot Fonteyn as Aurora and Robert Helpmann as Prince Charming, that the ballet in its entirety was to become standard fare for the West. This edition, with new décor by Oliver Messel, was introduced to the United States by the Sadler's Wells troupe at the Metropolitan Opera House in October, 1949, on their first American tour.

The 1921 presentation of *The Sleeping Beauty* by the Diaghilev company had been of particular splendor. Aurora was danced by Olga Spessivtzeva; Pierre Vladimiroff was the Prince Charming; Lydia Lopokova, the Lilac Fairy; and Carlotta Brianza—the original Aurora of the St. Petersburg première—the evil fairy, Carabosse. A further link with the past was signalized when Enrico Cecchetti, who had created the malignant witch at the Mariinsky, played it during the London season on the anniversary of his fiftieth year as a dancer. Igor Stravinsky provided certain orchestral transitions for this production, which differed slightly in schematic layout from that of 1890, and sketched the instrumentation for parts of the score, which, no longer available in full copy, came only in piano reduction. A few new dances, notably "The Three Ivans," were created for the last act by Bronislava Nijinska.

Intended for a long run, the lavishly mounted revival was not a financial success and vanished to the storehouse, where the sets were damaged by fire. During his company's season at the Paris Opéra in 1922, however, Diaghilev did salvage some of the great individual numbers and processionals from the ballet, incorporating them into a one-act *divertissement* which he called *Le Mariage d'Aurore* ("Aurora's Wedding"). This special abridgment was first presented in the United States by the Ballet Russe de Monte Carlo at the Metropolitan Opera House in October, 1935. Another series of extracts, *Princess Aurora*, containing much of the same material but with a finer sense of arrangement, was prepared by Anton Dolin for Ballet Theatre in a production launched at the Forty-fourth Street Theatre, New York, in 1941. Both versions were merely a reminder of the grandeur that is the full-length *Sleeping Beauty*, an enduring monument of Russian ballet. As in *Swan Lake* and *The Nutcracker*, the Tchaikovsky music is at the heart of the work. Certainly no more stimulating, colorful, and melodious score has been written for dance.

ACT ONE

SCENE ONE: A roaring theme sounds in the orchestra, the motive of the wicked fairy, Carabosse, who is to influence so drastically the course

of the plot. Then, as the music changes mood and takes on a ceremonious air, the curtain rises, revealing the gilded palace of King Florestan XXIV.

Lines of courtiers, dressed in the height of baroque splendor, descend the staircase into the great hall, where they are received by Cantallbutte, the royal seneschal. Then, to the rhythm of a stately march, the King

and Queen appear. Wearing regal ermine, they approach the cradle that is the center of all this festivity. The Princess Aurora, attended by nurses who sway the little bed with golden cords, lies within, awaiting the hour of her christening. Tenderly, the King bends over the sleeping infant, the Queen kisses her, and both monarchs ascend their thrones.

There is a fanfare of trumpets and a procession of benevolent spirits appears, bringing all the good fortune that the Princess might desire. These are crowned sprites of Nature, fairies named for the plants, flowers, or living creatures whom they represent: Pine Woods, Cherry Blossom, Carnation, Songbirds, Hummingbirds, Mountain Ash. As every one of them, followed by a page bearing her train, draws near the cradle with a special gift for the well-being of the child, the orchestra plays a sustained melody that marks the beginning of a formal *pas de sept*. The

seventh performer is the Lilac Fairy, whose entrance and solo—after the other spirits have ranged themselves before Aurora—bring the number to a climax.

Soon the long-drawn theme is transformed into a leaping echo of itself, and the messengers from Nature to Aurora at her birth dance swiftly, their attendants turning brilliantly in air. There follows a series of solo

MARGOT FONTEYN

Courtesy S. Hurok

variations, the most famous of which is the twinkling number for the
Fairy of the Songbirds, usually known as the "Finger Variation" because
of the animated fluttering of her hands.

When these spirits have done presenting their gifts, their guardian appears: the Lilac Fairy, loveliest of them all. Come with her own blessings for Aurora, she dances a waltz of extraordinary grace.

Suddenly, there is a clap of thunder. The King and Queen rise terrified from their thrones; one of the royal heralds runs in to report the arrival of the wicked fairy, Carabosse, ignored by the monarchs in their invitations to the spirit world. As the guests tremble, the orchestra sounds the same discordant theme that was heard at the beginning of the prelude (No. 1), and a black coach drawn by rats dashes into the hall.

A wizened old woman with straggling gray hair hobbles from the carriage. Attended by two sinister rats garbed as coachmen, she approaches the throne with her personal christening gift for the Princess: a gold cage containing a rodent. Indignantly, she demands of Cantalbutte why her name has been omitted from the list of honored guests. When the old seneschal, confused and overwhelmed, cannot answer, the witch pronounces a curse against the court of Florestan XXIV. . . . Aurora is to grow ever more beautiful until, in the prime of her youth, she will prick her finger and die.

At the climax of her harangue, the witch is raised, in the original version, triumphantly by her brigade of rats. In the Sadler's Wells production, this is eliminated. Then, seized with a desire to confront the child, she leaps to the ground and advances on the cradle; but she falls back— for there, above the sleeping girl, stands the Lilac Fairy with wand outstretched in protection.

As the furious Carabosse scampers into her coach and rushes from the hall, the Lilac Fairy promises the King and Queen that, instead of dying on the appointed day, the Princess shall slumber until awakened by a kiss from a King's son. As she makes this vow, to a vaulting musical theme which will be associated with the Lilac Fairy for the remainder of the ballet, the entire court kneels before her. Solemnly, she raises her

wand in token of happiness for the infant Aurora.

SCENE TWO: Sixteen years later, Aurora has grown to be one of the most beautiful of Princesses. Suitors from all over the world have come to seek her hand—among them the Princes of Spain, Italy, England, and India. Delighted at the presence of these four royal heirs, Aurora's father has decreed that a celebration be held in their honor. Not only the functionaries of the court have been invited, but also the people of the surrounding village.

The peasant folk mingle with the nobles in the palace gardens and dance merrily. Even the august Cantalbutte sways to their rythms; but he stops in alarm when he sees that some of the girls are carrying spin-

Courtesy S. Hurok

ACT I, SCENE TWO, FROM THE SADLER'S WELLS PRODUCTION

dles. Since all pointed objects have been banned from the neighborhood of the palace ever since the curse of Carabosse, on which the King still broods, the old man snatches them from the girls, warning of the punishment that goes with their possession. It is death.

Just at this moment, the King and Queen appear with the honored guests. Noticing Cantalbutte's agitation and learning of the spindles, the ruler is so unnerved that he orders the offenders executed at once. Only after the four Princes plead with him for the lives of the villagers and Cantalbutte intercedes does the King relent. In a burst of thankfulness, the peasants—carrying great garlands of flowers—perform a lusty waltz for the monarch and his Queen.

At last the Princess herself arrives in the garden: young, radiant, splendidly dressed. Supported by the Spanish Prince *en attitude*,† she gathers flowers from the four heirs—every one of them slowly turning her in a full circle with the acceptance of his bloom—during the Rose Adagio, one of the best-known portions of the ballet. As this episode nears its peak, the Spanish Prince withdraws and the girl remains balanced on point through her own technical command. The accompanying music is broad and noble, sustaining the Princess and her cavaliers in their every move.

When the ensemble has reached its end, an old woman steals across the garden among the villagers. Nearing the Princess, she opens her cloak to reveal a spindle. The girl, fascinated, snatches the object, waves it on high. Suddenly the dread point penetrates her finger. She whirls in a spasm of fright, and drops as if lifeless.

Now the old woman flings back the hood of her cloak and laughs malignantly. It is Carabosse. The four Princes draw their swords and close in on her; but, at their approach, she disappears in flame.

A moment of complete dejection follows. The rulers and their subjects stand helplessly about the fallen Aurora, until the Lilac Fairy appears. Comforting the parents and reminding them of her promise,

† On the point of one foot, the other leg extended to the rear, bent at the knee.

MOIRA SHEARER   *Courtesy S. Hurok*

she bids them carry the sleeping girl into the palace. Then she waves her wand; there is a sound of thunder, and an enchanted woodland springs from the ground, concealing the home of the King and placing it—until Aurora's awakening—under the protecting spell of this beneficent spirit.

ACT TWO

SCENE ONE: A hundred years have passed, and a hunting party is seen in a glade not too far from the magic wood. It is composed of young Prince Charming, his tutor, Gallison, and numerous courtiers with their ladies, all dressed in the rococo finery of a later age. As dusk is about to come over the forest, the party pauses beside a lake and the servants spread cloths for a repast.

Bored by a languorous countess who never leaves him and repelled by the childish antics of his tutor, the Prince sits by in a despondent mood. He barely looks at the game of Blindman's Buff that is being played, or at the exuberant dances of the noblewomen.

After the whole party has joined in a rousing farandole,* hunting horns are heard and the time for departure is sounded. All rise to leave except the Prince. Gallison, the tutor, urges him onward but, noting the youth's ill humor, withdraws. The others follow, and the Prince is left alone.

As the dusk fades imperceptibly into night, the Lilac Fairy appears on the lake in a fragile bark. Softly, the melody associated with her ancient vow is heard in the orchestra (No. 6). When the boat has neared the shore, she glides toward the Prince and draws him into a confession of his unhappiness at court, the dullness of his existence among people with whom he shares no interests. The Fairy listens intently to his sorrows; then, in answer, she tells of a sleeping Princess—destined to bring joy to a youth like himself—who awaits the kiss of a King's son to set her free.

The Prince, still ruled by melancholy, disbelieves the tale; but as the Fairy waves her wand, he sees a band of sprites invade the forest. Aurora, in an ethereal vision, hovers among them. The youth runs toward her and dances with the slumbering girl until, with the rest of the apparitions, she vanishes.

Now he begs the Lilac Fairy to lead him to the palace where the Princess lies. The Fairy conducts him to the bark, stands on the prow, and guides the boat gently through the waters, the Prince at her side. For a moment, as the darkness grows more intense, the vessel is lost to sight.

* A spirited group number, based on the prancing of serpentine columns, which had its origin in the south of France. It is not unlike the snake dance familiar to American college campuses.

ACT II, SCENE ONE, OF THE SADLER'S WELLS PRODUCTION

Then it appears on the horizon, etched against a mighty pile of stone. The voyagers are approaching the home of the spellbound Aurora.

SCENE TWO: After an orchestral interlude full of mystery, the curtain rises on an immense hall in the dwelling of King Florestan. Great shadows fall across the room, in the center of which is a raised slab on which Aurora lies asleep.

Led by the Lilac Fairy, Prince Charming emerges from the darkness, looking about him at the decay that seems to have eaten into the palace walls. Approaching the slab, he gazes reverently at the reclining figure; he bends over, kisses her lips. To a crash of thunder, Aurora opens her eyes. As she rises, the Prince lifts her to the ground and, with a fervent embrace, frees her from the curse pronounced by Carabosse.

ACT THREE*

All of the court, which was plunged into slumber with the Princess, now shares in her awakening. The palace shimmers with light as the dust of a century vanishes by magic and the King appears on the steps

* In the Diaghilev version of 1921, the transition from Aurora's awakening to the finale was instantaneous.

of the throne room, more resplendent than before. With him are the Queen, the courtiers, and the faithful Cantalbutte, magnificent in cloth of gold. It is he who leads the march through the lofty, colonnaded halls to celebrate the union of Aurora and her Prince.

By a happy stroke of dramatic invention, this closing scene brings as wedding guests several of the characters from Charles Perrault's collection of fairy tales, *Mother Goose,*[*] of which "The Sleeping Beauty" is a part. Entering to a festive polonaise, they entertain the court in a series

of fantastic *divertissements* which begins with a number for four sprites representing precious stones and metals.[†] These figures dance singly and in combination, their *pas de quatre* culminating with a coda in which

the two jewellike couples pair off.

The next *divertissement* offers Puss in Boots and the White Cat, a vignette of feline love. First the pair are full of affection. Later the White Cat, having had her fill of attention and tiring of it, scratches her suitor and runs off. He leaps after her.

This is succeeded by one of the most famous *pas de deux* in ballet, often taken from its place in *The Sleeping Beauty* and performed independently: the duet for the Bluebird and the Enchanted Princess Florine.[‡] The couple enter to a high-lying, exotically scored woodwind passage

and perform an opening adagio. There soon follows a breath-taking solo for the Bluebird in which a sequence of dazzling *entrechats,*[§] accompanied by the waving of the dancer's outstretched arms, gives the effect

[*] *Contes de ma Mère l'Oye* (1697).

[†] The Diaghilev revival introduced four *commedia dell' arte* characters at this point: Harlequin, Columbine, Pierrot, and Pierrette.

[‡] This was originally planned as a *pas de quatre* for Florine, the Bluebird, Cinderella, and her Prince. The entry and coda were to be danced by all four characters, the two variations performed as duets.

[§] See footnote on *entrechat* in *Cirque de Deux*.

THE WHITE CAT AND PUSS IN BOOTS FROM THE SADLER'S WELLS PRODUCTION

of a winged creature in flight; and its illusion is reinforced to no small degree by Tchaikovsky's soaring music. Immediately afterward come a

Allegro — tempo di valse

graceful variation for Florine and then a stunning finale in which both soloists—after many feats of combined technical prowess—leap brilliantly from the scene, Florine followed by the Bluebird in a giant arc.

Further *divertissements* at Aurora's wedding include numbers by Red Riding Hood and the Wolf, who gobbles his prey remorselessly just as she is on the point of escaping him; Hop O' My Thumb, his brothers, and the Ogre; and Cinderella, in a duet with her Prince. The Diaghilev revival of 1921 omitted both latter tales, adding in their place a sketch for Ariana and Bluebeard. It also interpolated—with music from other works by Tchaikovsky—two Oriental numbers and a Russian dance, "The Three Ivans." The Sadler's Wells version omits all three entrees.

Now the performances by the guests have run their course; the time has come for the *grand pas de deux* of Aurora and Prince Charming. Integrated perfectly into the massive act which surrounds it, this duo is spacious, noble, even austere—a balanced contrast to the glitter of the preceding *divertissements*, especially of the "Bluebird." The *grand pas* begins with a great, sweeping adagio; goes on through a dignified solo

Photo: *Alfredo Valente*   Courtesy *Ballet Theatre*
JOHN KRIZA AND RUTH ANN KOESUN AS PRINCE CHARMING AND AURORA
IN THE BLUEBIRD VARIATION

Andante non troppo

mf espressivo

variation for Aurora; and ends with a coda marking the dramatic, as well as the formal, climax of the ballet, for it is here that Aurora is bestowed upon her Prince.

The festivities are at an end; and *The Sleeping Beauty* closes with a joyous mazurka in which the visitors from Fairyland join the King,

Allegro brillante

Queen, court, and lovers in an apotheosis of movement, color, and orchestral sound.

Courtesy Ballet Theatre

KAREN CONRAD IN THE BLUEBIRD VARIATION

IGOR YOUSKEVITCH AND ALICIA ALONSO

Le Spectre de la Rose

THIS SHORT ballet in one act, with choreography by Michel Fokine, was designed as a vehicle for Vaslav Nijinsky in the Diaghilev season of 1911 at the Théâtre de Monte Carlo. The supporting role of the young girl was taken by Thamar Karsavina.

Through the scenario by J. L. Vaudoyer, based on a poem by Théophile Gautier, Fokine had every opportunity to exploit Nijinsky's famous elevations. Here was the spirit of a rose, bounding through the air, leaping into the room of a maiden and, after an enchanting *pas de deux*, soaring away on the breeze. If no dancer since Nijinsky—who created a sensation in the part—has managed even to suggest the aerial qualities associated with this role, the fault does not lie, as is often suggested, with the choreography. The work simply demands, for an adequate performance, a poet-athlete as its star; and in the absence of such a personage *Le Spectre de la Rose* should not be given. In its ideal state, this is one of Fokine's finest works, all of its movements stemming from a sensitive poetic scheme. Someday, when restudied, relighted, and recast (if the right protagonist can be found), its virtues will again be clear. As performed today, it is another "filler"—like *L'Après-Midi d'un Faune*— to be sandwiched in between two longer numbers.

The music employed is the "Invitation to the Dance" of Karl Maria von Weber. Originally written for pianoforte duet, the piece was orchestrated by Hector Berlioz in 1841 for a production at the Paris Opéra of Weber's *Der Freischütz,* in which it was interpolated as a ballet. This orchestral arrangement—a glowing realization of Weber's ideas—has been standard ever since.*

The curtain rises on the bedchamber of a demure young girl of the nineteenth century, as a solo cello plays a melody filled with nostalgic longing.

The young girl, flushed with the radiance of her first ball, has just come home. In her hand she holds a rose, her lover's token. Tired, yet too excited to go to bed, she sinks in her armchair. Then she dozes, and the flower drops from her hand.

There is a rustle in the air and, through the open window which looks out on the garden, in soars the spirit of the rose. This leap is accomplished to the proclamation by full orchestra of the chief waltz theme.

The young girl rises under a spell and dances with the spirit. Their own special waltz, as distinguished from the music of the spirit's entrance, is lyrical and tender.

* A more recent transcription of the piece by Felix Weingartner has not succeeded in replacing that by Berlioz.

Once more the girl seeks her chair—guided this time by her guest. For a moment he bends over her; then, with a final leap, disappears through the opposite window. Fokine's conception of this exit is rightly one of the most celebrated and inspired moments in all choreography.

As the nostalgic cello solo of the opening returns (No. 1), the young girl opens her eyes. Wondering whether or not her dream has been reality, she picks up the rose at her feet. Then—looking at the inanimate petals—she knows that only sleep and its illusions have given substance to the flower.

Photo: Mishkin   *Courtesy Anatol Chujoy*

VASLAV NIJINSKY AS THE SPIRIT
OF THE ROSE

Photo: Alfredo Valente
Courtesy Ballet Theatre

ANDRÉ EGLEVSKY AS THE SPIRIT
OF THE ROSE

THE FOUR CYGNETTES

Swan Lake

(LE LAC DES CYGNES)

THIS BALLET in four acts, with music by Tchaikovsky and book by V. P. Begichev and Vasily Geltzer, is one of the outstanding works in the repertory of romantic dance. First produced at the Bolshoi Theatre, Moscow, in February, 1877, it received an inadequate mounting. The choreographer on this occasion was Julius Reisinger, the prima ballerina, Pauline Karpakova, both artists relatively obscure in dance history. Tchaikovsky, humiliated by the ballet's failure, mistakenly attributed it to the shortcomings of his music. He planned later to rewrite the score for a new production, but he had not done it when he died in 1893.

In the following year, the idea of a revival of *Swan Lake* was proposed by the great choreographer Marius Petipa for the Imperial Theatre of St. Petersburg, the Mariinsky. Owing to a crowded schedule, however, only the second act * materialized in time for a Tchaikovsky

* Thus launching a tradition that has continued in many touring companies to the present day: the production of Act Two, a virtually self-sufficient dance drama, under the title of *Swan Lake.*

439

memorial program given in the capital on February 29, 1894. The full ballet, in revised choreographic form, did not appear at the Mariinsky until nearly a year later, with the celebrated Pierina Legnani in the leading role. The choreography for the new version was a joint affair, Petipa sketching the entire work and staging the third act. His associate, Lev Ivanov—already responsible for Act Two—produced the remainder.

The first American performance of the complete ballet took place at the Metropolitan Opera House in December, 1911, with Katerina Geltzer and Mikhail Mordkin in the leading roles. Since that time, Act Two (the capsule *Swan Lake* of frequent appearance) and Act Three (often given alone as *The Magic Swan*) have been familiar to United States audiences, but the work as a whole has remained a rarity. In its full-length form, *Swan Lake*—revived by Nicholas Sergeyev—is part of the repertory of the Sadler's Wells Company, which presented the ballet during its American tour of 1949.

This masterpiece contains, in performance, one extremely difficult assignment: the dual role of Odette, chaste Swan Queen of the second and fourth acts, and Odile, malignant villainess of the third—figures identical in appearance but entirely diverse in nature. To dance both these characters in a single evening, grasping the full range of their technical and dramatic contrasts, is a virtuoso undertaking for any ballerina.

Among the great dancers of this double part, following Legnani, have been Anna Pavlova, Thamar Karsavina, Mathilde Kchesinska, Olga Spessivtzeva, Vera Nemchinova, and Margot Fonteyn. Distinguished ballerinas who are noted for their performances of Odette in the separately produced second-act version of *Swan Lake*—a purely lyrical portrait—include Alexandra Danilova, Alicia Markova, Irina Baronova, Tamara Toumanova, Mia Slavenska, Rosella Hightower, Nana Gollner, and Nora Kaye. Every one of them has her adherents, and all excel in particular facets of the role.

There can be no doubt that a major portion of the magic of *Swan Lake* arises from the music. The orchestra not only creates an incomparable surge of rhythm on which the dancers can float: it sings for them, underlining in full the possibilities for expressive release to be found in this tale of the enchanted swan.

ACT ONE

A great festival is being held before a castle of long ago to celebrate the coming of age of Prince Siegfried. The youth stands on the lawn receiving his guests, chatting with them jovially. As part of the merry-making, a lad and two girls perform a *pas de trois*,* in which the brilliant

---

* This number has often been lifted from its context and placed in the second-act version of *Swan Lake*, at the discretion of the choreographer restaging the production. Sometimes the male variation alone is thus transferred, given to the artist who dances the part of Benno.

Photo: Fred Fehl

TAMARA TOUMANOVA AS ODETTE

Photo: Maurice Seymour
Courtesy Ballet Theatre

ALICIA ALONSO AS ODETTE

male variation, especially, calls for stellar technique and authority.

In the midst of this animation, only one disapproving note is sounded: Siegfried's mother appears, rebukes the Prince for the loose friendships he has cultivated, and reminds him that, at a ball to be held the following evening, he is to choose a bride and settle down to a more stable way of life. As she re-enters the castle, the guests dance a subdued, ceremonious waltz.

Suddenly, after a bit of diversion provided by the Prince's old tutor, who has drunk too freely, the attention of Siegfried and his friends is drawn to a flight of wild swans overhead. At this point, the mysterious musical motive which dominates the ballet is heard for the first time,

Andante

lending a portentous note to the action. As the Prince and his courtiers look upward at the flight, they agree to go hunting that night and snare the birds for themselves.

ACT TWO

The mysterious theme (No. 3) sounds again in the orchestra, and a mossy glade bordering a lake is revealed, with a ruined chapel in the background. This atmosphere, with its soft lighting and sense of the remote, nostalgic past, offers the quintessence of romantic ballet. As the curtain rises, a group of swans—of which the first wears a crown—rides the waters of the lake. They are seen for a moment and then disappear.

Now Siegfried's hunting party, led by the Prince's young friend Benno, enters the glade. The men look about them curiously; Benno beckons to Siegfried, who has been following at a distance. The wooded shore, with its stillness, must be the hiding place of the swans.

Photo: Alfredo Valente   *Courtesy Ballet Theatre*
NORA KAYE AND IGOR YOUSKEVITCH AS ODETTE AND
PRINCE SIEGFRIED

Courtesy S. Hurok
VIOLETTA ELVIN AND JOHN FIELD AS ODILE AND
PRINCE SIEGFRIED

Dismissing his friends, Siegfried stands alone in meditation. As he looks up, a vision in dazzling white appears—Odette, the Swan Queen. It is she who, wearing the crown, has led her band across the lake, hoping for deliverance at the hands of the Prince. Under an evil spell cast by the sorcerer von Rothbart, she can assume her natural form only from midnight to dawn. Her friends, too, suffer from the same enchantment. This story she communicates to Siegfried in flawless and poetic mime.

The Prince falls in love at once with Odette and dances with her. Both are dominated by the rapture of youth, by a purity of feeling that is heightened by the flow of the music. Just as they are about to embrace,

the sinister figure of von Rothbart * comes toward them from the ruined chapel. Siegfried defies him momentarily, then retreats, for he is powerless against the supernatural; and, with a warning gesture, the sorcerer withdraws.

* In early performances of *Swan Lake,* the enchanter appeared in the form of an owl hovering over the ruins. This detail was revived by the Sadler's Wells Company.

At this moment, the maidens who share Odette's enchantment make their appearance in a group, dressed in the *tutu* ° which is the hallmark of romantic ballet. As they descend a hill which slopes toward the lake, seeming to fly through the glade, the Prince's friends return, delighted at this chance of capturing their game. Siegfried restrains them with a commanding gesture; and the swan maidens, looking at him gratefully, circle the hunters in an idyllic waltz.

Soon the huntsmen withdraw to another part of the wood. The Prince is left alone with Odette. In a grand adagio, marked by a long-lined solo for violin,† he invites her to the ball at which he must choose a bride,

vowing it is she alone whom he will wed. The swan maidens, appearing in the background, dance in little rhythmic groups during this romanza, moving with subtle counterpoint against the sustained lines of the two principals.

Next, in the spirit of formalized ballet, come a group dance and solo variations. First is a number for four baby swans, famous for the descriptive, almost clucking quality of its woodwind color, as well as the precision which the young dancers must bring to it on stage. Then, when

the second act is given alone, a solo is usually inserted for Siegfried, based on a seldom-played excerpt from the *pas de deux* of Act Three. Finally, Odette herself performs one of the most winning variations in

---

° See introduction to *Les Sylphides*.

† Too often the tempo of this solo is slowed in performance through undue concessions to individual dancers, its scintillating runs reduced to meaningless dribbles.

MARGOT FONTEYN

the work, the delicate flexure of her limbs suggesting the bend of a swan's wings.

The happy hour in the glade has reached its end. Odette, warning the Prince that she cannot attend the ball unless the enchanter's spell is broken, exhorts him to keep his vow to her. If he should disregard it, both she and her friends must die.

Dawn approaches—the time for the Queen and her maidens to resume their bondage. Reluctantly, the girls withdraw from the hunters; Odette herself retires with a longing glance at Siegfried; and the entire band is seen once more, led by the crowned swan, riding the waters of the lake. When performed separately, this act concludes with the apparition of von Rothbart, who, as Siegfried tries to follow the swans, drives him back with a gesture that symbolizes doom.

ACT THREE

The ball at which Siegfried must choose his bride is taking place in the splendidly lighted castle. As the Prince and his mother are seated in state, guests throng the hall. Many of them, in costumes of the lands where they were born, perform national dances for the pleasure of their hosts. First comes a Spanish *divertissement,* then a Neapolitan tarantella, a Hungarian czardas, a Polish mazurka; but at the climax of the entertainment, the guests suddenly turn their attention from these dances to the arrival of an imposing stranger. It is von Rothbart, disguised as the Knight of the Black Swan.

With him is his daughter, the demonic Odile, who resembles Odette by magic. A sorceress in her own right, she is bent on destroying Siegfried. Even as she enters the hall, the unsuspecting Prince rises from his throne and hurries toward her. All the noble ladies who have danced for him that evening in the hope of being chosen have turned his thoughts only more strongly to Odette.

As Siegfried takes the enchantress in his arms, there follows a *pas de deux* that is among the most athletic in the repertory. It is here that Odile, in an outburst of malevolent joy, performs the thirty-two consecutive *fouettés* * which have become a feature of the scene. The

Prince, too, has his spectacular variation; and this *grand pas de deux* (often given by itself as a separate number) ends with a coda in which both performers engage in every sort of pyrotechnical display that balletic law allows.†

With the ending of the dance, the Prince announces that the daughter of the Knight of the Black Swan is his choice. Even as he takes her hand in token, a vision flutters outside the window: the Swan Queen (played by an obliging supernumerary), trying in vain to command Siegfried's attention. Triumphant that the Prince has broken faith, von Rothbart vanishes with his daughter, and, in the same moment, Siegfried realizes the deception. He rushes from the castle to find the real Odette.

ACT FOUR

Once more the dark, enchanted glade is seen. The maidens are dancing, awaiting the return of Odette from her flight to the castle. At last she arrives, brooding over Siegfried's perfidy.

There is a dramatic surge in the orchestra—which is used with almost operatic abandon throughout the act—and the Prince appears on the shore, running to meet Odette. The Swan Queen angrily turns away; but Siegfried advances, explains von Rothbart's trick, and begs her forgiveness. Odette, overwhelmed, falls in his arms.

This reconciliation is the beginning of a fresh trial. Now the sorcerer causes the lake to overflow, with the intent of overwhelming the swan maidens and their Queen. Ready to die with Odette, Siegfried carries her through the storm to a hill above the waves.

His gesture of sacrifice breaks the enchanter's spell. As the dawn comes up, the lake recedes and the swan maidens no longer ride its waters. They regain their human form, and Odette, freed by the Prince's love, is united with Siegfried. In the Sadler's Wells version, the Prince and the Queen of Swans both drown, and are seen at the ballet's end floating away in an elaborate shell-like bark.

* See footnote on *fouetté* in *Graduation Ball.*
† For a *reductio ad absurdum* of this style of dance, see *Cirque de Deux.*

BALLET THEATRE SYLPHS *Courtesy Museum of Modern Art*

Les Sylphides

IN ITS final form—there were two earlier versions—*Les Sylphides* is a *ballet blanc,** replete with the outer trappings of nineteenth-century dance: a high-lyrical background, formidable solo variations that are simple in technique but difficult in purity of style and motion. The costumes of soloists and *corps* follow the delicate lines of the skirt worn in the 1830's by Marie Taglioni, favorite ballerina of the time, reaching midway between the ankle and the knee. It was this evocation of the days of Louis Philippe, Adolphe Adam, and Victor Hugo that prompted Diaghilev to change the name of the ballet (produced originally in Russia by the choreographer, Michel Fokine, as *Chopiniana*) to *Les Sylphides*, when it was added to his own repertory. The great Taglioni

---

* The expression *ballet blanc* (literally "white ballet"), coined by Théophile Gautier in his critical writings on dance over a hundred years ago, has long been associated with romantic works such as the second act of *Giselle*, which employ in the course of their performance the traditional white ballet skirt, or *tutu*. It also refers, figuratively, to their poetic style.

had been especially identified at the Paris Opéra with a two-act ballet *La Sylphide*, forerunner of *Giselle*, telling of a spirit who floated into a mortal's life and became involved in human passions. In the newer work of Fokine, plotless but atmospheric, the entire group of sylphs discovered on stage at the rise of the curtain and uniformly dressed like lithographs of Taglioni would seem to justify the plurality of Diaghilev's title.

It is only outwardly, however, that *Les Sylphides* resembles the ballets of the mid-1800's. The choreography derives from traditional patterns, but with such a freshly developed sense of expressive power as to evolve almost a new basis for classical movement. One solo variation flows into another with masterful spontaneity. The supporting *corps* provides at times a fluid background for the soloists and at other moments assumes a motivating force of its own. *Les Sylphides* is Fokine's life-giving approach to formal ballet, his reanimation of an art that had grown prematurely sedate.

The first version of the work was offered privately in 1906 at St. Petersburg, where Fokine was teaching at the Imperial School of Ballet. Another presentation took place two years later, on March 21, 1908. Both performances were based musically on a suite of Chopin's piano pieces, orchestrated by Alexander Glazunov. Less than a month after the performance of March, 1908, Fokine revised his ballet completely. He had originally designed the work as a series of genre pictures—among them a Polish wedding mazurka and a Neapolitan tarantella—bound together dramatically by the figure of Chopin at the piano evoking these scenes in his imagination. For the occasion of April 6, 1908, a performance by Fokine's own class of girls at the Imperial School, the choreographer suddenly transformed the ballet into the plotless reverie that we know today. Except for the C-sharp minor Waltz, which was retained in Glazunov's orchestration, all of the music was given a fresh scoring by Maurice Keller.

Ever since the day that Keller was called in to do his revision, *Les Sylphides* has been—musically speaking—in a state of flux. Special arrangements of it abound in the libraries of various companies. The large number of instrumental versions by Taneyev, Stravinsky, Caillet, Britten, Rieti, Boutnikoff, and other less notable names would seem to indicate that Chopin's music—strongly pianistic by nature—offers a constant challenge to the transcriber for orchestra.*

Les Sylphides was first produced in its ultimate form by the Diaghilev Ballet at the Théâtre du Châtelet, Paris, June 2, 1909. Since that time it has become one of the staples of the repertory, a favorite work with audiences, and a severe testing ground for dancers. Only the elect can hope to get through its solo variations with distinction.

Anna Pavlova, Thamar Karsavina, Maria Baldina, and Vaslav Nijin-

---

* The special concert arrangement for Victor Records is the work of Leroy Anderson and Peter Bodge.

sky were the first to perform these variations. They have been followed
—with varying success—by an array of famous artists including Alexandra Danilova, Alicia Markova, Irina Baronova, Alicia Alonso, Anton
Dolin, Igor Youskevich, George Zoritch, and Yura Skibine.

Just as the orchestral arrangements for *Les Sylphides* shift with different companies, so is the scenery far from immutable. The original
Diaghilev setting was by Alexandre Benois. Subsequent changes have
been made in décor by A. Socrate and Léon Zack. At present writing, Ballet Theatre uses Eugene Dunkel's effective background inspired
by the style of Corot.

Architecturally, *Les Sylphides* consists of an orchestral prelude, a
formal introduction for soloists and *corps de ballet*, four solo variations,
a *pas de deux*, and finale. The *corps* is entirely feminine. There are three
female soloists and one male.

The opening bars, played in a darkened theatre, are an instrumentation of Chopin's A major Prelude, Op. 28, No. 7. This music, only six-

teen bars in length,* evokes before the curtain rises that other-worldly
mood which is the essence of *Les Sylphides*.

As the dancers are revealed—half-legendary figures in a moonlit
grove—the A-flat major Nocturne, Op. 32, No. 2, is sounded, with the

* Usually repeated, in ballet performances, to harmonize with the proportions of
the work as a whole.

four principals and *corps* grouped toward the rear of the stage. First the
corps advances slowly; then the principals join them; and soon the
opening section yields to the first solo variation—the waltz in G-flat
major, Op. 70, No. 1. Perhaps nowhere else in *Les Sylphides,* save in its

closing moments, do the spirits of music and dance unite so strikingly
as in this first variation. The soaring movements of the soloist are in full
rapport with the bold skips of the score.

The second variation, performed usually by the star ballerina to the
D major Mazurka, Op. 33, No. 3, demands extraordinary powers of ele-

vation, tempered by taste, imagination, and good classical style. When
done by too exuberant a dancer, the frequent leaps across stage and
disappearances into the wings can suggest the extravagant rather than
the poetic.

Next comes the C major Mazurka, Op. 67, No. 3, for male dancer, a

lyrical variation of floating quality. In this episode the performer is almost depersonalized, his body becoming a symbol in motion of abstract grace.

There follows the most nostalgic variation of all, based on a repetition of the A major Prelude that opened *Les Sylphides*. With the *corps* grouped in symmetrical clusters, the soloist becomes the touchstone of the whole moonlit mood sought by Fokine, to movements of great choreographic freedom.

Some versions of *Les Sylphides* differ in the order of their variations. Certain numbers may be reversed and, on occasion—as in recorded arrangements—fresh music added.* In stage performances, the moonlight solo is generally succeeded by the *pas de deux*, danced to the C-sharp minor Waltz, Op. 64, No. 2. Here again, the male dancer is no

* In the Victor album, the seldom-played F minor Waltz, Op. 69, No. 1, joins the other Chopin pieces making up the score.

Photo: Fred Fehl ANTON DOLIN AND ALICIA MARKOVA

more than an abstract figure, part of the nocturnal design; but the very poetry of his duo with the ballerina springs from the remote, elfin quality that lies at the heart of *Les Sylphides.*

The stage is emptied after the *pas de deux.* Now, to the brilliant introductory bars of the E-flat major Waltz, Op. 18, No. 1, the *corps*

enters. In the fluid interplay of groups and columns, this ensemble is at one with the architecture of the music, building a crescendo of motion simultaneously with the rising volume of the orchestra. At the height of the dynamic tension, the columns are transformed into a semicircular, exultant group which—as it passes the wings in a wide arc—is joined by the four soloists, who come leaping from offstage.

A decrescendo begins and the dancers move toward a point of repose. Throughout the nine bars of this dynamic recession, soloists and *corps*

gradually resume their pose of the opening tableau. A single measure of silence follows, then a great fortissimo chord, on which the final attitude is struck by most of the dancers. Two bars of waltz remain; and here the front line of girls comes forward, almost to the footlights, accompanied by three great orchestral chords. On the last note of the music they stand motionless—a period to the completed sentence—boldly counterbalancing the soloist and remainder of the *corps* as the curtain falls.

Sylvia

OR

THE NYMPH OF DIANA

THIS BALLET in three acts, with book by Jules Barbier and Baron de Reinach, choreography by Louis Mérante, was first produced at the Paris Opéra in June, 1876. As in the case of *La Source* and *Namouna*, both works of about the same era, scenic splendor and narrative intricacy—almost like that of grand opera—shared honors with dance and sometimes obscured it. *Sylvia*, however, remains an agreeable period piece, its shortcomings lessened by Léo Delibes's distinguished score. Much of the music has become standard in concert performance.

ACT ONE

There is a brief prelude, majestic in nature, and the curtain rises on

a legendary grove. Here, at the hour before dawn, fauns and dryads are frolicking near a statue of the god Eros, still illumined by moonlight. As the sound of human footsteps is heard, they hide and the shepherd, Amyntas, enters.

Throwing aside his crook and mantle, the youth thinks of another night—not long ago—when in this place he glimpsed a beautiful nymph dressed as a huntress. He has returned with the hope of seeing her again. Suddenly, distant horns are sounded and the nymph enters, followed by

her attendants. Amyntas hides.

It is Sylvia whom the shepherd has admired, ward of the chaste god-

454

dess Diana. As her companions bathe in a rustic stream, Sylvia swings gracefully on a bough above the water, watched not only by the hidden

Amyntas but also by Orion, the dark huntsman, scourge of the forests.

In a few moments the shepherd's crook and mantle are discovered by the nymphs. Angrily, Sylvia orders her friends to find the intruder. Orion vanishes; Amyntas is brought forth, and Sylvia draws her bow, aiming it at the youth. Then, on another impulse, she waves Amyntas aside—he is unworthy of her revenge. Instead, she will punish the all-motivating Eros, god of Love.

Amyntas runs to protect the statue, but he is pierced and falls to the ground. The statue, in turn, launches its own dart at the nymph. Sylvia trembles, places her hand over her heart; but when her comrades, running to her side and picking up the golden arrow, ask if she has been wounded, the nymph smilingly shakes her head.

The morning has grown lighter, and sounds from the village are heard. As Sylvia and her companions disappear, the sun rises and a band of peasants dance in with their girls, carrying fruit and wine. On their way to the harvest, they kneel before the statue of Eros, then go off along woodland paths. Only one young shepherd stays behind and hides as Orion approaches. The dark huntsman, in love with Sylvia, has returned to kill Amyntas. Seeing the youth already prostrate, he rejoices—then makes plans to abduct the nymph.

As he prepares a chain of gold with which to snare her, Sylvia emerges from the forest. She has come alone, drawn toward Amyntas by a feeling she cannot master. Just as she leans over the fallen youth, Orion casts his chain and captures her. There is a brief struggle, after which he carries her off.

Now the young shepherd in hiding calls to his friends for help. They enter, recognize the stricken Amyntas, try in vain to revive him. It is only when an old sorcerer appears, plucks a rose and brings it to his lips that the youth can breathe again. Learning that Sylvia has been carried off by Orion, he vows to free her and, in the moment of departure, prays to the statue of Eros. The image disappears and the god himself stands on the pedestal, pointing out to the youth the path which Orion has taken. As the peasants kneel reverently, Amyntas leaves on his journey.

ACT TWO

Held in the cave of Orion, Sylvia tries to flee but is caught by the huntsman, who threatens her with an ax. Then, as his mood calms, he offers her fruit and drink. Knowing she can win her freedom only through a ruse, Sylvia accepts the fruit and commands Orion's slaves to squeeze quantities of grapes into a goblet. This she offers to Orion.

As the nymph dances a bacchanale, the huntsman becomes inflamed with drink and love. His senses fail him; he falls to the ground in a drunken sleep. The slaves, too, who have gulped the wine, roll beside their master.

Still, the grotto is impassable; no way of escape seems clear. At the height of her anxiety, Sylvia prays not to the goddess Diana but to her former enemy, Eros. The god appears at once and leads her from the cave, which sinks into the ground. As a horn sounds far off, Eros reveals a vision of Amyntas to the nymph. He is grieving in solitude and awaiting her return.

ACT THREE

A vast stretch of seacoast may be seen, with a hill surmounted by the temple of Diana. As the curtain rises, a festival is being held in honor of Bacchus, with offerings of grapes to the god and the dancing of a bacchanale.

Moderato ben marcato

Amyntas appears in the midst of this revel. Despondent over his unsuccessful search for Sylvia, even the arrival of a galley from foreign lands fails to interest him. As the ship reaches the shore, Eros—disguised as a pirate—springs to the landing. With him are a number of veiled slaves whom he tries to sell. They all approach Amyntas, but only one can hold the attention of the melancholy youth. After she has danced for him to the melodious plucking of strings,* she raises her veil and Amyntas sees that it is Sylvia.

Allegretto ben marcato

* The famous "Pizzicato" from *Sylvia.*

At the climax of their reunion, Orion appears. While Sylvia flees to the temple of Diana, Amyntas stands his ground to do combat; but the huntsman, ignoring the shepherd, crashes his ax on the portals of the temple.

Clouds come over the scene, the roar of thunder is heard, and—on the third blow—the great doors swing open. Diana, with Sylvia kneeling beside her, stands on the threshold with drawn bow. As Orion leaps forward, she looses an arrow and the huntsman falls dead.

Now the goddess angrily demands why Sylvia has fallen in love with a mortal. As the nymph admits that she has been wounded by the dart of Eros, the god himself appears, throws off his pirate's disguise, and reminds Diana—by evoking a vision of the goddess visiting the sleeping Endymion—that she too has known love.

Diana, who would rather forget the incident, agrees to overlook Sylvia's indiscretion. Eros makes a sign, the apparition of Diana's embarrassing past disappears, and—as the goddess, together with Eros, ascends the steps of her temple—the sunlight returns, bathing Amyntas and Sylvia in its gold.

TANAQUIL LE CLERCQ, TODD BOLENDER, AND JOCELYN VOLLMAR TAKE BOWS AT THE
END OF A PERFORMANCE

Symphonie Concertante

THIS ABSTRACT ballet in three movements, set to one of the most beautiful of Mozart's compositions—the Sinfonia Concertante in E-flat major, No. 364 in the Köchel Catalogue, for solo violin, viola, and orchestra—was first produced by Ballet Society at the New York City Center in November, 1947. George Balanchine was the choreographer, and James Stewart Morcon designed the scenery and costumes. With a cast headed by Maria Tallchief, Tanaquil LeClercq, and Todd Bolender, the work scored an instantaneous success through its realization, in pure dance, of the lyrical and structural elements in Mozart's music.

FIRST MOVEMENT

Allegro Maestoso

The design begins immediately as the curtain rises on the broadly spaced opening chords of this Sinfonia, which, in everyday musical

vocabulary, might be called a double concerto for violin and viola. All of the girls in the ensemble enter at once. There are sixteen in the *corps,* six more in a separate, rather specialized group, and a pair of secondary soloists. Now the two principals appear, ballerinas who trace the musical lines of the solo violin and viola. As they dance with the special group of six—the violin dominating—the rest of the *corps* retires to the back and remains immobile. Then the opening pages of the concerto are repeated in abbreviated form, and the dancer representing the viola takes precedence.

At this point, when all the thematic material of the movement has been presented on stage and in the orchestra, soloists and *corps de ballet* go off, leaving the group of six girls alone on stage. These dancers give way in turn to the two ballerinas, who re-enter with a male partner.

The three principals perform a classical *pas de trois,* free rather than literal in its rendering of the musical content. At certain moments when the solo violin or viola cuts through the orchestral fabric, one or another of the ballerinas is favored correspondingly on stage; but, on the whole, this is an independent art work which, though inspired by Mozart's music, has an inner life of its own.

At the close of the first movement, there is an elaborate cadenza for violin and viola duplicated in dance by the two solo ballerinas. On the final chords, the ensemble leaves the stage.

SECOND MOVEMENT

Andante

To the opening bars of one of the most affecting movements in Mozart, based on a theme of extraordinary emotional surge, the group of six

dancers, led by the two secondary soloists, returns. The principal male appears, and then both ballerinas. Here there begins a design of great complexity in which the three principals circle about one another in ingeniously devised turns, while the two secondary soloists join the male of the group in a concentric pattern, which suggests the flowering of orchestral counterpoint in bodily form. At length these entanglements are resolved as the andante reaches its ending on a sustained, lyrical note.

THIRD MOVEMENT

Presto

For the concerto's sparkling finale the choreographer has created a

series of effective patterns that makes use of the entire ensemble. Everyone is on stage: the *corps*, the group of six special performers led by their soloists, the two chief ballerinas, and their cavalier. There are pirouettes for the male and short solos for his partners, and the ballet closes with a climactic dance design of the same clarity and elegance that lie at the base of Mozart's lovely score.

ROBERT BELSKY

Symphonie Fantastique

BALLET IN five scenes with choreography by Léonide Massine, music by Hector Berlioz. Its première took place at Covent Garden, London, on July 24, 1936, and the first American performance at the Metropolitan Opera House on October 29, 1936. The two principal roles on both occasions were danced by Mr. Massine as the Young Musician and by Tamara Toumanova as the Beloved. Marc Platoff and George Zoritch were the Old and Young Shepherds, Alexis Kosloff the Deer, and Yurek Shabelevsky as the Jailer completed the distinguished cast, which included bits by Alexandra Danilova and Nina Verchinina.

Symphonie Fantastique was hailed, at its première, as one of the great modern ballets. Subsequent performances have strengthened that impression. Although the plot is based on Hector Berlioz' own story—provided in the program notes to his famous "Fantastic" Symphony—certain moments of the action in Massine's ballet were created by the choreographer himself (notably in the third scene), filling in the gaps —for theatrical purposes—of the original scenario.

Berlioz wrote the music of *Symphonie Fantastique* as a young man of twenty-six in the highly charged atmosphere of Paris, 1829. Here, the romantic revolution in literature had already begun, and it was through this symphony—a truly historic work—that the kindred idea of tone-painting in music, the use of the orchestra as a gigantic spectrum, finally took root. Berlioz' instruments translated pictorial, sensuous impressions into architectural sounds. Massine remolded these ideas into a valid fusion of music and dance.

At the time Berlioz composed the *Symphonie Fantastique*, he was desperately in love with an Irish actress, Harriett * Smithson, who played such parts as Juliet and Ophelia with a visiting English company in Paris. At first unaware of the young composer's attentions and then indifferent to them, Miss Smithson became—in Berlioz' fevered imagination—the heroine of his symphony. In the programmatic scheme of the work, it was she who figured as the treacherous Beloved and Berlioz himself as the Young Musician. Interestingly enough, the composer—in real life—later married Miss Smithson. Their union was not a success.

The magnificent settings and costumes for the ballet are by Christian Bérard. Had it not been for a complicated copyright situation in which the performance rights to *Symphonie Fantastique* were held exclusively by the Original Ballet Russe long after Massine had left that troupe, this work would undoubtedly have become a popular favorite in the United States. It has been seen rarely, however, because of the long absences abroad by the de Basil company; and, on its revival by that organization at the Metropolitan Opera House in 1947, it emerged without the magic hand of its choreographer. At the date of writing, this country still awaits a full-scale reworking by Massine himself of his great symphonic ballets. The biggest stumbling block in adequately presenting *Symphonie Fantastique* today would lie in the audience's memory of Tamara Toumanova—now perhaps unavailable—as the Beloved. The part was created for her, and she for the part. One will not forget the unearthly beauty of her first scene, the haunting grace of her waltz, and the malignant fury with which she brought the work to a close. Any other artist than Massine, too, would be hard put in the role of the Young Musician, to which he brought perfection of miming.

* So called in the Berlioz biographies. The composer in his own *Memoirs* refers to her as Henrietta.

SCENE ONE

A Young Musician, alone in his room, is filled with uneasy and nervous thoughts, somber longings.* The vague nostalgia that he feels permeates the introduction to the symphony's first movement.

In a fit of despondency, he tries to end his life. The narcotic dose he has taken is too weak to cause death, but it throws him into a long sleep accompanied by the most extraordinary visions. At first the walls of the room seem to give way, revealing a dim background of a timeless place surmounted by a sphinx. Then, as the music erupts into a passionate allegro, the Beloved glides into the chamber *sur les pointes*. It is she who has caused the Musician's despair, she who—with an ever-recurring melody known as the Fixed Idea—keeps returning to plague his memory. The musical motive that accompanies her every appearance is the principal theme of the symphony.

Deathly white, with closely drawn black hair and haunting features, the Beloved hovers near the composer—and here Berlioz has introduced a lyrical and sustained theme; but as the Musician reaches out to touch

her, she floats away in company with a phantom band.

The Musican's desire mounts until, at last, he pursues the Beloved, seizes her, and lifts her in the midst of a swirling choreographic mass. She escapes again, leaving him in solitude.

* Much of this phraseology is Berlioz' own, taken from his program notes to *Symphonie Fantastique*.

SCENE TWO

The scene changes to a ballroom, where the Musician has gone for distraction. Before the melody of the waltz takes full shape in the orchestra, shadowy mutterings are heard in the cellos and basses, vague and anxious upsweeps in the harp. Then the waltz tune comes out, liquid and glowing.

In the opening of this scene, Massine has pointed up the dynamics of the music by ingenious theatrical means. Along with the crescendo of cellos, basses, and harps, he brings a gradual intensification of lighting to a dark, deserted stage until—just at the moment that the melody of the waltz sounds forth—an exquisitely proportioned room with columns is revealed and the dancers appear.

The Beloved arrives in the midst of the waltz and floats among the dancers. Again she is haunting, unearthly. The Musician tries to capture her, but in a moment she is gone. Feverishly, he rejoins the crowd of waltzers.

SCENE THREE

The Musician has left the city and taken refuge in pastoral surroundings. Here, in a purer and more relaxed atmosphere, he hopes to forget the Beloved. The setting provided by Bérard suggests the Roman Campagna, with broken columns, a ruined aqueduct, verdure, and an over-all sense of endless peace. The Musician is seated on a fallen shaft, at one with the countryside about him, yet strangely dreamy and abstracted. An old shepherd (English horn, in the orchestra) plays a nostalgic call on his pipe which is answered by a young shepherd (oboe).

A tranquil band comes upon the scene: young girls and children. A deer frolics among the classical ruins. One of the girls attracts the young

shepherd, who joins her in a chaste *pas de deux,* a delicately contrived impression of young love. Serenity is in the air; the Musician absorbs it gratefully as the orchestra plays the principal motive of this long, deeply inward movement.

Strange beings with wings, whom Massine called the Winds, suddenly appear; the afternoon light turns to evening; and, as cellos and basses play a new, ominous motive, the Musician thinks of his Beloved.

In the London première of Massine's work, the Beloved entered at this moment on wires, suspended above the scene in the manner of certain romantic ballets performed in Berlioz' own youth. This touch was eliminated—for practical reasons—in succeeding performances, and the presence of the Beloved indicated only through a growing turbulence in the orchestra (based on No. 2) and by the agitation of the Musician on stage.

At length peace returns to the scene, but it is the troubled quiet of evening. The girls and children have returned to their homes; the old shepherd plays his call and the young shepherd does not answer—he has gone off with the maiden who attracted him. Only the rumble of distant thunder replies to the older man's piping. And then—for many, the supreme point of this ballet—as the orchestra plays the long-drawn final cadence of the movement, which Berlioz has called a "sigh," the Musician rises and stares sorrowfully into the horizon. As done by Massine, this was the expression of all loneliness ever felt by the creative artist.

SCENE FOUR

Still under the influence of his deadly narcotic, the Young Musician dreams that he has murdered the Beloved and is being led to the scaffold. A march that is alternately somber and wild, brilliant and solemn, accompanies the procession.

In the stage version of Massine, the grotesque rhythms and instrumentation of the march are blended with sardonic portraits of the frolicking judges, the sadistic jailer, the gaping crowd. They torture the Musician with growing fury until—at the wail in the orchestra of the Fixed Idea (No. 2)—his life is torn from him on the scaffold. To the rolling of drums, the corpse is tossed aside.

SCENE FIVE

During the last of the ballet's five episodes (which correspond to the five movements of the Berlioz symphony), the Musician dreams that he is present at a witches' dance, surrounded by sorcerers and monsters who have come to attend his funeral. Groans are heard in the orchestra, shrill laughter and distant yells, which other cries seem to answer. The music grows increasingly wild and at last the monster-in-chief appears: the Beloved, in her true form as a primeval witch. Her theme has be-

Photo: Maurice Seymour   SCENE FOUR   *Courtesy Museum of Modern Art*

come twisted and ignoble, to suit her nature, played like a cheap music-hall tune by the shrill E-flat clarinet.

To the tolling of bells, shadowy monks bring the remains of the Musician on the scene. Two tubas and four bassoons (when all these instruments can be found at the same time in a ballet orchestra) play the savage old church chant, "Dies Irae."

Bells and chant give way to the frenzied measures of the witches'

467

round as—led by the Beloved—the spirits leap about the Musician's body
in celebration of their infernal Sabbath.

Suddenly they disperse, the music becomes low-pitched, and to the
whirring of violins and violas, the plucking of cellos and double basses,
the hollow voices of bassoons, the Beloved—her long black hair waving
about her—does a series of ghostly *fouettés*. She dances off, and the
train of attendant monsters returns.

It is here that Massine's mastery of the Berlioz idiom, his knowledge
of every facet of the orchestral score, is revealed at its most striking.
As the bass drum begins—almost inaudibly—a long, harrowing crescendo, and the cellos whisper the theme of the witches' round, the
monsters slither about the corpse of the Musician, slapping the stage
with their bodies. From this point to the end of the work, there is an incomparable gathering of resources on stage and in the orchestra. The
Beloved reappears to lead the fiends in their final rites, so furiously elemental that the entire host moves as one. With the cymbal crash of the
final measure, a satanic smile breaks out on the face of the Beloved.

MARIE-JEANNE AND HERBERT BLISS

Symphony in C
(LE PALAIS DE CRISTAL)

THIS BALLET in four movements, with choreography by George Balanchine, was first produced under the title *Le Palais de Cristal* at the Paris
Opéra in July, 1947, with a cast including Tamara Toumanova, Michel
Renault, and Max Bozzoni. Scenery and costumes were by Léonor Fini.
The work was revived by Mr. Balanchine for Ballet Society under the
title *Symphony in C* at the New York City Center in March, 1948, with
an ensemble headed by Maria Tallchief, Nicolas Magallanes, Tanaquil
LeClercq, Francisco Moncion, and Herbert Bliss. Presented in practice
dress, it was brilliantly successful.

The music underlying the dance is the youthful Symphony in C by
Georges Bizet, written in 1885 when the composer was seventeen years
of age. Neglected during Bizet's lifetime, the symphony was given its
world première in Basel under the direction of Felix Weingartner in
February, 1935. Since its rescue from oblivion, this score has become
standard repertory and forms an especially attractive background to the
ballet.

469

FIRST MOVEMENT

Allegro Vivo

The symphony begins squarely on the first theme, without introduction, as does Balanchine's choreography. Two groups of girls and secondary soloists move at once to the opening bars. Their assignment is

pure motion.

A solo note is introduced as the ballerina enters to the lyrical, long-lined melody of the second theme. When she has finished the phrase,

she disappears like a vision; all of the music played until now is repeated; and the dancers—including the ballerina—re-enact the design from the beginning . . . an utterly symphonic approach to dance.

Now two boys appear and engage the girl soloists briefly. In their wake comes the chief male dancer, who joins the ballerina. Meanwhile, the final part of the movement has been reached. The ballerina goes off, the opening theme is heard again, and the eight girls who had danced it at the beginning move as before—this time with the male principal in their midst. With the reappearance of her own haunting melody (No. 2), the ballerina returns and the movement builds to a brilliant conclusion.

SECOND MOVEMENT

Adagio

Since every one of the four episodes in *Symphony in C* has a different cast, a fresh *corps* of girls comes in on the opening bars of the adagio.

They are joined by secondary soloists and—to the sound of a sinuous oboe theme—by a new ballerina and her partner. Gently sustained group

patterns follow the slow unwinding of the score, a *pas de deux* occupying the central portion of the movement.

THIRD MOVEMENT

Allegro Vivace

With the announcement of a lively scherzo,* six girls enter, two solo

* Scherzo form is related to the structure of the old minuet: a first section, which is repeated; a contrasting episode known as a trio; and a return of the opening material. Balanchine's choreography follows these lines precisely.

Courtesy New York City Ballet
MARIA TALLCHIEF AND NICOLAS MAGALLANES

471

couples, then a leading ballerina with her cavalier. The pulse of the dance is an ebb and flow between principals and *corps*, the soloists alternately withdrawing and coming back at points that demand renewed impact and brilliance.

FINALE

Allegro Vivace

A new group appears, to a dashing perpetual-motion figure for

strings: *corps*, secondary soloists, ballerina and partner. From the very opening of this movement, a crescendo of tension builds on stage which never slackens till the final bar. Its cumulative effect, in mass and in motion, is hypnotic.

The dancers who have just arrived soon yield to the ensemble from the First Movement, who are brought back in a masterly stroke of design. These, in turn, give way—always with chiseled continuity—to the cast of the Second Movement, which, as the music grows in power, surrenders to the group from the scherzo.

Now a wave of thirty-eight girls advances: the four ballerinas and their attendant trains. All of the men enter in a surging band; and *Symphony in C* comes to an end on a crest of choreographic skill and brilliance.

Thamar

THIS NARRATIVE ballet in one act, with choreography by Michel Fokine and scenery by Léon Bakst, was first produced by the Diaghilev company at the Théâtre du Châtelet, Paris, in May, 1912. It had as its core the symphonic work, *Thamar*, composed in 1882 by Mili Balakireff, which had been inspired in turn by a poem of Michel Lermontoff dealing with a fabled princess of the Caucasus. The ballet, molded on an orchestral fantasy and using Near-Eastern coloring for its background, was perhaps inevitably devised by the same choreographer and scenic designer who, two years earlier, had created another Oriental spectacle in *Scheherazade* from the symphonic poem of Rimsky-Korsakov. *

Aside from their similarity of origin and color, the two works are strongly alike in plot-line. The sated Zobeide of *Scheherazade* becomes the degenerate Queen Thamar; her leaping slave has grown into the bounding stranger; there are the same heated revels, taking place this time in a Georgian throne-room instead of a Persian harem. Balakireff's colorful orchestral score provides the necessary impetus and dramatic background.

The title role was danced at the Paris première by Tamara Karsavina, and the part of the Stranger by Adolph Bolm. Given its American première at the Metropolitan Opera House in April, 1916, *Thamar* has not remained in the standard ballet repertoire.

Thamar, a beautiful and decadent ruler, is surrounded in the halls of her Caucasian palace by slaves and guards. She is crouched in an attitude of waiting; and when one of her maids, listening intently, gives her a sign, she springs toward a window and waves a scarf three times—signal of hospitality to unsuspecting travelers lost in the gorge that surrounds the house.

Almost at once, a stranger of princely bearing enters, muffled in a cloak. When he reveals his face, of extraordinary beauty, Thamar is dazzled. She offers him wine, then orders him led from the chamber. The Queen remains and her guards perform a dagger dance that grows constantly wilder until Thamar, unable to bear its intensity and the

* This difference should be noted, however: in *Scheherazade*, Fokine and Bakst disregarded the literary ideas on which Rimsky had based his music, while in *Thamar* they retained the outline of the poem that had motivated Balakireff.

longing that it arouses, stamps her foot, commanding that the stranger be brought to her.

Now he returns in splendid dress. The women of the court, beating tambourines, take part in the languorous dance about him. All this time, the Stranger looks passionately at Thamar, who feigns coldness. To gain her favor, he makes spectacular leaps in the air. The Queen soon joins the dance and at its climax—a long kiss—escapes through a green door of the throne-room, followed by her lover.

Another frenetic dagger dance by the guards takes place. Suddenly the Stranger re-enters, visibly shaken. The Queen comes after him, grimly intent. As she kisses the youth, two attendants—unseen by him—open a panel through which the waters of the river Terek are visible. Then, at the consummation of the kiss, Thamar stabs the stranger to the heart. He falls backward through the panel, which is closed immediately.

The murderess returns to her couch and takes up the waiting position in which she was seen at the opening of the ballet. One of her maids again listens intently and, at a given moment, whispers to Thamar. The Queen glides to the window and waves a scarf three times . . . Next!

SCENE WITH YOUSKEVITCH IN THE SPOTLIGHT

Theme and Variations

THIS *divertissement* in one act by George Balanchine, perhaps the pearl of all the choreographer's works in neoclassical style, was first presented by Ballet Theatre at the New York City Center in November, 1947. Woodman Thompson designed the superb scenery and costumes, and the ballet was given with a cast headed by Alicia Alonso and Igor Youskevitch. Since that time, Maria Tallchief has danced the leading part with marked success.

The orchestral background is the fourth movement—Theme and Variations—of Tchaikovsky's Suite No. 3 in G.*

The curtain rises almost at once on the introductory music, revealing a *corps* of twelve girls and the two principals. The ballerina, in a maize *tutu,* and her partner, clad in deep blue with a white-plumed beret, are framed by a setting of crystal chandeliers and long rococo galleries that lead to palace gardens beyond. Surrounding the soloist are twelve girls in groups of three, dressed in ecru and lilac. As the theme is announced

---

* A few colorful bars from the opening of the final variation have been added at the beginning of the ballet, as prelude.

by the orchestra, soloists and girls dance a simple choreographic state-

ment to its measures.

Variation One: The soloists go off, and the girls, in their opening elab-
oration of the theme, move deftly in group formation.

Variation Two: Here the ballerina returns, accompanied by the *corps,*
and uses several effective devices of classical dance—notably *fouettés—*
in the first of her solos.

Variation Three: Now the girls dance alone in groups of three—two lilac
and one ecru in every unit—their contrasting colors lending additional
point to the beauty of the choreographic patterns.

Variation Four: This is a solo for the male dancer, with breath-taking
beats and elevation. In the score itself, unexpected use is made by
Tchaikovsky of the violent old church chant, "Dies Irae," played in the
brasses as a rhythmic variant of the principal theme.

Variation Five: A short and vigorous interlude for the twelve girls follows.

Variation Six: In his second solo, the male dancer draws on still more of
the traditional weapons—especially *entrechats*—in the equipment of a
star performer. As plotted by Balanchine, this variation is neither trite
nor gaudy, but integrates every facet of virtuoso dance in a stunning
choreographic design.

Variation Seven: Here, to a short passage for woodwinds, the ballerina
enters pensively.

Variation Eight: Supported by the girls in lilac, she offers a variation marked by sustained poetic feeling and by the intertwining of individual figures from the *corps,* characteristic of Balanchine's earlier ballets.

Variation Nine: The ballerina, alone on stage, passes to a whimsical, then dazzling, variation, equaling in impact the most glowing previous efforts of her partner. As in all classical ballets, a sense of underlying competition between the two soloists, capped by their fusion in a *grand pas de deux,* is at the heart of the structure.

Variations Ten and Eleven: These two sections of the score, knowingly combined by the choreographer to form one unbroken line, make up the background for the *pas de deux.* The first of the sections, though symphonic in origin and not conceived by Tchaikovsky in terms of ballet, bears an uncanny resemblance to the *pas de deux* in *Swan Lake,* its long violin solo providing an ideal background for the adagio of the two soloists. In the second variation, as the original theme soars out in the strings and winds, the duo for the ballerina and her partner reaches a climax of courtly interplay.

Photo: Fred Fehl   MARIA TALLCHIEF AND IGOR YOUSKEVITCH

Variation Twelve: To the strains of a festive polonaise, eight men

Tempo di Polacca, molto brillante

enter in lavender jerkins and lilac tights, four more in rust and tan, all harmonizing with the costumes of the girls. Here Balanchine is at his most resourceful, creating solo and group combinations of a purity and brilliance that rank among his finest. At the climax of this finale, the entire ensemble, led by the two principals, swings into a great semicircular procession, affirming—in its evocation of Imperial Russian dance—the magnificence of the costumes and the background of rococo galleries and crystal chandeliers. *Theme and Variations* has a grandeur and inventiveness throughout that place it in the forefront of neoclassical ballets.

Courtesy Dance News

LÉONIDE MASSINE, DAVID LICHINE, AND TAMARA TOUMANOVA IN THE LEADING ROLES

The Three-Cornered Hat

(LE TRICORNE)

ONE OF the undisputed masterpieces of the ballet repertoire, *The Three-Cornered Hat* was given its first performance at the Alhambra Theatre in London by the Diaghilev company in July, 1919. A prodigious pooling of genius went into its production. Massine, in one of his great creative phases, was the choreographer; Manuel de Falla, Spain's most gifted composer of this century, provided the music; and Pablo Picasso contributed the décor. The ballet scored an overwhelming success at its première.

The story of *The Three-Cornered Hat* is based on a folk tale of the same name—*El Sombrero de Tres Picos*—by the Spanish author Pedro Antonio de Alarcón (1833–91). Its colorful dramatic possibilities appealed to the Austrian composer Hugo Wolf, who made it into an opera with German text: *Der Corregidor* (1896). Shortly before the composi-

479

tion of Massine's ballet, the Spanish author Martínez Sierra devised a pantomime on the same subject, with music by de Falla. It was well received in Madrid.

When Sergei Diaghilev and his ballet arrived in Spain during the First World War, the impresario met de Falla, heard part of the composer's music for Martínez Sierra's pantomime, and suggested that the score be revised for the requirements of dance. De Falla consented, making the necessary changes and adding two numbers: the famous farruca danced by the Miller and the brilliant jota with which the ballet closes.

Massine made an exacting study of Spanish national dance—with special emphasis on Andalusia—as preparation for his choreography. Touring the provinces of Spain, working with the natives, he evolved a stage work that is thoroughly Spanish in spirit but has remained pure ballet. This is no literal imitation of Iberian Style.

Time has dealt more kindly with *The Three-Cornered Hat* than with most other ballets of the Diaghilev era. Revivals of the work have always drawn fresh admiration for the beauty of the music, the superb imagination of Massine's choreography, the color of Picasso's settings and costumes. Massine created the role of the Miller and has been dancing it incomparably—at the time of writing—for thirty years. Tamara Toumanova has been the best of recent exponents of the Miller's Wife, while the part of the Corregidor has been well taken in this generation by David Lichine and Marc Platoff.

The orchestra sounds a brilliant introduction: the insistent pounding of a festal rhythm, played by brass and percussion. Cries of *"Olé! Olé!"* are heard off stage with the tapping of heels, the clicking of castanets.

For a moment, the revelry stops. A dark singing voice is heard in the distance, prophesying evil. Then the pounding of the drums is resumed, and the curtain rises.

In the center of a great plain stands a prosperous Spanish village. The white walls of the houses give off the glint of the noonday sun. No one is about but the Miller. He is standing before a bird cage, teaching his blackbird to whistle the hours of the day.

As he gestures that it is two o'clock, his pet (through the medium of the orchestra) perversely answers three. The Miller angrily tries to correct the bird, but only confuses it more. Now his young and beautiful wife appears. She whistles two o'clock and the blackbird gives the right answer.

Both the Miller, youthful himself, and his wife are very much in love. They embrace; then the Miller goes about his work, drawing water from a well. Suddenly a boyish Dandy is seen on the bridge over a near-by stream. He prances along, trailing a kite, and blows a kiss to the Miller's Wife—who seems responsive—as the orchestra plays his vapid motive.

The Miller looks up from his work, runs in pursuit toward the bridge, but the Dandy disappears. Almost immediately, the sound of marching men is heard. The orchestra plays a pompous tune, and the Miller sees

a litter approaching, borne by massive footmen. At their side walks a stooping figure: the Corregidor, governor of the province. Behind him stride six officers, their pock-marked faces streaked with powder. The Corregidor's young bride is inside the litter.

During the passing of this procession, the Miller's Wife looks with interest at the Corregidor. To her surprise, she notes that her glance is returned. The old man, richly dressed in knee breeches and a three-cornered hat, is by temperament a satyr.

He lags behind his escort, peers at the Miller's Wife, and lets his elaborately woven handkerchief fall to the ground. Rather than antagonize him, the Miller's Wife picks it up. The Corregidor chuckles amiably, thanks her, and trots onward with the procession. His indulgent gestures indicate that he is planning a return visit.

Three workmen enter with large sacks of flour. As the Miller watches them carry their burden to the storehouse, he notices a handsome village girl bearing a pitcher of water on her head. She has for him the same physical charm that the Dandy had exercised on the Miller's Wife; and now it is the young bride's turn to be jealous.

The village girl and the helpers go their way. All is quiet on the plain; husband and wife are reconciled after a short exchange on the subject of fidelity. And as the Miller goes into the house, the woman remains alone, dancing an exultant fandango.

She is observed at a distance by the Corregidor, who has come back. Soon he limps nearer to make advances, but the Miller's Wife is too quick for him. She seizes a cluster of grapes from the vine, holds them out to the roué, and retreats at the same time. Eager to reach her, the old man begins the chase in earnest, snatching a grape now and then, but missing the real object of his pursuit. Finally he falls in exhaustion.

The Miller, who has seen this performance from the house, runs to his wife's assistance. They raise the governor from the ground and, with derisive gestures, show him their contempt. The Corregidor limps away, swearing vengeance. But his threats mean little to the Miller and his wife. Both of them have joined in the exuberant fandango. While they dance triumphantly, shadows fall across the Spanish plain.

Here, the first half of the ballet—both story and music—reaches its natural climax; the action flows into the second portion without pause. Late afternoon sunlight gives way slowly to evening; and the orchestra plays a long-lined, relaxed melody as a group of neighbors come to the mill.

They are at hand for a midsummer celebration. Taking their places

Photo: Fred Fehl SIMON SEMENOFF AS THE CORREGIDOR

near the bridge, four of the men tap their heels and click their castanets. Soon all of the neighbors join the dance, in homage to the Miller and his wife.

The Miller, who has greeted them warmly, enters his house, returning with a wineskin and a number of cups which he sets before his friends. Then, as the neighbors stretch upon the ground, the Miller draws himself to his full height. Snapping his fingers and advancing with short, determined steps, he begins the impassioned farruca.

This is the heart of *The Three-Cornered Hat;* and, as performed by Massine, who spins crescendi of inward tension and outward movement in perfect unison, it provides one of the most electrifying solos in theatrical dance.

At length the farruca is done. Night has come upon the plain, deep and starlit. As the neighbors drink a final toast, they hear the tramp of marching men. Only two kinds of people would be abroad at such an hour: outlaws from the hills, or soldiers of the Corregidor.

Soon the bodyguards of the governor draw up before the house, place the Miller under arrest, and lead him away. The neighbors disperse, and the Miller's Wife is left alone. From far off in the night comes a dismal song. Within the house a cuckoo clock strikes nine; and as the moon bathes the plain in light, the blackbird whistles nine in answer.

The Miller's Wife sighs. Suddenly she hears pattering footsteps; and the Corregidor stands close by. His appearance is heralded in the orchestra by a grotesque bassoon figure.

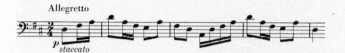

Now that the Miller has been disposed of, the Corregidor's advances are bolder. He tries to embrace the Miller's Wife, grapples with her, is flung to the ground. Then he regains his footing and follows the woman to the bridge. Another struggle takes place. With a major effort, the Miller's Wife wrenches herself free. The Corregidor, thrown off his balance, topples from the narrow span into the river.

The situation has become absurd, and the Miller's Wife bursts into laughter at the sight of the elderly lover flapping about in the water. Putting her fears aside, she hoists him to the shore. But no sooner is he out of the stream than the chase begins again. This time the Miller's Wife reaches for a musket that hangs in the doorway of her house, levels it at the governor, retreats across the bridge, and makes her escape.

With the flight of this beautiful woman, the Corregidor's ardor dampens. He grows conscious of his dripping clothes, his miserable condition. Taking off most of his soaking garments, he lays them out to dry. Near his clothes, he rests the emblem of his caste: the three-cornered hat. Then, shivering with cold, he invades the Miller's home and falls exhausted on his rival's bed.

At dawn the Miller, escaped from the police, creeps toward his house. To his dismay, he sees the three-cornered hat in front of it and the Corregidor's clothing . . . then the old man himself, who steals out of the house in a borrowed nightshirt and fantastic sleeping cap. First the Miller is enraged. Then an impish thought of revenge takes hold of him, and with a bit of chalk, he draws the face of the Corregidor's young bride on the wall of his house. Taking the governor's clothes and the three-cornered hat, he sets out to pay court to the Corregidor's wife.*

The governor's troubles have only just begun. Left to ponder the meaning of the caricature on the wall, he is set upon by his own body-

---

* This, according to the original story. As now performed, the Miller scrawls a libelous portrait of the Corregidor himself on the wall and then runs off.

Photo: Fred Fehl   ARGENTINITA AS THE MILLER'S WIFE

guards—who mistake him, in his borrowed nightgown, for the escaped Miller. Drawn by the uproar, all of the people in the village come running to the scene: old and young, peasants, beggars with crutches and long beards, neighbors—and, at length, the Miller and his wife. They have met each other wandering on the plain. And here begins one of the most magnificent finales—for musical and dramatic values—of any work in ballet.

The orchestra starts it with the surging measures of the jota: full, insistently brilliant.

485

Inflamed by the brutality of the Corregidor's police, the people rise against them. Dragging the wretched governor—whom they have recognized too late—to safety, the once-feared bodyguards make their retreat before the threats of the crowd. And now joyous anarchy reigns in the village.

The young Dandy appears on the bridge as he had done the afternoon before, when he flirted with the Miller's Wife. This time, however, instead of trailing a kite, he carries a straw dummy representing the Corregidor. As he tosses the dummy skyward, the crowd waits to catch the image and fling it up again. The dancing of the villagers has continued all this time, the massive opening measures of the jota giving way to a light, tripping tune:

But the music again grows in volume. The Miller and his wife, happily reunited, lead the rejoicing. And as the dummy of the Corregidor whirls in the air, symbolizing the shattered rule of the three-cornered hat, the ballet ends in an irresistible blend of color, sight, and sound.

Le Tombeau de Couperin

THIS *divertissement* in high romantic style formed part of the repertory of the Ballet Suédois, an organization of Scandinavian dancers which was created in Paris by Rolf de Maré, patron of the arts, together with the Swedish choreographer Jean Borlin, in 1920, and continued its activities until 1924, with tours throughout Europe and America.

Le Tombeau de Couperin, a series of pieces evoking the style of the early eighteenth century—the era of François Couperin, famous harpsichordist to King Louis XIV—was originally written by Ravel as a piano suite in six sections, each of which was dedicated to a comrade who had fallen in the First World War. The work was completed in November, 1917. Soon after publication of the piano suite, Ravel scored four of these sections—the Prelude, Forlane,* Rigaudon,† and Toccata—for small orchestra. His transcription, which has become part of the standard symphonic repertory, was first given in Paris in February, 1920.

In November of the same year, Borlin's choreographed version of the score, with décor by Pierre Laprade, was presented by the Ballet Suédois at the Théâtre des Champs-Élysées. Like the music of Ravel, Borlin's choreography sought to conjure up the symmetry and elegance of a vanished epoch, the golden age of court life at Versailles.

With graceful gardens in the background creating an atmosphere reminiscent of the paintings of Watteau, men and women in eighteenth-century dress—white wigs, ribbons, panniers—take part in the dances of the time.

First comes the Prelude, subtlest of the four movements of this suite,

* *Forlane*—an old Venetian dance form which found its way into France toward the end of the sixteenth century. Its original Italian spelling was *furlana.*

† *Rigaudon*—still another dance form, supposed to have originated in the south of France. A certain M. Rigaud is said to have invented it.

graceful in its line and complex in its harmony; then the Forlane, alter-

nately whimsical and nostalgic; the Minuet, of a poignancy which sug-

gests more a dream of bygone days than actuality; and finally, the
brilliant closing Rigaudon.

All of these dances, arranged for the stage by Borlin with Laprade's
delicate décor, struck a note completely in harmony with Ravel's distinguished score.

La Tragédie de Salomé

Long vanished from the stage as a ballet, *La Tragédie de Salomé* survives as a name because of the stunning orchestral score written for it by Florent Schmitt. This work, with scenario based on a poem by Robert d'Humières and with choreography by Boris Romanoff, was first given at the Paris Opéra, July, 1913, in a Diaghilev season. The title role was taken by Thamar Karsavina. A revival at the same theatre, six years later, with staging by Nicola Guerra, featured Ida Rubinstein as the Princess. Cast in a single scene that contains three diverse dances for Salome, the ballet is a free adaptation of the Biblical story, lavish in its use of symbolism. Its general atmosphere is one of lush decadence.

The first portion of the ballet is preceded by a prelude, voluptuous in mood; then the curtain rises to reveal a terrace of Herod's palace on the Dead Sea. The hills of Moab enclose the horizon; Mount Nebo may be seen in the distance; the sun is setting. Torches light the scene and strike with their rays a jewel box into which Queen Herodias is plunging her hands, bringing forth pearl necklaces and golden veils. Her daughter Salome appears, fascinated with the jewels, and performs her first dance.

There follows the second portion; Salome disappears. Shadows envelop the ruler Herod, lost in thoughts of luxury and fear, while Herodias spies on him from a corner of the terrace. Fantastic visions creep from the sea. The orgies of Sodom and Gomorrah, rising from their

Allegro

ashes, draw Salome back. She hears a solitary voice—the tones of John the Baptist. Herod, too, listens. As thunder rumbles in the distance, Salome begins to dance. Herod rises.

Gradual darkness envelops the scene. Crazed with lust, Herod seizes Salome and tears off her veils. At this moment John appears, come to purge the sin-ridden palace, but Herodias delivers him at once to the executioner. Her daughter Salome gladly receives the head. Suddenly agitated, the girl throws her trophy into the sea, which turns blood-red. The head reappears, transfixing Salome with its glance; it multiplies, becoming a veritable ocean of heads.

And then the concluding section of the ballet begins with a dance of fright as Salome is trapped by the wrath of Nature. A hurricane breaks loose. Mount Nebo belches flames. Branches are ripped from the trees, and the stones of Herod's fortress crumble. The storm breaks with infernal delirium and destroys the dancer.

The Triumph of Neptune

THIS PANTOMIMIC ballet in two acts and twelve scenes is important today chiefly for its attractive score by Lord Berners and for the fact that it was the first stage work of any magnitude choreographed by George Balanchine. First produced by the Diaghilev company at the Lyceum Theatre, London, in December, 1926, it had a scenario by Sacheverell Sitwell. Among the principal dancers in a notable cast were Alexandra Danilova as the Fairy Queen, Serge Lifar as the Sailor, Lydia Sokolova as the Goddess, and Mr. Balanchine as the Negro. The ballet has not been performed in the United States.

ACT ONE

The plot of *The Triumph of Neptune* concerns itself with the search for Fairyland by two British adventurers: a newspaperman and a sailor. At the opening, on London Bridge, a crowd has gathered to look through a magic telescope which is trained on the fairy kingdom. Glimpses may be had of sprites dancing among the clouds.

No sooner do the two explorers take off than the Sailor's wife succumbs to the advances of a dandy. The travelers, en route, are shipwrecked and rescued by a sea goddess. Even as the London papers try to get news of them, they head for an enchanted forest filled with snow.

ACT TWO

The Sailor's wife has begun to pass her time more often with the dandy. One evening they dance a polka together and then go inside the lady's house, where their figures are seen outlined against the shade. Suddenly the Sailor's spirit returns, knife in hand, to defend the honor of his house. Constables rush to arrest him but lay hold only of a shadow. He has gone back on his journey to Fairyland.

The two explorers join forces again in a grotto, through which they fight their way to an ogre's castle. Here the Newspaperman is captured and sawed in half. The Sailor escapes, but all hopes of his return to

England are dashed when a drunken Negro on London Bridge upsets the magic telescope. Disillusioned by his wife's conduct, the Sailor decides to renounce humanity; and so, transformed into a sprite, he weds Neptune's daughter, who joins him in a conjugal hornpipe.

The ballet concludes with the elaborate ceremonies that unite the new Fairy Prince to his consort.

DANIELLE DARRIANCE AND JEAN BABILÉE

Tyl Eulenspiegel

THIS WORK in one act, with choreography by Vaslav Nijinsky and décor by Robert Edmond Jones, was given its première in the autumn of 1916 at the Manhattan Opera House, New York, by the Diaghilev Ballet Russe under the sponsorship of the Metropolitan Opera. The choreographer danced the title role. Mr. Jones, in an article * written many years after the première, called *Tyl Eulenspiegel* retrospectively a great ballet. Nijinsky's wife, Romola, in her biography of the dancer, has also referred to *Tyl* as an important work. The verdict of the public, how-

* For *Nijinsky*, a collection of essays assembled by Paul Magriel (1949).

ever, was negative, and with the retirement of Nijinsky from active public life, his ballet was seen no more.

The scenario followed the story outline of Strauss's symphonic poem, which was used as musical background. In his famous score, introduced in 1895, the composer offered a tone-portrait of a medieval rogue whose story was first recounted by a German author of the sixteenth century, Dr. Thomas Murnau.

Structurally, Strauss's work is in rondo form, based on the return and development of two principal motives representing the hero.

The first of these, vaulting and propulsive, does not apply so much

to Tyl in person as to his type in the world—the eternal buffoon. By way of contrast, the second theme—with its high-pitched, impish quality—

represents Tyl directly, the scoundrel who puts housewives to flight in the market place, disguises himself as a priest, falls occasionally—but hopelessly—in love, mocks the burghers of medieval Brunswick as they march in solemn procession, and finally—for having committed the crime of being too individualistic in a society that calls for complete conformity—is taken before a tribunal, charged, and hanged.

These episodes were followed with more or less fidelity in the Nijinsky stage version. In the words of the choreographer's wife, the dancer became—in his re-creation of the folk-rascal—at once rogue, priest, cavalier, professor, and social prophet. It is unfortunate that Nijinsky's mental illness, which came soon after the ballet's première, prevented him from polishing the work and seeing it incorporated into the repertoire. Its dramatic scheme promised much.

MICHAEL KIDD AND LILLIAN LANESE

Undertow

THIS BALLET in one act, with choreography by Antony Tudor and music by William Schuman, was first presented by Ballet Theatre at the Metropolitan Opera House in April, 1945. The central role of the Transgressor was danced by Hugh Laing. Diana Adams appeared as Cybele, Shirley Eckl as Volupia, Alicia Alonso as Ate, Nana Gollner as Medusa— the four women in the Transgressor's life—and Lucia Chase contributed an amusing bit as Polyhymnia, a street-corner reformer.

Undertow was a further exploration by Tudor, following his epochal

Pillar of Fire, into the realms of psychiatric drama and represented, in its searing and violent conclusions, perhaps the final word that could be said by the choreographer in this field. It is significant that Tudor, in his next ballet, *Shadow of the Wind,* turned away completely from the erotic introspections of *Jardin aux Lilas, Pillar of Fire,* and *Undertow* to find creative impulse in the chaste and lyrical. His drama of the Transgressor, however, remains a commanding work, held by its choreographer to be his finest. The background—an urban slum—carries inevitably sordid overtones; but for those who hold that theatrical dance is as valid a mirror of life as any other art form, Tudor's sensitive and resourceful treatment of the theme has raised it above the morbidly specific and made it part of human experience.

William Schuman's music, as nervous and violent as the ballet for which it was composed, adds enormous impact to the movement on stage. This score, often given separately in concert form, had its symphonic première in a performance by the Los Angeles Philharmonic Orchestra in November, 1945.

PROLOGUE

To the soft but insistent repetition by strings and bass drum of sustained, low-lying chords, topped by the plaintive sound of a solo clar-

inet, the curtain rises to reveal the birth of the Transgressor. No sooner has the child come into the world than his mother * ignores him and gives her attention instead to the man who has been her lover. This first defeat in the sphere of human affection warps the child and turns him inward.

THE DRAMA

The scene changes and a public square is revealed in a run-down section of a big city. The monumental nature of the square, with its statues of winged horses everywhere, serves to emphasize by contrast the mean-

---

* In the classical nomenclature adapted by Tudor for the persons of the drama, she is known as Cybele. This system of names, allegorical in purpose, often becomes needlessly obscure and is not followed closely in the present account.

ness of the people who have come to live there. It is here that the Transgressor—on the verge of manhood—has been reared. Now, as the squalid
inhabitants of the place stroll by in the early evening, he appears on
the street, playing games with a little girl; but his attention soon wanders from the child to a hard-bitten prostitute, Volupia, who has come
to ply her trade.

As the Transgressor looks on, his formative mind taking in every one
of Volupia's actions, the first of the streetwalker's prospects crosses the
square. Poorly dressed, in the seamy mode of the neighborhood, he
saunters up to the woman, accosts her, and follows her off. A gang of
young toughs dashes by, wrestling with each other, filling the streets
with gutter revelry.

Now Volupia returns, on the alert for new clients. At once, she notices
a fat, aging tradesman whose desires lead him toward the streetwalker
but whose fears compel him to look at her secretively without daring an
approach. The situation remains static for a moment: Volupia awaits
his advances; he stands rooted in cowardly longing. Finally the woman
turns on him angrily and drives him off.

Other inhabitants of the slum, all closely observed by the Transgressor,
stroll by. In their midst comes a middle-aged crusader, Polyhymnia, on
her way to conduct a prayer meeting. Radiating sanctity, she exhorts the
down-at-the-heels strollers in the square to reform, as a solo trumpet
plays the type of sentimental hymn generally heard on the streets.

Now one of the most perverse inhabitants of the quarter enters, drawn
by the noise of Polyhymnia's meeting. It is Ate, who has the body of a
child and a face ravaged by evil. As performed with mastery by Alicia
Alonso—usually identified with romantic parts—this character conveyed
a sense of decadence terrifying to the last details of make-up, her repul-
siveness heightened by movements of undisciplined obscenity grafted on
to classical dance.

The vicious young girl makes advances to the Transgressor but creates
no impression. As she settles for an ex-client of Volupia and runs after
him, a young bridal couple goes prancing by. They are envied by the
Transgressor, who has never known happiness. In their wake come
three drunken women, staggering through the streets and mouthing a
ribald version of Polyhymnia's anthem.

Once more Ate is seen. Now she has joined forces with the crowd of
sidewalk toughs, fanning their passions until, in a gang, they drag her

off to the darkness of an alley. All this time the Transgressor has stood by, his undirected emotions rising at the sight of first Volupia and then Ate. As the depraved little girl returns from her carousing with the toughs, the Transgressor moves toward her. His hands are about to reach her throat when, saved by the return of one of the drunken women, Ate escapes. The child who played games with the Transgressor before the appearance of Volupia is a bystander. Terrified by the actions of her friend, she runs off. The youth remains—inflamed and in a turmoil.

Suddenly, this procession of the women in the Transgressor's life comes to a climax. Medusa appears, one notch above the station of Volupia, since she is nonprofessional, but nonetheless hard and sordid. After trying her charms on a few of the other men still lurking in the neighborhood, her gaze falls on the Transgressor. About to draw him on, she is interrupted by the persistent Polyhymnia, again in the midst of a prayer meeting for the jaded inhabitants of the square. The Transgressor, eager to be saved from himself, joins the group, but Medusa turns furiously on the near-converts, drives them away, and stays behind with the youth.

Now all the hatred and longing stored in the warped boy come out in elemental form. First he makes love to Medusa, then he seizes her and—

at the climactic moment—crushes out her life. The combination of dance and music at this climax—the composer has indicated in his score that, in addition to full orchestra, the pianist's left hand and forearm must pound all the black keys on the instrument at once—is overwhelming. No other theatrical work has gone so far in the direction of unbridled violence.

EPILOGUE

The lights go out at once on the fearful strangulation, and when they come on again the Transgressor stands alone. Strange visions of the square rise behind him; the winged horses seem to be soaring. Fearful that his deed will be discovered, he writhes in anxiety, makes strange, spasmodic movements. In the midst of one of these unresolved attempts to escape from himself, his former playmate appears, carrying a balloon. When she looks again at the youth she had seen flex his hands about

NORA KAYE AND HUGH LAING

Ate's throat, she knows him as the undoubted murderer of Medusa. The other inhabitants of the run-down section appear at her call; and, as the little girl's finger goes out accusingly toward the Transgressor, her balloon floats skyward.

It is the moment for which the Transgressor has waited. Now that his deed has been exposed, his tension is over; and he goes off slowly, heedless of the crowd about him, ready to pay for the crime whose impulse has ruled him from earliest memory.

LA VALSE AS PERFORMED AT THE RADIO CITY MUSIC HALL

La Valse

THIS CHOREOGRAPHIC poem in one act, with scenario by Bronislava Nijinska, settings and costumes by Alexandre Benois, was first produced at the Paris Opéra in 1929, with Ida Rubinstein and Anatole Vilzak in the leading parts. The core of the work is Maurice Ravel's superb score of the same name. In accord with the music, Mme Nijinska's ground plan is built on the lines of a long crescendo. While the symphonic waltz of Ravel carries within it subtle intimations of Hapsburg decadence, the ballet lacks these overtones and is French Empire in feeling.

The curtain rises on an almost empty stage, as a shadowy rhythmic pattern is outlined in the orchestra.

The setting is a luxurious ballroom in gilt and crimson, with huge mirrors, re-creating the elegance of Paris, 1860. A few figures are seen, seated in formal conversation. Then they rise, start to waltz, and the chief motive of Ravel's score emerges from the orchestra.

Other dancers appear, splendidly dressed. An adjoining ballroom may be seen in the background. The brilliance of the waltz's principal theme alternates with a languorous second subject.

At times the waltzers in the foreground suggest the brilliant principal theme while those in the other room convey the languor of the second theme; then the contrast is shifted. Finally, as the music reaches its climax, all of the dancers join in a dazzling finale.

MELISSA HAYDEN, PAULA LLOYD, AND BARBARA COLE

Waltz Academy

THIS BALLET in one act (sometimes known as *Six Waltzes*), with choreography by George Balanchine, was first produced by Ballet Theatre at the Metropolitan Opera House in October, 1944. Leading roles were danced by Nana Gollner, Nora Kaye, and Paul Petroff. The scenery was by Oliver Smith and costumes were by Alvin Colt. As musical background, Balanchine chose a suite by Vittorio Rieti known as *Second Avenue Waltzes*, whose individual numbers had been dedicated to friends of the composer living in the vicinity of Queensboro Bridge, New York.

This is an abstract ballet—a series of concert dances bound by a slight connecting story. Its outward action takes place in the hall of a ballet school during a waltz competition by the students.

The curtain rises on a vigorous orchestral introduction, and then the first waltz begins, danced by a group of six girls. A short interlude leads to the next piece, presented by two girls and two boys.

Now, after another musical bridge, comes a number for three dancers,

lyrical in style, followed by a second *pas de trois*, with different participants, more brilliant than the first.

It is only natural that the culminating point of such a competition

GROUP WITH ALICIA ALONSO AND DIMITRI ROMANOFF IN THE CENTER

should be a *pas de deux*, performed by a boy and a girl of the academy

who are in love. They join in a tender duo, yielding to a final waltz in which the whole group takes part.

The Wise Virgins

THIS FANTASY-BALLET, in a single scene, is based on William Walton's arrangement of selected music by J. S. Bach.* The choreography is by Frederick Ashton, the scenery and costumes by Rex Whistler. *The Wise Virgins* was first performed in April, 1940, at the Sadler's Wells Theatre, London, with Margot Fonteyn as the Bride and Michael Somes as the Bridegroom.

As the prelude sounds, an inner curtain in Italian Renaissance style is revealed. It has painted pink walls and, in the center, an archaic lamp pouring smoke which provides the decorative frame for a scroll—supported by angels—of the parable of the Wise and Foolish Virgins, as related in the Gospel of St. Matthew, Chapter 25, 1-13.

Now the drop curtain rises on the inner scene and another pink wall is disclosed, with stairs leading to a gold door. As a group of cherubs take their places on the steps, the Wise Virgins enter, followed by the Bride and her parents, then by the Foolish Virgins.

Just as in the parable, they come with lamps. First, the Bride moves to a chaste and quiet measure. Then, when the Virgins recline on the ground—the Wise ones with their lamps extinguished, and the others with their vessels lit—the chosen one has a vision of a host of angels who raise her to her feet. The Bridegroom enters with a shining crown; and here the ballet reaches its high point as the couple meet. Soon the vision fades and the Groom disappears.

In the reality that follows, a burst of music announces the actual coming of the Bridegroom. The Virgins rise—the Foolish ones setting off to buy oil for their depleted lamps. Then the door at the summit of the stairs is opened by a cherub, and the Bridegroom appears. As he takes the Bride in his arms, the attendant spirits adorn her with the robe of Chastity. The Wise Virgins are escorted through the doorway to Heaven by angels, who walk with them in pairs. The Bride and Groom follow; and the door is closed behind them.

* The melody "Sheep May Safely Graze" serves as motto.

Now the Foolish Virgins return, their lamps replenished. Brashly, they beat on the celestial door—which suddenly opens. A troop of angels emerges to force them back, and they kneel in humility before the Bride and Bridegroom, who, surrounded by the five Wise Virgins and five companion spirits, stand in the center of the heavenly host.

Selective Discography of RCA Victor Recordings

ADÉLAÏDE, OU LA LANGAGE DES FLEURS
Maurice Ravel: *Valses nobles et sentimentales:* Monteux—San Francisco Symphony Orchestra; DM-1143.

ALEKO
Peter Tchaikovsky: Trio in A Minor: Rubinstein-Heifetz-Piatigorsky; in preparation.

EL AMOR BRUJO
Manuel de Falla: *El Amor Brujo:* Stokowski-Merriman—Hollywood Bowl Symphony Orchestra; WDM-1089 or LM-1054.

APOLLON MUSAGÈTE
Igor Stravinski: *Apollon Musagète:* Stravinski—RCA Victor Orchestra; WDM-1424 or LM-1096.

APPALACHIAN SPRING
Aaron Copland: *Appalachian Spring:* Koussevitzky—Boston Symphony Orchestra; DM-1046.

L'APRÈS-MIDI D'UN FAUNE
Claude Debussy: *L'Après-Midi d'un Faune:* Stokowski and his Symphony Orchestra; 49-0942 or 12-1119.

BACCHANALE
Richard Wagner: *Tannhäuser: Overture and Venusberg Music:* Stokowski and his Symphony Orchestra; WDM-1383 or LM-1066.

LE BAISER DE LA FÉE
Igor Stravinsky: *Le Baiser de la Fée:* Stravinsky—RCA Victor Symphony Orchestra; WDM-1202.

LE BEAU DANUBE
Johann Strauss, Jr.: *The Beautiful Blue Danube Waltz:* Stokowski and his Symphony Orchestra; 49-1076 or 12-1160.

BILLY THE KID
Aaron Copland: *Billy the Kid:* Bernstein—RCA Victor Symphony Orchestra; WDM-1333 or LM-1031.

BOLERO
Maurice Ravel: *Bolero:* Koussevitzky—Boston Symphony Orchestra; WDM-1220 or LM-1012.

LA BOUTIQUE FANTASQUE
Gioacchino Rossini: (Suite arranged by Respighi): Goossens—London Philharmonic Orchestra; DM-415.

CAPRICCIO ESPAGNOL
Nicholas Rimsky-Korsakov: *Capriccio Espagnol:* Fiedler—Boston Pops Orchestra; 11827 and 11828.

LE CARNAVAL
Robert Schumann: *Carnaval Suite,* Op. 9: Goossens—London Philharmonic Orchestra; DM-513.

CHOPIN CONCERTO
Frédéric Chopin: Concerto No. 1 in E Minor: Brailowsky-Steinberg—RCA Victor Symphony Orchestra; WDM-1317 or LM-1020.

CHOREARTEUM
Johannes Brahms: Symphony No. 4 in E Minor, Op. 98: Munch—Boston Symphony Orchestra; WDM-1399 or LM-1086.

CHOUT
Sergei Prokofiev: *Chout:* Koussevitzky—Boston Symphony Orchestra; final side of WDM-1241.

CONCERTO BAROCCO
J. S. Bach: Concerto for Two Violins: Both solo parts by Heifetz—RCA Victor Orchestra—Waxman; WDM-1136 or LM-1051.

COPPÉLIA
Léo Delibes: Suite from *Coppélia:* Sevitzky—Indianapolis Symphony Orchestra; WDM-1305 or LM-1032.

LE COQ D'OR
Nicholas Rimsky-Korsakov: *Le Coq d'Or:* Fiedler—Boston Pops Orchestra; DM-797.

THE CREATURES OF PROMETHEUS
Ludwig van Beethoven: *The Men of Prometheus: Overture:* Toscanini—NBC Symphony Orchestra; final side in WDM-1098.

DANSES CONCERTANTES
Igor Stravinsky: *Danses Concertantes:* Stravinsky—RCA Victor Orchestra; WDM-1234 or LM-1075.

DAPHNIS ET CHLOÉ
Maurice Ravel: *Daphnis et Chloé Suite No. 1:* Monteux—San Francisco Symphony Orchestra; DM-1143. *Suite No. 2:* Toscanini—NBC Symphony Orchestra; WDM-1374 or LM-1043.

DIM LUSTRE
Richard Strauss: Burlesque in D Minor: Arrau-Defauw—Chicago Symphony Orchestra; DM-1216.

FACSIMILE
Leonard Bernstein: *Facsimile:* Bernstein—RCA Victor Symphony Orchestra; DM-1142.

FANCY FREE
Leonard Bernstein: Three Dances from *Fancy Free:* Fiedler—Boston Pops Orchestra; 11-9386.

FRANCESCA DA RIMINI
Peter Tchaikovsky: *Francesca da Rimini:* Koussevitzky—Boston Symphony Orchestra; DM-1179.

GAITÉ PARISIENNE
Jacques Offenbach: *Gaité Parisienne:* Fiedler—Boston Pops Orchestra; WDM-1147 or LM-1001.

GALA PERFORMANCE
  Sergei Prokofiev: Classical Symphony: Koussevitzky—Boston Symphony Orchestra; DM-1241.

GAYNE
  Aram Khatchaturian: *Gayne Ballet Suite:* Rodzinski—Chicago Symphony Orchestra; WDM-1212.

GISELLE
  Adolphe Adam: *Giselle:* Irving—Royal Opera Orchestra, Covent Garden; WDM-1397 or LM-1092.

THE GOLDEN AGE
  Dmitri Shostakovitch: Polka from *The Age of Gold:* Golschmann—St. Louis Symphony Orchestra; 11-8592.

GRADUATION BALL
  Johann Strauss, Jr.: *Graduation Ball:* Dorati—Dallas Symphony Orchestra; WDM-1180 or LM-1061.

HELEN OF TROY
  Jacques Offenbach: *Helen of Troy Suite:* Dorati—Minneapolis Symphony Orchestra; WDM-1381 or LM-22.

L'HISTOIRE D'UN SOLDAT
  Igor Stravinsky: *L'Histoire d'un Soldat:* Bernstein—Boston Symphony Orchestra; WDM-1197.

THE INCREDIBLE FLUTIST
  Walter Piston: *The Incredible Flutist:* Fiedler—Boston Pops Orchestra; DM-621.

JARDIN AUX LILAS
  Ernest Chausson: Poème for Violin and Orchestra; Menuhin—Symphony Orchestra of Paris—Enesco; 7913 and 7914.

JEUX
  Claude Debussy: *Jeux:* de Sabata—Symphony Orchestra of the Augusteo, Rome; WDM-1276 or LM-1057.

MOTHER GOOSE
  Maurice Ravel: *Ma Mère l'Oye:* Koussevitzky—Boston Symphony Orchestra; WDM-1268 or LM-1012.

LABYRINTH
  Franz Schubert: Symphony No. 9: Toscanini—NBC Symphony Orchestra; WDM-1167 or LM-1040.

THE NUTCRACKER
  Peter Tchaikovsky: *Nutcracker Suite No. 1:* Stokowski and his Symphony Orchestra; WDM-1468 or LM-46. *Suite No. 2:* Fiedler—Boston Pops Orchestra; WDM-1164 or LM-1029.

L'OISEAU DE FEU
  Igor Stravinsky: *The Firebird:* Stokowski and his Symphony Orchestra; WDM-1421 or LM-1098.

ORPHEUS
  Igor Stravinsky: *Orpheus:* Stravinsky—RCA Victor Symphony Orchestra; WDM-1320 or LM-1033.

PAGANINI
  Sergei Rachmaninoff: Variations on a Theme by Paganini: Artur Rubinstein—Philharmonia Orchestra—Susskind; WDM-1269 or LM-26.

PETER AND THE WOLF
Sergei Prokofiev: *Peter and the Wolf:* Eleanor Roosevelt-Koussevitzky—Boston Symphony Orchestra; WDM-1437 or LM-45.

PETROUCHKA
Igor Stravinsky: *Petrouchka:* Stokowski and his Symphony Orchestra; in preparation.

PILLAR OF FIRE
Arnold Schönberg: *Verklärte Nacht:* Golschmann—St. Louis Symphony Orchestra; DM-1005.

POLOVTSIAN DANCES
Alexander Borodin: *Prince Igor:* Dances of the Polovetzki Maidens: Stokowski and his Symphony Orchestra; WDM-1386 or LM-1054.

LES PRÉSAGES
Peter Tchaikovsky: Symphony No. 5 in E Minor: Koussevitzky—Boston Symphony Orchestra; WDM-1057 or LM-1047.

QUELQUES FLEURS
François Auber: Overtures: Fiedler—Boston Pops Orchestra; WDM-1274 or LM-1049.

RAYMONDA
Alexander Glazounov: *Raymonda:* Fiedler—Boston Pops Orchestra; DM-1072.

RODEO
Aaron Copland: *Rodeo:* Dorati—Dallas Symphony Orchestra; WDM-1214.

ROMEO AND JULIET
Sergei Prokofiev: Ballet Music from *Romeo and Juliet:* Koussevitzky—Boston Symphony Orchestra; DM-1129.

LE ROSSIGNOL
Igor Stravinsky: *The Song of the Nightingale:* Goossens—Cincinnati Symphony Orchestra; DM-1041.

RUSSIAN SOLDIER
Sergei Prokofiev: *Lieutenant Kije Suite:* Koussevitzky—Boston Symphony Orchestra; DM-459.

LE SACRE DU PRINTEMPS
Igor Stravinsky: *Le Sacre du Printemps:* Monteux—San Francisco Symphony Orchestra; DM-1052.

EL SALON MEXICO
Aaron Copland: *El Salon Mexico:* Koussevitzky—Boston Symphony Orchestra; DM-546.

SCHEHERAZADE
Nicholas Rimsky-Korsakov: *Scheherazade:* Monteux—San Francisco Symphony Orchestra; WDM-920 or LM-1029.

THE SEASONS
Alexander Glazounov: *The Seasons:* Dorati—Dallas Symphony Orchestra; DM-1072.

SERENADE
Peter Tchaikovsky: *Serenade for Strings:* Koussevitzky—Boston Symphony Orchestra; WDM-1346 or LM-1056.

SEVENTH SYMPHONY
Ludwig van Beethoven: Symphony No. 7: Munch—Boston Symphony Orchestra; WDM-1360 or LM-1034.

THE SLEEPING BEAUTY
Peter Tchaikovsky: *Sleeping Beauty Ballet:* Stokowski and his Symphony Orchestra; WDM-1205 or LM-1010.

LE SPECTRE DE LA ROSE
Carl Maria von Weber: *Invitation to the Dance:* Stokowski and his Symphony Orchestra; WDM-1394 or LM-1083.

SWAN LAKE
Peter Tchaikovsky: *Swan Lake:* Golschmann—St. Louis Symphony Orchestra; WDM-1028 or LM-1032.

LES SYLPHIDES
Frédéric Chopin: *Les Sylphides:* Fiedler—Boston Pops Orchestra; WDM-1119 or LM-10.

SYLVIA
Léo Delibes: *Sylvia:* Sevitzky—Indianapolis Symphony Orchestra; WDM-1305 or LM-1032.

SYMPHONIE FANTASTIQUE
Hector Berlioz: *Symphonie Fantastique:* Monteux—San Francisco Symphony Orchestra; DM-994.

THE THREE-CORNERED HAT
Manuel de Falla: Dances from *The Three-Cornered Hat:* Fiedler—Boston Pops Orchestra; DM-505.

TYL EULENSPIEGEL
Richard Strauss: *Tyl Eulenspiegel:* Koussevitzky—Boston Symphony Orchestra; DM-1029.

LA VALSE
Maurice Ravel: *La Valse:* Munch—Boston Symphony Orchestra; 12-1207 or 49-1213.

THE WISE VIRGINS
J. S. Bach (Arranged by Walton): *The Wise Virgins:* Walton—Sadlers Wells Orchestra; DM-817.

Index of Choreographers

Index of Composers

517

General Index

Adam, Adolphe, 7, 210, 211, 448
Adams, Diana, 160, 175-177, 228, 229, 279, 495
Alarcón, Pedro Antonio de, 479
Alford, Walter, vi
Algeranoff, Harcourt, 134
Allatini, Eric, 163
Alonso, Fernando, 242, 300
Alonzo, Alicia, 17, 63, 175, 207, 223, 226, 269, 279, 297, 416, 436, 441, 450, 475, 495, 497, 503
Altman, N., 209
Amberg, George, 354
Andersen, Hans Christian, 50, 95, 369, 370
Anderson-Ivantzoff, Elizaveta, 265
Anderson, Leroy, 449
Andreù, Mariano, 89, 163
Angiolini, Gaspare, 7, 10, 162, 163
Anisimova, N. A., 209
Anjou, Due d', 2
Anne, Empress, 10
Ansermet, Ernest, 233, 264
Arbeau, Thoinot, 2, 3
Arbos, Enrique, 33
Arensky, Anton, 92
Argentinita, 33, 89, 90, 485
Armstrong, John, 167
Ashton, Frederick, 49, 107, 108, 167-168, 305, 335, 396, 505
Auber, Daniel François, 341
Auberjonois, René, 233
Augusta, Mme., 212
Aulnoy, Marie Catherine d', 258
Aveline, Albert, 140

Babilée, Jean, 493
Bach, Johann Sebastian, 114, 115, 505
Bakst, Léon, 43, 92, 148, 187, 249, 397, 398, 422, 473
Balakireff, Mili, 473
Balanchine, George, vi, 13, 14-15, 16, 19, 20, 37, 38, 49, 52, 53, 82, 114, 115, 116, 145, 212, 213, 227, 228, 250, 259, 260, 275, 285, 288, 323, 325, 332, 345, 370, 407, 408, 410, 458, 469, 470, 471, 475, 476, 477, 478, 491, 502
Baldina, Maria, 449
Ballard, Lucinda, 213
Ballets and Divertissements:
Abandoned Wife, The (from *The Shadow of the Wind*), 418
Adélaïde, ou la Langage des Fleurs, 25-26
Afternoon of a Faun, The (see *L'Après-Midi d'un Faune*)
Aglaë, or Cupid's Pupil, 357
Aleko, 17, 27-32
Amor Brujo, El, 33-35
Amphion and Thalia, 335
Apollo (see *Apollon Musagète*)
Apollon Musagète, 36-39
Après-Midi d'un Faune, L', 43, 44-45, 147, 232, 384, 437
Appalachian Spring, 21, 40-42
Aurora's Wedding (from *The Sleeping Beauty*), 423
Bacchanale, 46-48, 170, 253, 255
Baiser de la Fée, Le, 37, 49-52
Ballet Ballads, 20
Ballet Comique de la Reine, 2
Ballet for Martha, 40
Ballet Imperial, 53-56, 410
Ballet Mechanique, 245
Beau Danube, Le, 57-60, 89, 199, 223
Biches, Les, 250
Billy the Kid, 16, 19, 61-67, 354
Bluebeard, 17, 68-74, 229
Bogatyri, 75-78
Bolero, 79-81
Bolt, The, 221
Bourgeois Gentilhomme, Le, 82-84
Boutique Fantasque, La, 85-88
Cappriccio Espagnol, 89-91
Captive Princess and Her Hero (*On Stage!*), 281

521

ABOUT THE AUTHOR

At present, Mr. Lawrence is permanent conductor of the Phoenix (Arizona) Symphony Orchestra and Associate Professor of Music in Tempe State College, also in Phoenix. He went to the Southwest after serving as ballet critic and associate music critic for several years on the New York Herald Tribune, *acting as guest conductor with a number of symphony orchestras and ballet companies, and serving two years in the U.S. Army Air Force—mostly in Italy, where he conducted opera.*

Mr. Lawrence is author of fifteen other books on ballet and opera, and may be heard frequently on the Saturday afternoon Metropolitan Opera broadcasts, where he almost invariably comes up with the correct answers on the Intermission Opera Quiz. He is also a frequent contributor to The Saturday Review of Literature *on musical subjects.*